|
thinking
outside
the box
|

thinking outside the box

A Contemporary Television Genre Reader

Edited by
Gary R. Edgerton
and Brian G. Rose

THE UNIVERSITY PRESS
OF KENTUCKY

Publication of this volume was made possible in part
by a grant from the National Endowment for the Humanities.

The University Press of Kentucky
Scholarly publisher for the Commonwealth, serving Bellarmine University, Berea
College, Centre College of Kentucky, Eastern Kentucky University,
The Filson Historical Society, Georgetown College, Kentucky Historical Society,
Kentucky State University, Morehead State University, Murray State University,
Northern Kentucky University, Transylvania University, University of Kentucky,
University of Louisville, and Western Kentucky University.
All rights reserved.

Editorial and Sales Offices: The University Press of Kentucky
663 South Limestone Street, Lexington, Kentucky 40508-4008
www.kentuckypress.com

09 08 07 06 05   5 4 3 2 1

Library of Congress Cataloging-in-Publication Data

Thinking outside the box : a contemporary television genre reader / edited
by Gary R. Edgerton and Brian Rose.
    p.   cm.
 Includes bibliographical references and index.
 ISBN-13: 978-0-8131-2365-3 (hardcover : alk. paper)
 ISBN-10: 0-8131-2365-8 (hardcover : alk. paper)
 1. Television programs. 2. Television program genres. I. Edgerton, Gary
R. (Gary Richard), 1952– II. Rose, Brian Geoffrey.
 PN1992.55.T47 2005
 791.45'6—dc22
                              2005028377

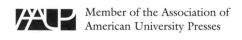 Member of the Association of
American University Presses

contents

acknowledgments

We would like to thank Leila Salisbury for her unflagging encouragement from start to finish on this project, as well as her colleagues at the University Press of Kentucky for all their help in preparing and publishing this book. We also express our deepest thanks to our families and friends for their continuing love and support.

introduction

television genres in transition

Gary R. Edgerton and Brian G. Rose

> Some important new critical theories have challenged the primacy of
> genre as a basic critical concept. The next important task of genre
> theory is to examine these objections in order to discover to what
> extent they require revision of the theory of popular genres and to
> what extent they may require us to go "beyond genre."
>
> —John G. Cawelti, "The Question of Popular Genres Revisited," 1997[1]

Genre has been a fundamental tool in analyzing television ever since the
publication of Horace Newcomb's *TV: The Most Popular Art* (1974)
and the first edition of his widely used anthology, *Television: The Critical View* (1976).[2] Both of these books were landmarks in the development of television studies as a discipline, encouraging a younger
generation of scholars to approach TV from a decidedly humanistic approach rather than from the preprofessional orientation that had gripped
broadcasting as a field of study during the previous fifty years. Part of
the discipline's folklore has it that Edward R. Murrow took the first
radio announcing class ever offered in the United States at then Washington State College in 1928. Whether or not this course was a historical first is beside the point; what is important for our purposes is that
Murrow's formative educational experience in broadcasting was tellingly
skills oriented, thus setting the appropriate example for the literally tens
of thousands of students who followed in his fabled footsteps over the
next half century.

In the beginning, radio and later television studies in American higher education received far too many of their developmental cues from the industry that they purported to analyze and critique. Historical-critical scholarship, in particular, was largely a peripheral concern. One glaring exception to this early tendency was Erik Barnouw's groundbreaking and highly influential three-volume history of broadcasting in the United States—*A Tower in Babel* (1966), *The Golden Web* (1968), and *The Image Empire* (1970).[3] The seminal impact of this trilogy cannot be overestimated. Nor can the influence of Newcomb's *TV: The Most Popular Art* and his follow-up *Television: The Critical View*. Many of us who were young graduate students at the time greeted these breakthrough texts as welcome breaths of fresh air. The traditional social science perspective no longer needed to be the only way that TV could be studied. Instead, more humanities-based approaches rapidly emerged over the next quarter century, with a marked upswing in scholarly work on television history, theory, criticism, genres, authorship, reception, political economy, institutional structures, and other cultural matters such as gender, race, ethnicity, nationality, and class. Finally we felt freer to consider the centrality of TV in the intellectual life of our own culture as well as globally.

As a doctoral student at the University of Chicago, Horace Newcomb came under the tutelage of John Cawelti, the preeminent genre theorist and critic in popular culture studies. Newcomb naturally began to conceptualize television from a genre perspective, just as Cawelti had done earlier with popular fiction and film, thus influencing his own mentor's growing interest in TV in turn. Cawelti worked out of a classical liberal arts tradition, tracing his genre analyses back to Aristotle's notion of mimesis, or art being an imitation of life. Genre criticism from this classical viewpoint focuses primarily on the artworks themselves—be they literary or otherwise—examining them for the types of articulation and the kinds of actions they reveal. In short, Aristotle organized the entire literary canon into three classes: the *lyric* (uttered throughout in first person), the *epic narrative* (spoken by a narrator who is giving voice to many characters), and the *drama* (where the characters speak for themselves). This tripartite schema placed the analytical emphasis squarely on the text and ultimately led to the curricular divisions of poetry, novels, and drama in university and college English courses.

Cawelti's greatest contribution to the nascent field of cultural studies was basing his work on the foundational ideas of several earlier critics, ranging from Gilbert Seldes in *The Seven Lively Arts* (1924) to Stuart Hall and Paddy Whannel in *The Popular Arts* (1964), thus following

The beginning classical stage of television genre criticism was primarily concerned with conceptualizing programming into distinct and identifiable
categories, such as Westerns, epitomized by the long-running *Gunsmoke*
starring James Arness as Marshal Matt Dillon. Courtesy of CBS Television.

their lead in applying the rigors of genre analysis to all sorts of popular artistic expressions.[4] Cawelti also recalled that "television, too, has been vitally influenced by the concept of genre in its recent development. Beginning with Horace Newcomb's pioneer work of 1974, *TV: The Most Popular Art*, the concept of genre has become an increasingly important aspect of television criticism, dominating anthologies like Newcomb's *Television: The Critical View* (1976), Adler and Cater's *Television as a Cultural Force* (1976), and Kaplan's *Regarding Television* (1983), as well as the pages of the *Journal of Popular Film and Television*, which has published much outstanding work in the study of popular genres."[5]

The high point in this first, "classical" stage of analyzing TV from a genre perspective came with the successive appearance of Stuart Kaminsky and Jeffrey Mahan's *American Television Genres* and then Brian Rose's *TV Genres* in 1985.[6] Both of these books sketched out the scholarly parameters of conceptualizing television programming into distinctive and identifiable categories. *American Television Genres* examined quiz and game shows, police stories, soap operas, science fiction and horror, comedy, detective programs, and news; the more extensive *TV Genres* surveyed police series, detective shows, Westerns, medical melodramas, science fiction and fantasy TV, situation comedies, soap operas, American made-for-TV movies, docudramas, news, documentaries, sports telecasting, game shows, variety shows, talk shows, children's programming, educational and cultural programming, religious programming, and television commercials. A good first step had clearly been taken in organizing the world of TV into recognizable program categories based on recurring formulaic patterns. Still, the analytical emphasis remained mainly on textual matters, such as setting, plot structure, characterization, iconography, theme, technique, and style.

By the mid-1980s, many practicing genre critics, led by John Cawelti, Horace Newcomb, and others, felt the need to go "beyond genre," or at least to envision genre in far more expansive ways. The influx of a wide assortment of critical-cultural theories made it abundantly clear that the then current definitional approach to TV genre criticism was far too focused on *text* rather than *context*. Spurred further by the pioneering work of Raymond Williams, television scholars began asking what the proper unit of analysis was for analyzing television content. Was it genre? Or was it an episode, several programs, a series, a full network schedule? Or was it the "flow" of programming as experienced by the viewer, as Williams contended?[7] Or was it Newcomb and Hirsch's slightly

"Smile, you're on *Candid Camera!*" was the punch line of one of the earliest examples of reality television. (Left to right) Co-host Durward Kirby and creative producer and host Allen Funt. Courtesy of Bob Banner Associates.

different notion of the "viewing strip," referring to a string of programs minus those elements "within and between"?[8]

According to John Hartley (writing in 1984), "Television is recalcitrant when it comes to identifying where the text should stop," adding succinctly that "television is equally resistant to classification into texts."[9] A contemporaneous case in point is the endlessly malleable genre of reality TV. Previously ranging from the harmless, staged voyeurism of *Candid Camera* (which premiered in 1948 on ABC) to the warts-and-all drama of PBS's *An American Family* (1973) to Fox's true-life crime series *Cops* (1989–) to audience participation shows like *America's Funniest Home Videos* (ABC, 1990–), reality TV has spread its roots in every conceivable direction since 2000. The germinating seed was *Survivor* (CBS, 2000–), whose shrewd combination of quiz show, adventure program, and soap opera elements boosted the fortunes of CBS almost overnight. Its success, in typical television fashion, unleashed a torrent of avid imitators, including Fox's *Temptation Island* (2001–3) and *Boot*

Camp (2001–2), NBC's *Fear Factor* (2001–), and ABC's *The Mole* (2001–3). In just as natural a progression, the reality eruption also led to the development of numerous genre hybrids, including MTV's *The Osbournes* (2002–5), with its breakthrough melding of sitcom and documentary; Fox's *Murder in Small Town X* (2001), which blended mystery and adventure as ten contestants tried to solve a fictional murder in an actual town in Maine; and Fox's slick mixture of talent and variety shows, *American Idol* (2002–).

One of the curious developments of reality TV's success is that it opened American television's usually closed doors to international programming concepts. CBS's *Big Brother* (2000–) was originally developed in Holland, before spreading to more than a dozen countries throughout the world. (Interestingly, the U.S. version was never able to achieve the phenomenal popularity earned by the show's foreign counterparts, a fact perhaps attributable to the absence of the open eroticism unabashedly displayed by its European cousins.) Fox's *American Idol* came from England, as did TLC cable network's surprise hit *Trading Spaces* (2000–), adapted from BBC-1's *Changing Rooms* (1997–). Originally the Food Network didn't even bother with reformatting but simply rebroadcast the Japanese program *Iron Chef* (Fuji Network System, 1993–99), though it did add an English translation. Whether U.S. audiences are ready for other overseas reality hits, such as Argentina's *Human Resources* (where studio audiences choose which unemployed contestant to reward with a full-time job) or Germany's *Krazy Krauts*, remains to be seen.

The eagerness with which U.S. programmers looked abroad during the last few years may be a new trend, but in many ways it stems from the same spirit (and anxiety) that has always led networks to search for some novel aspect of formula production to exploit or in most cases rework and recycle. Especially since the mid-1980s, genre TV programming has rarely operated according to precise formal categories or strict style and content conventions. The competitive pressures of seven broadcast networks and currently more than 330 cable channels have led producers and programmers to embrace concepts that deliberately cross "traditional" boundaries and fuse the widest assemblage of elements (as the foregoing descriptions of reality TV series reveal). The frenzied search for audiences, particularly those targeted for their demographic desirability, has forced those executives responsible for selection and scheduling to recognize the importance of ever more varied formula menus and broader genre mixes.

Not surprisingly, the study of television genres is again making a comeback in scholarly circles in response to this unprecedented mixing and matching of traditional generic forms. No longer is genre being viewed as a *fixed entity* where programs are being evaluated either deductively against some ideal conception of what a particular genre should be, or inductively alongside an ever-widening collection of similarly structured texts. Nor are genres even thought of anymore as some kind of macrotext or supertext; instead they are viewed as part of a much broader system of signification that derives its deeper meanings from the interrelationship between an assortment of creative, technological, industrial, institutional, and reception-related practices. Current critical-cultural theories have enabled the idea of genre to be reconceptualized as a *process* rather than a static category, infusing a new range of possibilities to television genre criticism in general. "There is no reason to junk the notion of genre (and subgenre)," argues popular media scholar Gregory Waller, just "because cultural products cannot be categorized and classified as precisely and objectively as natural flora or fauna."[10] We heartily agree with this assertion and thus offer this volume as a renewed examination of how TV genres form, operate, change over time, interact with each other, and signify much about the people who produce and watch them on a regular basis.

The time is again ripe to revisit the rich potential of studying television genres, only now from a second-stage "critical-cultural" perspective. *Thinking Outside the Box: A Contemporary Television Genre Reader* is intended as a cross section of some of the best and most challenging scholarship currently being conducted in this subject area. In part 1, "The Contemporary Agenda," we begin this collection with three theoretical and critically informed overviews to orient the reader; this is followed in part 2, "Traditional Genres in Transition," with four successive analyses of generic transformations that have occurred in children's programming, sitcoms, soap operas, and talk shows; leading to explorations in part 3, "New Directions in Television Genres," of several unique generic hybrids, including reality programs, teen-oriented science fiction/fantasy/supernatural series, "quality drama," and the recent upswing in networking genres; and concluding in part 4, "Television Genres in Global Perspective," with three comprehensive investigations into the current worldwide reach and development of television genres, as well as an epilogue that serves as a convenient bibliographic guide for future study. Our ultimate goal in *Thinking Outside the Box: A Contemporary Television Genre Reader* is to be interpretive and detailed in our research and writing, rather than exhaustive and all-encompassing in a more general and surface-level way. We are also bringing together some of the most prominent and accomplished senior scholars in television studies with several of the more promising and innovative newcomers to the field.

We are pleased to lead off this collection with Horace Newcomb's historical and biographical chapter, "Reflections on *TV: The Most Popular Art.*" As previously noted, this book—more so than any other—influenced humanities scholars to first try television criticism (especially from a generic perspective) more than thirty years ago. Newcomb's recollections offer an illuminating snapshot of how the earliest textual analyses of TV emerged out of literary and popular culture studies. He also explains why less aesthetic, more ideological approaches to television eventually took precedence. Moreover, Newcomb's "reflections" of growing up in Mississippi during the late 1940s and 1950s subtly reveal the sociopolitical dimension of TV as a cultural practice as he incisively links his early viewing experiences with the racial climate at the time.

Continuing in part 1, Jason Mittell builds on similar assumptions in "A Cultural Approach to Television Genre Theory" by arguing that genres surpass the boundaries of media texts and operate within the larger contexts of industry, audience, and culture. He presents a television-specific approach in his chapter, incorporating contemporary cultural theory, discourse analysis, and the music video genre as a representative example, as he hones in on Michael Jackson's trio of successful MTV hits from 1983—"Billie Jean," "Beat It," and "Thriller." Completing this first part, Christopher Anderson investigates the recent shift in television as an industry and institution away from stories created by writers, brought to life by actors and directors, and presented in a reassuring rhythm of daily and weekly episodes. Instead, he clarifies in "Television Networks and the Uses of Drama" how evolving economic priorities in TV have profoundly undercut many of the medium's long-standing fictional formulas, such as lawyer, cop, and doctor shows, replacing them with a fundamentally new and different kind of small screen storytelling based loosely on the reality of actual people, places, and events.

Norma Pecora begins part 2 with her historical overview, "The Changing Face of Children's Television." In this chapter, Pecora conducts an institutional analysis—emphasizing audience, economics, industry, and technology—as she delineates a half century of change in programming aimed at toddlers, tweens, and teens. Pecora underscores how children have always been targeted as little consumers, even as they have contributed to the transformation of this genre by the consumptive activities they engage in and the creative choices they make. Next, Richard Butsch performs a large-scale content analysis of television's arguably most durable genre in "Five Decades and Three Hundred Sitcoms about Class and Gender." The author in this chapter adopts a macro perspective spanning fifty-seven years and literally dozens of specific examples, as he identifies how male and female stereotypes on TV intersect with the depiction of class, acquiring different meanings according to whether they appear in working-class or middle-class contexts.

In "Soap Opera Survival Tactics," Ellen Seiter and Mary Jeanne Wilson consider some of the more recent generic innovations by which this popular programming staple sustains its appeal for a whole new generation of television watchers. This chapter focuses specifically on changing viewing contexts, shifting audience appeals, and alterations in this genre's traditional narrative schemes and configuration of characters. The authors look closely at the question of the soap opera's long-term survival by analyzing the cases of the cable channel SoapNet, the supernatural soap opera *Passions,* and the prime-time teenage soap *The O.C.* In "Beyond Genre: Cable's Impact on the Talk Show," Jeffrey Jones argues that although the inherent recombinant features of this programming category have always produced a level of generic uncertainty and change, the expansion of cable over the last decade has led to a situation where the talk show may no longer be a meaningful designation. In particular, Jones examines the hybridization of comedy talk and public affairs programming starting with *Politically Incorrect* when it appeared on Comedy Central between 1993 and 1996; the transformation of cable news channels into networks largely composed of talk shows, beginning with Fox News in 1996; and the problem of generic purity in an era when reality shows of all sorts, such as MTV's *The Real World,* rely so heavily on talk as one of their principal ingredients.

In part 3, Ron Simon highlights how reality programming has become one of the most dynamic and successful genres on TV, largely to the consternation of critics, network executives, and the Hollywood creative community. He points out in "The Changing Definition of Reality Television" that the medium has always attempted to integrate ordinary persons into unscripted situations of which producers and participants theoretically do not know the outcome. In today's television environment, though, as Simon indicates, reality TV presently comprises a hy-

Both set in Manhattan apartments, *I Love Lucy* and *Seinfeld* are indicative of the dramatic changes in style and sensibility that occurred in the situation comedy from the early 1950s through the late 1990s. (Above, left to right) William Frawley as Fred Mertz, Lucille Ball as Lucy Ricardo, Vivian Vance as Ethel Mertz, and Desi Arnaz as Ricky Ricardo in *I Love Lucy*. Courtesy of CBS Television. (Below, left to right) Julia Louis-Dreyfus as Elaine, Michael Richards as Kramer, and Jerry Seinfeld in *Seinfeld*. Courtesy of Columbia TriStar Television.

brid blend of program types that were once discrete but now blur the line between true life and prime-time entertainment. In "Unreal TV," Rhonda Wilcox likewise describes how series such as *Buffy the Vampire Slayer, The X-Files, Twin Peaks, Northern Exposure, Xena: Warrior Princess, Star Trek: The Next Generation, Lois and Clark, Roswell, Smallville,* and *Angel* have all explored new generic territory in their own special ways. Wilcox notes that these programs contain elements of fantasy, science fiction, the supernatural, or the surreal not merely for plot convenience or escapist action but to layer these shows with symbolic depth, which in turn attracts large and intense fan followings.

Part 3 continues with Al Auster examining original cable programming in his chapter, "HBO's Approach to Generic Transformation." Auster recounts how HBO's series such as *The Larry Sanders Show, The Sopranos, The Corner, The Wire, Oz, Six Feet Under,* and *Sex and the City,* free of the broadcast webs' restraints regarding obscenity, nudity, and content, have together pioneered a new sensibility in TV drama and comedy, while at the same time remaining true to their original generic roots. In "'I Want My Niche TV': Genre as a Networking Strategy in the Digital Era," Gary Edgerton and Kyle Nicholas next identify the main technological, institutional, and cultural reasons behind the recent explosion in TV networking, describing the creative interplay between industry and audiences in the formation and evolution of many wide-ranging television formats. All told, they analyze the profound transformation that is now occurring in, between, and across TV genres in light of continued consolidation of media ownership, both in the United States and globally, along with the related impact of digital convergence, which extends the boundaries of generic expression beyond television to the Internet, CDs, DVDs, videotape, video games, and print.

The worldwide expanse of TV genres is the primary focus of part 4, beginning with Timothy Havens's institutional analysis, "Globalization and the Generic Transformation of Telenovelas." Havens provides a history of the telenovela, an overview of its international circulation, and an exploration of the various economic and cultural reasons behind the genre's widespread popularity. He furthermore observes how telenovelas offer the dominant screen representations of Latino identity now available throughout most of the world. Michael Curtin, in his chapter, "From Kung Fu to Imperial Court: Chinese Historical Drama," additionally covers why heritage programming has emerged as the signature genre in East Asia. By exploring a wide variety of political, cultural, and economic influences, Curtin illustrates how television producers throughout Greater China collaborate, coproduce, and exchange historical and other kinds of programs as never before. Shanti Kumar then critically examines cultural polarities such as "Western" versus "Indian" or "global" versus "local" in international TV genres such as music videos and sports shows on satellite networks such as Channel [V] and ESPN in India. In "Innovation, Imitation, and Hybridity in Indian Television," Kumar employs close textual analyses to reveal how various programming formats and hybrid characters represent an in-between class of Indians that creatively innovates and imitates established conventions of global television genres to deal with complex issues of national identity, regional diversity, and local communities in postcolonial India.

Brian Rose concludes our collection with an extended review of the literature entitled "Reading TV Genres." Rose surveys how scholars began addressing the subject of television genres in the 1970s as a way of establishing a cultural and artistic legitimacy for the medium (as opposed to previous works concentrating on its sociological and industrial dimensions). He explicates how, more recently, TV genres have been addressed in a variety of challenging ways, either through detailed individual genre studies or by a reexamination of genre as a complex web of cultural practices involving industry, technology, aesthetics, economics, and reception. Overall, we both hope this bibliographic essay and the chapters that precede it will encourage additional scholarly work in television genres as both a critical approach and a subject of serious study.

Notes

1. John G. Cawelti, "The Question of Popular Genres Revisited," in *In the Eye of the Beholder: Critical Perspectives in Popular Film and Television,* ed. Gary R. Edgerton, Michael T. Marsden, and Jack Nachbar (Bowling Green, Ohio: Bowling Green State University Popular Press, 1997), 71.

2. Horace Newcomb, *TV: The Most Popular Art* (New York: Anchor Press, 1974); Horace Newcomb, ed., *Television: The Critical View* (New York: Oxford University Press, 1976).

3. Erik Barnouw, *A Tower in Babel: A History of Broadcasting in the United States to 1933* (New York: Oxford University Press, 1966); Erik Barnouw, *The Golden Web: A History of Broadcasting in the United States, 1933–1953* (New York: Oxford University Press, 1968); Erik Barnouw, *The Image Empire: A History of Broadcasting in the United States from 1953* (New York: Oxford University Press, 1970).

4. Gilbert Seldes, *The Seven Lively Arts* (New York: Harper and Brothers, 1924); Stuart Hall and Paddy Whannel, eds., *The Popular Arts* (New York: Pantheon, 1964).

5. Cawelti, "Question of Popular Genres Revisited," 70–71; Richard Adler and Douglass Cater, eds., *Television as a Cultural Force* (New York: Praeger, 1976); E. Ann Kaplan, *Regarding Television: Critical Approaches—An Anthology* (Frederick, Md.: University Publications of America, 1983).

6. Stuart M. Kaminsky with Jeffrey H. Mahan, *American Television Genres* (Chicago: Nelson-Hall, 1985); Brian G. Rose, ed., *TV Genres: A Handbook and Reference Guide* (Westport, Conn.: Greenwood Press, 1985).

7. Raymond Williams, with an introduction by Lynn Spigel, *Television: Technology and Cultural Form* (1974; repr., Hanover, N.H.: Wesleyan University Press/ University Press of New England, 1992), 80–112.

8. Horace M. Newcomb and Paul M. Hirsch, "Television as a Cultural Forum: Implications for Research," in *Interpreting Television: Current Research Perspectives,* ed. Willard D. Rowland Jr. and Bruce Watkins (Beverly Hills, Calif.: Sage, 1984), 66.

9. John Hartley, "Encouraging Signs: Television and the Power of Dirt, Speech, and Scandalous Categories," in Rowland and Watkins, *Interpreting Television,* 120.

10. Gregory A. Waller, "Flow, Genre, and the Television Text," in Edgerton, Marsden, and Nachbar, *In the Eye of the Beholder,* 61.

1 | the contemporary agenda

1 reflections on *TV: The Most Popular Art*

Horace Newcomb

By way of beginning, it is important to note that so far as I recall, and without rereading every page, the word "genre" does not appear in *TV: The Most Popular Art*.[1] The reasons for that rhetorical choice are telling. They recall early discussions surrounding the study of popular culture, the importance of personal situations and influences, and attempts to invent strategies for dealing with television, a topic/problem/subject matter fraught and freighted with a range of existing analyses that had positioned the medium in specific ways. "Reflecting" on that book, then, a book published thirty years ago, in the winter of 1974, requires various digressions into personal, autobiographical circumstances, as well as reconsideration and analysis. Here is the first digression.

In the winter quarter of 1968 at the University of Chicago, John Cawelti offered what I believe was his first course in the study of popular culture. At the request of English department chair Gwin Kolb, that course was titled "Literature and Popular Culture." By that date I, and a number of equally interested and intrigued doctoral students in English, had completed course work and, with the assistance of grants from the Ford Foundation, were writing dissertations. The Ford grants had gone to a cohort of about twenty students who had fulfilled all requirements prior to the dissertation in a plan to shorten the time taken to complete doctorates in the humanities. Most of us had entered graduate school together three years earlier, had either completed a one-year M.A. or arrived with that degree in hand, and had passed a written admission examination for the doctoral program, six quarters of courses, two language examinations, and "The Seventy-five-Book Examination," an oral examination conducted by three professors on a list of books compiled by each individual candidate. I mention this because in this group were a number interested in broadening our study to encompass more social and sociological questions, more history. In general we wished to develop more contextual approaches to the study of literature. It was, after all, 1968, and graduate students in the English department had recently held meetings with faculty regarding an appropriate role for the study of the humanities in times of social upheaval, and Chicago had recently held a university-wide set of colloquiums on the topic "What Knowledge Is Most Worth Having?"

I do not recall if Cawelti's course was offered at the undergraduate or graduate level, but a number of graduate students audited at least part of the course. I was then in the midst of a dissertation dealing with American literary "naturalism," focused on the late-nineteenth-century efforts of Theodore Dreiser, Stephen Crane, and Frank Norris to forge a new approach to representing human experience, individual and social, in fiction. My work dealt with what might now be referred to as "ancillary" materials available from these authors, their own philosophical writing, their journalism, their reviews and commentary, their letters, lectures, and other pronouncements. John Cawelti was the director of the project. I attended several meetings of the popular culture course but was more intent on completing the degree in order to receive the full salary of my first job, secured later that winter, at Cornell College in Mount Vernon, Iowa. In the spring, however, I accepted a part-time position teaching freshman composition at Northwestern, and in June our son was born. Thus, the dissertation was not finished until December, which meant the salary was reduced from $10,000 to $9,500. I defended the dissertation in April 1969 and received the degree in August.

A year later Cawelti was named to chair the panel "Literature and the Other Arts" at an annual meeting of the Midwest Modern Language Association (MMLA). I proposed a paper dealing with television, sent him a very rough draft, received notes in response, altered the focus of the paper in accordance with those notes, and presented the new version, an analysis of the narrative structure of soap opera, in the spring of 1971.

A digression within the first digression: I had chosen to write a dissertation dealing with "minor" literary figures, "noncanonical" American writers, for specific reasons. Dreiser, Crane, and Norris, and William Dean Howells, the figure I posed to establish context for their work, were well enough respected, sometimes taught as secondary figures in courses on the novel or in surveys of American literature. But they were greatly overshadowed by Hawthorne, to some extent Poe, certainly Melville, and of course Henry James. Whitman, with poetry, staked down pretty much the entire other side of the tent, linked occasionally to Dickinson and a bevy of truly minor figures. In the study of American literature the naturalists were at best seen as "transitional" figures working between Hawthorne, Melville, and James on one side and the great modern trio, Fitzgerald, Hemingway, and Faulkner, on the other.

For me, however, the ponderous, dread-filled, often violent, always detailed novels of the naturalists spoke deeply of "real" lives. Enamored as I was (and remain) of James's sentences, I cared not a whit for his people. In spite of the dominant perspective on the naturalists, I did not find them particularly pessimistic. I did not find them belittling human experience, making helpless pawns of characters overcome by "nameless forces" that ground them to oblivion. True enough, that happened with some frequency in the tales, but I always found great sympathy for those individuals, and not a little dignity in their plight, both qualities carefully constructed by the authors. In the conclusion to the dissertation I referred to a narrative strategy resulting in a "rhetoric of defense," through which we are made to care about the characters and thereby understand a great deal more about life and lives, perhaps our own.

All this (not only my efforts, but those of most of my colleagues) was done without recourse to "theory." We had Northrop Frye, of course, and in our own hallways, Wayne Booth, whose *Rhetoric of Fiction* was crucial.[2] (Mr. Booth's commentary on my pretentiously titled seminar paper, "Idea, Form, and Naturalism," was most helpful in completing the dissertation.) Sheldon Sacks, another faculty member, had just published *Fiction and the Shape of Belief,* a book closer to my own interests.[3] In his seminar Sacks offered a definition of the novel I continue to find helpful, especially in the study of television. A novel, he suggested (and I paraphrase), is a long, made-up story dealing with characters about whom we are made to care. Students there also had the legacy of the "Chicago critics," most notably R. S. Crane,[4] who often focused on genre (in the sense to which I will shortly return). More important, these individuals had instilled in their own students (Booth among them), and all students of literature at the time, the necessity for "close reading."

Our budding efforts at literary scholarship, then, focused primarily on our own interpretive strategies, individual arguments grounded in careful examination of specific passages selected, to support our conclusions, from primary texts. A fundamental requirement was to see how "parts relate to the whole," in good Aristotelian manner. We recognized that other interpretations of the same material were to be expected and that, as I later came to understand and try to explain in my own classes, discourse and progress in the humanities would be seen as a grand continuing dialogue, a symposium of sorts among those who wish to understand more sufficiently the (perhaps endless) possibilities layered in expressive forms.

A larger point emerges here. Some of those who began to study popular culture did so knowing that more battles would have to be fought, that arguments would have to be made not only about the works examined but about the reasons—the necessity, in some views—for doing so. Stronger political shadings would be added to these arguments soon enough, a digression to come later. One fairly thin explanation was essentially sociological—it is important to study these materials because they attract millions, entertain them (a liability, of course), distract them, and so on. The most immediate question in many quarters was, What is the relation of these previously ignored and often scorned materials to "high culture"? Which brings me to "genre."

The term was narrowly focused and applied. Drama, poetry, prose fiction, and nonfiction were genres. Drama could be subdivided into comedy and tragedy. Fiction could be subdivided less easily into those same two large cases, but narrower definitions usually described "movements" or "styles" or "narrative strategies" such as "the picaresque," "the epistolary," and so on. Satire was often singled out as a topic for study and, despite the focus on authors such as Swift, was only tenuously defined as a "genre." Nonfiction could be defined in a range of ways, with the "personal essay," "the diary," or "the autobiography" providing sufficient material for large studies. More often one studied, wrote about, and later designed courses dealing with authors or periods. Genre study was of growing importance, but relatively closely defined.

Return to personal account digression: The draft paper I sent to John Cawelti as a submission for the MMLA meeting was titled "The Problem of Repetition in Television." The argument merely expanded the title, grousing about the predictability of stories presented on TV. I castigated the medium for presenting endless numbers of comedies, predictable from the first scene, mysteries that made conclusions clear from commission of crime, Westerns lacking the richness of filmic heritage. These qualities were presented as "flaws," diminishing the potential I found in the medium for complex storytelling. (I had watched a lot of television, a point to be discussed later.)

When *TV: The Most Popular Art* was published in 1974, *The Waltons* was featured as one of the narratively complex "new shows." (Left to right) Ralph Waite as John Walton, Michael Learned as Olivia Walton, and Richard Thomas as John Boy Walton. Courtesy of Warner Brothers Television.

Some days later I received a package containing a typescript of a very long essay called, at the time, "Prolegomenon to the Study of the Western." This work became Cawelti's masterful book *The Six-Gun Mystique*.[5] The note accompanying the essay had words to this effect, again paraphrasing: Take a look at this. There are other ways and reasons to think about repetition, and I am considering some of them here. Your passages about soap opera are intriguing. Why not focus the paper on that topic?

I did so, and a version of that paper became something of a "target" in organizing *The Most Popular Art*. In the book the chapter title is "Soap Opera: Approaching the Real World." It's a giveaway. Soaps, I suggest there, offer "probability" missing in the "repetitive" forms of sitcom, mysteries, Westerns, doctors and lawyers, and the other organizing figures of television narrative. Probability was considered a good thing, closer to "high art," another good thing, because it pushes "us" into different (better?) relations with the ideas, concepts, and problems found in the programs.

The analytical term Cawelti applied in his study of the Western, the term I adopted for the study of television, was not "genre"—still reserved for "high art"—but "formula." In retrospect it seems somewhat condescending. It is mechanical or at best chemical, a mixture of elements that, if done correctly, done the same way by anyone, will end in the same result. It sounds as if it could be written down, handed over, passed along. It's a recipe and not at all coincidental to the rise of the "packaged" foods such as cake mixes, home hair treatments, and toothpaste with new "whitening" formulas advertised on television.

The strange thing is, the attempt was to have the material taken seriously, not to add to its dismissal. But the term was available and well defined after Cawelti's achievement. Using it indicates something of the tentative qualities common in many early studies of popular culture. Moreover, a major problem for the study of "television" (an attempt to cover the entire medium) was basically one of organization. What would later and now be called television "genres" was the handy answer.

A brief digression on a general problem in the study of popular culture: Genre study and the variants that have come to be known as "genre theory" have been central to the study of popular expressive culture. This has much to do with the vast amounts of available material. Which of Mickey Spillane's or Zane Grey's novels, which popular song, which issue of *Superman* would stand the scrutiny paid to a poem by Chaucer, a novel by George Eliot? Individual "authorship" offered another organizational strategy, and there are indeed more studies of Spillane or Grey than of their individual works. But as one skeptical colleague put it in the early seventies, disdain dripping at the edges of the comment, "What's next, the oeuvre of Harold Robbins?" For the most part, then, the "form," the "organizing principle," the "formula" or "genre" becomes the object of study. Close reading, close analysis involves study of multiple examples of the genre (and opens the scholar to ridicule for treating even these examples so seriously). Meaning resides in the genre, the pattern, and explaining it, tracing it, interpreting it becomes the work. While I agree with all these statements, I would also argue that the work is thus made easier. It is easier to argue for "significance" in this manner. Is one Tarzan novel, one Hopalong Cassidy movie "better," even "more important," than another, or is it the "pattern" that establishes import, tells the story, Tarzan's, Burroughs's—the scholar's? This examination of patterns of meaning construction explains part of the later move to more formalized "cultural studies."

Back to *The Most Popular Art:* In the late sixties there were few models drawing on the humanities for treating television seriously as a storytelling medium. The small body of existing attempts were for the most part fugitive essays in general readership magazines. A handful of collections provided very early academic discussions of television fiction. *TV as Art: Some Essays in Criticism,* edited by Patrick D. Hazard, collected "papers originally commissioned by the Television Information Office for the National Council of Teachers of English Television Festival" and was published by the National Council in 1966.[6] It contained essays by Hazard, George Bluestone, George Dessart, and Raymond Williams, among others. Even in this collection attention was frequently paid to the ways in which television affected, or intervened in, the lives of children. Two seminars held at the Asilomar Conference Center in California produced essay collections.[7] In general, however, there was little on which to build.

This lack is important because one purpose of *TV: The Most Popular Art* was to respond to, angle off of, circle around, or otherwise enter a conversation dominated by social scientific approaches to the medium. This did not mean engaging these dominant approaches in a substantial manner. The fact is that I knew little and understood less of what those approaches were attempting to do. My reading in the area was limited to the simpler preparations and summaries for general audiences because these had often led to public discussions of the medium. My concern was that "everyone" *knew* that television should be treated as a social problem. Almost all other approaches and attendant questions were simply ignored.

I probed books such as Hazard's, the better magazines, collections of essays by specific authors in search of materials that would throw hints toward the kind of analysis I wished to pursue, hoping in vague, unstated fashion to do something resembling Robert Warshow's great achievement in *The Immediate Experience*.[8] When I had gathered a sufficient number of essays working in this direction, I wrote a proposal focused on the difficulty of studying television from a humanities perspective and sent it with a table of contents to a number of editors. None was interested. One, William Whitehead at Doubleday/Anchor, responded by saying the publication series did "not do well with anthologies," but asking if I would be interested in writing a monograph about television. I thought this was a good idea that had actually been tossed over the transom by a publisher. The anthology proposal became *Television: The Critical View*,[9] the first edition published two years after *The Most Popular Art*.

At Whitehead's request I wrote a new proposal. It began with an overview of other (mostly social scientific) approaches to television. Somewhere toward the end of the book would be a version of the analysis of soap opera, a "formula" I continued to insist was more narratively complex than most on television, and one I wished, in some small way, to "rescue" from the bottom of the cultural pit. Between these chapters would be others, dealing with other television "formulas"—comedies, mysteries, Westerns, doctors and lawyers, and so on—as they were presented in the schedule or subtitled by *TV Guide*.

The proposal was written, if memory serves, during 1970 and 1971, important years for television. *All in the Family*, *The Mary Tyler Moore Show*, and other interesting examples were appearing, suggesting to me that something even more intriguing than I had imagined was going on. These programs, with others, were to be discussed in a chapter added after the proposal was accepted, under the heading "The New Shows." The final chapter of the book, "Toward a Television Aesthetic," may have been part of the original proposal, but I do not recall if that was the case.

TV: The Most Popular Art is, by today's standards, a terribly simple, indeed naive, book. Some of its limitations can be blamed on the lack of models and guides discussed in this chapter. But it is also true that for all the interest among those who turned to the study of popular culture from training in literary study, sociology, or history, television generally remained the most disdained instantiation of popularity. Popular fiction was grounded in literary relations and linked to the rise of literacy. Films were increasingly placed in the curricula of the humanities, though the focus was often on "art film," "cinema," "foreign" films. More than any of these other expressive forms, television was blatantly burned with the brand of crass commercialism, superficiality, industrial production, predictability, and repetition—all detriments of the "formulaic."

Study was also severely hampered by the inability to engage in "close" analysis. The videocassette recorder had not been developed. Archives existed but were difficult to use. Even visits to the Library of Congress Motion Picture Division were not very helpful given the limited holdings and time required for viewing. As a result, my examples were drawn from programs currently on the air or, more likely, because I wished to trace and compare earlier material, from memory.[10] That strategy is dangerous and not recommended.

The Most Popular Art is a "back-broken" book. It attempts to explore two main lines of analysis, two major questions. As inadequate as it now appears, however, the two questions remain central to the study of television. Put in very direct terms, the first question is, How does television tell its stories? To answer, I turned to descriptive analysis of narrative strategies, comparison and clarification of relationships among formulas (genres), discussion of television's versions of these patterns as related to those in other media. General conclusions regarding features crossing all the formulas were outlined to argue for a television aesthetic, distinctive features of the medium that made television's version of common formulas more similar to one another than to their antecedents in other popular forms.

The second question, again in simplest form, is, What is the relation of television's stories and storytelling strategies to American (and, by implication, any other) society and culture? Here the focus was on the subject matter of programs and again presented large, "patterned" cultural "themes." Problems and issues presented in specific individual texts (episodes) were claimed to be versions of concepts such as "order," "justice," "authority," and, most common and most important, "family."

Important aspects of both sets of questions are missing from the book. As stated earlier, my "choice" to use genre—and from this point I will drop "formula"—as an organizational strategy merely followed the industrial organization of commercial American television. Although there are references to previous versions in literature and film, no effort was made to trace and explore the full implications of those categories in specific historical fashion illuminated by attention to industry, regulation, or economics. Indeed, one intention was to bracket the study of television "content" and narrative strategy from economic structures and industrial practices, placing economically grounded explanations of the medium with other "social scientific" approaches. Such an omission now seems amazingly shortsighted. Similarly, attempts to "interpret" cultural connections without any developed theory of culture also seem extraordinarily weak. This is especially the case given that European theories of culture and communication, media and society, were available, even if not yet widely examined and applied in departments of literature or, at the time, in formally constituted American studies programs such as the one in which I was appointed.

All this changed very quickly. More sophisticated approaches to these questions developed, particularly in Britain, as television came to be seen as a legitimate object of study grounded in the humanities. Raymond Williams, in *Television; Technology and Cultural Form,* of course challenged any simple notion of genre with his observations on televisual "flow."[11] Two books in this country developed from Aspen Institute seminars dealing with television were soon published. One of them, *Television as a Cultural Force,* contained some explorations of television genre.[12] Most notable among them was David Thorburn's superb essay "Television Melodrama," which remains one of the most cogent explanations of television fiction yet published.[13] In 1978, John Fiske and John Hartley's *Reading Television* also used genre as part of its organizational strategy but offered a succinct and far more complex understanding of "culture" as context for the specific topics, especially as they linked television *and* culture to "ideology."[14]

Among the most revealing analyses of genre and popular culture in my own continuing education was *Hollywood Genres: Formulas, Filmmaking, and the Studio System,* by Thomas Schatz, my colleague at the University of Texas.[15] His 1981 study of Hollywood movie genres (applying the term "formula" in a more precise industrial manner than that in *The Most Popular Art*) drew on European cultural theory, most especially for Schatz, Lévi-Straussian structuralism. Even more important, Schatz explored genre as an industrial/economic strategy while also presenting industrial and economic strategies *as* cultural strategies. This insight was powerfully instructive, suggesting that the move away from "literary" models of analysis would be far more appropriate for the study of television even though "textual analysis" could and should remain prominent.

In this same period the study of television was increasingly guided by the growing influence of cultural studies, which primarily meant the influence of the Birmingham Center for the Study of Contemporary Culture. Stuart Hall's essay "Encoding/Decoding" was circulated widely, even before publication in 1981.[16] It, too, called attention to industrial practices, but interestingly, and significantly, the "decoding" aspect of Hall's polarity attracted far more attention, and studies of television audiences proliferated.

But the real impact of what came to be known as British cultural studies lay in the growing focus in media studies on ideology, especially as elaborated in the works of Antonio Gramsci.[17] Analyses of television increasingly turned to questions of how the medium reinforced and, in some rare instances, challenged "dominant ideology."

The study of particular genres, the study of any history of formal characteristics, the study of ranges of meanings linked to other expressive forms were all in some ways set aside. The focus turned to understanding (or simply "demonstrating") the overarching ideological tendency of "television." This development is well illustrated in the work of Todd Gitlin, first in his essay "Prime Time Ideology: The Hegemonic Process in Television Entertainment"[18] and later in *Inside Prime Time*.[19] In the essay, Gitlin specifically discusses the role of "genre" in perpetuating a "leaky hegemony" characteristic of television entertainment. In the book, one of the most significant contributions to the study of the medium to date, he explores ideas and ideological formations as constructed and practiced inside the television industry. Many examples and discussions again focus on the role of genre. All, in the general argument of the book, lead to a pessimistic view of the medium as a central component of a flawed dominant ideology.

Throughout these long arguments over television's ideological role, genre has continued to play a crucial role as analytical device, industrial practice for organization and production, and rhetorical strategy. This is certainly the case in the essay I coauthored with Paul M. Hirsch, "Television as a Cultural Forum: Implications for Research."[20] Drawn into the discussion of ideology and away from vaguely defined "aesthetic" concerns, we argued that genre provides ideological "inflection," that the same social issue or problem, the same ideological struggle (for or against dominance), would be shaped differently in different generic constructs and that even individual instances of a single genre (police shows, medical shows, etc.) were sufficiently distinct from one another to alter meaning and significance. Our focus was on cultural processes, drawing on symbolic anthropology to complicate the discussion of ideology. In part, our aim was to respond to approaches such as "cultivation analysis," which claimed that the most important aspect of television lay in its common demographic features rather than in distinctive formal and narrative characteristics. Another goal was to challenge easy notions of "hegemony," also dependent on charting similarities rather than differences in television content.

Still, even in this essay the dual concerns of *The Most Popular Art* drove the analysis: How does television tell stories, and how do those stories process sociocultural concerns? The argument that the storytelling device was presented as "the schedule," and that that "text" was filled with a range of approaches to those concerns, was certainly more complicated than any "close reading" of a single television program would have suggested. But the first problems remained to be explored, which requires comment on yet another example of *TV: The Most Popular Art*.

Even though genre was used primarily as an organizational device in the book, there is a specific trajectory to the general argument. It claimed to move from the most fundamental and "simple" genre, the situation comedy, to the most complex, "the new shows," exemplified by programs such as *All in the Family, The Waltons,* and various British miniseries. Implicit in that arc was the "development" from "least artistic" to more, if not "most," artistic, development toward "high culture," toward the significance of the book's title, toward a redemption of "the popular" if not a diminution of "art." Despite the insistence that "popular culture" was worthy of study, that forms appealing to mass audiences were rich sites for analysis, what I now find more embarrassing is precisely the insistence that certain forms of cultural expression (sitcoms?) are inherently limited. Even the turn to *All in the Family, M*A*S*H,* and other programs sought to claim for them a kind of high-culture propriety, grounded in that other thrust of the book, cultural analysis. The duality, the ambivalence, is evident throughout. For example: "The audience [for *M*A*S*H*] is caught between its laughter and its realization—gently prodded when things get too lighthearted—that the war provides the theater for the humor. Even so, the choice has been made to emphasize the comedy and to reduce the specific social commentary. This show and 'All in the Family' are strong indications that comedy is now the chief vehicle for social criticism on television, a belief that is self-consciously shared by writers and producers of 'Maude's' alcoholism segment."[21] The passage goes on to quote those writers and producers regarding their intent in that episode of *Maude* to use this medium for noble purposes. But even this realization did not return,

The audience for $M*A*S*H$ is caught between its laughter and its realization that the war provides the theater for the humor. (Left to right) First row: Alan Alda as Captain Hawkeye Pierce; second row: Mike Farrell as Captain B. J. Hunnicut, Harry Morgan as Colonel Sherman Potter, Loretta Swit as Major Margaret Houlihan, and David Ogden Stiers as Major Charles Emerson Winchester; third row: William Christopher as Father Francis Mulcahy and Jamie Farr as Captain Maxwell Klinger. Courtesy of 20th Century Fox Television.

would not at the time have returned, my attention to *I Love Lucy* to recognize some of the same, more deeply embedded possibilities.

The final chapter of the book tries to go beyond summary and push the argument "for" television more strongly. That discussion, too, bears upon the uses and study of genre and on the study of television generally. It is not, in any strict sense, a discussion of "aesthetics." Rather, it merely attempts to define some common features, techniques, and characteristics of "the medium." There and in other places the book claims that television modifies existing "formulas" into its own "television version" of those categories, a claim I believe retains some validity. But the question is whether and how "intimacy, continuity, and history," the three distinctive "aesthetic" features I attribute to television, relate to genre. My concern is also with how they might relate today as well as thirty years ago.

I still find these descriptors/devices/characteristics useful, but some of the terms and implications should be modified. "Intimacy" I would retain, despite some reliance in the initial description on the size of the television screen. I maintain that television fiction, news, documentary, and recent versions of programming known as "reality" continue to be fascinated with and reliant on narratives recounting intimate matters in intimate ways. In some instances intimacy has been extraordinarily intensified. We have been made privy to decisions regarding "marriage," "birth," and "death," that could alter lives. We have observed as individuals are ridiculed and embarrassed. We have been allowed to witness alterations of the body, procedures that in many cultures might be considered sacred. We have been afforded the voyeur's perspective, even as we are aware that the "real" people we observe are equally aware of their exhibitions, are "performing" for us.

"Continuity," however, should give way to seriality. This is what I attempted to elevate as narrative device in admiration of soap opera and miniseries. In the earlier work the praise was pointed toward "realism," toward "probability," and the goal was to place (force, guide) audiences into a more immediate encounter with content. Believing serious treatment of contemporary issues to be somehow diminished by narrative closure (a common assumption among far harsher critics of television than I), I considered continuity a rhetorical strategy of great significance.

The fact that almost all television genres today exhibit a degree of seriality, and that some are built primarily on this device, suggests that it remains a major factor in television storytelling. Indeed, I suggest that the turn to serial narrative in prime-time television confirmed the value

The Mary Tyler Moore Show was the first situation comedy to wrap up its serial narrative with a special finale. (Left to right) Mary Tyler Moore as Mary Richards, Edward Asner as Lou Grant, and Ted Knight as Ted Baxter. Courtesy of MTM Enterprises, Inc.

of soap opera strategies and enabled the creation of some of television's most outstanding content. Even those "series" that deny, or defy, seriality, the *Law & Orders*, the *CSIs*, are defined by their rejection of seriality. Clearly, the narrative strategy is in part a function of a commercially supported, advertiser-driven system of electronic communication, developed in radio and carried over to television as a means of attracting audiences in a regularized, routinized manner. But serialized narratives are prominent in television systems around the world, and the use of segmented, regularized time, no matter the economic underpinning, fosters this narrative mode. As a result, one Aristotelian dictum—that stories have beginnings, middles, and ends—can be shattered. It rarely is, of course. Most serial narratives in non-U.S. systems come to an end, as do miniseries or "limited" series. But many other American series, heavily serialized, merely stop, their ending left hanging "in the air." And even those forms that previously used more submerged forms of seriality, such as the situation comedy, have increasingly placed it at the forefront of their narrative strategies. Series such as *Friends* and *Frasier,* like *M*A*S*H* and *The Mary Tyler Moore Show* before them, "wrap up" their serial aspects in "finales." Only, in some cases, to reappear years later, as (regrettably) did *The Dick Van Dyke Show* in 2004.

Seriality allows genres to be deeply mined for content, for exploration of character, for inflection of issues. Writers, producers, actors are afforded opportunities to expand their work in interesting ways, presumably in hopes of interesting audiences in interesting ways. Represented actions, plot points, and events can reveal new motivations, altering directions for the future of the narrative and clarifying past actions or shedding new light on significant decisions. It is no surprise, then, that the more recent "reality" programs rely heavily on serial narrative, even piquing viewer interest with the fact that the "ending" has occurred long before the program airs and that "some" participants know what is "going to" happen.

The term "history" must also be replaced in a description of television's common characteristics. Already in 1974 its application was fragile, artificial. Had the Western not so recently been so central to television programming, or had the first successful miniseries imports not traded so heavily on historical topics, the device I was attempting to describe might have been differently named. It was not until the preparation of the "Cultural Forum" essay, following increased attention to symbolic anthropology, that a more appropriate description became evident. The work of Victor Turner, Clifford Geertz, and Mary Douglas was a crucial opening in this regard.[22] Most specifically, Turner's exploration of "liminal" and "liminoid" occasions, spaces, and events provided a different way to think about the manner in which television narratives both remove us from and place us inside social and cultural events, problems, topics, themes. Even the most immediate detective program, such as those in the *Law & Order* franchise, makes urban space and headline narratives into something removed from our experience but touching us directly. The settings and strategies of "reality" programming—remote geographic locations, enclosed houses, isolation, intense social interaction, contests, observation by outsiders—are manufactured versions of liminal experience. Rules are both broken and affirmed in these sites.

When intimacy, seriality, and liminality are merged and concentrated, as in *The Sopranos* or *Six Feet Under,* in *Scrubs* or *The Office,* even, at times, in *Frasier* and *Friends,* television's rich possibilities are exhibited. The past merges with the present—special makeup and memory sequences reveal the "fat Monica" and explain much about her obsessions and professions. Dreams inform "reality," but it is the reality of "fiction." Fathers die but continue to appear, playing key roles in the lives of sons and daughters.

Most significantly, genres blur, lose specific meaning, intent, import. "Formulaic" expectations are subverted. Boundaries fail to hold in the narratives, but also in the industry, where writer-producers explore worlds in which we laugh at the amount of food consumed in the back room of the Bada-Bing, only to become nauseous at the sheer physical effort required to murder with bare hands. Time is altered when days are extended across the television "season" in twenty-four episodes, playing with and in chronology as in another kind of dream sequence.

Finally, I will suggest that television has come nearly full circle, has returned to an almost classical sense of narrative, to a very basic and fundamental sense of genre. From one perspective, all television is melodrama as defined and explored by Peter Brooks in *The Melodramatic Imagination*.[23] Citing the origins of the form in the decline of firm belief in any transcendent power, Brooks suggests that melodrama provides society with potent but occluded accounts of good and evil, positive and negative alternatives grounded in the social rather than external moral or religious realms.

But melodrama must continually represent social and cultural structures and shifts in some "contemporary" manner. We probably do not accept television's doctors and lawyers, policemen and firefighters, mobsters and mothers as "analytically accurate." But in their liminal arenas they somehow ring true, reminding us of what we value and what a difficult thing it is to value anything. They offer stories in which we find some "ideological formations" repressive, some alternatives attractive, some memories deplorable, some decisions—in fiction or in the news reports—reprehensible. This occurs even in those television "comedies" that turn suddenly into something more "serious," when Samantha announces her breast cancer in *Sex and the City* or death intervenes unexpectedly in *Scrubs*. These, too, are melodramatic moments offering patterns available for our own choices.

Perhaps, then, we are left with the two great seriocomic masks. On the one hand, the upturned smirk of comedy. On the other, not the droop of tragedy but the twisted, enigmatic Mona Lisa–like half grin of melodrama, the genre that perhaps defines our present moment in history.

Concluding digression: Why television? Because he was working in a radio and television sales and repair shop in the small Mississippi town where we lived, my father brought a television set into the house in 1952, early for most people like us. We viewed whatever was on, just as we had entertained ourselves with variety, drama, and comedy and informed ourselves with news on radio. I watched television throughout my formal study of literature as I had, with the usual exception of late high school and the college years, for most of my life.

During graduate school days, watching TV was a pleasant distraction from the library, though the study of literature was in no way diminished by my fascination with the other medium. The great live dramas were ending, but I had for years observed very classy examples of "high art" there, adaptations of Faulkner, Hemingway, the usual Shakespeare. And I had noted the original dramas for the medium, work by Rod Serling, Horton Foote, and a bevy of outstanding writers who presented social problem plays to the mass audience. More significant in immediate terms, however, programs such as *The Defenders, Route 66, Peter Gunn, Have Gun, Will Travel,* other Westerns, police and detective programs, medical melodramas—all these probed topics that surrounded us. What I noted most was that almost no one had asked what I considered truly interesting questions about these fictional forms.

Some years after the publication of *The Most Popular Art,* I regularly assigned my undergraduate students an exercise I called a "television autobiography." I asked them to write about how television was part of their lived experience. They wrote extensively about programs they remembered, series and episodes. But they wrote more often about how TV affected family dynamics, how they learned social behaviors, how they accepted and rejected models they found there. My own autobiographical impulses made me realize that I was writing about television because the medium had changed my life, most vividly in social and cultural terms, terms fundamentally political.

Growing up in Mississippi in the forties and fifties meant growing up in a closed society. Television opened a vast array of options to that closure, most crucially in the way it dealt with "race." Sometimes it presented issues in veiled form, as when Matt Dillon defended a "minority" character on *Gunsmoke.* Sometimes it took issues by the throat, as in *The Defenders* or in a particularly vivid episode of *Dr. Kildare.* At other times, and increasingly in the years in which I was watching less but thinking more, it pushed terrible images into our living rooms. The Freedom Riders pulled from buses and the students beaten at lunch counters were being filmed very close to my home, and this had an enormous impact, radically altering the ways in which I conceived of "race relations," leading to some considerable degree of personal and social discomfort, and to minor activism.

For most viewers around me, friends or family, teachers or preachers, the images and narratives did not have the same effect. The fact that the images were available, however, created the attention I still pay the medium. Turning an analytical interest to those fictions that moved, annoyed, embarrassed, or amused me hardly seems a long step. It was, despite any ideological analysis or lack of it, despite any criticism of the medium or apology for it, undertaken as a "political" choice as much as a professional one. The "curriculum," the "canon" in which I had been educated needed, in my view, this opening. I remain convinced that television viewing is, as Michael Saenz so carefully describes, "a cultural practice."[24] Its significance is profound. Not a medium that "polices," "instructs," "affects" us, television presents repertoires—some as despicable as others are noble—and the elements we select from those offerings of meaning, belief, behavior, emotion, and performance fit variously into our experience. It does these things in ways that continue to change, still drawing me to the screen and to the questions that seem never to be fully and satisfactorily answered.

Notes

1. Horace Newcomb, *TV: The Most Popular Art* (Garden City, N.Y.: Anchor Press, 1974).

2. Wayne C. Booth, *The Rhetoric of Fiction* (Chicago: University of Chicago Press, 1961).

3. Sheldon Sacks, *Fiction and the Shape of Belief: A Study of Henry Fielding, with Glances at Swift, Johnson and Richardson* (Berkeley: University of California Press, 1964).

4. See, for example, Ronald S. Crane, *The Languages of Criticism and the Structure of Poetry* (Toronto: University of Toronto Press, 1953).

5. John G. Cawelti, *The Six-Gun Mystique* (Bowling Green, Ohio: Bowling Green University Popular Press, 1971).

6. Patrick D. Hazard, ed., *TV as Art: Some Essays in Criticism* (Champaign, Ill.: National Council of Teachers of English, 1966).

7. Stanley Donner, ed., *The Future of Commercial Television* (London: Times Publishing, 1965); Stanley Donner, ed., *The Meaning of Commercial Television* (Austin: University of Texas Press, 1966).

8. Robert Warshow, *The Immediate Experience: Movies, Comics, Theatre and Other Aspects of Popular Culture* (New York: Atheneum, 1971).

9. Horace Newcomb, ed., *Television: The Critical View* (New York: Oxford University Press, 1976).

10. A small personal digression: I was teaching three courses each semester and, from early 1973 through the spring of 1974, when much of the writing was done, also writing six hundred words a day, five days a week, as the television

columnist for the *Baltimore Morning Sun*. As the acknowledgments for the book state clearly, the book would not have been written without the assistance of Sara Newcomb, who cared for our household, which included two young children.

11. Raymond Williams, *Television; Technology and Cultural Form* (London: Fontana, 1974).

12. Douglass Cater and Richard Adler, eds., *Television as a Cultural Force* (New York: Praeger, 1976). See also Douglas Cater and Richard Adler, eds., *Television as a Social Force: New Approaches to TV Criticism* (New York: Praeger, 1975).

13. David Thorburn, "Television Melodrama," in Cater and Adler, *Television as a Cultural Force*.

14. John Fiske and John Hartley, *Reading Television* (London: Methuen, 1978).

15. Thomas Schatz, *Hollywood Genres: Formulas, Filmmaking, and the Studio System* (Philadelphia: Temple University Press, 1981).

16. Stuart Hall, "Encoding/Decoding," in *Culture, Media, Language: Working Papers in Cultural Studies, 1972–79*, ed. Stuart Hall, Dorothy Hobson, Alan Lowe, and Paul Willis (London: Hutchinson, 1981), 128–38.

17. See, for example, Antonio Gramsci, *Selections from the Prison Notebooks of Antonio Gramsci*, ed. and trans. Quentin Hoare and Goeffrey Nowell Smith (London: Lawrence and Wishart, 1971).

18. Todd Gitlin, "Prime Time Ideology: The Hegemonic Process in Television Entertainment," *Social Problems* 26, no. 3 (1979): 251–66.

19. Todd Gitlin, *Inside Prime Time* (New York: Pantheon, 1983).

20. Horace Newcomb and Paul M. Hirsch, "Television as a Cultural Forum: Implications for Research," *Quarterly Review of Film Studies* 8 (Summer 1983): 45–56.

21. Newcomb, *TV: The Most Popular Art*, 226.

22. See Victor Turner, "Process, System, and Symbol: A New Anthropological Synthesis," *Daedalus* (Summer 1977); "Liminal to Liminoid, in Play, Flow, and Ritual: An Essay in Comparative Symbology," *Rice University Studies* 60, no. 3 (1974); Clifford Geertz, *The Interpretation of Cultures* (New York: Basic Books, 1973); Mary Douglas, *Implicit Meanings: Essays in Anthropology* (London: Routledge and Kegan Paul, 1973).

23. Peter Brooks, *The Melodramatic Imagination: Balzac, Henry James, Melodrama and the Mode of Excess* (New Haven, Conn.: Yale University Press, 1976).

24. Michael Saenz, "Television Viewing as a Cultural Practice," *Journal of Communication Inquiry* 16, no. 2 (1992): 37–51.

2 | a cultural approach to television genre theory

Jason Mittell

Genres are a part of every aspect of television. Most texts have some generic identity, fitting into well-entrenched generic categories or incorporating genre mixing (like "dramedies" such as *Ally McBeal* [1997–2002] or blends like *Make Me Laugh* [1997], a comedy/game show). Industries use genres in producing programs, as well as in other central practices like self-definition (channels such as ESPN or Cartoon Network) or scheduling (locating genres within time slots, as in daytime soap operas). Audiences use genres to organize fan practices (generically determined organizations, conferences, and Web sites), personal preferences, and everyday conversations and viewing practices. Likewise, academics use generic distinctions to delineate research projects and special topic courses, while journalistic critics rely on genres to locate programs within a common framework. Even going to the video store or skimming through *TV Guide* reveals genre as the primary way to sort out television's vast array of textual options. Despite this virtual omnipresence of genre within TV, little theoretical research has been aimed at explaining how genres work specifically for television.

A number of factors explain this lack of theoretical exploration. Some scholars may view the vast body of genre theory produced within literary and film studies as sufficient, able to explain genre in any medium. Much literary and film genre theory, however, cannot account for some of the specific industry and audience practices unique to television, or for the mixture of fictional and nonfictional programming that constitutes the lineup on nearly every TV channel. Importing nonindigenous genre theories into television studies without significant revision creates many difficulties when accounting for the specifics of the medium.

The greatest obstacle to television-specific genre theory stems from the assumptions of traditional approaches to genre. Most genre theory has focused on issues that seem outdated to some media scholars, whether they be the formal and aesthetic mechanics of texts or structuralist theories of generic meanings that seem incompatible with contemporary methods. The central questions motivating many media scholars today—how do television programs fit into historically specific systems of cultural power and politics?—appear distant from those that typify genre theory.[1] Thus a return to genre theory might imply theoretical backtracking, either to structuralism, aesthetics, or ritual theories, all of which take a backseat to current cultural studies paradigms within television studies. Even the most comprehensive discussion of television genre theory, Jane Feuer's essay in *Channels of Discourse*, ultimately concludes that genre analysis as a paradigm does not work as well for television as it has for film or literature.[2] So what's a media scholar to do?

The answers to this question so far have not been fully satisfying. Many television genre studies seem content to take genres at face value, using the categorical labels that are culturally commonplace without much consideration of the meanings or usefulness of those selfsame labels. Television scholars who do "stop to smell the theory" have been quick to employ film and literary theories, often (though not always) with brief disclaimers noting the flaws inherent in these paradigms, while adding the now-ubiquitous phrase "More work in this area is needed." This chapter is a first step toward "more work in this area." It proposes an alternative approach that can better account for the cultural operations of television genre than can traditional approaches. This theoretical offering is admittedly brief and does not put this theory into detailed practice, which I do elsewhere.[3] Despite these caveats, this chapter might at least put the topic of television genre theory more squarely on the academic agenda for media scholars and provide some ideas for further discussion.

In examining the assumptions of genre theory and putting forward a cultural approach to television genres, two aspects of my argument require clarification. First, while I offer a television-specific approach to genre, many of my theoretical points are applicable to (and derive from) work in other media, especially cinema studies. The conceptual basis for my argument could be applied to any medium and is not dependent on any essential qualities of television. The focus on television examples in this chapter both provides a more detailed account of genre than a transmedia approach could offer and avoids the tendency toward generalization and abstraction that typifies some genre theory. Second, although I may appear critical of other methods of genre analysis, I do not wish to suggest that my approach is the only "correct" way to examine genres—I embrace methodological eclecticism, acknowledging that neither my approach nor any other could possibly answer every question about every generic instance. Yet I think it is important to note that traditional approaches to genre have relied on a number of assumptions that should be examined and reappraised in light of contemporary theoretical paradigms.

Traditional Genre Analysis and the Textualist Assumption

Media scholars have traditionally looked at genre as a textual component, using a variety of guiding questions and theoretical paradigms. One tradition poses *questions of definition,* looking to identify the core elements that constitute a given genre by examining texts to delimit the formal mechanisms constituting the essence of a given genre.[4] Another approach, probably the most common in media studies, asks *questions of interpretation* by exploring the textual meanings of genres and situating them within larger social contexts.[5] Within this interpretive approach, a number of specific theoretical orientations have emerged—ritual, ideological, structuralist, psychoanalytic, and cultural studies, just to list some central (and potentially overlapping) paradigms.[6] A third (and less developed) form of genre analysis poses *questions of history* to emphasize the evolutionary dynamics of genres, looking at how changing cultural circumstances bring about generic shifts.[7]

Despite this variety of methods and paradigms, most examples of genre analysis primarily consider genre as a textual attribute. We might characterize this central notion about genres as the "textualist assumption," a position that takes many forms. Some scholars (more commonly in literary theory) make explicit claims that genre is an intrinsic property of texts.[8] Media scholars more frequently *imply* genre as a textual component through a number of practices—situating genre within larger discussions of texts (as opposed to industries, audiences, or culture),[9] mapping an internal-external distinction onto texts versus "other factors,"[10] or methodologically examining a genre primarily through textual analysis.[11] This textualist assumption seems to have contributed to the decline in genre analysis; as cultural media scholars have moved away from textual analysis, genre has been left behind with topics like narrative and style as perceived relics of extinct methodologies.

So what is wrong with the textualist assumption? Aren't genres just categories of texts? Certainly genres do categorize texts. We might consider that genres categorize industrial practices (such as the self-definition of the Sci Fi Channel) or audience members (such as sci-fi fans), but in these instances the textual category of "science fiction" precedes the industry's and audiences' use of the term—science fiction programs are the implied unifying factor within both the industry and audience categories. This is not to suggest that genres are not primarily categories of texts, but there is a crucial difference between conceiving of genre as a textual *category* and treating it like a textual *component*, a distinction that most genre studies elide.

The members of any given category do not create, define, or constitute the category itself. A category works primarily to link a number of discrete elements together under a label for cultural convenience. Although the members of a given category might all possess some inherent trait binding them together, there is nothing intrinsic about the category itself. Think of our contemporary understanding of racial difference—while all people who are categorized under the label of "black" might have dark skin (although certainly this is not always true), there is nothing inherent about dark skin that makes it a racial category. Eye color or hair color have no categorical equivalents to skin color; these are all differing physical components of human bodies, but only some components are culturally activated into salient and used categories. We can accept the distinction between a biological trait (like skin color) and the cultural category that activates it into a system of differentiation (namely, race)—these are related, but not identical, physical and conceptual elements. If we shifted the same biological bodies into another cultural system of difference, other physical traits could become activated into operative categories of differentiation (such as height). The physical elements do not change, but the category does, suggesting that the category itself emerges from the relationship between the elements it groups together and the cultural context in which it operates.

The same type of distinction also holds for media texts. We do not generally differentiate between shows that take place in Boston and those that take place in Chicago, but we do differentiate between programs set in hospitals and those set in police stations. Texts have many different components, but only some are used to define generic categories.

As many genre scholars have noted, there are no uniform criteria for genre delimitation—some are defined by setting (like Westerns), some by actions (like crime shows), some by audience affect (like comedies), and some by narrative form (like mysteries).[12] This diversity of definitional attributes suggests that there is nothing internal to texts mandating how they are to be generically categorized. In fact, some scholars have pointed to instances where the same text becomes "re-genrified" as cultural contexts shift.[13] If the same text is open enough to be categorized under various genres, then it follows that it is problematic to look for generic definitions solely within the confines of the text.

Genres are not found within one isolated text; *Wheel of Fortune* (1975–) is not a genre in and of itself, but rather is a member of the generic category "game show." Genres only emerge from the intertextual relations between multiple texts, resulting in a common category. But how do these texts interrelate to form a genre? Texts cannot interact on their own; they come together only through cultural practices such as production and reception. Audiences link programs together all the time ("this show is just a clone of that one"), as do industry personnel ("imagine *Friends* meets *The X-Files*"). Texts themselves do not actively link together without this type of cultural activity. Even when one text explicitly references another (such as in the case of allusions, parodies, spin-offs, or crossovers), these instances become activated only through processes of production or reception. If we watch *The Jeffersons* (1975–85) without the knowledge that it spun off from *All in the Family* (1971–79)—as surely many audience members have—then we cannot usefully claim that intertextuality is relevant or active at that moment of reception. Thus if genre is dependent on *intertextuality*, it cannot be an *inherently textual* component.

Most genre scholarship has analyzed texts because they are the most imminent and material objects of media. Logic and tradition authorize this analytic mode as well; if we want to understand the biological taxonomy of frogs, we need to look at the members of that category (namely, frogs). Traditionally, we do the same for genres: if you want to understand music videos, watch as many as you can.[14] But unlike frogs, music videos do not reproduce on their own. We cannot understand why *Unsolved Mysteries* (1987–) followed *America's Most Wanted* (1988–) just by watching the shows; there is no causal mechanism or active process of generic continuity in the programs themselves. Processes of genre reproduction, such as creating new sitcoms and newsmagazine programs, occur only through the actions of industries and audiences, not texts themselves.[15] Likewise, there is no inherent genetic code that forbids cross-genre mating; whereas a biological imperative maintains a natural distinction between frogs and tulips, nothing genetic prevented the creation of the generically mixed music video/police drama, *Cop Rock* (1990). But the creation of *Cop Rock* did not stem from texts themselves—*Hill Street Blues* (1981–87) and "Like a Virgin" (1984) did not create their own sordid offspring. The mixing of genres is a cultural process, enacted by industry personnel, often in response to audience viewing practices. While we may want to study frogs in order to understand their biological category, texts themselves are insufficient to understand how genres are created, merge, evolve, or disappear. We should look outside the texts to locate the range of sites in which genres operate, change, proliferate, and die out.

Instead of biological taxonomy, a better parallel for genre analysis might be brands of automobiles. Most people would locate the difference between Chevrolets and Toyotas within the internal mechanics of the two brands, noting different designs, machinery, and engine systems. While this may be an important site of differentiation, it is not necessarily the primary way the two brands differ. Many differences in automobile brands are established through industrial practices (manufacturing styles, labels, marketing, corporate reputation, and nationality) and cultural circulation (driver preferences, press accounts, consumer ratings, and advertising). In some extreme cases, the two brands might contain identical parts, be assembled in the same plant, and utilize indistinguishable internal mechanics; for instance, car experts Tom and Ray Magliozzi of *Car Talk* fame wrote in 1993, "Chevy and Toyota build a car together in California. At Toyota dealers, they call it a Corolla, and at Chevy dealers, it's called the Geo Prizm."[16] In this case, the differences are completely cultural instead of mechanical, but cars are always cultural products, accruing meanings and associations through their widespread production and usage, linkages that are not guaranteed by their mechanical essence or internal design. They are also clearly historical—few would argue that the essence of a Chevy is the same today as it was in 1920. Mechanical designs, corporate structure, consumer usage, and cultural associations have all shifted dramatically, yet some scholars treat genres as timeless essences defined by an inner core rather than constituted by changing cultural practices, using taxonomic biological parallels that are less apt than those of cultural technologies like automobiles.

Thus genres are *not* intrinsic to texts; they are constituted by the processes that some scholars have labeled "external" elements, such as industrial and audience practices. But we cannot simply replace an intrinsic textual approach to genre with an extrinsic contextual theory. The dualities between text and context, internal and external, are artificial and arbitrary.[17] We need to look beyond the text as the locus for genre and instead locate genres within the complex interrelations among texts, industries, audiences, and historical contexts.[18] The boundaries between texts and the cultural practices that constitute them (primarily production and reception) are too shifting and fluid to be reified. Texts exist only through their production and reception, so we cannot make the boundary between texts and their material cultural contexts absolute. Genres transect these boundaries, with production, distribution, promotion, and reception practices all working to categorize media texts into genres. Emphasizing the boundaries between elements "internal" and "external" to genres only obscures how genres transect these fluid borders.

Let me sum up my argument thus far. Genres have traditionally been treated as textual components. Although genres are categories of texts, texts themselves do not determine, contain, or produce their own categorization. Generic categories are intertextual and hence operate more broadly than within the bounded realm of a media text. Even though texts certainly bear marks that are typical of genres, these textual conventions are not what define the genre. Genres exist only through the creation, circulation, and reception of texts within cultural contexts. Textual analysis cannot examine media genres as they operate at the categorical level—there are texts that are categorized by genres, but their textual sum does not equal the whole of the genre. Instead, we must separate the practice of analyzing generically labeled texts from an analysis of the genre as a cultural category. Analyses of generic texts are certainly worthwhile, but they cannot explain how genres themselves operate as categories. We thus need to rethink genres in different terms and propose their analysis using different methods. But what is this new approach to genre?[19]

Discursive Practices and Generic Clusters

Decentering the text within genre analysis might cause some methodological hesitation. If genres are components of texts, there is a clear site of analysis on which to focus our critical attention. But if genres are not textual properties, where exactly might we find and analyze them? While there are certainly many theoretical approaches that we might adopt to explain how a category becomes culturally salient, it is more useful to conceive of genre as a *discursive practice*. By regarding genre as a property and function of discourse, we can examine the ways in which various forms of communication work to constitute generic definitions and meanings.

This discursive approach emerges out of contemporary poststructuralist theories, as genre seems to fit perfectly into the account of discursive formations offered by Michel Foucault.[20] For Foucault, discursive formations are historically specific systems of thought, conceptual categories that work to define cultural experiences within larger systems of power. He notes that discursive formations do not emerge from a centralized structure or single site of power but are built bottom-up from disparate micro-instances. Even though discursive formations are often marked by discontinuities and irregularities, they do follow an overall regularity and fit into a specific cultural context's larger "regime of truth." Discursive formations often appear to be "natural" or internal properties of beings, such as humans or texts, but they are actually culturally constituted and mutable. Like Foucault's notion of the "author function" of discourses, we can approach genre as a function of discourse that is neither intrinsic nor essential to texts.[21] All these features of discursive formations hold for genres as well.

To examine generic discourses, we should analyze the contextualized generic practices that circulate around and through texts. We might look at what audiences and industries say about genres, what terms and definitions circulate around any given generic instance, and how specific cultural concepts are linked to particular genres. These discursive practices can be broken down into three basic types by how they work to constitute genres: *definition* ("this show is a sitcom because it has a laugh track"), *interpretation* ("sitcoms reflect and reinforce the status quo"), and *evaluation* ("sitcoms are better entertainment than soap operas").[22] These discursive utterances may seem to reflect on an already established genre, but they are themselves constitutive of that genre; they are the practices that define genres, delimit their meanings, and posit their cultural value. If genres are formed through intertextual relationships between texts, then the discursive enunciations that link texts become the site and material for genre analysis.

This discursive approach offers a new framework by which to examine media texts—instead of examining texts as bounded and stable objects of analysis, we should view texts as sites of discursive practice. A discursive approach to genre necessitates that we decenter the text as the primary site of genre, but not to the extent that we ignore texts. Media texts still function as important locales of generic discourses and must be examined on a par with other sites, such as audience and industrial practices. Television programs explicitly cite generic categories, and advertising, promotions, parodies, and intertextual references within shows are all vital sites of generic discursive practice. In decentering the text from genre analysis, we cannot jettison the text as a site of discursive generic operation; rather, we should simply acknowledge that an isolated text does not define a genre on its own.

Generic discourses are best examined and mapped in their surface enunciations, instead of interpreted and "read into" like media texts. We should not attempt to interpret generic discourses by suggesting what statements "really mean" or express beneath the surface. Instead, we should focus on the breadth of discursive enunciations around any given instance, mapping out as many articulations of genre as possible and situating them within larger cultural contexts and relations of power. For example, to examine the quiz show genre, we should look beyond singular sites such as texts or production practices. Instead, we should gather many diverse enunciations of the genre from the widest possible range of sources, including corporate documents, press reviews and commentaries, trade journal accounts, parodies, regulatory policies, audience practices, production manuals, other media representations, advertisements, and the texts themselves. Linking together these numerous generic discourses will begin to suggest more large-scale patterns of generic definitions, meanings, and hierarchies, but we should arrive at these macro-features through an analysis of micro-instances. Although discontinuities and ruptures among definitions, meanings, and values will certainly emerge, generic discourses point toward larger regularities that provide a genre's appearance of stability and coherence.

Our goal in analyzing generic discourses is not to arrive at a genre's "proper" definition, interpretation, or evaluation but to explore the material ways in which genres are culturally defined, interpreted, and evaluated. Shifting our focus away from projects that attempt to provide the ultimate definition or interpretation of a genre will enable us to examine the ways in which genre definitions, interpretations, and evaluations are part of the larger cultural operations of genre. Instead of guiding questions such as, What does a given genre mean? or How can we define a genre? we might look toward widespread cultural practices of genre interpretation and definition, leading to questions such as, What does a given genre mean for a specific community? or How is a genre's definition strategically articulated by socially situated groups? This approach requires much more specific and detailed research into a genre at a given historical instance, suggesting that sweeping accounts are likely incomplete. This is not to say that genres do not have large-scale diachronic and cross-media histories—these larger trends are valid objects of study, but the abstract and generalized mode of media history most common to generic historiography tends to efface specific instances in the name of macro-patterns. We can begin to build a more satisfying macro-account of a genre's history from the bottom up, by collecting micro-instances of generic discourses in historically specific moments and examining the resulting large-scale patterns and trajectories. This bottom-up approach reflects how genres actually form and evolve—out of the specific cultural practices of industries and audiences, not out of macro-structures.

Since genre discourses do not stem solely from a central source—be it industrial or ideological—we need to look at genre history as a fluid and active process, not as a teleological tale of textual rise and fall. Instead of typical questions of definition or interpretation, we should foreground *questions of cultural process* in our attempts to analyze media genres. The notion of genre as a discursive process has been proposed by a number of scholars, although it has only recently been explored as a more fully realized approach.[23] The key work in this area is Rick Altman's recent book *Film/Genre*. Although Altman provides many compelling and convincing arguments for a process-based approach to genre—points that are congruent with my approach—he finally argues for augmenting his influential textualist semantic/syntactic theory of genre with a consideration of the pragmatic aspects of genre as well. This traditional structuralist account of texts is not easily compatible with his more revisionist poststructuralist account of generic processes and pragmatics. Despite Altman's foregrounding of cultural processes, textual structure remains central to his approach, making it difficult to provide an account of how generic categories operate outside the bounds of the text.

We should examine the cultural processes of generic discourses prior to examining the generic texts that have been traditionally viewed as identical to the genre itself. Specifically, genre theory should account for how generic processes operate within cultural contexts, how industry and audience practices constitute genres, and how genres can be fluid over time yet fairly coherent at any given moment. We should also examine the specificities of the medium—Altman convincingly argues that the film industry promotes multiple genres around any single movie to maximize audience appeals. Even though we may find similar trends in television, we cannot simply import such an argument into a distinct medium with vitally different industrial imperatives and audience practices. We should carefully adapt the theoretical advances offered within film studies to the particularities of television genres, as well as developing specific insights emerging from the detailed analysis of television genres. This approach to genre synthesizes previous accounts of generic processes to offer a model specifically concerning television genres, while offering theoretical notions that might be useful for other media as well.

Approaching genres as discursive formations enables us to balance notions of genre as both active process and stable formation. Although genres are constantly in flux and under definitional negotiation, generic terms are still salient enough that most people would agree on a common working definition for any genre. Even if we cannot provide an essential definition of a genre's core identity, we all still know a sitcom when we see one. Discourse theory offers a model for such stability in flux—genres work as *discursive clusters,* with certain definitions and meanings coming together at any given time to suggest a coherent and clear genre. But these clusters are contingent and transitory, shifting over time and taking on new meanings and definitions within differing contexts. In addition, these generic clusters are hollow. Discursive genre clusters are formed from the outside, with the gathering and linking of meanings that create the appearance of a generic core, but this center is just as contingent and fluid as the more "fringe" discourses. At any given moment, a genre might appear quite stable, static, and bounded; however, the same genre might operate differently in another historic or cultural context. Using this approach to generic clusters, we can see how genres work simultaneously as fluid and static, an active process and a stable product. Genre historiography, then, should provide a genealogy of discursive shifts and rearticulations to account for a genre's evolution and redefinition, not just a chronology of changing textual examples.

Another central facet to this approach is that the generic discourses within a given cluster are *not* solely media texts. The discourses that constitute a generic cluster are the enunciations and practices that *locate* a text within a genre (including textual discourses as well). In the case of quiz shows, for example, it is not the individual programs that constitute the genre but the production and reception discourses that articulate programs together and situate them within the genre. The texts themselves are certainly brought into the genre and are components of the cluster, but they cannot be seen separately from the ways industries and audiences (broadly conceived) position them within or in relation to the genre. Thus, *Win Ben Stein's Money* (1997–2002) should be examined not as a textual example (or counterexample) of a quiz show but as a site of generic discourse in which competing (and harmonious) voices and practices work to position the text in relation to the genre.

Needless to say, this cultural approach to genre is of a somewhat different order than the traditional methods of genre analysis. The three typical approaches to genres outlined here—definitional, interpretive, and historical—all engage in *textual generic criticism,* looking at genre texts to uncover and identify definitions, meanings, and changes. Other approaches to genre analysis, such as psychological examinations of generic pleasures, also begin with the text in order to analyze the larger operations of the genre.[24] While we might accept all these methodological options in the name of theoretical pluralism, we must recognize that if we conceive of genres as cultural categories, then most typical approaches do not actually analyze *genres* per se. Rather, they use generic categories to delimit their textual projects but do not engage in the level of categorical analysis that an account of genre necessitates. It is putting the cart before the horse to analyze the texts of a given genre in the name of analyzing the genre itself; instead, we must explore the categorical operation of a genre before looking closely at its component texts if we want to understand the genre in cultural practice.[25] Once we chart out how genres are culturally constituted, defined, interpreted, and evaluated, we might look to other methods to analyze common textual forms, psychological pleasures, or structuring principles, but we should first understand how genres operate culturally to utilize the assumed generic terms that delineate such a study.

Exemplifying Genre Analysis with Michael Jackson's Music Videos

As I have argued, genres are categorical clusters of discursive processes that transect texts via their cultural interactions with industries, audiences, and broader contexts. We might begin a genre analysis by starting with a textual example, an industrial practice, a historical shift, or an audience controversy, but our study of generic processes needs to account for how all these realms work in interactive tandem. To study

The success of Michael Jackson's early music videos, such as the prototypical dance/performance piece "Billie Jean," helped change MTV's racially segregated programming policies. Courtesy of Optimum Productions.

genres as cultural categories, we must examine discourses that run through texts but are not found solely within them. Using abstract theory is not conducive to this cultural studies model, however, because the ultimate goal is to study genres as they actually occur in specific instances.

As an exemplary case in point, how might Michael Jackson's trio of successful music videos from 1983, "Billie Jean," "Beat It," and "Thriller," be understood within the context of the music video genre? Traditional methods of genre analysis might offer specific text-based approaches to the case study. A hypothetical definitional approach might try to isolate the core elements that constitute the genre, positing that the genre is defined by the musical song, with the video elements taking a secondary role. These videos would represent a spectrum from core ("Billie Jean" as prototypical dance/performance piece) to periphery ("Thriller" as a generic exception, with fourteen minutes of narrative mixed with song and dance), with "Beat It" residing on the genre's fringe (with its integration of narrative and a brief nonmusical segment). An interpretive approach to the genre might relate these videos to their social situation by showing how the music video is symptomatic of cultural anxieties or concerns. Thus, these videos might be read as embodying rebellion as a countercultural urge (the "Beat It" gang fight, the monsters of "Thriller"), yet recuperating the status quo by the end in the name of dominant ideology.[26] A typical historical approach might chart the shift from performance-centered videos like "Billie Jean" to the narrative model of "Beat It," with "Thriller" representing the extreme possibilities of a narrative music video that would rarely be matched. This approach might situate the videos within the context of industrial practices and cultural contexts but would look primarily to the videos themselves for the site of genre definition and meaning.

All these approaches might offer valuable insights, but some questions cannot be adequately addressed through these paradigms: How do MTV's practices help constitute the genre? How do audiences use genre distinctions to understand these videos? How do other systems of cultural differentiation, such as race, impact the genre? How do musical generic categories operate in this case study? In presenting a brief analysis of this specific instance, the following account of these videos is intentionally narrow in scope, focused solely on the industrial practices involving these music videos, especially MTV's role in defining the genre. Since this approach to genre analysis looks at specific instances in action, as opposed to broader accounts of the genre as a whole, this case study will not focus on the same scope as the hypothetical analyses offered here. Instead, I will illustrate how the music video operated as a cultural category for MTV at this particular historical moment concerning this trio of videos. By emphasizing the realm of industrial practice, this analysis will not address how audiences, critics, artists, and texts all contributed to the generic cluster at this historical moment—an entire article (at least) would be necessary to address these aspects adequately. This case study does, however, exemplify how generic categories are mobilized in specific instances and how industrial practices work to define genres, linking them to cultural hierarchies and systems of difference.

In 1983, MTV was a comparatively new entity, still establishing its industrial practices and constructing an audience.[27] While the channel was known for featuring the emergent music video genre, MTV used a particularly narrow definition of the genre to reach its target audience: the channel notoriously excluded black artists in the name of featuring only "rock" videos.[28] MTV's industrial practice is not separable from an abstract notion of the genre's definition, because MTV effectively defined the music video through its choice of what to program and what to exclude. This is not to say that if MTV excluded a video, it would be unrecognizable as a music video; rather, the commonsense definitions of the genre as circulating within American culture were expressly tied to (and constituted by) MTV's industrial practices. MTV defined the *dominant* conception of the genre. Press accounts of the music video in the early 1980s mention white artists such as MTV staples Duran Duran, Culture Club, and the Stray Cats as typical music video stars, while few articles name any black artists before Jackson's breakthrough in 1983. There were other outlets for music video exhibition, but they either directly followed MTV's white-centric lead (like NBC's *Friday Night Videos* [1983–87]) or offered explicit counterprogramming (like newly formed BET's *Video Soul* [1981–2000]), thereby allowing MTV to define the mainstream generic terms. Prior to Jackson's videos and subsequent crossover success, MTV delimited the boundaries of the music video genre by using its narrow notions of target audience (white suburban youth) and musical style (new wave, heavy metal, classic rock, and white pop).

MTV drew upon previously held generic discourses constituted within the popular music and radio industries, using a definition of "rock" music to definitionally exclude black artists and audiences, a move that effectively effaced the racially hybridized origins of rock as a musical style.[29] Through its industrial practices, MTV actively linked a number of cultural discourses within the generic cluster of the music video: commodified rock rebellion, segregated suburban culture, "rock" performance style specifically embodying a straight white male identity, and a posture of cutting-edge newness and anticommercial style. MTV's practices constructed a particularly narrow target audience of young white suburban straight boys, although the crossover into female and gay tastes was far less resisted than the racial line, as many early MTV stars (e.g., Cyndi Lauper and Culture Club) transgressed gender and sexuality boundaries.[30]

Although industrial practices have been discussed as important for the constitution of genres, this case study highlights some of the specifics of television that film models cannot address.[31] Traditional accounts that examine production practices in constituting genres cannot explain MTV's practices, as the channel did not produce any of the music videos it aired (or excluded). Yet MTV's practices of selecting videos, highlighting particular artists and musical styles, framing videos through VJ introductions, and bringing the generic texts to cable-wired households all worked to shape the genre's definitions, meanings, and cultural values. An analysis of the television industry's generic practices must look beyond production to note how exhibition, advertising, and textual framing all work to constitute television genres.

Into this context of MTV's "white-only" programming came the release of what would turn out to be the best-selling musical album of all time, Michael Jackson's *Thriller*. MTV maintained its controversial policy by initially refusing to play the first two videos from *Thriller*, "Billie Jean" and "Beat It." Jackson's label, CBS Records, saw the crossover commercial potential of Jackson's album and pressured MTV to program Jackson's videos in their lineup, allegedly threatening to withdraw all CBS artists from MTV if Jackson continued to be excluded. Facing this pressure (as well as Jackson's tremendous success in record sales), MTV yielded and featured "Billie Jean," eliciting tremendous audience response. "Beat It" followed soon thereafter, with both videos in heavy rotation on MTV by March 1983.[32] The third video from the album, the title track "Thriller," was even more unusual for MTV—a fourteen-minute high-budget narrative film integrating the song into a larger horror story. MTV gladly accepted this video, given Jackson's overwhelming commercial success both with album sales and on MTV. The network featured "Thriller" prominently in December 1983, with significant promotion and fanfare. The success of Jackson's videos helped change MTV's racially segregated programming policies, bringing in additional black artists like Prince and Tina Turner, and adding legitimacy to the emerging music video format.

But MTV's industrial practices alone did not define the terrain of the music video in 1983; active audience voices countered MTV's policies. These voices are not easily accessible, except when they come from locations of cultural capital and access to major media. We are left with a number of public press accounts and critiques of MTV's segregation policies, protests of MTV by outspoken artists like Rick James and David Bowie, the anti-MTV practices of BET and CBS Records, and the staggering sales of Jackson's album and *Making Michael Jackson's "Thriller."* These voices and practices criticized MTV's conception of the genre by positing different discursive links within the generic cluster—calling attention to the implicit racism in the channel's "rock-only" policy, opening up the music video to a wider range of audiences, and highlighting the crossover appeal of black artists like Jackson. MTV altered its policies in reaction to these voices, not just because the marketplace demanded change (as it alleged) but because of industrial threats from CBS and high-profile white artists like Bowie. This is not to claim that

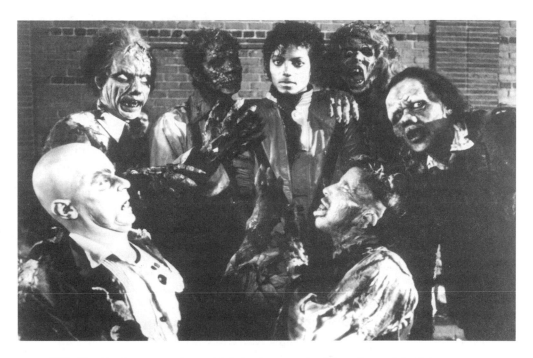

"Thriller," a fourteen-minute high-budget music video directed by John Landis, debuted on MTV in 1983 and provided overwhelming commercial success for both the network and the album of the same name. Courtesy of Optimum Productions.

the constitution of the music video genre is simply a top-down practice, with the industry mandating public tastes. Instead, I am using the more accessible industrial discourses to examine this moment of generic shift; to expand this account of these videos, I would look to other sites of discourse such as fan practices and alternative press accounts.

While MTV justified its racial ban primarily in terms of musical genre (rock instead of R & B or soul) and target audience, the channel also referenced the textual form of the opening shot of "Beat It": a twenty-second prologue without musical accompaniment. MTV, claiming that this was not truly a music video, would play the video only after editing out this nonmusical beginning.[33] Although this policy was not upheld for long, and later videos regularly incorporated nonmusical segments (although few to the degree of "Thriller"), this moment is a very specific instance of the processes of generic differentiation activated in a public cultural forum. MTV, an invested and powerful player in the music video business, made a brief claim for the genre's proper formal definition, using form as an excuse to maintain a controversial policy. Generic practices like this occur often, whether a network forces a program to "genre" itself more explicitly (e.g., ABC's imposition of a laugh track on *Sports Night* [1998–2000]) or public controversies ensue over a genre's appropriate content (like adult themes in the cartoon shows *Beavis & Butt-head* [1993–97] and *South Park* [1997–]). Previous modes of genre analysis have trouble accounting for these cultural practices because they occur outside the boundaries of the text. The ability to analyze how genre definitions, meanings, and evaluations all intermingle with cultural power relations is the primary advantage to an approach examining genres as discursive processes.

Thus, in this case study, we see the music video genre at the nexus of a number of crucial discourses and practices—race-based distinctions and hierarchies, industrial debates over the genre's proper target audience, assumptions of the genre's textual "essence," Jackson's growing star persona, and public protests over MTV's exclusionary policies. No single one of these elements defined the genre in full; rather, we must look at the conjuncture of these various discourses into a generic cluster. Needless to say, other cases would necessitate considering many more cultural, industrial, and audience practices as formative of the genre's meaning, definition, and cultural value at a given moment.

Conclusion: Five Principles of Cultural Genre Analysis

This brief example shows the necessity of exploring media genres in detailed specificity, not overarching generalities. We can never know a genre's meaning in its entirety or arrive at its ultimate definition because this is not the way genres operate; the music video is a wide-ranging cluster of discourses, not a uniform transhistorical essence. Genre definitions are always partial and contingent, emerging out of specific cultural relations rather than abstract textual ideals. We need to examine how genres operate as conceptual frameworks, situating media texts within larger contexts of understanding. The goal of studying media genres is not to make broad assertions about the genre as a whole but to understand how genres work within specific instances and how they fit into larger systems of cultural power. This new approach to television genre analysis can better our understanding of how media are imbricated within their contexts of production and reception, and how media work to constitute our vision of the world. In conclusion, five core points can be highlighted to summarize this cultural approach to genre analysis.

Genre Analyses Should Account for the Particular Attributes of the Medium

We cannot simply superimpose genre definitions from cinema or literature onto television. Certainly, medium distinctions are becoming increasingly blurred with the rise of technologies such as home video and integrated digital media, and thus we cannot regard "medium" as an absolute fixed category (any more than genre). But film genre processes cannot account for many of television's specific practices; indeed, television's constant integration of fiction and nonfiction, narrative and nonnarrative, especially confounds the dependence on narrative structure typical of most film genre criticism. Similarly, film has few equivalents to the genre-defined channels or genre-delimited scheduling practices that are commonplace for television, especially today.[34] Audience practices of genre consumption and identification also seem to be different for television, featuring more active practices of fan involvement with ongoing series, especially serials.[35] While we should not essentialize television's medium-defining practices, we need to consider a medium's particular features as a component of a larger push toward specificities in genre analysis.

Genre Studies Should Negotiate between Specificity and Generality

Obviously, genre is a categorical concept and therefore somewhat transcends specific instances. But traditional genre analysis has tended to avoid detailed specificities in favor of sweeping generalizations. A more nuanced approach can account for this tension more effectively. There are two general directions from which to approach any genre analysis. One way might start with a genre and analyze one specific element of it: focusing on a historic turning point (like the quiz show scandals), isolating a core social issue (like representations of minorities on sitcoms), or tracing a genre's origins (like the prehistory of music videos). By narrowing the focus to a specific aspect of a genre's definition, meaning, history, or cultural value, we can avoid the problems of overgeneralization and simplification that have been typical of many traditional genre studies.

The second way to approach genre analysis would start with a specific media case study and analyze how genre processes operate within this specific instance, as in the case of MTV and Michael Jackson's music videos. Such projects might isolate a variety of starting points—an industrial formation (like Cartoon Network), audience practices (like science fiction fan conventions), a textual instance (like genre parody in *The Simpsons* [1989–]), a policy decision (like educational programming mandates), or a moment in social history (like the coverage of civil rights struggles in news and documentaries). These specific topics each may serve as the nexus point of analysis, but we cannot let them dictate the methodological terrain of the entire study. We may start with a textual case to motivate our study, but we still must examine how genres transcend textual boundaries and operate within audience and industry practices as well. We can start with isolated instances, but our analysis must incorporate the interrelated operations of genre that weave through the multiple realms of media.

Genre Histories Should Be Written Using Discursive Genealogies

Genre histories have traditionally chronicled generic texts, often using both definitional and interpretive approaches. To understand genres as cultural categories, we need different methods; generic discourses are not deep repositories of hidden meanings, formal structures, or subtextual insights. Rather, we should follow the model of Foucauldian genealogy, emphasizing breadth over depth, and collecting as many discursive instances surrounding a given instance of generic process as we can.[36] In viewing the surfaces of discursive genre clusters, large-scale patterns and meanings will emerge, but we should resist plugging these findings into old systems of macro-structures or interpretive generalizations. Insights into genre can best emerge out of detailed research and specific cultural articulations of definition, interpretation, and evaluation, rather than from critical analyses of form or text. To accommodate this attention to discursive process, genre analysis should gather instances of genre activity in interrelated sites of audience, industrial, and cultural practices.

Genres Should Be Understood in Cultural Practice

As noted previously, genres are cultural processes that are best examined in specific historical instances. But one important aspect of genre studies builds upon literary critic Tzvetan Todorov's distinction between "historical" genres (those that are found in cultural practice) and "theoretical" genres (those that form ideal categories for scholars).[37] Theoretical genres can be useful for positing linkages among texts and practices that have not been previously operative, positing new categories that might be later taken up as more widespread genres (such as with film noir).[38] Before trying to posit ideal categories and look beyond the historical operation of genres, however, we should study how genres are operative and constituted in everyday life. Attempts to establish theoretical models of a genre's formal mechanics or deep structures of meaning cannot tell us how genres work within a historical context, how they evolve and emerge, or how they fit into larger relations of power. If our goal is to understand genres as cultural categories, we should first examine the discourses that constitute the category before examining the texts that seem delimited by the genre. While certain instances might dictate the proposal of new categories, in general it seems that analyzing the operation of historical genres and their relation to cultural power is a more pressing concern for media scholars.

Genres Should Be Situated within Larger Systems of Cultural Hierarchies and Power Relations

The goal of most cultural media scholarship is not to understand the media in and of themselves but rather to look at the workings of media as a component of social contexts and power relations. One of the reasons that genre studies have been generally absent within cultural approaches to the media is that genre has been traditionally conceived as a formal textual element and thus not conducive to the study of mediated politics. Even when scholars do approach genre by foregrounding cultural power relations, such as in the traditions of ideological and structuralist criticism, they tend to analyze genres at a level of abstraction ill suited to understanding the specifics of cultural practice. By looking at genre as a contextual discursive process, we can situate genres within larger regimes of power and better understand their cultural operation. Since genres are systems of categorization and differentiation, linking genre distinctions to other systems of difference can point to the workings of cultural power.

The ways in which these linkages might play out are limitless. Although there is certainly a strong tradition linking genre analysis and gender differences, for instance, we can broaden this approach to include other axes of identity differentiation as well, such as race, age, sexuality, class, and nationality. We might also look at how genre differences are imbricated within hierarchies of cultural value, both between genres and within one specific genre. Drawing upon the influential studies of cultural distinctions by Pierre Bourdieu, we could map a genre like the talk show onto larger distinctions such as aesthetic value, audience identity, codes of realism, and hierarchies of taste.[39] This analysis would produce a spectrum of generic conventions and assumptions (such as "tabloid" versus "hard" news) that are explicitly tied to greater systems of cultural power and differentiation. This approach to genre distinction avoids the tradition of text-centered analysis, accounting for the ways in which cultural agents articulate genre differentiation as constitutive of genre definitions, meanings, and values. Using this mode of examination, cultural media scholars can turn to genre analysis without abandoning their larger political projects.

This approach to genre not only enables us to deal with cultural politics but also requires that we situate genre within power relations. Just as Foucault asserts that discourses are always processes of power, genres are also constituted by power relations. Genres are not neutral categories but are situated within larger systems of power and thus come "fully loaded" with political implications. This is not to suggest that we limit our genre analyses to cases where cultural politics are obviously foregrounded. Instead, we should look for the political implications and effects of genre distinctions in seemingly "nonpolitical" case studies as well. If we accept that genres are constituted by cultural discourses, we need to acknowledge that those enunciations are always situated within larger systems of power and the political can never be effaced from these generic processes. For instance, the importation of film cartoons to television in the 1950s might seem most relevant as part of a (potentially apolitical) industrial history. But in doing such a history, we can also be attuned to the political implications of this industrial shift—the scheduling of cartoons on Saturday mornings effectively created a marginalized location for the genre that redefined films designed for mass audiences in movie houses into "kids-only" fare. This generic redefinition linked a number of hierarchies of cultural value, assumptions of "proper" content (such as controversies over violence and the excision of racial stereotypes), and limited visions of children's entertainment into the discursive cluster of the cartoon genre. Even in cases where politics might appear secondary, foregrounding how specific articulations of genres emerge out of power relations can point toward some important insights concerning both genres and larger cultural issues.

This overall approach to television genre analysis—examining genres as clusters of discursive processes running through texts, audiences, and industries via specific cultural practices—places genre analysis back onto the agenda of critical media studies. The traditional scholarly practices of analyzing generic texts will not—and should not—simply disappear. Much has been gained by all these prior methodological and theoretical approaches, ranging from more careful formal understandings of horror narratives to critiques of the structures underlying the typical Western film. Nonetheless, we need to question the "given" in these approaches—that there is an already established generic category that can serve as the foundation for genre analysis. By first examining genres as cultural categories, unpacking the processes of definition, interpretation, and evaluation that constitute these categories in our everyday experiences with media, we can arrive at a clearer and more comprehensive understanding of how genres work to shape our media experiences, how media work to shape our social realities, and how generic categories can then be used to ground our study of media texts.

Notes

1. This is not true for all approaches to genre. Certainly this type of political question motivated many ideological and structuralist accounts of film and television genres. Nonetheless, contemporary media studies has shifted toward more specific accounts of power and away from the broad macro-examinations that typify structuralism.

2. Jane Feuer, "Genre Study and Television," in *Channels of Discourse, Reassembled,* ed. Robert C. Allen (Chapel Hill: University of North Carolina Press, 1992), 157. Feuer's essay is certainly the most-read overview of television genre analysis and has defined the field of genre studies for television for more than a decade.

3. In *Genre and Television: From Cop Shows to Cartoons in American Culture* (New York: Routledge, 2004), I trace out the major trends in genre theory, consider some of the more subtle nuances and theoretical implications of my approach, and offer a number of case studies to put my theory into practice.

4. For one of the few definition-based analyses of television genres (in conjunction with film), see Steve Neale and Frank Krutnik, *Popular Film and Television Comedy* (New York: Routledge, 1990); for a paradigmatic example of this approach within film studies, see Noël Carroll, *The Philosophy of Horror, or Paradoxes of the Heart* (New York: Routledge, 1990).

5. For a range of typical interpretive accounts of television genres, see John Dennington and John Tulloch, "Cops, Consensus and Ideology," *Screen Education,* no. 20 (1976): 37–46; E. Ann Kaplan, *Rocking around the Clock: Music Television, Postmodernism, and Consumer Culture* (New York: Methuen, 1987); David Marc, *Comic Visions: Television Comedy and American Culture,* 2nd ed. (London: Blackwell, 1997); Laura Stempel Mumford, *Love and Ideology in the*

Afternoon: Soap Opera, Women, and Television Genre (Bloomington: Indiana University Press, 1995); and Horace Newcomb, *TV: The Most Popular Art* (Garden City, N.Y.: Anchor Press, 1974). For more influential film examples, see Will Wright, *Six Guns and Society: A Structural Study of the Western* (Berkeley: University of California Press, 1975); Thomas Schatz, *Hollywood Genres: Formulas, Filmmaking, and the Studio System* (Philadelphia: Temple University Press, 1981); and John G. Cawelti, *The Six-Gun Mystique,* 2nd ed. (Bowling Green: Bowling Green State University Popular Press, 1984).

6. Note that some of these critical schools do not examine texts solely for meanings. This is especially true of cultural studies, the paradigm that I wish to foreground in my own approach to genre. However, some cultural studies work does pose core meanings to genres, even as it denies the intrinsic and textual basis of these meanings.

7. A paradigmatic historical genre analysis is Feuer's account of the sitcom. A more satisfying and complex historical account of a film genre is Rick Altman, *The American Film Musical* (Bloomington: Indiana University Press, 1987), although Altman refutes a number of his positions in his more recent work in genre theory, *Film/Genre* (London: BFI Publishing, 1999).

8. Literary scholar E. D. Hirsch offers a theory of one correct "intrinsic genre" corresponding to the author's intended meaning. E. D. Hirsch Jr., *Validity in Interpretation* (New Haven, Conn.: Yale University Press, 1967).

9. For one typical example, see Graeme Turner, *Film as Social Practice,* 2nd ed. (New York: Routledge, 1993), 85–93. Turner places genre under the chapter "Film Narrative," even though he defines genre as produced by texts, industries, and audiences. Another example is Leah R. Vande Berg, Lawrence A. Wenner, and Bruce E. Gronbeck, eds., *Critical Approaches to Television* (Boston: Houghton Mifflin, 1998), which places generic criticism in the chapter "Text-Centered Approaches to Television Criticism."

10. Feuer specifically divides her analysis between media developments that are "internal to the genre"—namely, textual form and content—and those that are external, such as cultural and industrial changes. While this division may seem useful, I argue that this false internal-external binary leads us away from how genres operate within cultural contexts. Under Feuer's model of history, the genre itself is a collection of texts that all bear "internal" markings of the sitcom; "external forces" are useful in understanding the meanings and changes in these texts at any time, but they are not directly constitutive of the genre itself. Feuer, "Genre Study and Television," 151. For another example, see Mumford, *Love and Ideology in the Afternoon,* 17–18. In arguing against a definition of the soap opera based on audience pleasures or uses, she calls for a definition "that focuses instead on the specific characteristics of the genre itself"—namely, the text.

11. This mode of analysis is typical of nearly all the approaches to genre described earlier in the chapter.

12. Altman suggests that traditionally genres have been viewed as equal to the corpus that they seem to identify and that this corpus is defined by a common structure and topic. He goes on to consider Wittgenstein's concept of "family

relations" concerning genres but argues convincingly that genre definitions are contingent and historical, arriving through "use," not internal structures. Altman, *Film/Genre*, 22–24, 96–99.

13. See Steve Neale, "Questions of Genre," in *Film Genre Reader II*, ed. Barry Keith Grant (Austin: University of Texas Press, 1995), 159–83, for his discussion of *The Great Train Robbery*'s reclassification from crime film into Western, drawing on Charles Musser's research. Altman also addresses similar cases in the film genres of musicals and biopics; Altman, *Film/Genre*, 30–44. I also deal with a similar instance concerning animated short films from the 1930s and 1940s, which became recategorized as children's cartoons in 1960s television, in an unpublished larger project.

14. For a detailed discussion of the role of the biological analogy in literary genre theory, see David Fishelov, *Metaphors of Genre: The Role of Analogies in Genre Theory* (University Park: Pennsylvania State University Press, 1993), especially chap. 2. Altman discusses the tradition of evolutionary models for film genres; *Film/Genre*, 62–68.

15. Altman offers the most compelling and detailed account of the specific processes that film industries engage in to create and modify genres, an account that is less developed in television studies; *Film/Genre*, chaps. 3–5.

16. Quoted on http://cartalk.cars.com/Columns/CC/CC4021TXT.html, June 7, 1999.

17. For a provocative debate on the boundaries of the text, see John Fiske's "Moments of Television: Neither the Text nor the Audience" and Charlotte Brunsdon's "Text and Audience," both in *Remote Control: Television, Audiences, and Cultural Power*, ed. Ellen Seiter, Hans Borchers, Gabriele Kreutzner, and Eva-Maria Warth (New York: Routledge, 1989), 56–78, 116–29.

18. This approach to media studies—examining the integrated relationships between industry, audience, text, and context—is drawn from Julie D'Acci, *Defining Women: Television and the Case of* Cagney & Lacey (Chapel Hill: University of North Carolina Press, 1994); see also Stuart Hall, "Encoding/Decoding," in *Culture, Media, Language*, ed. Stuart Hall et al. (London: Hutchinson, 1980), and Richard Johnson, "What Is Cultural Studies Anyway?" *Social Text* 6, no. 16 (1987): 38–80.

19. A potential answer to this question was offered by a prescient early essay, Andrew Tudor, "Genre," in Grant, *Film Genre Reader II*, 3–10. Although his argument was not as influential as it deserved to be when it first appeared in the 1970s, Tudor's early critique of genre criticism highlighted what he called "the empiricist dilemma" of genres—genre critics isolate a group of texts to establish a genre's definitional criteria but by doing so merely reproduce the initial assumptions that led to their sample of films. Tudor proposes a rough vision of what might replace this paradoxical mode of genre criticism, namely, an account of how genres operate in the "interplay between culture, audience, films, and filmmakers"; "Genre," 8. While Tudor does not offer a fully realized model for this analysis, he keenly points out that attempts to analyze genre texts are not effective ways to examine genres themselves but rather just another mode of textual analysis. I

wish to extend Tudor's critique into a mode of genre analysis that highlights the categorical aspects of genres over their textual attributes.

20. For his most central account of discourse, see Michel Foucault, *The Order of Things: An Archeology of the Human Sciences* (New York: Vintage, 1970); Michel Foucault, *The Archeology of Knowledge and the Discourse on Language*, trans. A. M. Sheridan Smith (New York: Pantheon, 1972); Michel Foucault, *The History of Sexuality: An Introduction*, trans. Robert Hurley, vol. 1 (New York: Vintage, 1978); and Michel Foucault, *Power/Knowledge: Selected Interviews and Other Writings, 1972–1977*, ed. Colin Gordon (New York: Pantheon, 1980).

21. James Naremore, *More Than Night: Film Noir in Its Contexts* (Berkeley: University of California Press, 1998), offers a similar link between Foucauldian theory and media genres in theorizing his "history of the idea" of film noir. Naremore's work shows the rich analytic possibilities of this approach, although he does not develop this theoretical link in depth; *More Than Night*, 11.

22. There is an obvious (if misleading) parallel between the three modes of discursive practice for genres (definition, interpretation, and evaluation) and the three models of genre theory typified at the beginning of this chapter (definition, interpretation, and history). I do not mean to equate these trios through this parallel. While certainly there are more popular modes of generic historicization and scholarly modes of evaluation, historical approaches are an academic model that do not have an equal in the general cultural practices; in addition, evaluative practices are much more important in everyday discourse than in scholarly research. Thus, when I discuss these discursive practices throughout the rest of this chapter, I am not suggesting that they are equivalent to the scholarly traditions outlined here.

23. See Neale, "Questions of Genre"; Robert C. Allen, "Bursting Bubbles: 'Soap Opera,' Audiences, and the Limits of Genre," in Seiter et al., *Remote Control*, 44–55; Tony Bennett, *Outside Literature* (New York: Routledge, 1990); and Ralph Cohen, "History and Genre," *New Literary History* 17, no. 2 (1986): 203–18.

24. Psychological approaches primarily refer to either psychoanalytic or cognitive accounts of the pleasures found within genres. For examples of psychoanalytic approaches, see Robin Wood, "Return of the Repressed," in *Planks of Reason: Essays on the Horror Film*, ed. Barry K. Grant (Metuchen, N.J.: Scarecrow Press, 1984); Margaret Tarratt, "Monsters from the Id," in Grant, *Film Genre Reader II*, 330–49; and Kaplan, *Rocking around the Clock*. For examples of cognitive approaches to genre, see Carroll, *Philosophy of Horror*, especially chap. 4; Torben Grodal, *Moving Pictures: A New Theory of Film Genres, Feelings, and Cognition* (Oxford: Oxford University Press, 1997); and Noël Carroll, "Film, Emotion, and Genre," in *Passionate Views: Film, Cognition, and Emotion*, ed. Carl Plantinga and Greg M. Smith (Baltimore: Johns Hopkins University Press, 1999).

25. This argument (and most appropriate cliché) is made most clearly in Tudor, "Genre," 10.

26. Altman suggests that the representation of countercultural behavior and its eventual narrative recuperation is a defining feature of generic entertainment, an argument that I find too broad to be particularly convincing. Altman, *Film/Genre*, 144–65.

27. MTV debuted in 1981, but most commentators felt that this cable network did not have a significant impact until its debut on the Manhattan and Los Angeles cable systems in September 1982. See Tom McGrath, *MTV: The Making of a Revolution* (Philadelphia: Running Press, 1996), 88–91.

28. Ibid.; Andrew Pollack, "Music on Cable TV Provoking a Debate," *New York Times,* November 29, 1982.

29. MTV head Robert Pittman was quoted in *Variety* justifying his station's "rock-only" policy: "We hope to find more black musicians doing rock 'n' roll and new music. It's not a color barrier—it's a music barrier." Richard Gold, "Labels Limit Videos on Black Artists," *Variety,* December 15, 1982, 78.

30. See Lisa A. Lewis, *Gender Politics and MTV: Voicing the Difference* (Philadelphia: Temple University Press, 1990).

31. See Schatz, *Hollywood Genres,* for an influential structuralist account of how Hollywood studios produce genres. Altman heavily revises Schatz's account, highlighting how marketing techniques and exhibition work in film genres in addition to (and sometimes counter to) production practices. Altman, *Film/Genre,* chaps. 4–7.

32. For documentation of this chronology (with a few inconsistencies), see McGrath, *MTV,* 99–101; Steven Levy, "Ad Nauseum: How MTV Sells Out Rock & Roll," *Rolling Stone,* December 8, 1983, 37; J. Randy Taraborrelli, *Michael Jackson: The Magic and the Madness* (New York: Birch Lane Press, 1991), 322; Christopher Andersen, *Michael Jackson Unauthorized* (New York: Simon and Schuster, 1994), 108–9; and Dave Marsh, *Trapped: Michael Jackson and the Crossover Dream* (New York: Bantam, 1985), 216–20.

33. This aspect of MTV's policy is difficult to research; I have found no documentation of MTV's practices involving "Beat It" and the opening prologue. My discussion of this facet is based on my recollection as reported on MTV when it first featured the "Beat It" video. Whether or not this was a serious concern for the channel or just an excuse to continue to exclude Jackson's videos (I would guess the latter) is less important than how the rationale serves as an example of how conceptions of a genre's definition are culturally operative in specific instances such as this one.

34. Some similar film practices include differentiated film bills in the 1930s and 1940s, with separate newsreel, animation, A feature, and B feature slots, genre-defined theaters (such as art houses or porn theaters), and generically delimited film festivals or screenings. Yet film genre analysis mostly ignores these issues, and any attempt to translate between these practices and television scheduling and channel delineation would need to be rethought significantly.

35. The exceptions to this difference include film series, such as *Star Wars,* but certainly television serializations are far more common than film ones.

36. Note that in arguing for "breadth" over "depth," I am not calling for studying a genre broadly. Rather, breadth must encompass the widest range of discourses and sites of genre operation as possible, all focused on a specific historical instance framing the genre study.

37. Tzvetan Todorov, *The Fantastic: A Structural Approach to a Literary Genre,* trans. Richard Howard (Ithaca, N.Y.: Cornell University Press, 1975), 13–14.

38. Such theoretical genre creation has been less common for television studies than for cinema, with few examples that seem to take hold as widespread generic terms. An attempt to pose a theoretical television genre that falls short is Nina C. Leibman, *Living Room Lectures: The Fifties Family in Film and Television* (Austin: University of Texas Press, 1995). Leibman attempts to redefine the 1950s domestic sitcom as family melodrama but in doing so neglects to account for the centrality of comedy and humor within both the texts and their cultural circulation.

39. See Pierre Bourdieu, *Distinction: A Social Critique of the Judgement of Taste,* trans. Richard Nice (Cambridge, Mass.: Harvard University Press, 1984), and Pierre Bourdieu, *The Field of Cultural Production: Essays on Art and Literature,* trans. Randal Johnson (New York: Columbia University Press, 1993). I map out the talk show genre onto other cultural hierarchies in *Genre and Television.*

3 television networks and the uses of drama

Christopher Anderson

Once upon a time, when homes had antennas and the world was young, American television told stories. Certainly television bore witness to real events, bringing a distant world closer through news and documentaries or displaying the range of human emotion revealed in contests and performances, but mostly it told stories—created by writers, brought to life by actors and directors, dispensed in a reassuring rhythm of daily or weekly episodes. Television drama began as fiction for the age of mass marketing, produced on a grand scale according to a few standard formulas, delivered as efficiently to a mass audience scattered across the continent as to a single viewer seated before the television set. It was in this context that television drama took form, its tendencies slowly becoming habit, its habits becoming a language shared by producers and audiences alike. It was in this context that the fictional world of television drama became the domain of lawyers, cops, and doctors.

The hour-long television drama series emerged and developed as a result of constitutive choices made during the first thirty-five years of American television, when the broadcast networks—CBS, NBC, and ABC—controlled more than 90 percent of the audience. During this long period of stability, the institutions that made up the television industry—networks, affiliate stations, advertisers, and studios—hammered out a set of relationships that essentially defined the medium of television in the United States. The constitutive choices made by these institutions served corporate interests first and foremost, but they also shaped the cultural experience of American television for generations. As generally happens with institutions, contingent decisions made to achieve particular economic or organizational goals took on weight and gravity with the passage of time, until they came to seem as natural, as inevitable, as the passing of the seasons.

For the networks in the years before cable there was little incentive to tinker with the status quo once it had been established. For viewers this meant that television was defined by program scarcity. Viewers could select only from the few choices made available by the networks. The experience of television was beyond the control of individual viewers, who had no option but to build their lives around network schedules. To watch a program you had to be in front of a TV set when it aired. If two equally desirable programs were on at the same time—a common occurrence due to the networks' tactic of counterprogramming against one another—you had to choose between them. In an age before the VCR and remote control, network executives considered it axiomatic that viewer tastes were subject to "tuner inertia"; viewers were reluctant to change the channel because of the effort required to raise oneself off the couch. The hour-long drama series became a staple of television programming during the comfortable days of inertial viewing, when the audience was reliably anchored to the three networks.

Television drama evolved in conditions that no longer exist. Successive waves of technological innovation have given viewers a greater selection of programming and more control over the viewing experience. An entire generation has come of age with cable, home video, and video games. A new generation has added the Internet to the mix. These viewers wouldn't recognize the environment of program scarcity and tuner inertia that gave rise to traditional one-hour dramas. Their tastes and viewing patterns, developed under radically different conditions, have replaced tuner inertia with tuner promiscuity—a restless awareness of the alternatives available at any moment. As the television industry courts these viewers, American television is no longer *primarily* a medium for storytelling—or at least not for fiction. While most program formats reveal, to one degree or another, the deep influence and lasting appeal of narrative, fictional series are now merely one item on television's abundant menu of programming.

Because one-hour dramas are the most costly type of program to produce, television dramas face intense economic pressure while trying to compete for the attention of viewers who have a wider range of program choices than ever and no particular allegiance to the conventions of fictional drama series. In fact, the audience for drama series is disproportionately composed of viewers old enough to have developed their tastes before the era of cable and remote controls—not to mention video games and the Internet. Young adults, the demographic group most desired by advertisers, have not shown an affinity for hour-long dramas. Under these new conditions, in which drama series are no longer supported by the habitual viewing practices in which the genre evolved, what is the fate of television drama? What will happen to all those lawyers, cops, and doctors if viewers continue to discover other formats, such as reality TV, that provide the narrative satisfactions of a drama series at less cost to the networks? Can television drama survive in these new conditions? Or is the familiar one-hour drama a vestigial remnant of an earlier stage in the medium's history? These are the questions facing the television networks and studios as they contemplate the future of television drama.

After All These Years, What Is Television?

Imagine that you're watching the second episode of *Lost,* a new series from executive producer J. J. Abrams, creator of *Alias* (2001–) and *Felicity* (1998–2002). This program premiered on ABC in September 2004. Your television set is state-of-the-art HDTV: a whisper-thin, seventy-inch plasma screen that virtually floats on air. A surround-sound audio system envelops you in a three-dimensional soundscape. Your viewing conditions are magnificent. The screen may be a bit smaller, but by any other measure your home theater rivals that of the multiplex on the outskirts of town. You've spent a small fortune to achieve this effect, and *Lost* rewards your indulgence. Each episode costs more than $2 million—with two or three times that amount spent on the pilot episode—and the money, as they say in the business, is on the screen.[1]

Lost is the story of a few dozen people who survive the crash of a commercial airliner and now must endure life on an uncharted tropical island while they await a rescue that may never take place. With its obvious echoes of *Survivor* (2000–), *Lost* is the first drama to capture the narrative appeal of the reality TV series. Directed by Abrams himself, the pilot episode opened with a stunning sequence that surpassed any moment on the big screen this year for visual imagination and narrative audacity. The episode begins with a cold opening—no titles or credits. An eye, filling the screen, blinks open. The camera cranes upward, revealing a man in a business suit (Matthew Fox) lying amid dense foliage on the jungle floor. He glances around, struggling to regain his senses.

Lost is the story of a few dozen people who survive the crash of a commercial airliner and now must endure life on an uncharted tropical island while they await a rescue that may never occur. (Left to right) Evangeline Lilly as Kate, Ian Somerhalder as Boone, and Dominic Monaghan as Charlie. Courtesy of Touchstone Television.

A dog, a beautiful Labrador retriever, wanders past. Bruised and bleeding, the man pulls himself to his feet and staggers through bamboo, gnarled trees, and tall grass; the camera rushes alongside, attempting to hold him in close-up. The sound track becomes eerily quiet except for the sound of his labored breathing. As he steps out of the forest and looks ahead, the camera pans to reveal what he sees: an alluring white sand beach brushed gently by azure waves. No viewer would be surprised if this turned out to be a dream sequence. The languorous pace and lush, yet disconcerting, images that open the sequence, sharpened by intensely subjective camera work and staccato editing, create an experience that is both vivid and perplexing. These are familiar cues for a dream, and Abrams—who has been known to obscure the boundaries that separate memory, dream, and reality on *Alias*—enjoys playing with such expectations. If this were a dream, now would be the time for a quick cut: the man sits bolt upright, the dream evaporates, real life begins.

Instead, the camera pauses to luxuriate in the tropical imagery for a moment before a distant scream pierces the sound track. The camera

Creative producer J. J. Abrams and his production team skillfully
obscure the boundaries that separate memory, dream, and reality in
Alias. (Left to right) Jennifer Garner as Sydney Bristow and Victor
Garber as Jack Bristow. Courtesy of Touchstone Television.

glides down the beach, quickly picking up speed to keep pace with the
man racing into the frame. He runs toward something not yet revealed
by the camera, something that drives him forward even as he struggles
to find his footing. He passes people scattered along the beach—some
lying motionless, others racked with pain. The long focal length of the
camera lens now compresses space, stacking people and objects in a be-

wildering jumble. More people wander past the camera, as if figments of a dream. Pieces of wreckage appear scattered about. The sound track fills with a growing cacophony—people wail, a turbine engine whines, flames crackle. The man rushes forward, and the camera reveals an enormous, shattered airliner fuselage protruding violently from the sand. The sound track fills with the natural sounds of the scene, and it becomes clear that this is not a dream at all but a horrifying reality. There are echoes of a similarly disorienting sequence that opens Peter Weir's movie *Fearless* (1993), in which Jeff Bridges survives a similar crash, but this is nevertheless a moment of brilliant, original filmmaking.

Clearly, *Lost* isn't shot in some Vancouver botanical garden dressed to look like a tropical isle. Nor does it cheat with tight compositions to camouflage a piece of Southern California real estate last used as a location for *Baywatch*. No, *Lost* is shot on location in Hawaii, and the added expense is apparent: in the blazing sunshine that bleaches the sand bone white and the iridescent raindrops that dangle from moist green leaves; in the large cast that populates each scene and fills the background with activity; in the stunning image of the ruined airliner; and in the extended tracking shot that reveals these extraordinary circumstances as they are experienced by the character who will almost certainly become the moral center of the series. These are physical details that forge a perspective on events and draw a viewer deeply into a narrative world. Each detail serves a purpose in the narrative, and the scene would not be as effective without them. But each detail also carries a hefty price tag. There are certainly less expensive ways to shoot and edit a scene like this, but the Disney corporate empire, which produces the program through its Touchstone studio and broadcasts it on its ABC network, looks to have spared no expense in a bid to win back the many viewers who have drifted from the network over the past few years.

The final touch that burnishes your experience of *Lost* comes courtesy of your digital video recorder. It's impossible to get the kids in bed before 8:00 P.M. Wednesday, the hour when ABC insists on scheduling this tense and potentially violent drama, but your digital video recorder has recorded the program and saved it on its hard drive, where it awaits a time that's more convenient for you. You view the program on your own schedule, not that dictated by network executives. With a feature that allows you to fast-forward through commercials at sixty times normal speed, you haven't watched a commercial or network promotion in months. Your experience of *Lost* has achieved an almost cinematic purity. Ensconced in your own private theater, freed from the network schedule and commercial interruptions, you are able to lose yourself in the narrative world fashioned by J. J. Abrams and his collaborators. You have almost forgotten that this is television.

Now you've reached the climax of the second episode, also directed by Abrams. A small band of survivors has volunteered to carry a radio transceiver through the jungle to a mountain peak towering in the distance; at a higher elevation perhaps the signal will have a greater range. The scene is racked with tension. The group is fractious, driven by suspicion and fear. The most hot-tempered member carries a pistol uncovered in the wreckage. The batteries on the transceiver are running low. And something horrific lurks in the jungle, a howling, unseen presence that already has attacked and eviscerated the pilot. The actors are framed in intense, sweaty close-ups, as the camera swirls vertiginously around them. Suspense coils tightly with each step. Suddenly, the sound track bursts with a ferocious roar and a terrifying blast of music. A beast attacks. Fleeting images capture the terror: crashing foliage, panicked flight, a flash of white fur, gunshots fired. The beast, mortally wounded, crashes dead at their feet. It's a polar bear. (Wait a second! A polar bear? In a jungle?) Before they have time to fully register this bizarre attack, the transceiver squawks—a woman's voice, speaking French. Who is she? What is she saying? Perhaps they aren't alone after all! Does anyone in the group speak the language? Quickly—the batteries are running low! Characters scream at one another. A woman clasps the speaker to her ear and begins to translate: "She's saying—please help me! Please come get me . . . !"

At this moment of supreme tension in the episode's final moments— so artfully performed by the actors, so carefully orchestrated by the director—something inexplicable occurs. In the bottom right corner of the TV screen, the translucent ABC network logo (known in the industry as a "bug") fades away. Without warning, three small red squares, stacked one upon the other, materialize and begin to spin. They align themselves, forming a narrow red column that runs halfway up the screen on the right. Inside the column, a tiny man in a tailored suit looks upward at the woman who is translating the distress signal, then turns to face the camera. He folds his arms smugly and smiles directly at you, the viewer. Alongside the column stands the word "next." At the bottom sits the ABC network logo. After a few seconds this apparition spins wildly and dissolves. You're wrapped up in the story, transported by the storytelling and the pleasure of your home theater, so it takes an instant to register what you've seen. For a second you wonder whether it has something to do with the admittedly puzzling story. What the hell was it? As you ask yourself this question, the spell has been broken. You have been dislodged from the story and may even have missed the crucial narrative information that deepens the island's enigma: this mysterious voice is a recorded distress call that has been playing repeatedly . . . for sixteen years!

As a viewer you've seen something no less bizarre than a polar bear in a jungle. You have witnessed a "snipe," the industry's term for a network promotion embedded into a broadcast—in this case, a promo for *The Bachelor,* the ABC program immediately following *Lost*. Networks have begun using these digitally inserted devices more frequently over the past year. Digital technology makes it a simple effect to achieve. But the real question is, *Why* would a network use it? A network programmer might describe it as a service, a friendly programming reminder for viewers overwhelmed by options in a multichannel universe. A more cynical observer might speculate that networks have embedded promos like this to secure the attention of viewers who switch channels during commercial breaks or those who use digital video recorders to eliminate breaks altogether.

Viewers of sports and cable news have grown accustomed to a screen peppered with incongruous text and graphics. At the cable news networks, text scrolls continuously across the bottom of the screen, while information and graphic designs layer the image. Digitally inserted commercial logos and network promos share the screen with athletic feats during most sports programs. But those are not scripted dramas. They don't rely for effect on their ability to convey a viewer into a credible narrative world. In their fragmentary design and modes of direct address, news and sports programs are inherently interruptible. That's what makes them such ideal formats for television.

Most networks that superimpose snipes onto situation comedies and dramas have tended to insert them at a moment when they'll be least intrusive—for instance, immediately upon returning from a commercial break. In the case of *Lost,* the programmers at ABC showed no such discretion. By superimposing their distracting whirligig onto an intensely dramatic scene—without a thought for the integrity of the story or the experience of a viewer who might actually be engaged in the story—the network programmers have shown that this is, after all, commercial television.

It doesn't matter that J. J. Abrams—as writer, director, and executive producer—has collaborated with a large cast and production staff to build to this moment over the course of two carefully executed episodes. Nor does it matter that ABC's corporate sibling, Touchstone, has millions of dollars invested in Abrams's captivating illusion. And it certainly doesn't matter that you, the viewer, have tried to liberate yourself from the rigid schedules and annoying interruptions of commercial television in order to savor this story. Auteurs and aesthetes be damned! This is still commercial television. Networks still schedule programs and orchestrate promotions to maximize the flow of viewers from one program to the next, because commercial networks are still in the business of delivering viewers to advertisers.

As revealed by this incident, the tension at the networks must be excruciating—nearly as intense as the drama on-screen. To attract the young adult viewers most desired by advertisers, networks must attempt to create dramas that lure and reward a discriminating audience. In the past, this audience may have been dissatisfied with commercial networks for interrupting or otherwise interfering with a drama, but they could only dream of an alternative. Today a flick of the remote control takes them directly to uninterrupted drama series available on HBO and Showtime, collected in DVD box sets, or created through the do-it-yourself capabilities of digital video recorders. Discerning viewers are still drawn to drama series, but they have acquired a taste for an unadulterated viewing experience.

The networks are aware of these shifting tastes and have made small gestures of accommodation. In recent years, the networks occasionally have negotiated with advertisers to present season-opening episodes without commercials. Temporarily freed from commercial interruptions by the sponsorship of the Ford Motor Company, the Fox drama *24* (2001–) and ABC's *Alias* have compensated by using Ford vehicles throughout the series (including one curiously extraneous chase in *Alias* that showed a new Ford model from a number of flattering angles without advancing the plot at all). Certain network dramas, including *ER* (1994–) and *The West Wing* (1999–) have shifted to wide-screen, or "letterbox," aspect ratios once favored only by video connoisseurs but now increasingly familiar to anyone who watches DVDs or the drama series on HBO (and eventually to become the new standard with the widespread adoption of HDTV sets). In its rejection of the standard television aspect ratio for the dimensions of the big screen, the letterbox format stands as a clear mark of distinction for television series. Of course, the networks may gesture toward the discerning viewer with these small adjustments, but the economic model of commercial television ultimately won't allow them to indulge the taste for an unadulterated viewing experience. If viewers aren't watching commercials, network television can't exist.

I haven't singled out this fleeting incident from fall 2004 because I think that *Lost* is different from other commercial television programs. Like all television series produced for the broadcast networks, *Lost* has a narrative structure designed for the conditions of commercial television—to allow for commercial interruptions, to accommodate viewers who may not have seen previous episodes, to establish a narrative framework capable of sustaining the central dilemma and generating new conflicts for years to come. It isn't that *Lost* deserves to be viewed in a state of concentration and sensory immersion like that I've described, but it is rich enough in detail and potent enough in its storytelling to reward such a deeply engaged mode of viewing. Even at a moment in the history of television when a commercial network has developed a series that invites viewers to step outside the flow of commercial television and experience television drama *as drama,* the network is compelled to reassert its presence by literally stamping its economic priorities onto the drama. The snipe is a reminder that television drama on a commercial network is still a form of *television* before it is a form of drama.

From the standpoint of a network programmer, who must respond to new technologies and new modes of viewing, these digitally inserted promos make sense, but they carry the scent of desperation. They are brutal, oddly self-defeating solutions to long-term problems posed by new technologies, heightened competition for viewers, and the changing tastes of audiences. By ordering a series like *Lost,* ABC presumably hopes to lure back viewers who are drawn to ambitious television storytelling. But these are also the viewers most likely to be alienated by such reckless disregard for the integrity of a story. The irony deepens when one considers the contradictions that this incident reveals within the Disney empire. Touchstone has invested millions to produce the series, which it hopes will become a valuable corporate asset by finding an audience on ABC and surviving for years. Yet the producers find their storytelling undermined by the short-term promotional agenda of their putative corporate allies. A studio like Touchstone needs credibility in Hollywood's creative community in order to attract the most talented individuals, and many producers have begun to complain openly about the use of snipes by the networks. The curious incident of the snipe in the jungle reveals just how difficult it has become to balance the competing interests of a television network.

In a nod toward the discerning viewer, *The West Wing* is shot in a wide-screen or "letterbox" aspect ratio familiar to anyone who watches DVDs or the drama series on HBO. This format stands as a clear mark of distinction for a television series. (Left to right) First row: John Spencer as Leo McGarry, Martin Sheen as President Josiah Bartlet, and Bradley Whitford as Josh Lyman; second row: Rob Lowe as Sam Norman Seaborn and Allison Janney as C. J. Cregg. Courtesy of Warner Brothers Television.

Lost began the new season as an unexpected hit for ABC. The second episode finished ninth in the weekly Nielsen ratings with 16.5 million viewers. *The Bachelor,* however, came in fortieth place with only 8.5 million viewers.[2] If there is any justice in the television universe, the snipe promoting *The Bachelor* actually chased off the other 8 million viewers who had been watching *Lost*. By the time ABC broadcast the third episode, *Lost* was blessedly free of snipes. It can't be a coincidence. Somewhere in Disney management, someone must have recognized that the snipe was bad for business. But the snipe was just a symptom of larger problems at the networks, and those won't disappear as easily.

The Burden of History

The media conglomerates were supposed to become masters of the universe, marshaling vast resources and functioning with ruthless efficiency to program each of us as cheerful Manchurian Candidates of the shopping mall. But seamless corporate synergy is more easily imagined than achieved—as Disney and ABC remind us almost weekly. The contradictions between corporate divisions cannot be resolved by executive mandate because they are inherent in institutional practices and economic relations forged during an earlier stage in the history of television. In attempting to adapt to the changing conditions of American television, the broadcast networks are weighed down by the burden of history.

It has become a cliché to speak of the crisis facing network television. The crisis has lasted now for nearly twenty years, as the networks have seen their market share diminish year by year since cable arrived on the scene in the 1980s. Each fall begins with network executives confidently proclaiming, as they have again this year, that "viewing levels will go up" or that "more people will be watching network television." Each spring brings the news that the networks' share of the audience has declined yet again. The crisis facing the networks is less the shock of an earthquake than the relentless rain of a slow-moving storm front. The six current broadcast networks—CBS, NBC, ABC, Fox, WB, and UPN—have lost almost a quarter of their audience over the past decade, and the 2004–5 season was the first in which cable regularly captured more than half of the total audience.[3] Young males, in particular, have turned to cable, home video, and the interactive appeal of the Internet and video games. In the year 2003 alone, the number of young male viewers watching the networks fell by almost 10 percent. Meanwhile, advertising rates have continued to rise, and advertisers have begun to ask why they should be asked to pay more for less. One major advertiser, Mitsubishi Motor Company, pulled its advertising off prime time network programs. Only two of the networks—CBS and NBC—earned profits for their corporate parents over the past few years.[4]

Of course, the conglomerates that own the broadcast networks are in no danger of collapsing. As these corporations have observed the decline of the broadcast networks, they have responded by forming their own cable channels or by acquiring competitors. A diversified portfolio of broadcast and cable networks now allows the parent companies— General Electric, Viacom, Disney, Time Warner, and News Corporation—to reconstitute much of the audience lost to the networks over the past two decades. When counting the ratings for their combined broadcast and cable networks, these companies still reach more than 80 percent of viewers in prime time.[5] Seen from the lofty heights of corporate ownership, particularly for those concerned about who owns the media, the American television industry hasn't changed all that much since the days when three networks dominated the industry. Power is still concentrated in very few hands.

On the other hand, the conditions that affect the television drama have changed considerably as the mass audience of the broadcast era has splintered. While cable networks cumulatively control more viewers than the broadcast networks, no single cable network captures more than three million viewers on a monthly average.[6] This means that the television audience is fragmented along lines of demography and taste and widely dispersed across a range of channels—and the trend is likely to intensify in the coming years as the distribution technologies (cable, satellite, Internet) increase channel capacity. This change in the constitution of the television audience has clearly altered the market for television programming. Networks no longer have the luxury of creating one-size-fits-all programming for a mass audience. Instead, programs are tailored for the tastes of a demographic segment targeted by particular advertisers. The broadcast networks—which require substantially larger audiences in order to earn a profit—must try to develop programs capable of building a coalition audience from among these scattered audience segments.

With a smaller audience base—and therefore lower advertising revenues—available for any single network, the networks have sought to develop less costly program formats. By importing reality formats that originated overseas and entered American TV via cable, the networks have helped to create a new distinction in the television industry between "scripted" and "unscripted" programming. Scripted programs are simply more expensive to produce than unscripted programs, and the hour-long drama series is the most expensive of all. While an unscripted hour-long program costs on average $1 million per episode, the majority of network dramas now cost $2 million or more per episode. With reality programs like *Survivor, American Idol* (2002–), and *The Bachelor* (2002–) drawing ratings that often surpass those of dramas, traditional drama series look increasingly like an extravagance that survives from a distant era of television.

In the United States the standard form of prime-time television drama is the hour-long episodic series, organized around a set of recurring central characters who interact with one another and with occasional new characters in a recognizable, bounded social setting. The series consists of twenty-two to twenty-six episodes that are broadcast on a weekly basis (with occasional breaks) over the course of a thirty-five-week season that runs from September to May. Each episode is designed to accommodate at least three interruptions for commercials and network promotions. Episodes may consist of self-contained plots, in which conflicts are raised and resolved within the episode, or serial plots, in which major conflicts are left unresolved and continue through subsequent episodes. If a series meets the network's definition of success (a judgment based on a variety of factors, but always dependent on an evaluation of ratings), it is renewed for another, identically structured, season and continues in this manner until either the network decides to cancel the series or the studio ceases production. Of course, the vast majority of series never survive for a second season.

This description of television drama is so familiar that it will be self-evident to anyone who watches TV in the United States. Yet even the most fundamental characteristics of American television drama are contingent upon choices made long ago—often during the radio era—by the institutions that defined commercial broadcasting. These choices then became institutionalized—sometimes by contract, often by convention—and solidified into strategies and procedures that still govern network television. In carrying the cumulative weight of history, these constitutive choices made during an earlier period of American television inhibit change at the broadcast networks. The weight of history can be seen in three defining characteristics of American television: the *network schedule,* the *television season,* and the *open-ended structure* of series narrative.

First, consider the *network schedule*. The idea of a weekly series built around recurring characters and a familiar setting, broadcast regularly at the same hour each week, is only necessary in a system based on advertising revenue. A network must be able to predict, with a high degree of certainty, how many consumers of a particular type it can gather together at a given time to watch a commercial message. This requires the network to develop a schedule engineered to carry viewers from one program to the next. The networks discovered that episodic series best served this purpose because they had the ability to hook viewers with an ongoing story and familiar characters, reliably drawing viewers back at the same time each day or week. Without the need for such predictable viewing patterns, the networks might be better suited to attempt novel onetime programs, limited series, or other alternatives to the continuing series. In the era of network monopoly, there were many different drama formats beside the continuing series, including anthologies (featuring a new, unrelated story each week), made-for-TV movies, and miniseries. But with the dispersal of viewers in the cable era, these formats have virtually disappeared from the networks, revived only occasionally for high-profile special events.

The demands of the network schedule also pose unique challenges for producers and programmers. Open-ended serials with ongoing, unresolved conflicts can generate a high degree of viewer involvement, but they also carry risks—particularly in an environment in which viewers have so many other options. The concern among programmers is that viewers who have not watched a series from the first episode may feel unprepared to join it already in progress, and those who miss one or two episodes along the way may simply give up. Over the years, the industry has discovered that serials also suffer steep ratings declines when shown again on the networks or in syndication. This obviously limits their value for studios and networks, which rely heavily on the revenue from repeats.

To serve the demands of the network schedule, the safe bet is the episodic series that features a small group of recurring characters involved in plots that are resolved by the end of the episode. This narrative structure, which relies on a high degree of redundancy and repetition, makes fewer long-term demands on viewers, who are able to come and go, or to begin watching at any time, without fear of confusion. The procedural dramas *Law & Order* (1990–) and *CSI: Crime Scene Investigation* (2000–) exemplify this type of series, in which each episode centers on a criminal investigation that ends with a clear resolution. Any form of narrative complexity that diverges from the episodic model of

Law & Order exemplifies the procedural drama in which each episode centers around a criminal investigation that ends with a clear resolution. (Left to right) Michael Moriarty as Assistant DA Ben Stone, Richard Brooks as DA Paul Robinette, and Steven Hill as DA Adam Schiff. Courtesy of Wolf Films.

these procedurals—such as the "real-time" storytelling of *24,* in which each episode covers one hour of a twenty-four-hour period, or the use of a single story retold from multiple perspectives on NBC's short-lived *Boomtown*—presents networks with the challenge of how to add unfamiliar viewers over the course of a season. As a result, two decades after the serialization of prime-time dramas kicked into high gear with the success of programs like *Dallas* (1978–91) and *Hill Street Blues* (1981–87), the majority of network dramas have reverted to self-contained, plot-driven episodes that wouldn't have seemed out of place to a viewer in the days of *Perry Mason* (1957–66) or *Hawaii Five-O* (1968–80).

Next, consider the idea of the *television season.* Each autumn the networks introduce new programs and then broadcast original episodes through the winter and spring, with summer traditionally reserved for repeats. Because the networks provide a program service to affiliate stations, they are obliged to supply a full schedule of original programming during the season. The commitment to providing original episodes over such an extended period requires networks to order at least twenty-two episodes each season (down from as many as thirty-nine in the first two decades of television). The large program orders have always presented a challenge to producers, who have to meet the demands of high-volume production, no matter how it affects the quality of a series. Within this system, regardless of how one might like to organize the creative process, an executive producer must adopt the division of labor and bureaucratic management structure developed over the years to facilitate series production; the high volume of production allows for no other option. The writer-producer responsible for creating and supervising a series can be replaced for failing in these management duties, whether falling behind schedule or going over budget (as happened with Stephen Bochco on *Hill Street Blues* and Aaron Sorkin on *The West Wing*). Once-promising series like *Wiseguy* (1987–90) and *Twin Peaks* (1990–91) collapsed under the weight of such high demands but might have thrived in a system that required only eight to twelve episodes per season.

The commitment to the conventional television season also imposes an annual rhythm on the television industry that may not be the most effective way of organizing the creative process. To unveil new programs in the fall, the networks have evolved a "development season" that runs from January to March. During this period, while many producers are still working on the current season of their ongoing series, the networks order dozens of pilot episodes as potential series for the upcoming season. The pool of directors, actors, and production crews in Hollywood often find themselves wildly overworked during this intense period—often at overtime wages—and then virtually unemployed as they wait to see which programs the networks will pick up. While it almost certainly would be more rational to develop new television series throughout the year, this is the system that has developed over the years to meet the timetable created by the television season.

The networks are committed to the season not simply because they must provide thirty-five weeks of original programming but also because they depend on the seventeen weeks in the summer when they have traditionally scheduled repeats. The pattern was imported from radio, where networks discovered that overall audience levels decline in the summer months. Over the years the networks have benefited from the summer lull because it freed them from the greater expense of having to provide fifty-two weeks of original programming each year. By paying a license fee to the studio, a network has the right to broadcast an episode two or three times over the course of a year, and those repeats are crucial for network profits because the advertising revenue from the first broadcast alone seldom equals the cost of the license fee. Although repeats never attract as many viewers as original episodes, the networks need to air most programs a second time to earn a profit. Due to the competition from cable and the activities of viewers who increasingly program their own repeats using episodes archived on DVD or the hard drives of their digital video recorders, network programmers frequently propose shifting to a year-round schedule of original programming. But it's simply not feasible under the existing economics of network television. Because the networks cannot break the need for repeats without turning to substantially less expensive programming, they favor episodic dramas like *Law & Order* and *CSI* that see smaller drops in ratings when aired a second or third time.

Finally, consider the *open-ended structure* of the television series. The American television industry has a deep commitment to the creation of long-running television series because networks and studios both depend financially on those few series that remain on the air for several years. The network's central goal with scripted series is to cultivate long-term commitment by viewers, particularly at a time when it is difficult to convince viewers to watch new programs. This dovetails with the studio's need to accumulate at least eighty episodes so that a series can be sold in lucrative secondary markets, which include local stations and cable networks in the United States and in countries around the world.

The television industry might have developed a system in which the networks pay a license fee that covers the entire cost of production. Instead, competition among the studios encouraged deficit financing, in which the production budget surpasses the license fee, which usually covers only 50 to 60 percent of the studio's cost. The networks benefited from this arrangement because they received programs with stars and production values that far exceeded the amount paid to the studio. The studios accepted it because they covered their deficits and often earned enormous riches by selling these programs, already partially subsidized by the networks, in secondary markets following the network run. The extraordinarily high cost of production has created a powerful barrier to entry for any organization or individual thinking of challenging the existing networks and studios. With the cost of a one-hour network drama now roughly $2 million to $2.5 million per episode, studios can run up a deficit of $20 million or more per season for each series lucky enough to be chosen for the network schedule. Studios need the revenue from secondary markets not only to pay for the deficits accumulated on successful series but also for those many series canceled by the networks that never generate enough episodes to make it to secondary markets. Therefore, studios and networks are as committed as ever to creating drama series that can sustain a narrative indefinitely without calcifying in formulaic repetition or sliding into absurdity (a phenomenon identified and labeled by fans as "jumping the shark"). Although it may be stopped at any time by network decision, a network drama must begin with an interminable narrative; individual episodes may conclude, but the narrative can never end.

The standard form of the television drama in the United States is certainly not the only pattern for a drama series, simply the version that developed in response to the constitutive choices that defined American television in the era of network monopoly. Virtually every television network outside the United States produces limited series that consist of a finite number of episodes and are designed to end, or continuing series that offer a limited number of episodes annually. Cable channels in the United States have adopted these more modest and flexible formats with startling success. They have the freedom to pursue alternative formats because they are either partially or entirely independent of the advertising-supported economic model of the broadcast networks.

During the 1990s, the broadcast networks saw their status as the source of quality drama supplanted by HBO, which has developed a reputation for creating the most innovative drama series—*The Sopranos* (1999–), *Six Feet Under* (2001–5), *The Wire* (2002–), and *Deadwood* (2004–). As a subscription-based service, HBO doesn't have to provide a full program service or to attract an audience for advertisers; it simply has to give people a reason to pay the cost of a monthly subscription. This leads HBO to focus on creating a few series that attract inordinate attention from the media, critics, and viewers, while also contributing to the value of the HBO brand. It also frees HBO from the scheduling constraints of the broadcast networks. HBO has succeeded in part by repeating new episodes at least three times in a week, which recognizes the more abundant choices available to viewers by offering several opportunities to find a program in the schedule. HBO doesn't have to premiere all its series at one time in the fall or commission twenty-two episodes per season; it can develop series year-round, allowing its producers to concentrate on making a dozen high-quality episodes—at their own pace—instead of scrambling to provide twenty-two. Most worrisome for the broadcast networks, HBO's acclaimed series siphon off the viewers most prized by advertisers. HBO doesn't sell these audiences to advertisers, but if they're watching HBO, they aren't available for the broadcast networks.

Basic cable channels like Lifetime, FX, A&E, and ESPN have begun to develop original drama series for similar reasons. Basic cable channels differ from both broadcast networks and pay cable in that they have two sources of revenue: advertising and transmission fees from cable and satellite systems. While broadcast networks rely on advertising sales alone, and pay cable relies on viewer subscriptions, cable channels earn money both from selling commercial time and from charging transmission fees to cable and satellite delivery systems, which are then passed along to viewers as higher service rates. Cable channels have an incentive to develop series that not only attract a core audience for advertisers but also enhance the network brand, which increases the value of the network in negotiations with cable and satellite operators.

As a result, cable drama series are designed to reinforce a channel's particular brand identity, often by placing a slight spin on the most traditional drama franchises in order to appeal to the channel's target audience. Lifetime pursues its audience of young adult women with female-inflected variations on the police and medical drama, such as *The Division* (2001–) and *Strong Medicine* (2000–). With *The Shield* (2002–), *Nip/Tuck* (2003–), and *Rescue Me* (2004–), cable channel FX has established a brand by introducing charismatic, deeply flawed male heroes in the *Sopranos* mold to conventional dramatic franchises (cops, doctors, firefighters). Because the cable channels cannot afford a full schedule of original programs, they tend to concentrate on developing one or two limited-run signature dramas that serve to create an identity for the entire channel. The cable channels concentrate marketing and promotion budgets to raise the profile of a single series at a time in order to create a phenomenon that attracts media attention. Given that these channels draw only two or three million viewers, the drama series aren't expected to earn an immediate profit, but to serve as loss leaders, gradually building a constituency of viewers for the network, while enhancing the value of the network as a marketable brand.

The Conclusion, If Not the End

Although it is tempting to forecast the future of television drama, the history of television is littered with failed predictions from the past. Several times in the history of television, we've read premature obituaries for one genre or another. The situation comedy was thought to be moribund by the early 1980s, before it roared back to life with *The Cosby Show* in 1984; the same was true for the hour-long drama before its revival with *ER* in 1994. Instead of trying to predict the future by looking forward, it might be useful to pause for a glance backward. Network television has its origins in constitutive choices made during the era of broadcasting, when three national networks had monopolistic control of the airwaves. Those conditions no longer exist, but the structures created by networks, advertisers, stations, and studios in that period still exert a powerful influence on television programming, favoring certain program forms over others, encouraging or constraining innovation. This is certainly the case for the drama series, which is a capital- and labor-intensive form of programming that also requires a significant investment on the part of media corporations and viewers, who must devote precious time, attention, and even emotion to remain engaged in an ongoing narrative. For these reasons, the drama series is a genre resistant to quick or convenient transformations. It is likely to remain the domain of lawyers, cops, and doctors for the foreseeable future.

In speaking about contemporary drama, I haven't spent much time talking about the formal characteristics or the history of the genre. Instead, I have given my attention to the *uses of drama series* by the institutions that define American television. I have tried to point out the constitutive choices that give drama series a particular form on American television. Broadcast networks and cable channels have developed very different uses for drama series, and these different uses favor different types of drama. The cable networks are creating the most complex and innovative dramas at the moment because they aren't subject to the same constraints as the broadcast networks. It isn't just that they're freed from certain obvious constraints on language and the behavior of characters, but that they have a license to introduce a greater number of characters, and those characters need not demonstrate clear and consistent motives. They are able to develop messy, open-ended plots without the need for temporary resolutions along the way. How have the cable channels gotten this license? They don't need drama series to function as a building block in a comprehensive program service, to attract fifteen to twenty million viewers per episode, or to earn an immediate profit from the broadcast; instead, they use select dramas as loss leaders to forge a brand identity for an entire channel. With these expectations, they prefer drama that rewards the intense devotion of a committed viewer to that which strives to be accessible to the irregular viewer who may occasionally sample an episode.

The broadcast networks are obviously aware of the alternatives available on cable, but they have difficulty adapting those alternatives to the conditions of network television. Limited-run series, such as NBC's *Kingpin* (2003) and ABC's *Kingdom Hospital* (2004) and *The D.A.* (2004), haven't found an audience. For the networks, which need to promote an entire schedule, it is difficult to draw attention to a limited-run series in the midst of an ongoing season. Unlike the cable channels, the networks cannot repeat an episode several times a week to accumulate viewers as the cable channels have. The networks have begun to repeat some programs (they call it "repurposing"), especially as they have given up trying to provide original programming on Saturday night, but they can't afford to schedule too many repeats during the season without degrading the value of the program service in the eyes of affiliates and viewers. And the networks have little room for error, whether experimenting with new programs or scheduling repeats. Any program that fails to captivate a viewer, for whatever reason, becomes an invitation for that viewer to look elsewhere.

With viewers dispersed across dozens of channels and using their television sets for activities other than watching television, networks have had a difficult time launching regularly scheduled programs and even less success inserting occasional programs into their schedules (does anyone remember the "television special"?). It's not just that the networks are failing to gauge the tastes of contemporary audiences, but that the audiences for drama are simply not as accessible as they once were. When viewers are not concentrated around a few channels, they must be collected, and that has become an enormous challenge at a time when viewers who don't tune in to a particular network will never be exposed to its promotional messages. For this reason, the networks have had to be more aggressive in taking their promotional efforts to potential viewers—which is why, for instance, one now sees advertisements for television series among the previews at movie theaters. It has become so difficult to draw attention to new drama series that NBC and CBS would rather clone a new edition of *Law & Order* or *CSI* than try to reinvent the television drama.

There are still some network dramas that risk dense, ongoing story lines with multiple characters, dramas that dare to test the waters beyond the domain of doctors, cops, and lawyers. The phenomenal early success of *Lost* and *Desperate Housewives* on ABC in 2004–5 offers hope for the survival of something other than police procedurals on network television. But viewers have a reason for remaining skeptical of even the most promising network dramas for fear that the series will either be canceled or given an extreme makeover by network pressure to appeal to casual viewers.

The case of *Alias* can serve as a cautionary tale. For one and a half seasons, *Alias* wove an intense, almost impenetrably dense conspiracy plot that rewarded dedicated viewers and almost certainly left new viewers bewildered. Then ABC decided to hype the series by placing it in the coveted spot following the Super Bowl in 2003. Given this opportunity to relaunch a series that had never garnered strong ratings, ABC ordered the producers to simplify the convoluted story and create a more inviting narrative for unfamiliar viewers by focusing on core characters, clarifying relationships, and offering the satisfaction of neat resolutions. Otherwise, the series risked cancellation. As a result, *Alias* wrapped up the entire conspiracy plot in that single episode. It was a cynical act of betrayal that unexpectedly stamped the imperatives of the commercial network onto a series that had earned the devotion of committed viewers who had invested thirty hours in the story. How could we have forgotten? Viewers who turn to the networks expecting the sort of innovative or challenging dramas that have become routine on HBO would be wise to harden their hearts. There is assurance in cable, but with the "free" television provided by the networks, it's strictly caveat emptor.

Notes

1. Laura M. Holson, "The Wonderful World of Succession," *New York Times,* October 24, 2004, 3:1.

2. "The Ratings," *Entertainment Weekly,* October 22, 2004, 85.

3. Denise Martin, "Cable Makes Inroads into Autumn," *Variety,* October 25–31, 2004, 26.

4. Bill Carter, "As Season Begins, Networks Struggle in Cable's Shadow," *New York Times,* September 19, 2004, 1; Emily Nelson, "Nielsen Ratings Come under Fire," *Wall Street Journal,* November 17, 2003, B10.

5. Martin Peers, "Show of Strength: How Media Giants Are Reassembling the Old Oligopoly," *Wall Street Journal,* September 15, 2003, A1.

6. Megan Larson, "The Lure of Limited Series," *Mediaweek,* January 5, 2004, 14.

2 | traditional genres in transition

4 | the changing face of children's television

Norma Pecora

It is only recently that there has been any serious attempt to apply genre theory to children's television. Overwhelmingly the work on children's television, both past and present, has addressed media effects often in the context of violent content. When programming is discussed, it is generally as format or formal features.[1] Piling argues that children's television is associated with cartoons that are seen as "unworthy of critical attention."[2] The limited and dated work on children's television that does exist tends to explore controversies surrounding children's television,[3] the protectionist nature of the medium,[4] or the commodification of children's culture.[5] More recently the turn has been toward the genre of teen dramas represented by work on *Buffy the Vampire Slayer* (1997–2003), *Felicity* (1998–2002), and *Dawson's Creek* (1998–2003); here the interest is most often in the construction of identity and material consumption.[6]

In part, this lack of attention is not surprising, for "children's television" is not a single content category but cuts across numerous formats that reflect adult programming—drama and action adventure, comedy, game shows, news, and information. What distinguishes children's television from adult forms is its dependence on audience age as a defining characteristic. It is, as Máire Messenger Davies explains, the only genre "defined by the people who watch it, rather than the characteristics of the text."[7] We speak not of children's dramas or comedies but of television for the preschooler, for ages six to eleven, or for teens or tweens.

Consequently, we have yet to discuss this genre in a way that takes into full account the range of texts that it represents, but more important, we have yet to define it in what Mittell argues is genres as "cultural categories."[8] Messenger Davies begins that discussion with her attention to age as a defining category. Building on previous work representing children's television in the context of genre theory by Stoddard and Davies, and beginning with an attempt to contextualize it historically, this chapter will examine the development of children's television genre as it has been shaped by the audiences, industry economics, and emerging technologies. Such a discussion is important if we are to understand the "social function"[9] of children's television or the "demands of audience and advertisers"[10] or if we are to "explore the material ways in which [this genre is] culturally defined, interpreted, and evaluated."[11]

According to Mittell, while text is not to be ignored, genres are "cultural categories that surpass the boundaries of media texts and operate within industry, audience, and cultural practices." He goes on to explain that "industries rely on genres in producing programs as well as in other central practices such as self-definition (channels such as ESPN or Cartoon Network) and scheduling (locating genres within time slots, as in daytime soap operas). Audiences use genres to organize fan practices (generally determined organizations, conferences, and Websites), personal preferences, and everyday conversations and viewing practices."[12] Children constitute a somewhat different audience from adults, but we can see Mittell's definition play out in the children's television industry: Disney and Nickelodeon are, by definition, channels for younger children, whereas MTV, Cartoon Network, and WB and UPN are for tweens and teens. Scheduling practices have also led to the Saturday morning "ghetto" of children's cartoons. While young children do not have the authority to "organize fan practices," they do have "personal preferences" that become a part of their everyday culture.[13] Fan practices are articulated by older children, tweens and teens, through Web sites and chat rooms devoted to their favorite media personalities.

This alternative approach to "genre as text" allows us to "locate genres within the complex interrelations among texts, audiences, and historical contexts."[14] By doing so we can understand, for example, the new genre of teen dramas like *Dawson's Creek* that come out of a recognition of teens, particularly teen girls, as an important consumer audience and the need for new channels such as WB and UPN to compete creatively against well-established networks. These teen dramas have interesting textual constructions that fit within well-defined genre categories, but

Winky Dink and You was one of the first interactive television shows. Children were encouraged to draw with crayons upon a special plastic sheet that clung to the screen, thus taking part in the telling of a Winky Dink adventure story. (Left to right) Host Jack Barry, Mae Questel (the voice of Winky Dink), and Winky Dink. Courtesy of Barry & Enright Productions.

they are more interesting to us a "cultural category."[15] Thus it is so for children's television in general.[16]

From Winky Dink to Jimmy Neutron

In fall 1953, *Winky Dink and You* (1953–57) was introduced on a Saturday morning by the CBS network as a new and innovative program that offered interactive television for children. With a "Winky Dink Kit" children could participate in the adventures of Winky Dink, and parents could be assured their children were engaged in "wholesome entertainment and active self-expression."[17] Nearly fifty years later a new hero— *The Adventures of Jimmy Neutron: Boy Genius* (2002–)—was introduced by the Nickelodeon cable channel in a complex marketing strategy that involved preproduction licensing agreements, multimedia platforms, and a promotion campaign unmatched in children's television. McAllister and Giglio illustrate one level of this marketing campaign in their description of a Saturday morning paraphrased here:

> At 8:55 on Saturday, January 26, 2002, the promotional space in the "squeezed credits" featured a music video by a current teen star performing the music to the film *Jimmy Neutron: Boy Genius* (still in theatrical release at that time). Four minutes later the program separator featured Jimmy Neutron controlling a robot and including a Nickelodeon logo. At 9:10 another promo included Jimmy Neutron on the cover of *Nickelodeon.* Fifteen minutes after that a spot commercial for the *Jimmy Neutron* movie appeared; at 9:44 a promotion for the Jimmy Neutron videogame available at nick.com was played followed by two more commercials for *Jimmy Neutron.* At 10:58 he was featured once again.[18]

In one hour, children saw Jimmy Neutron eight times in a seamless move between program and product—what McAllister and Giglio call "commodity flow." In that time the film, a song (available on CD), *Nickelodeon Magazine,* and a Jimmy Neutron video game were featured. *The Adventures of Jimmy Neutron: Boy Genius,* the television program, first aired the following fall, and children were primed.

While both Winky and Jimmy are bright, brash young men out to help the world—Winky with his crayoned bridges and Jimmy with his scientific inventions—in many ways they serve as markers for the changes in children's television over the past fifty years. Where Winky was a simple, hand-drawn figure, Jimmy is the animated product of CGI technology; Winky's helpfulness came in the form of a bridge over water or an umbrella in the storm; Jimmy's inventions involve robotrons and chemical formulas, the latest in science and technology. Winky was a product of television, Jimmy of a wide array of media platforms and corporate demands. No longer is children's television driven by what is inside the box; what is outside the box also serves to create an identity and audience for the character.

The changes that have occurred between the 1950s introduction of Winky Dink and the introduction of Jimmy Neutron fifty years later illustrate the transformation of children's television that is grounded in the cultural and material practices by which genres are defined.[19] For example, in the 1960s, with the introduction of new technology that made animation less labor-intensive and therefore more cost-effective, animation became a more viable approach for children's television pro-

Fifty years after Winky Dink, the Nickelodeon cable channel introduced another bright, brash young man out to save the world—only this time using the latest in science and technology. (Left to right) Jimmy Neutron and his dog, Goddard. Courtesy of Nickelodeon/Paramount Pictures and Viacom International, Inc.

duction, with consequences for particular genres—live-action variety programs like *Super Circus* (1949–56) experienced audience decline, to be replaced by cartoons with talking animals such as *Yogi Bear* (1958–88). Later, with new marketing partners in retail licensing and the toy industry, up-front costs were spread over several venues but created a need for more marketable characters—Yogi Bear now needs a posse of characters to be sold separately as in *The Smurfs* (1981–89) or *He-Man and the Masters of the Universe* (1983–90). And children who are raised on computers have little patience with a piece of plastic and magic crayons. Finally, Winky Dink was introduced at a time when there were only three broadcast channels, but Jimmy must compete against a widening array of media outlets, including cable, videocassettes, video and computer games, books and magazines, and a motion picture industry that has discovered the young audience.[20] The world of Jimmy Neutron is a very different one from that of Winky Dink.

Genre as Text

First and foremost, audience age is the defining factor for children's television genres. However, as Mittell argues, text cannot be ignored. In many ways, text and age come together in children's genres. For example, when we speak of content categories in children's television, the texts can be filled with the pathos, humor, and richness of adult dramas, comedies, or documentaries, but always the particular interests, abilities, and needs of the child are kept in mind. Most important, age is always a characteristic of text. While in the past it was more ambiguous, children's television has always had an element of being "different" from adult programming. Nowadays it is recognized that adventure stories for preschoolers must have uncomplicated plots, bright colors, and simple language. Successful characters in preschool adventures are often animals that take on human characteristics appealing to a preschooler's life stage and interests—think *Winnie the Pooh*. By the time a child is six to eleven years old, he or she has greater language skills that allow for more sophisticated humor and plotlines. Children of this age have an immense curiosity about the world. They are interested in relationships, news and documentaries, and action adventures with heroes who are involved in morality plays between good and evil—*Doug* (1991–99), *Nick News* (1992–), and *Spider-Man* (1994–98), for example. Stories for this age are more likely to involve geopolitical issues and moral conflicts, issues the children are struggling to understand. Older youths tend to watch adult programming and MTV, though increasingly there are teen dramas that develop cultlike followings—such as *Buffy the Vampire Slayer, Degrassi High* (1989–92), and *Saved by the Bell* (1989–93). If we reflect on the content categories of children's television, it is obvious many of the texts have similarities to those of adult genres but always, as Messenger Davies points out, for an audience that is "special," one that comes to the text with limited world experience.

Episodic Dramas

As with adult programming, children and youth dramas are based on interpersonal conflict, usually with exaggerated emotions and tensions focusing on the everyday problems of the child.[21] Dramas for tweens follow much the same structure as teen drama but are less likely to focus on romance and more likely to speak to camaraderie and friendships. Recent examples would include *Saved by the Bell, Buffy the Vampire Slayer,* and *Dawson's Creek.*

Action Adventure

In many ways similar to drama, action adventure tends to focus on action rather than characters. More recently these programs have been dominated by animation.[22] The adventure revolves around the conflict between good and evil, with a single hero and his (rarely her) group of supporting characters acting as a team. Action adventure is perhaps the primary genre of children's television and can include a range of categories such as comedic adventures like *Yogi Bear, The Smurfs,* and *The Care Bears* (1985–88) and mythical adventures represented by *He-Man and the Masters of the Universe, Transformers* (1984–87), and *Superman* (1952–58).

Ellen Seiter, in her analysis of *Ghostbusters* (1986–87) and *My Little Pony* (1986–92), two examples of this content category, revealed gendered and structural differences embedded in genres. *Ghostbusters* is representative of action adventure stories for boys and *My Little Pony* as that for girls. According to Seiter, these programs are distinguished by the following characteristics:

Ghostbusters	*My Little Pony*
The hero as our equal	The heroine as our better half
Hierarchical group	Democracy of peers
Emotions masked	Emotions valued as truth
Playful attitude toward work	Play put aside to save others
Fear as enjoyable	Overcoming fears
Blast enemy away	Persuade enemy to change
Violent conflict	Moral persuasion
Technology	Nature
Urban setting	Pastoral setting
Dystopia	Utopia[23]

This kind of analysis can be useful in distinguishing not only genres but also the structural differences in gendered programming. The 1990s saw a new gendering of action adventure television with shows like *The Powerpuff Girls* (1998–), blending some of the genre characteristics of "boy" and "girl" action adventure shows. The Powerpuff girls are likely to blast the enemy away, but there is also an attempt at moral persuasion and always with a sense of fair play.

Comedy

The adult world of television is dominated by situation comedies that are often set in the home. Family-oriented sitcoms, with their familiar structure of mother/father/children, are particularly appealing to children.[24] Nickelodeon and Disney relied heavily on this genre when they introduced programming targeted to the tween girl audience with *Sabrina* (1996–2003), *That's So Raven* (2003–), and, in an animated version, *Daria* (1997–2002).

The examples mentioned so far have addressed "programming made for children," that is, creative content designed specifically with the child audience in mind. Situation comedies represent "programming children watch," or programs made for adults but with an expectation that children will also watch these shows. In the early days of Nickelodeon, when the channel was building its audience and brand, Nick at Nite utilized vintage situation comedies to fill the evening hours and draw in an adult audience with the expectation that children would also watch these programs and stay with Nickelodeon, thus conflating children and adult genres.

Other adultlike genres are a part of children's television. Variety programs were an important part of early children's television; game shows, popular among eight- to eleven-year-olds, who tend to be competitive by nature, can occasionally be found on Nickelodeon. For instance, *Double Dare* (1986–94), with its green slime, is one of the network's signature programs. News programs and documentaries tend to be for older children who can understand more abstract representations, who can distinguish between fantasy and reality, and are cognitively prepared to follow story lines that are rarely found on any of the channels for children. More recently, reality shows and do-it-yourself programs have begun to move into the youth and tween market with cooking programs, household decorating shows such as juvenile versions of the popular *Trading Spaces* (2002–), and junior versions of adult reality programs like *Survivor* (2000–).

Historically, children's television as a genre has cut across numerous content categories or formats that imitate adult genres. With few exceptions children's television reflects adult formats—for example, educational programming like *Sesame Street* (1969–)—and, as in adult television, particular genres have come into and gone out of style. In the early 1970s locally produced, lunchtime cartoon shows hosted by an Uncle Bob or Captain Joe were very popular when children walked home from school for lunch; however, these shows no longer exist as a consequence of the Federal Communications Commission (FCC) ruling on host-selling, the consolidation of school districts and the consequent decline in local schools, and a move by local stations to design noon news shows to attract adult audiences. It is, as Mittell points out, the way genre works within material practices.

Genres as Cultural Categories

Mittell's notion of "cultural categories" is important if we are to understand the "demands of audience and advertisers," both of which drive the children's television industry. When motion pictures were introduced, children were among their first audiences. Radio taught children they could "get Mom to buy" a wide array of cereals and snack foods. Consequently, television found in children an active and loyal audience and an eager and willing consumer group. This is not to say children are dupes of the system or an easy mark—the field is littered with failed products and programs; rather, children, particularly those aged six to eleven, are curious, inspired, imaginative, and interested in the world around them. As a rule, they are also open to trying new things while being part of a peer group that is important in developing their sense of self. In the almost sixty years of television they have become very savvy as audience members and consumers.

Television was introduced into the home in the late 1940s, at a time when children received toys as presents only for their birthdays and on other special occasions. The child-rearing philosophy of the day was "seen but not heard," and attending school before age six was a rare occurrence. "Media" meant books and comic books, radio dramas, vinyl records, and a yearly Disney movie. Toys were generic dolls or Western-style six-shooters, building blocks, and crayons.[25] Advertisers and television executives thought of this audience as "children," though there were clearly age-specific interests and demands. In one of the first studies of children's television, using 1952 data, Leo Bogart identified some of these age-related differences when he questioned children about their television program preferences. He found that *Howdy Doody* (1947–60) was the most popular program among children aged 6 and under, and 7 to 8, and 9 to 10; *I Love Lucy* (1951–57) and *The Milton Berle Show* (1948–67), both adult programs, were the most popular among children aged 11 to 12, 13 to 14, and 15 to 16.[26]

Gradually over the history of children's television, the industry has refined its parameters of this audience, although six- to eleven-year-olds still rule. When television was new, the networks programmed an occasional series for older or younger ages. *American Bandstand* (1957–89) was an extremely popular teen program in the 1950s, and programs like *Ding Dong School* out of Chicago and *Aunt Fran's Playmates* from Columbus, Ohio, attempted to both entertain and teach those children who did not yet attend school. It was the six- to eleven-year-old audience, though, that was most sought after. Preschoolers were seen as having no consumer value because they had neither expendable income nor shopping savvy; the conventional wisdom said teens, who had allowances to spend, did not watch television, and when they did, they were more likely to watch adult programming. However, as television evolved, so too did the concept of the child audience.

During these early years, the television and advertising industries targeted children in two ways. First, many of the early children's shows were aired during the evening hours as the industry tried to sell television sets to parents. How better to do so than with entertainment that brought the family together.[27] Second, carrying over the advertising model from radio, many of the children's programs were sponsored by snack foods, breakfast cereals, and other disposable household products.[28] For example, Miss Frances on *Ding Dong School* tells the children to "go get Mom" so she can extol the virtues of Johnson's No-Tears Baby Shampoo—selling the product to both the child and the mother. In addition to the Winky Dink kits, children were able to nudge parents for toys like Davy Crockett hats and Toni dolls. (My prized possession was a Dale Evans cowgirl outfit, complete with six-shooter, that I received for a birthday.) Children now became active participants in the consumer market by virtue of the products advertised to them and those, like the toys, they found attractive.

In the 1960s the industry continued to refine its definition of the child audience. With the overwhelming success of *Sesame Street,* the preschool audience gained credibility. While still not seen as an important consumer market, preschoolers were now clearly a distinct target audience. Several events came together in the 1960s to bring about other changes to children's television. During the 1950s most television programs were either fully supported by a single sponsor or funded by the network on a sustaining basis. With increased production costs, television moved to multiple or participating sponsorship.[29] This would open the advertising up to new products because now four advertisements might be shown where previously only one had been. According to Turow, another important development was a new technology that made animation less expensive (although the change to color would concomitantly add to costs). Much of the animated programming in the 1950s consisted of theatrical cartoons sold to broadcast television. In the late 1950s, Hanna and Barbera came up with a "limited animation" process that made cartoon production more cost-efficient. In addition, the networks were preparing for color broadcasting, which came during the mid-1960s, creating a demand for programs "in living color" that were far more expensive to produce than black-and-white shows. Even with the new Hanna-Barbera process, the expense of color broadcasting led to a need to share costs and to amortize expenses, which further encouraged participating sponsorship and multiple showings of a series. As Turow states, "The networks, for their part, encouraged the move to participation because it gave them control over series development, and often over profits from series successes. In addition, participation allowed the networks more discretion than ever before regarding program lineups and, by extension, programming strategies."[30] Three things came together at this point—advertisers' demand for an audience, a more simple form of animation that made the production of children's television more practical, and a move away from children's television in the evening hours because there was no longer a need to create demand for television sets. By the end of the 1960s the structure of children's television was well established as animated, Saturday morning, action adventure cartoon shows, a strategy that worked well for both advertisers and the networks.[31]

The 1960s also brought about an alternative to the advertiser-supported children's program. In 1967 the public broadcasting service introduced *Sesame Street* and *Mister Rogers' Neighborhood* (1968–2001). The first was the result of a partnership between the academic and creative communities; the second was a well-received, locally produced program. Both were commercial free but created a new audience segment, preschoolers, as the popularity of *Sesame Street* demonstrated that children would watch high-quality educational programming. For the most part commercial broadcast television has ignored this audience and invested in the larger and more affluent audience of six- to eleven-year-olds who are consumers in training.

Once established, this model of commercial children's television—Saturday morning animation for six- to eleven-year-olds—continued through the 1970s with relatively minor changes. However, the stage was being set for licensed characters, which have come to define children's entertainment. During the late 1970s the Prime Time Access Rule (PTAR) and Financial and Syndication Ruling (FinSyn) opened the television industry to new outlets. As a result of these two legislative moves, the number of independent television stations increased dramatically, and with that came a need for programming to fill their hours.[32] This need was met with cheaply produced, first-run animation for children, often in partnership with toy companies. The clearest example is *He-Man and the Masters of the Universe*, which was developed in partnership with Mattel.[33] He-Man came with at least twenty-six other characters (sold separately), an array of weapons and methods of transportation, and a castle. Each episode of the program featured a villain or sidekick that became that week's "must-have" toy. The growth of children-friendly superstores and Toys "R" Us made shopping for these new products all the easier; after all, who didn't want to be a Toys "R" Us kid?

Changes in the Landscape: Enter Cable and VCRs

Until the 1980s, the three networks had no competition for the child audience, but three events occurred in the 1980s to change that: the growth of independent television, the introduction of cable channels, and the development of home video recording. By the end of the decade, the children's television landscape looked very different. As a result of PTAR and FinSyn in the late 1970s, independent stations not affiliated with the major networks became a dominant force in the industry, as they went from 85 stations in 1976 to 225 stations in 1985.[34] Like network television in the 1940s, these stations went for a children's audience by programming afternoon cartoons. Often undercapitalized, independent stations used off-network animated shows, giving new life to old programs, and first-run syndicated cartoons that were cheaply produced and frequently created in partnership with toy companies. These new stations allowed for an exponential growth in the children's television marketplace. When cable, as a content provider, came on the scene in the early 1980s, children were yet again seen as a way into the home. Nickelodeon was one of the first cable channels to be developed when its parent company, Warner Communications (WCI), expanded *Pinwheel* (1979–89), a children's program that had been part of WCI's QUBE experiment with cabled communities.[35] Parents were encouraged to subscribe to cable not for themselves but for their children, and, in addition to *Pinwheel,* WCI filled Nickelodeon with inexpensive programming. Nickelodeon's early days had no advertising, making the channel particularly attractive to parents. Disney, USA Network, and Cartoon Network were also all a part of early cable. The adoption of cable and the shift from the networks to these new outlets have been dramatic. Within ten years of its introduction, more than 77 percent of the children's audience was watching cable; during that time, the networks went from 98 percent of the audience to 15 percent.[36]

Perhaps the most significant change of this time, though, was the development of home video equipment. In 1984 slightly more than 10 percent of the households in the United States had this equipment; by 1988, more than half the homes in the United States owned a VCR. Disney initially sued to stop the sales of these machines because of copyright infringement, but later it embraced the technology, and children's videos became the largest and most popular section of video rental stores.[37] This technology gave children control over their viewing. They could watch what they wanted, when they wanted, and as many times as their parents would allow. Many characters, like Strawberry Shortcake, went straight to the home video market, and some programs had such success in the home video market that they have become popular television programs, such as characters Builder Bob and Postman Pat. This technology gave children the opportunity to use "television" on their own terms. Anyone who spends time around young children can supply anecdotal evidence of their proficiency at using VCRs and now DVD equipment beginning as early as three years old. The 1980s brought a new sense of "children's television."

Thinking Outside the Box—Literally

Children's television is now more than "just TV," since its reach extends to many other media as well. Any program in development must consider merchandising and book possibilities, gaming potential, music ancillaries, movie rights, and perhaps a live concert. A program now is a "concept" that brings with it toys, movies, books, games, DVDs and CDs, retail goods, snack foods, and promotions—all outside the box. As we have seen, the changes from Winky Dink as a television show to the complex marketing of Jimmy Neutron are the consequence of technological advancements, economics of the industry, and audience demand that have occurred over time. The 1990s continued that transformative pattern.

During the 1990s the growth of the Internet and the World Wide Web created a generation of technologically savvy young people who can control their media environment through videocassette and DVD technology or the computer. Children's television programming, particularly for younger children, is no longer just television but also VHS,

DVD, and Web sites with games and adventures. The Web site for Nickelodeon (www.nick.com) includes backstories on the characters, games and craft projects, a chat room, streaming video of upcoming events, and advertising. Toy technology and the links to television have also become more sophisticated. A current example is the relationship between Warner Bros., producers of the superhero series *The Batman* (2004–), and Mattel, a leading toy manufacturer. Kids' WB! announced that in fall 2004 *The Batman* cartoon would use a new technology, video encoded invisible light (VEIL), where the image on the screen makes toys featuring this technology light up and move.[38]

All the while, our definition of "children" is changing. Bogart's research of the 1950s demonstrated that people were thinking of young television viewers by age, but this was an organizing variable more than an attempt to understand age-related differences. As a rule the industry considered children as one large cohort. It was not until the late 1960s, and the success of *Sesame Street,* that there began to be a consideration of preschoolers and a fine-tuning of audience segmentation. This notion of age-specific programs was reinforced when, in the 1970s, Action for Children's Television demanded such programming. Public broadcasting now brings us *Boohbah* (2000–2003), noticeable for its characteristics designed to attract the attention of preliterate children, such as bright colors, recurring sounds, and repetitive patterns. Naturally, there is also a Web site and a line of retail products even for the youngest of ages. Nickelodeon and Disney extended the concept of targeting specific children's groupings as they refined and targeted their programming schedules to bring particular audiences to the television. Over its twenty years as a cable channel, Nickelodeon began with "children's television" and later added Nick at Nite for the tween, Nick Jr. for the preschooler, and Nick Jr. Baby.[39]

The 1990s saw an expansion of the children's audience both up and down with the development of tween and teen genres and pre-preschool programming. Perhaps the most significant new segment has been the teen dramas. While Nickelodeon, Disney, and the Public Broadcasting System were "discovering" the youngest audience, the new networks WB, UPN, and Fox were attracting an older, teen audience with programs like *Felicity, Dawson's Creek,* and *Buffy the Vampire Slayer.* Again, teens have long been an audience for the media, but now media consolidation has both fragmented that market and multiplied its texts and products.[40] Osgerby argues that teen dramas come from a long tradition of "teen girl" television, but what has occurred more recently is differ-

While Nickelodeon, Disney, and PBS were aggressively targeting children in the 1990s, newer networks such as WB were aiming at a slightly older audience with teen dramas like *Felicity*. (Left to right) Keri Russell as Felicity Porter and Scott Foley as Noel Crane. Courtesy of Warner Brothers Television.

ent in both substance and scale.[41] With new outlets like WB and UPN and the expansion of the consumer market, these shows take on the serious issues of identity, sexuality, and relationships as branded clothing lines, jewelry, and cosmetics are sold on companion Web sites. As McAllister and Giglio have demonstrated in their analysis of the commodity flow of television, these commercial channels now offer a seamless flow of products—both retail and media.

The synergistic relationships that are forming as a result of media consolidation are also evident in the children's television industry. With the Children's Television Act of 1990 came the first regulatory process that obligated all television broadcast stations to demonstrate that they met their public interest responsibility by programming for the educational and entertainment needs of the young audience; this obligation was strengthened in 1995 with the Three Hour Rule, which requires broadcasters to document at license renewal time that they program an average of three hours of age-specific, educational programming per week. ABC and CBS stations meet this obligation by using programming "at hand" from their parent companies—Disney and Nickelodeon—content that is vetted as "educational." NBC is now fulfilling this requirement by "renting out" the Saturday morning block to Discovery Channel, a cable channel that has a well-established reputation for quality documentary programming.[42] The consequences of this regulatory policy are that children now see the same programs on the networks as they do on Nickelodeon and Disney. During the prime hours of Saturday morning in 2000, ABC programmed *One Saturday Morning* (1997–2002), *Doug* (1991–94), and *Pepper Ann* (1997–2000)—all Disney productions and all promoting prosocial messages. CBS programmed *Franklin* (1997–), *Kipper* (1998–), *Little Bear* (1995–2000), and *Little Bill* (1999–), all preschool programs with prosocial messages distributed on Nickelodeon's Nick Jr. The format of choice for Saturday morning children's television has become palatable prosocial animation for the preschooler, no more the action adventure superheroes of the 1950s and 1960s for children aged six to eleven.

Economics drive the U.S. commercial television market, perhaps nowhere more so than in the children's television industry. Early TV sets were promoted as important for children, a technique used later by cable and emerging networks. Once each was established, the amount of children's programming declined. When cable was first introduced, Nickelodeon, the Cartoon Network, and USA all programmed heavily for children. Disney soon followed. The Cartoon Network and USA no longer program for children, and, although hundreds of new cable channels have been added since cable was first introduced, Noggin is the only new children's channel. WB and UPN initially programmed for children and teens, and though WB now has a children's block (Kids' WB!) both have eliminated their programming for teens.

Children's television is not a genre to be considered as a monolith serving a singular audience; like adult television, it is the consequence of the economy, technology, and politics of the time. Jason Mittell calls for an analysis of genre situated within power politics. He asks that we "look for the political implications and effects of genre distinctions in seemingly 'nonpolitical' case studies," providing the example of the motion picture industry's sale of theatrical cartoons to the television networks.[43] This "articulation of genres . . . can point toward some important insights concerning both genres and larger cultural issues."[44] Most important, Mittell argues that "we can arrive at a clearer and more comprehensive understanding of how genres work to shape our media experiences, how media work to shape our social realities."[45] Let this chapter be a beginning of the articulation of children's television not as just cartoons or other content categories that are "unworthy of critical consideration."[46]

In approaching the genres of children's television critically, it is evident that Winky Dink and Jimmy Neutron are more than brash young men[47] who represent children's animated television; instead, they embody the changing nature of childhood. Fifty years ago Winky came on the scene to a naive audience of children (and parents) who were just beginning to understand the potential of television. Few dreamed of its possibilities to take us to the moon, exotic places, or a war zone. Children today have seen much more on their TV screens. If they are bored with a program, they can push a button and access a hundred other channels, as well as an array of videotapes or DVDs. Jimmy Neutron and his clever gadgets and his high-tech solutions to everyday problems reflect the child of this millennium. The technology of Winky's and Jimmy's worlds replicates the worlds they live in. Crayons were the communication tool of Winky Dink's generation; today it is not unusual for a middle-class preschool child to be familiar with a computer,[48] and most teens text message their friends with cell phones.

These two series also serve as markers for the changing economics of the industry in both the obvious (three networks/multiple platforms) and the not so obvious ways, for example, the transition of children from a special audience to sophisticated consumers. McAllister and Giglio's aforementioned description of a Saturday morning on Nickelodeon illustrates how entertainment and marketing are now seamlessly blended. Much the same can be found on the broadcast networks and the Disney Channel, and as the number of corporations that own media channels diminishes, one can expect such synergistic practices to increase. The consumer power of today's children is evident in high-end products like minivans, cell phones, and computers that are targeted toward them. The array of products featuring licensed characters is no longer unique and is far too extensive to list.

Children are the future not as citizens in a democracy but as consumers in an economic system that targets their purchasing power. It is critical that we think of children's media as a cultural category if we are to understand the "social function"[49] of children's television, the "demands of audience and advertisers,"[50] and if we are to "explore the material ways in which [this genre is] culturally defined, interpreted, and evaluated."[51] As Winky would say, boys and girls, get out your crayons—we have work to do.

Notes

Thank you to Kem Saichaie for his work on an earlier draft.

1. There are parallels between previous analyses of the content of children's television and genre theory, but, like most of the research on children's television, the discussion has been in the context of social science research. Only recently have some scholars begun to apply the lens of cultural studies—theoretical home of genre analysis—to children's popular culture. Therefore, this chapter will fold previous work on children's television programming into this discussion.

2. J. Piling, *A Reader in Animation Studies* (Sydney: John Libbey, 1999), quoted in Máire Messenger Davies, *"Dear BBC": Children, Television Storytelling and the Public Sphere* (Cambridge: Cambridge University Press, 2001), 226.

3. Karen Stoddard, "Children's Television Genres," in *TV Genres,* ed. Brian G. Rose (Westport, Conn.: Greenwood Press, 1985), 353–65.

4. Máire Messenger Davies, "Studying Children's Television," in *The Television Genre Book,* ed. Glen Creeber (London: British Film Institute, 2001), 96–97.

5. Ellen Seiter, *Sold Separately* (New Brunswick, N.J.: Rutgers University Press, 1993); Stephen Kline, *Out of the Garden: Toys, TV, and Children* (London: Verso, 1993); Norma Pecora, *The Business of Children's Entertainment* (New York: Guilford Press, 1998).

6. See, for example, Glyn Davis and Kay Dickenson, *Teen TV* (London: British Film Institute, 2004).

7. Davies, *"Dear BBC,"* 96.

8. Jason Mittell, "A Cultural Approach to Television Genre Theory," *Cinema Journal* 40, no. 3 (2001): 3.

9. R. Altman, *Film/Genre* (London: BFI Publishing, 1999), quoted in Graeme Turner, "The Uses and Limitations of Genre," in Creeber, *The Television Genre Book,* 4.

10. Rose, *TV Genres,* 9.

11. Mittell, "Cultural Approach to Television Genre Theory," 9.

12. Ibid., 3.

13. Merris Griffiths and David Machin, "Television and Playground Games as a Part of Children's Symbolic Culture," *Social Semiotics* 13, no. 2 (2003).

14. Mittell, "Cultural Approach to Television Genre Theory," 7.

15. Ibid., 5.

16. In this chapter the generic term "children's television" refers to programming that can include ages birth to eighteen, although the focus is on younger children.

17. CBS press release in Anthony M. Maltese, "A Descriptive Study of Children's Programming on Major American Television Networks from 1950 through 1964" (Ph.D. diss., Ohio University, 1967), 101.

18. Adapted from Matthew P. McAllister and J. Matt Giglio "The Commodity Flow of U.S. Children's Television," *Critical Studies of Media Communication* 22 (March 2005).

19. Mittell, "Cultural Approach to Television Genre Theory," 9.

20. Since the 1950s, movies have been made for an increasingly younger audience. The 1950s and 1960s brought teen movies, but more recently the industry has been producing entertainment for an even younger audience, including the Harry Potter movies and Disney fare such as *Finding Nemo.*

21. Joseph Turow, *Entertainment, Education, and the Hard Sell* (New York: Praeger, 1981), 126.

22. Toby Miller, "The Action Series," in Creeber, *The Television Genre Book,* 17.

23. Seiter, *Sold Separately,* 185.

24. J. Hartley, "Situation Comedy," in Creeber, *The Television Genre Book,* 66.

25. This is not to say that licensed products did not exist. In the early 1930s Mickey Mouse could be found on T-shirts and notebooks, and Toni, a maker of home permanents, licensed its name to dolls with beautiful blond curls.

26. Leo Bogart, *The Age of Television,* 2nd ed. (New York: Ungar, 1958), 253.

27. Cy Schneider, *Children's Television: How It Works and Its Influence on Children* (Lincolnwood, Ill.: NTC Business Books, 1989).

28. Pecora, *Business of Children's Entertainment,* 12.

29. For daytime and prime-time programming in 1964–65, 48 percent of the network ads were participating; by 1968–69, almost 100 percent of commercials were thirty-second spots. See Christopher H. Sterling and John M. Kittross, *Stay Tuned: A Concise History of American Broadcasting,* 2nd ed. (Belmont, Calif.: Wadsworth, 1990), 393.

30. Turow, *Entertainment, Education, and the Hard Sell,* 54.

31. See ibid., 50–83, for the development of this argument.

32. Pecora, *Business of Children's Entertainment,* 34.

33. Ibid., 69.

34. Ibid., 42.

35. Norma Pecora, "Nickelodeon Grows Up," in *Nickelodeon Nation,* ed. Heather Hendershot (New York: New York University Press, 2004), 15–44.

36. D. Petrozzello, "Cable Competition for Kids Intensifies," *Broadcasting and Cable,* July 27, 1998, quoted in Alison Alexander, "Broadcast Networks and the Children's Television Business," in *Handbook of Children and the Media,* ed. Dorothy G. Singer and Jerome L. Singer (Thousand Oaks, Calif.: Sage, 2001), 497.

37. Sterling and Kittross, *Stay Tuned,* 378.

38. Jill Goldsmith, "Batman Has His Eye on You," *Variety,* 14–20, June 2004, 6.

39. Advertisement in *Women's Day,* September 2004.

40. Valerie Wee, "Selling Teen Culture: How American Multimedia Conglomeration Reshaped Teen Television in the 1990s," in Davis and Dickenson, *Teen TV,* 89.

41. Bill Osgerby, "'So Who's Got Time for Adults!': Femininity, Consumption and the Development of Teen TV," in Davis and Dickenson, *Teen TV,* 83.

42. "NBC Rents Saturday Morning to Discovery," *Pittsburgh Post-Gazette,* May 9, 2002, region edition, C6.

43. Mittell, "Cultural Approach to Television Genre Theory," 19.

44. Ibid.

45. Ibid., 19–20.

46. Piling in Davies, *"Dear BBC,"* 226.

47. That there are few brash young ladies is the topic for another paper.

48. In 2004 IBM released a PC branded with Nickelodeon's *Blues Clues* (1996–); not to be upstaged, Macintosh has just announced the release of a Disney computer with large buttons, an easy-to-use keyboard for little fingers, and the easily recognized Mickey Mouse profile.

49. Altman, *Film/Genre,* quoted in Turner, "Uses and Limitations of Genre," 4.

50. Rose, *TV Genres,* 9.

51. Mittell, "Cultural Approach to Television Genre Theory," 9.

5 | five decades and three hundred sitcoms about class and gender

Richard Butsch

Since *I Love Lucy,* situation comedy has been the mainstay, the bread and butter, of prime-time television. It has been the most durable of genres: at least four hundred sitcoms have appeared during prime time. Three hundred were domestic sitcoms depicting families; many of the rest were constructed as artificial families of friends or coworkers. Many lasted only a few weeks, some lasted for years, but each year they were key to network profits. Overall they reliably provided good ratings, and they were cheaper to produce than drama and far more sellable as reruns than any other form.

Situation comedy is built around a humorous "situation" in which tension develops and is resolved during the half hour. In episode after episode the situation is re-created. In many sitcoms, particularly those featuring a well-known comic, the comic situations are embodied in a character who is always getting himself into trouble. David Grote said comic characters are traditionally of three types, the Innocent, the Fool, and the Scoundrel. The Scoundrel is rare in TV sitcoms, Sergeant Bilko being the most famous exception. Many domestic sitcoms feature children, Innocents, as the comic characters. This was typical of idyllic middle-class families depicted in sitcoms such as *The Brady Bunch, The Cosby Show,* and *Seventh Heaven.*[1] The parents are cast as wise in contrast to the innocent children. These shows evoke a warm glow more than a loud laugh.

However, the most memorable sitcoms have been built around a Fool, such as Lucy, Archie, or Homer. Sometimes the fool is a supporting character, such as Raymond's father in *Everybody Loves Raymond*. The buffoon or fool is a classic type in comic drama, traditionally cast as someone of inferior status, slaves or servants, women, peasants and lower classes, subordinate races, and so forth. The fool has been used in ancient Greek and Roman drama, in Renaissance drama, in nineteenth-century minstrelsy, in ethnic humor of vaudeville. The ground was well trod long before the creation of situation comedy.[2]

Inferior statuses are represented using negative stereotypes of women, blacks and other minorities, the old and the young, and other low statuses. Already embedded in the larger culture, these stereotypes are useful for their familiarity. Over time, stereotypes are merged into character types that recur and have a special importance in the culture as stock images—the country bumpkin, the dizzy blonde—used to construct a culture's tales and even to type each other in everyday life. They become codes that audiences can be expected to know and that writers can use to advance dramatic goals without having to explain. This is especially useful in a short form of drama like the twenty-two-minute sitcom. The foolishness in sitcoms is almost always attached to a character's lower status, by representing well-known stereotypes of this status group.

A higher status can be denied by representing a person as having opposite characteristics. Men are devalued by characterizing them as feminine. Adults have been devalued by characterizing them as childlike. When a person has two contradictory status positions, such as rich woman, black middle class, working-class man, the higher status can be undercut to resolve the contradiction in favor of the lower status. Demasculinizing working-class men—that is, applying descriptors that contradict the culturally accepted definition of masculine—not only devalues them as men but also uses gender to affirm their subordinate class status.[3]

Television sitcoms have continued the tradition of representing lower-status groups as inferior. They also have valued one status by manipulating other status traits. One of the most striking patterns in the fifty years of television situation comedy is the consistency in devaluing working-class men's masculinity and thus confirming that class as a deserved lower status. This dramatic mechanism has been a central part of television sitcoms throughout the form's history. Working-class men have been persistently represented as fools, middle-class men seldom so.

There have been times, before television, when working-class men were not represented as fools. The Depression and World War II were the most recent eras when public discourse acknowledged the positive contribution of manual labor. Muscle was depicted as heroic and patriotic—not the sculpted muscle of the gym, but muscles for work, ones on which the nation depended to rebuild itself during the Depression and defend itself during the war. The Roosevelt administration celebrated these working men as strong and vital through Works Progress Administration (WPA) arts and building projects.

By the time television arrived, something had changed America's cultural discourse. From the 1950s on, the admiration of physical labor steadily declined. No longer were construction workers, steelworkers, miners, and craftsmen represented positively. Manual labor instead came to represent stupidity and failure, the only alternative for those men who were not smart enough to be educated to achieve mental work occupations. The mental worker, the middle class, was ascendant in cultural discourse. Since the 1950s manual workers, especially white working-class men, have been characterized as uncouth beer-bellied loud-mouths, couch potatoes, wife beaters, the silent majority, racists, supporters of right-wing causes.

Nowhere has this been so consistently represented to so large an audience as in television domestic sitcoms. For generations, television has presented this message, so long that few people have any memory of sympathetic, let alone heroic, images of working men who perform manual labor. White working-class men have been reduced to Homer, Archie, Fred, Ralph. Every American is familiar with these characters. They are the representatives of working-class men. They are not positive images. They confirm other discourses about America's working class that demean these people and, in doing so, resign them to their fate of low income and little respect.

Sitcoms' predominance on prime-time television throughout its history and their consequent share of the television audience over this history mean that they are preeminent examples of dominant culture, steadily presented to the largest population over the longest time. Pervasive and persistent images crystallize as cultural types. Alternative and oppositional images and readings appear within this context and typically refer to it. Character types that recur across series and across time, and contrasts between types, which may be evident only when we look at the panorama of series taken together, are of especial importance.

What does this half century of dominant culture say? While there can be many readings of these hundreds of sitcoms, there are also patterns of consistency that are powerful means to reproduce and naturalize certain views. A wealth of studies document television images of women and of African Americans. Some have documented images of men. An older research tradition has tabulated occupational frequencies. A handful of studies have examined class or the intersection of gender and class.[4] Almost all these have looked at a specific point in time. Innumerable studies have focused on the text of a single television show. Almost none have examined the pattern of images across many series and over several seasons, what we might call the historical tapestry of television culture.

Analysis across many shows and many years can reveal persistent and pervasive images. It also enables us to discover important contrasts that otherwise would not be noticeable. For example, when we observe the treatment of men and women across shows of different classes, we discover contrasts in the representations of men and women depending on class. Such analyses add depth to our understanding of the traditional types in our culture's tales.

Richard Butsch and Lynda Glennon surveyed three decades of prime-time network domestic situation comedies from the beginning of network television in 1946 to 1980 and found persistent patterns throughout. In previous publications I extended this work to 1989.[5] This chapter extends the earlier work through the 2003–4 season. This research is based on lists of all domestic situation comedy series compiled from Tim Brooks and Earle Marsh's 1999 edition of *The Complete Directory to Prime Time Network Shows,* the annual *TV Guide* fall preview issues, and the epguides.com Web site (http://epguides.com), which provides situation and episode summaries for hundreds of shows. It includes all domestic sitcoms appearing on the six broadcast networks; it does not include series appearing on cable networks or solely in syndication.[6]

I concentrate here on successful series that had five or more first-run seasons, the determinant of successful sale on the syndication market, or that ranked in the top twenty of the annual Nielsen ratings. These are the series and characters that sedimented in the national culture and conversation, shows that most Americans know something about even if they haven't seen them. I will contrast working-class to middle-class series over the five decades.

Most sitcoms featured upper-middle-class families of professionals and businesspeople, but the vast majority were not successful series. Working-class family sitcoms were relatively scarce through most of the nearly six decades of broadcast network television. They were more common during transitional times for network television, seeming to be chosen only when network executives were desperate. Once on television, however, a remarkable percentage became television classics (*The Honeymooners,*

The Flintstones, All in the Family, The Simpsons) and created a vivid cultural type of the working-class man. Also illustrating their exceptional success, only three prime-time animated series have aired more than one hundred episodes: *The Flintstones, The Simpsons,* and *King of the Hill.*[7] All three depict working-class families.

Simpler Times: The 1950s and 1960s

The sitcom began as a radio genre, gaining success in the 1940s due in part to its lower costs compared to comedy-variety shows with big-name stars and orchestras. Even on radio the most common situation was a family. Many of the 1950s radio sitcoms became the first television sitcoms. Even *I Love Lucy* was copied from the radio show *My Favorite Husband,* in which Lucille Ball had starred. As J. Fred MacDonald summed up, "Radio situation comedies were middle-class morality tales. The American family was portrayed as a vital institution in which love, trust and self-confidence were best developed."[8]

Television production costs were many times those of radio, which affected the form of sitcom adapted to television. Advertisers were less willing to pay such costs. The networks moved to a magazine format of programming in which they owned and produced or controlled production of the programs, selling commercial time between programs. Networks benefited from efficiencies of scale, since they were producing many more programs than any advertiser or ad agency could expect to do. The breakthrough was the use of film, which allowed the rerun and syndication of programs, spreading the costs over repeated use and sales.

To sustain a mass audience, the networks preferred blandness in sitcoms. Each network had a censorship office, called standards and practices, to weed out anything controversial.[9] No threatening world impinged on these early TV families, not the bomb or the cold war; not 1960s Vietnam, riots, protests; not sex or drugs. These families seldom struggled. All problems were simple and internal to the family. Almost everyone was content about their place in the family and in the world. With this reassuring formula, the characters were inevitably oversimplified stereotypes that were rather consistent from series to series.

Working-Class Stereotypes

In working-class sitcoms of the period, the man is more or less a buffoon, dumb, incompetent, irresponsible, immature, lacking good sense. His saving grace, for audiences to like and continue to watch him, is that he has a good heart and cares about his family. He is simply not capable of fulfilling his role as father and husband. Humor was built around some variant of his inadequacy as a man. The man was typically caught in a situation of his own making.

This characterization is accentuated by contrasts to the wives and children in these working-class series, as well as by contrasts to the middle-class men in other series. Typically the working-class wife and sometimes the children were portrayed as more intelligent, rational, sensible, responsible, and mature than the man. Mother, not father, typically knew best. Often she had to help him out of situations. The children were often smarter than their fathers, and their successes contrasted to their father's failures. At best father was benign but inferior, at worst an embarrassment.

This formula was the core of the successful 1950s series *The Honeymooners, The Life of Riley,* and *I Remember Mama.* Chester, the father on *The Life of Riley,* was continually concocting schemes to help his family. He attempted to fix a school election so his daughter would win, but he succeeded only in embarrassing her. His incessant failures were expressed in his closing line for each episode, "What a revoltin' development this is!" His wife, Peg, was tolerant of Chester's fiascoes and helped him, sometimes enlisting the children, to save face. The children were Chester's intellectual superiors. While Chester tripped over the English language, Junior headed for college.

The main characters in *The Honeymooners* lived in a bare Brooklyn apartment with few amenities. Consequently, husband Ralph was obsessed with success and modest affluence, at which he constantly schemed but invariably failed. He wanted to afford simple comforts such as a television for his wife, Alice. He tried get-rich-quick schemes, such as marketing what he thought was Alice's homemade sauce, only to learn it was dog food. Alice always quipped, "I told you so." He occasionally tried more conventional means, such as applying for a promotion or trying a self-improvement program—means Alice approved of, but which also got nowhere. Alice's logic and sarcasm invariably bested Ralph in arguments, which typically ended with Ralph saying, in angry frustration, "Just you wait, Alice, one of these days, pow, right in the kisser." She recognized the foolishness of his schemes and sometimes got him out of the messes he'd gotten them into.

I Remember Mama, a sentimental reminiscence of early-twentieth-century family life, was one of the few working-class series in which a working-class family was taken seriously. No one was the butt of humor, yet Lars, the father in this Norwegian immigrant family, was an "earnest bumbler," in the words of the show's scriptwriter.[10] Frequently Mama had to conspire to help him save face. The children went to Mama for advice.

Only one working-class domestic situation comedy was aired through the entire decade of the 1960s. *The Flintstones* was a cartoon version of *The Life of Riley* and *The Honeymooners*. Fred Flintstone's loudmouth brashness was like Ralph Kramden's, but Fred was more amiable, like Chester Riley. Fred's wife, Wilma, exhibited motherly tolerance of Fred's shenanigans, as Peg did of Chester Riley's. Typically Wilma was aware of Fred's surreptitious schemes from the beginning and provided both a safety net for him when he failed and a punishment, much as a mother would for a child. When Fred persuaded his friend Barney to play hooky from work to attend a ball game, Wilma and Barney's wife, Betty, caught them; for their punishment, the "boys" had to take their wives to the opera.

All four of these successful working-class series presented a consistent picture of working-class men as bumblers who were inadequate to fulfill their manly roles of supporting and leading their families. Failing as men confirmed the appropriateness of their lower class status, especially when compared with the middle-class TV husbands of the time.

Middle-Class Stereotypes

In most middle-class series, both parents were intelligent, sensible, and mature. They were calm and affable, in stark contrast to the hysteria that typified the slapstick comedy of the working-class series. In these programs the situation was typically a problem involving one of the children. The parents, seldom perplexed, guided the child through a solution, providing a moral lesson along the way. They were what Glennon and Butsch called superparents.[11]

Moreover, the fathers tended to be more than usually affluent and successful, further accenting the difference from working-class men. Glamorous, prestigious professions predominated over more mundane ones, for example, stars over struggling actors, doctors over nurses, lawyers over accountants; within a given profession, characters were very successful or young, with much promise. Occupational success like this affirmed their manhood, which, in turn, buttressed their class status.

The successful middle-class series of the 1950s included *The George Burns and Gracie Allen Show, The Stu Erwin Show, I Love Lucy, The Adventures of Ozzie and Harriet, Make Room for Daddy, Father Knows Best,*

The patriarch of *Father Knows Best* provided an ideal of 1950s middle-class masculinity. He was a successful and self-assured father who was loved and admired by his wife and children. (Left to right) Billy Gray as Bud Anderson, Robert Young as Jim Anderson, Lauren Chapin as Kathleen Anderson, Elinor Donahue as Betty Anderson, and Jane Wyatt as Margaret Anderson. Courtesy of Screen Gems Television.

Leave It to Beaver, and *December Bride*. *Father Knows Best* is, of course, the prototype of its title, the completely self-assured and successful father, admired by his wife and children, the ideal of 1950s middle-class masculinity. Jim Anderson was always calm, reasonable, and ready with the answers. When the children forgot his birthday, his wife, Margaret, got upset. Jim, unfazed, admonished her for getting angry. Ozzie Nelson wrote the scripts for *Ozzie and Harriet* to express his view of child rearing as relaxed but moral guidance.[12] The title *Make Room for Daddy* made clear who was important in that program's family, in contrast to *I Remember Mama*.

Occasionally a middle-class series was built around a fool as the source of humor. In these cases, however, the fool was almost always the wife, some variant of the movies' stock character the "dizzy blonde." This stereotype confirmed the lower status of women while it avoided under-cutting the middle-class status of the family by preserving the reputa-tion of the husband and head of house. Gracie Allen of *The Burns and Allen Show* was the prototype of the dizzy blonde, interjecting inane statements into the conversations of her husband, George. In *December Bride* the mother-in-law played the scatterbrain. The title character of *I Love Lucy*—and its various reincarnations, *Here's Lucy,* and so on—was the singular example of the woman as buffoon, with the husband as the mature and sensible one, though occasionally he was driven to distrac-tion by his wife's antics. Lucy reversed the gender roles of *Riley* and *The Honeymooners.*

The Stu Erwin Show was the one exception to the rule, reflected in the show's other title, *Trouble with Father.* Comic actor Stu Erwin played a middle-class version of the bumbling father, a high school principal out of his depths at home, based on his stock character from movies since the 1930s.

In the working-class vacuum of the 1960s, middle-class superparents reigned with *The Donna Reed Show, The Dick Van Dyke Show, Petticoat Junction, Bewitched, Green Acres, My Three Sons,* and *Family Affair. The Donna Reed Show, My Three Sons,* and *Family Affair* were classic superparent series. In each the parents were calm and rational. Donna Reed was nicknamed "Mother Knows Best," but the father, a pediatri-cian, was not ineffectual; his wife merely filled the traditional role of providing the primary child care. The same traditional division of labor was a continuing theme in *My Three Sons,* which often depicted the dif-ficulty an all-male household had with domestic matters. The widowed father, an engineer, however, is more than adequate in helping his sons grow up, despite minor mishaps at home. His success as a man is further attested by the continual stream of women who are attracted to him while he is engrossed in his fatherly role. *Family Affair* revived the *Bach-elor Father* formula, in which a prosperous bachelor inherits children and becomes a devoted father. *The Dick Van Dyke Show* also reinforced traditional gender roles: the wife, Laura, typically asked the questions or posed the problem, and husband, Rob, provided the answer. The stum-bling physical humor that was Van Dyke's signature as a comic was mostly absent from the show.

Petticoat Junction and *Green Acres* were part of a rural nostalgia pe-riod of 1960s television. *Petticoat Junction* featured a widow with three beautiful daughters. Its principal theme centered on how to be feminine and attract a husband. Its spin-off, *Green Acres,* featured a stereotypical "dumb blonde" wife, à la Gracie Allen, opposite a successful husband who gave up his Manhattan law practice to become a gentleman farmer. In *Bewitched,* Samantha, the wife, was a clever witch often tempted to use her powers to get her way or help her husband's career, but she also wanted to abandon witchcraft to please her husband, Darrin. Darrin was sometimes befuddled by the supernatural shenanigans but otherwise was depicted as sensible and a competent advertising executive. The 1960s domestic sitcoms uniformly continued the theme of confident, mature, and successful middle-class men posed against the caricature Fred Flintstone, the only representative of working-class men.

Changing Times: The 1970s and 1980s

CBS had been the dominant network of the 1960s, but by 1970 many of its top shows were aging badly. Several had begun in the 1950s, and their audiences were similarly aging and shrinking. Rather than seeking to please everyone, advertisers and networks began to target specific demographic groups, particularly younger audiences aged eighteen to forty-nine. CBS brass decided it was necessary to take some risk, dropping old standbys like comic Red Skelton and introducing new shows that might attract a younger, more savvy viewership. They bought *All in the Family* and began broadcasting it in January 1971.

Norman Lear and MTM Productions began to modify situation comedy in the 1970s.[13] Life in their shows was less idyllic, the characters were less one-dimensional than during the 1950s, and more mediating themes appeared. Lear, who produced *All in the Family, Sanford and Son,* and *Good Times,* introduced real-life problems such as racism, poverty, and abortion that were nonexistent in 1950s and 1960s sitcoms.

While introducing many controversial topics, Lear built this new style on the old and familiar stereotype of the blustery and none-too-bright working-class man. Archie Bunker of *All in the Family* and Fred Sanford of *Sanford and Son* were reminiscent of Ralph Kramden and Chester Riley; James of *Good Times* was a good deal like Lars of *I Remember Mama.* In *All in the Family,* Lear intentionally made Archie a ridiculous character whose prejudices were illogical and senseless. Archie's malapropisms made him the butt of humor, just as Chester Riley's did in the 1950s. Archie also engaged in harebrained schemes like Ralph Kramden's and Chester Riley's.

Edith was not as evidently superior to Archie as the earlier wives were. She was much more hesitant in her criticism of Archie, but she tried

Norman Lear's groundbreaking and controversial *All in the Family* introduced more realistic issues and problems into the situation comedy, such as racism, poverty, and abortion. (Left to right) Sherman Hemsley as George Jefferson and Carroll O'Connor as Archie Bunker. Courtesy of Norman Lear/Tandem Productions.

timidly to advise him against his schemes. The foil for Archie was Mike, his son-in-law, a college graduate who served as the spokesperson for Lear's upper-middle-class viewpoint. He was the liberal to Archie's silent majority, the highbrow to Archie's lowbrow. In one episode Archie changed the television channel from a Beethoven concert that Mike was watching to midget wrestling.

Sanford and Son was a black version of *All in the Family.* Widower Fred Sanford was as bigoted and ignorant as Archie. His son, Lamont, like Mike, was oriented to improvement and middle-class manners. He was embarrassed by his father's behavior. George, the father in *The Jeffersons,* although a businessman, fit the same mold as Archie and Fred, namely, loud and bigoted. The theme song, "Movin' on Up to the East Side," expressed the fact that Jefferson was not born and bred middle-class. His misbehavior, in other words, reflected not on the middle class but on his working-class roots. Like Lamont, his wife and family were embarrassed at the things he said. He and Fred, despite class differences, were devalued in the same way white working-class men were. Race worked as the equivalent of class, illustrating that lower statuses were interchangeable for the purpose of creating a dramatic fool.

Good Times was a black version of *I Remember Mama*. The mother, Florida, was the mainstay of the family. James, like Lars of *I Remember Mama*, was not a buffoon but nevertheless was unable to fulfill his role as breadwinner and father figure. He was often unemployed and hot-tempered as well. The role of fool fell to teenage J.J., the oldest son, who was the one with endless get-rich-quick schemes. Rather than a fool, however, he was an irreverent jokester with a quick wit, in contrast to his father's inadequacies. His irreverence appealed to audiences, so producers enlarged his role. Thelma and Michael were model children and ambitious: she attended college, he was very bright and was talked about as a future president.

The 1980s continued the tradition of stereotyping working-class men in *Alice*. The show blended work and family. The surrogate father was Mel, the owner and cook of a greasy spoon Arizona diner, who was a loudmouth like Archie Bunker. Alice was the wise and calm surrogate wife, like her namesake in *The Honeymooners,* and the mother of a twelve-year-old son who respected her. In *Gimme a Break*, a widowed police captain—a managerial occupation with working-class ties and traditions—was an ineffective father; his black maid bailed him out when he got himself into a domestic jam.

Middle-Class Sitcoms in the 1970s and 1980s

Through the 1970s and 1980s, TV's middle-class parents became fallible, made mistakes, got upset. But they soon regained control of the situation and resolved the problem, like the mothers and unlike the fathers of working-class series. They allowed their children to speak to them much more as equals than those in the earlier series, yet they remained unflappable and ultimately retained their roles as guides and models to their children. They co-opted the high ground by admitting their mistakes and summarizing the moral lesson both for their children and for the audience.

Of the successful middle-class sitcoms of the 1970s, *The Brady Bunch* maintained the 1950s tradition of *Father Knows Best*. The parents had the answers to all their children's questions. When vacationing at the Grand Canyon they explained the canyon and the traditions of the local

Hopi tribe as if they were trained guides. They consistently approached problems calmly and rationally, even in an episode in which one of the children was lost. The mother in *Happy Days* was a bit of a dizzy woman, a tamer version of Lucy. The father, Howard Cunningham, was reasonable and sensible. Fonzie, a young working-class friend of the family whom the kids admired and women found irresistible, typically supported the father's moral authority.

But other shows diverged from the earlier formula, as situation comedy expressed a new irreverence toward professionals and experts. *The Bob Newhart Show* featured a psychologist who hesitated, had self-doubts, and often was caught in his own words. His office mate, a dentist, was a schemer, and his neighbor, Howard, was a divorced airplane pilot and a buffoon. The title character of *Maude* was an outspoken feminist woman whose demands continually exasperated her husband, Walter. Although Walter was a match for Maude, his friend Arthur, an M.D., was a buffoon. As just discussed, George Jefferson, the husband in *The Jeffersons,* who owned a dry-cleaning chain, was an uncouth loudmouth. Notably, none of these series that deviated from the calm, competent middle-class man included young children to witness their limitations, as in most working-class series.

Through the early 1980s shows continued their questioning of upper-middle-class professionals and authority in *Benson, Newhart* (a new show), and *Who's the Boss?* Bob Newhart continued to play the stuttering, flummoxed character from his old show, but now as the owner-operator of a Vermont bed-and-breakfast. *Benson* featured a white, widowed upper-middle-class man who was a klutz as a governor and a father. His black butler, Benson, regularly rescued his white male boss. Confirming his ability, Benson was successively promoted from butler to budget director, then to lieutenant governor; in the last episode he was a candidate for governor, an unusually positive portrayal of a black male character.

The mid-1980s returned to the superparent tradition. The classic middle-class father appeared in *The Cosby Show, The Hogan Family, Family Ties,* and *Growing Pains. Full House* was most like the saccharine 1950s shows, with a calm, understanding widowed sportscaster father skillfully shepherding three cute daughters. In *The Cosby Show* the father joked around with his children but also made it clear who was the boss. *Growing Pains, Family Ties,* and to a lesser degree *The Hogan Family* featured slightly more fallible parents. In one episode of *Growing Pains* the parents insist that their daughter plead guilty to a charge of resisting arrest

The Cosby Show was a return to the superparent tradition, where the father joked around with his children but also made it clear that he was still the boss. (Left to right) Bill Cosby as Dr. Cliff Huxtable, Tempestt Bledsoe as Vanessa Huxtable, Keshia Knight Pulliam as Rudy Huxtable, Lisa Bonet as Denise Huxtable, and Phylicia Rashad as Clair Huxtable. Courtesy of Carsey-Werner Productions.

to avoid a trial. The daughter refuses to lie; the judge respects this and lets her off. The parents, however, regain the high ground by approving her behavior and summarizing the lesson. The teen son of *Family Ties* was a bit too bright for his parents, yet he was held in check and still respected them. While the fathers and mothers exhibited foibles and flaws absent in series of the 1950s, they were nonetheless parents who knew best.

Who's the Boss? complicates the trend with its gender reversal between Angela, the quintessential upper-middle-class professional, and the ethnic working-class Tony as the housekeeper. But, as the title suggests, Angela is not such a success at home. Tony is a wiser parent and better housekeeper than Angela, an advertising executive. This class reversal, however, is veiled by the gender reversal that is the heart of the situation. Both are succeeding at what their gender is *not* supposed to do, and the woman fails in what she *is* supposed to do.

Postmodern Times: The Late 1980s and 1990s

VCRs and communication satellites changed the television industry through the 1980s and 1990s. Satellites made it economically feasible for smaller networks to distribute programming. This in turn created a large supply of programming that made cable television attractive and multiplied the number of channels available to viewers. VCRs were a second alternative to broadcast, once movies were released and rental began.[14] These changes were complemented by the growth of independent television stations and the beginning of Fox, the first new broadcast network since DuMont in the 1940s. The three networks that dominated network and radio for fifty years, and that accounted for 90 percent of the prime-time TV audience for thirty years, watched their ratings erode steadily. In this climate networks were willing to try things they would not consider in good times. The Reagan-era Federal Communications Commission enabled this experimentation by relaxing rules on language and subject matter for TV. By the late 1980s all these pieces were in place, and a new era of sitcom blossomed.

The shift began perhaps with two developments, *Roseanne* (1988), in which the Carsey-Werner production company spread its wings in ways it could not do with *Cosby;* and the arrival of Fox with programming that pushed the envelope, like *Married with Children* (1987), *The Simpsons* (1990), and several shows featuring black performers. Fox was ready to use sassier scripts to gain a foothold against its established competitors.[15] These new shows were noted for regular use of irreverence, sarcasm, irony, and even insult in the dialogue, forms uncommon in earlier sitcoms. They were more likely to include risqué lines about sex than to introduce social issues as Lear did in the 1970s. In general, sitcoms shifted away from the morality tales typical since radio to programs about flawed families.

Working-Class Shows of the Late 1980s and 1990s

Yet for all the talk about postmodernism at the time, sitcom scripts were not as postmodern as one might expect. All these changes were still built on decades-old character types. While *The Simpsons* and *Married . . . with Children* were ruder, even gross, at the same time they used the old stereotypes of working-class men as inadequate breadwinners and models for their children.

The Simpsons began its sixteenth season in fall 2004. In its earlier years, Homer Simpson barely brought home the bacon. The children's "college fund" contained $88.50. The family couldn't afford a new TV until Homer received double his money back for guaranteed family therapy that failed. He caused a nuclear accident while waving to his son touring the nuclear power plant where he works. Repeating the tradition's negative contrasts between father and mother, Marge, like Edith Bunker, is somewhat more levelheaded than Homer. The kids are embarrassingly smarter than their dad; second grader Lisa wins against him at Scrabble, and Bart consistently beats him in a boxing video game. Both better Homer in arguments, with Homer resorting to shouting.

One episode of *The Simpsons* even encapsulated the continuing tradition of working-class sitcoms. Lisa Simpson realized she had the same genes as her dad and became depressed. Then she realized all the male relatives were jerks like her dad. By contrast, she discovered the females were all successful, with careers as surgeons, professors, or scientists.

Married . . . with Children portrayed a family of uniformly unlikable people. The show was a spoof of the goody-goody TV family. The contrast was not between family members but to the wholesomeness of other TV families. The father, Al Bundy, a shoe salesman, was dumb but not lovable as in the traditional working-class type. He lied and smelled bad. The show was an endless stream of put-downs. Al's wife, Peg, regularly complained of his lack of money and sexual inadequacy. Peg's friend described Al as having no skills and no brain. Peg and her daughter, Kelly, were also depicted as dumb. Peg couldn't remember what channel her favorite TV show was on; Kelly did not know what the word "simpleton" meant. The son, Bud, was the only one with any intelligence, and he was an oversexed adolescent.[16]

A more conventional sitcom, *Family Matters* moderated the traditional working-class stereotype father. At first the father, a black policeman, bungled his efforts. He got lost taking a shortcut, gave the wrong directions to rescuers, said the wrong things trying to impress his boss. But soon the role of fool shifted to the neighbor boy Steve Urkel, who became an unexpected hit with audiences. The father began to fade as the featured fool, and the role of Urkel was expanded, much as had occurred with the role of J.J. in *Good Times* in the 1970s. Yet consistent with the tradition of working-class wives, Harriet, the wife, was the more sensible person in the family.

Somewhat of an exception to the traditional stereotype was Dan Conners, the father of *Roseanne,* who, while a bit wild, was also sensible about the kids. In one episode Dan was the voice of wisdom when he advised Roseanne not to engage in a power struggle with teenage Becky.

The characters in *Roseanne* refused to apologize for their
working-class background and lifestyle and thumbed their
noses at middle-class propriety. (Left to right) Roseanne Barr
as Roseanne Conner and John Goodman as Dan Conner.
Courtesy of Paramount Pictures.

More striking about *Roseanne* was its refusal to apologize for the family's
working-class ways or to accept middle-class manners as superior. Dan
and Roseanne were content with their working-class tastes. They could
use more money, but they were not conflicted about behaving "properly," and they did not aspire to cultural upward mobility.

The Bundys of *Married . . . with Children* also were unapologetic for not being upper-middle-class and rather metaphorically thumbed their noses at those expectations. For the first time, working-class characters were allowed to be themselves instead of inferior copies of middle-class characters.

Of fifty-three new domestic sitcoms from 1990 to 1999, sixteen featured working-class families. Eleven series featured black families, indicating another trend toward more representation of subordinate groups. Yet several notable series that did not survive five seasons reproduced the working-class stereotype. The father in *The Dinosaurs* was a Jurassic Archie Bunker. The father in *Joe's Life* was an unemployed houschusband whose wife supported the family. *Bless This House,* which featured a macho postal worker with a feisty wife and sassy daughter, was described as *The Honeymooners* with kids.[17] In 1991 *Roc* featured a not-too-bright black garbage man with a stereotypical macho attitude and a more educated wife who worked as a nurse. In the new *Cosby,* the husband was an unemployed airport worker whose wife co-owned a flower shop and whose daughter was a lawyer. *Costello* was criticized for its crude stereotypes of working-class men. Strong, working wives and mothers ran their families and, in some shows, overshadowed their husbands. The title characters in *Jesse* and *Thea,* among others, were single mothers who exhibited strength and good character that put their men to shame. Many 1990s shows featured dysfunctional families, but the more serious dysfunctions existed in blue-collar families. Alcoholism, spousal abuse, child abandonment, and children being put up for adoption appeared in working-class shows like *Grace under Fire.* Divorce and quirky personalities were more typical of middle-class shows.[18]

In *Grace under Fire,* the working-class father was an unreliable drunken "good-for-nothing" who abandoned the family. Grace held a traditionally male job in an oil refinery and did better than most of the men. Two of her male friends were relaxed and comfortable, a middle-class pharmacist and a local TV reporter. She dated a series of stable, apparently middle-class men.

In the late 1990s' *King of the Hill,* Hank, a Texas propane gas salesman, wears white T-shirts and jeans and drinks beer from cans with his buddies, and is often clueless when his son tries to ask him questions. His son and wife are also not too bright. His live-in niece-in-law, Luanne Platter, is frustrated and embarrassed by them. Hank's friends are a divorced military barber, a paranoid with an obsession for government conspiracy theories, and a man who just mumbles. All the males are of limited intellect. Unlike in older working-class series, however, so is everyone else.

The main character of *King of Queens* is Doug, a UPS driver whose wife, Carrie, works in a law firm and is a little too bright for him. He is a couch potato who loves to watch sports with his buddies on his seventy-inch television. Husband and wife are young, fun-loving, and not quite ready to become parents. But Carrie is interested in self-improvement for both of them, for example, by going to highbrow events. She tries to reform Doug's bad habits, such as too much eating and TV. It's a bit like a 1990s version of Fred and Wilma's relationship.

Thus, while there were more shows featuring working-class people in the 1990s, the men continued to be stereotyped as immature and not too bright, immature, in contrast to their more capable and responsible wives or adult female relatives. With few exceptions the working-class male leads were inadequate in their masculine roles. Undercutting their status as men in turn confirmed their lower status as working-class and resolved the contradictory statuses of adult white male, on the one hand, and working-class, on the other.

Middle-Class Sitcoms of the Late 1980s and 1990s

Unlike working-class characters of the 1990s, who continued to be true to stereotype, middle-class series came in all forms and sizes. One show briefly featured an ex-husband who was a fired soap opera actor, another a con artist who moves in with his successful lawyer sister, another a hyperactive party planner on her third husband, and another a suspended professional athlete who moves in with his professor brother. There were four black middle-class families and one mixed-race couple. Jack, the father in *The Wonder Years,* is a businessman who wears a suit and tie to work. He is singularly uninvolved in his family. When asked, he advises the kids, "Do what your mother said."

But there continued to be plenty of warm and fuzzy middle-class families, including some with slightly offbeat parents. Most were short-lived. *Something So Right* was described as *The Brady Bunch* with taboo subjects; *Cleghorne!* was called a dysfunctional *Family Ties;* and *Parenthood* was likened to *thirtysomething. Harts of the West, Something Wilder, The Tony Danza Show,* and *The Gregory Hines Show* featured wholesome families. While quirky or even a bit dysfunctional, these families were still warm and comforting, with competent parents.

More long-lasting were two conventional shows. *Step by Step* was called *The Brady Bunch* for the 1990s. Frank, the father, owned a contracting company. He carried a lunch box to work but bought pro basketball game tickets for a "client." His wife, Carol, owned a beauty salon, although she also graduated from college. He was an outdoorsy type who was permissive with the kids, while Carol was more compulsive. The children were the focus of situations.

Seventh Heaven is another saccharine *Brady Bunch* look-alike that has survived a decade. A minister and a stay-at-home mom are perfect parents to five children whose trials of growing up are the subject of the show. Issues have included dating crises, teen suicide, sibling rivalry, gang violence, hate crimes, violence in schools, drug use, vandalism, drinking and driving, teen pregnancy, and homelessness. The show has thrived presenting old-fashioned moral lessons in the security of an old-fashioned ideal middle-class family.

More written and talked about were *Home Improvement, Mad about You,* and *Everybody Loves Raymond.* Magazine and newspaper articles have commented on how these fathers/husbands were portrayed less positively than in the old days. Some attributed this to women becoming the majority on writing teams for several sitcoms and holding important executive positions at the networks.[19] But, while these men are not fathers who know best, neither are they buffoons, like the men of working-class series.

Tim, the father in *Home Improvement,* is the star of his own TV show. At home, the focus is on the antics of the father rather than the children. But his antics involve his asserting his own independence and macho masculinity, rather than making a fool of himself. He reaffirms his manhood rather than undermining it, the masculine answer to feminism, a role model for the contemporary man. *Mad about You* explored the little annoyances and knots of relationships and in doing so also revealed the flaws and insecurities of both the man and the woman. At the same time, both were professionals with promising careers; both worked together to sort out their differences; both were mature and intelligent adults.

The social class of *Everybody Loves Raymond* is anomalous, and the main character does not conform to stereotypes of the middle-class man. Raymond is a sportswriter and joins a private golf club, but in other ways the show is similar to the working-class form. Raymond's brother is a policeman, and his parents are stereotypical ethnic New Yorkers. His father, in particular, is the classic working-class television type, modeled on Ralph and Archie: loud, gruff, overbearing. Moreover, Raymond appears several times on *King of Queens* as a friend of Doug, the UPS driver. Raymond is cowed by his wife and his parents. He lies and concocts schemes to avoid confronting them. Yet he is professionally successful, and his children are toddlers and thus are too young to outsmart or disrespect him, as is the tradition in working-class series.

While the 1990s continued the trend to show middle-class people as imperfect, the variety of representations avoided the stereotyping in working-class series. Like the characters of urban sitcoms described by Michael Tueth, these middle-class men are well-educated professionals, successful, intellectually superior, and emotionally intense, while also being emotionally confused and childish to a degree.[20]

The New Millennium

In the new millennium, a bounty of new black and working-class sitcoms were scheduled for prime time by the six broadcast networks. Joining *King of the Hill* and *King of Queens,* which began in the 1990s, were two more successful white working-class shows, *Grounded for Life* and *Still Standing,* as well as three unsuccessful shows, *The Fighting Fitzgeralds, The Mullets,* and *My Big Fat Greek Life.* Ten new black family sitcoms appeared, including *My Wife and Kids, One on One,* and *Bernie Mac.* Only two of the ten black families are working-class; the rest feature very successful heads of house, mostly as entertainers. Five of the ten programs appeared on UPN and WB, where they represented half the minor networks' new sitcoms. Two Hispanic families and two gay shows set in families also appeared. Broadcast networks were clearly looking for the unconventional more than ever to stem the decline in ratings.

Sean of *Grounded for Life* is a grown-up kid, but he's also an echo of the old stereotype. He's continually screwing up, like Ralph and Fred. He tries to help his daughter, Lily (who has been given detention for wearing too short a skirt to school), by taking pictures of the other girls, all of whom have short skirts. The principal gives all the girls detention and tells them it's Lily's fault. Sean's son wants to go home to work on a science project, but Sean insists on staying at a fair to listen to the Ramones. Sean writes a note to school explaining why his son did not finish the project; the boy gets in trouble, and Sean feels guilty. When he gets $1,500 from his mother's inheritance, Sean buys a guitar, then returns it out of guilt to pay for a ski trip for his daughter.

Still Standing is about a working-class Chicago couple who came of age in the 1970s and still love rock and roll but now have three kids.

The wife, Judy, is supposed to be smarter than her husband, Bill, who always screws up. He tries to make Judy feel better by telling her the husband of a woman she envies is cheating on her. This backfires when Judy tells everyone. The difference here is that the wife also screws up. These two shows present couples similar to the one in *King of Queens*.

The Fighting Fitzgeralds presented a rather positive portrayal of a retired fire captain, a managerial position, but one rooted in working-class culture. Unfortunately, the show was canceled after only ten episodes. *The Mullets,* about two brothers described as "dumb and dumber," is a classic case of laughing at white trash.[21] These new shows again portray working-class men as irresponsible and immature. The difference is that some middle-class men are now being portrayed in this way, whereas this was rarely the case before the 1990s.

Malcolm in the Middle and *According to Jim* continue the unashamedly irresponsible middle-class men of the 1990s. Malcolm's father, Hal, works in an unspecified office but finds plenty of time for all kinds of fun and trouble. He hijacks the kids from school to take them to car races. He has a chance to drive a steamroller and gets a hankering to crush things. Hal has a wealthy father, and one might explain the character as an eccentric who never learned to worry about practical matters like money. The mother, Lois, has the bigger part of the job of civilizing their four exceptionally rowdy boys.

Jim of *According to Jim* is a contractor in partnership with his architect brother-in-law. Jim can't give up his motorcycle. He's also in a hurry to go to a Bears game, sticking his wife's dead cat in the freezer instead of burying it. He has his sister-in-law pick out presents for his wife rather than doing it himself.

One on One and *Two and a Half Men* feature bachelors with child-rearing responsibilities suddenly thrust upon them. These shows are a new version of the old formula of the affluent bachelor father, such as the 1960s *Family Affair,* which was revived in 2002 but soon canceled. In the past the bachelors experienced a strain between their former unencumbered single life and their new obligations, and attempted to live up to those obligations. The father in *One on One* is a black version of the bachelor father. While he enjoys sports, his buddies, and women, he's concerned about protecting and properly bringing up his daughter, Breanna.

Charlie of *Two and a Half Men* is another adolescent man. He is a prosperous bachelor with a Malibu beach house, a Jaguar, and success with women. But when his brother's marriage falls apart, Charlie takes in him and his fourth-grade son, creating the situational conflict be-

tween his social life and the boy. To resolve the conflict Charlie sometimes includes the boy in his activities such as shopping for women and
playing poker.

These programs depicting grown men behaving as adolescents are
surrounded by shows that settle for a quirky twist on the old formula.
Even Stevens is a show about a perfect family that focuses on a seventh-
grade boy. The parents, a successful attorney and a state senator, remain
in the background, while the boy stumbles through life; when he has
problems, the parents and older kids help him put things back together.
My Wife and Kids features a successful businessman who becomes a
househusband so his wife can pursue her career. He trips up, but he also
creates a warm and fuzzy feeling at home. Similarly, *Bernie Mac,* featuring a successful comedian whose wife is a corporate executive, welcomes
into his home and takes care of his sister's kids. Bernie is blustery but
well-meaning. These are slightly jazzier versions of *The Cosby Show,* and
even the two programs that feature a gay character are rather tame. In
both *The Ellen Show* and *Normal, Ohio,* the gay character returns to a
family and hometown and by and large is accepted.

Conclusion

The five decades of television sitcoms can be summed up in the French
phrase "Plus ça change, plus c'est la meme chose" (The more things change,
the more they stay the same). While there have been variations and exceptions, the stock character of the ineffectual, even buffoonish, working-
class man has persisted as the dominant image. In the prime-time tapestry
he is contrasted with consistently competent working-class wives and children and manly middle-class fathers—a composite image in which working-class men are demasculinized and their class status justified.

The persistence of the working-class male stereotype contrasts with
the changes in representations of middle-class families. Although middle-
class families were stereotypically perfect in the 1950s and 1960s, from
the 1970s on their depictions progressively broadened to include a wide
range of character types and situations. Nevertheless, the superparent
continued to be a common representation of the middle class, and middle-
class men, while sometimes represented as irresponsible, were not demasculinized and continued to be unusually successful in their careers.

Major upheavals in American society and culture during the 1960s
and 1970s, followed by major changes in television industry and television technology in the 1980s and 1990s, brought innovations to TV's

domestic sitcoms and broadened and deepened their characterizations. But they have not dislodged the pattern of class representations that are at the core of more than three hundred domestic sitcoms that have been consumed nightly by the American people. If there has been any change in the class representations, it has been to leaven the starchy image of a perfect middle class. There is no sign of a return to the more positive representations of working men that were more common in the popular culture of the 1930s and 1940s and that slowly passed away with the appearance of television.

Notes

1. David Grote, *The End of Comedy* (Hamden, Conn.: Shoestring Press, 1983), 39–41, 87–88. For alternate definitions of sitcom, see Jane Feuer, "Genre Study and Television," in *Channels of Discourse,* ed. Robert C. Allen (Chapel Hill: University of North Carolina Press, 1987), 113–33, and Susan Horowitz, "Sitcom Domesticus: A Species Endangered by Social Change," in *Television: A Critical View,* 4th ed., ed. Horace Newcomb (New York: Oxford University Press, 1987), 106–11.

2. Grote, *End of Comedy,* 41–43; Stuart Hall and Paddy Whannel, *The Popular Arts* (Boston: Beacon Press, 1967); Orrin Klapp, *Heroes, Villains, and Fools: The Changing American Character* (Englewood Cliffs, N.J.: Prentice-Hall, 1962).

3. Joan Scott, *Gender and the Politics of History* (New York: Columbia University Press, 1988); Ava Baron, "Questions of Gender: Deskilling and De-masculinizing in the U.S. Printing Industry, 1830–1915," *Gender and History* 1 (Summer 1989): 178–99.

4. Beth Olson and William Douglas, "The Family on Television: Evaluation of Gender Roles in Situation Comedy," *Sex Roles* 36, nos. 5–6 (March 1997): 409–27; Sally Steenland, "Content Analysis of the Image of Women on Television," in *Women and Media: Content, Careers and Criticism,* ed. Cindy M. Lont (Belmont, Calif.: Wadsworth, 1995); Steve Craig, ed., *Mediated Males: Men, Masculinity and the Media* (Beverly Hills, Calif.: Sage, 1992); Herman Gray, "Television and the New Black Man: Black Male Images in Prime Time Situation Comedy," *Media, Culture and Society* 8 (April 1986): 223–42; Dallas Smythe, "Reality as Presented by Television," *Public Opinion Quarterly* 18 (Summer 1954), 143–56; Mark Crispin Miller, "Deride and Conquer," in *Watching Television,* ed. Todd Gitlin (New York: Pantheon, 1986), 183–228; Sari Thomas and Brian Callahan, "Allocating Happiness: TV Families and Social Class," *Journal of Communication* 32, no. 3 (1982): 184–90; H. Leslie Steeves and Marilyn Crafton Smith, "Class and Gender in Prime-Time Television," *Journal of Communication* 11, no. 1 (Winter 1987): 43–63; Marjorie Ferguson, "Images of Power and Feminine Fallacy," *Critical Studies in Mass Communication* 7 (September 1990): 215–30.

5. Richard Butsch, "Class and Gender in Four Decades of Television Situation Comedy," *Critical Studies in Mass Communication* 9, no. 4 (December 1992): 387–99; Richard Butsch and Lynda Glennon, "Families on TV: Where Was the

Working Class?" *Television* 7, nos. 2/3 (1980): 11–12; Richard Butsch and Lynda Glennon, "Social Class: Frequency Trends in Domestic Situation Comedy, 1946–1978," *Journal of Broadcasting* 27 (Winter 1983): 77–81; Lynda Glennon and Richard Butsch, "The Family as Portrayed on Television, 1946–1978," in *Television and Behavior: Ten Years of Scientific Progress and Implications for the Eighties,* vol. 2, *Technical Reviews,* ed. David Pearl, Lorraine Bouthilet, and Joyce Lazar (Washington, D.C.: U.S. Department of Health and Human Services, 1982), 264–71.

6. The occupation of the head of household was used to distinguish the class represented in the sitcom. For consistency I continue to use the same guidelines as when I began this research three decades ago, following Harry Braverman, *Labor and Monopoly Capital* (New York: Monthly Review Press, 1974), 377–80.

7. John Consoli, "Network TV," *MediaWeek* 11, no. 9 (February 26, 2001): 9.

8. J. Fred MacDonald, *Don't Touch That Dial* (Chicago: Nelson-Hall, 1979), 132–45, quotation on 141; Jess Oppenheimer, *Laughs, Luck and Lucy* (Syracuse, N.Y.: Syracuse University Press, 1996), chaps. 10–11.

9. Robert Pekurny, "Broadcast Self-Regulation" (Ph.D. diss., University of Minnesota, 1977); Alfred R. Schneider, *The Gatekeeper: My 30 Years as a TV Censor* (Syracuse, N.Y.: Syracuse University Press, 2001).

10. "From the Old Country," *Time,* February 26, 1951, 86.

11. Glennon and Butsch, "Family as Portrayed on Television."

12. James Joslyn and John Pendleton, "The Adventures of Ozzie and Harriet," *Journal of Popular Culture* 7 (1973): 23–41.

13. Feuer, "Genre Study and Television," 113–33; Ella Taylor, *Prime-Time Families* (Berkeley: University of California Press, 1989).

14. Richard Butsch, *The Making of American Audiences* (Cambridge: Cambridge University Press, 2000), chap. 18; FCC Network Inquiry Special Staff, Preliminary Reports, FCC, 1980.

15. Kristal Brent Zook, *Color by Fox: The Fox Network and the Revolution in Black Television* (New York: Oxford University Press, 1999).

16. Rick Marin, "Nuking the Nuclear Family," *Newsweek,* April 29, 1996, 70.

17. David Hiltbrand, "Tube," *People,* September 18, 1995, 21; Helen Arthur, "Love in the Time of AIDS," *Nation,* September 25, 1995, 327.

18. Caryn James, "Dysfunction Wears Out Its Welcome," *New York Times,* December 3, 1995, H1, H37.

19. Erica Scharrer, "From Wise to Foolish: The Portrayal of the Sitcom Father, 1950s–1990s," *Journal of Broadcasting and Electronic Media* 45, no. 1 (Winter 2001): 23–41; Hilary De Vries, "In Comedies, Signs of a New Women's Movement," *New York Times,* February 25, 2001, AR19, AR36.

20. Michael Tueth, "Fun City: The Urban Sitcom of the 1990s," *Journal of Popular Film and Television* 28, no. 3 (Fall 2000): 98–108.

21. On representations of white trash, see Dwight Billings, Gurney Norman, and Katherine Ledford, eds., *Confronting Appalachian Stereotypes* (Lexington: University Press of Kentucky, 1999); Matthew Wray and Annalee Newitz, eds., *White Trash* (New York: Routledge, 1996).

6 soap opera survival tactics

Ellen Seiter and Mary Jeanne Wilson

Soap operas have recently diminished in ratings and numbers of programs aired, yet the genre still influences audiences and producers, who have borrowed such conventions as seriality and cliffhangers to enliven everything from *Friends* (1994–2004) and *Sex and the City* (1998–2004) to *CSI* (2000–) and *The Sopranos* (1999–). Reality shows are just the most recent example of a genre that has newly adopted soap opera conventions (cliffhangers and implausible plotlines; a paranoid obsession with disputed paternity and sexual relationships) with spectacular success. Though soap operas remain the lowliest of genres among popular culture critics and television professionals, they hold a significant place as one of the most enduring and global of genres. Soaps have also inspired some of the liveliest and most sustained debates within the scholarly literature of feminist television studies.

In this chapter, we consider soap opera's ability to sustain its appeal to changing generations of television audiences. With their diminishing audiences and increased competition from cable, current soaps have employed a number of innovative survival tactics to revitalize interest in the genre. This chapter suggests new possibilities for the scholarly critique of soaps: changing viewing contexts, shifting audience appeal, and alterations to the genre's traditional narrative schemes and configuration of characters. We first take a look at how academic debates around the notion of "quality" may serve as useful tools in reevaluating soaps as individual programs that differ widely within the genre. We then turn to the question of the soap opera's long-term survival as a distinct genre by examining three new manifestations of the form: soap operas broadcast in rerun on the cable channel SoapNet, the supernatural soap opera *Passions* (1999–), and finally the prime-time teen soap *The O.C.* (2003–).

Quality TV and Soap Operas

The one thing that the industry, scholars, and viewers might agree on is that the daytime soap opera does not fall under anyone's definition of "quality" TV. Within television studies, soaps have been widely discussed in terms of their gendered address and fan interaction. Rarely have the differences among individual soaps been looked at in terms of markers of quality TV. While our intent is not to define soap operas as quality TV, we do think soaps may be evaluated according to a critical hierarchy. Television studies debates around quality have tended to limit the discussion to certain genres, while others, like soaps, have been discussed only in terms of the popular. Yet the same debates around quality exist within the production world of soaps and their fans. All soaps are not created equal, and fans make judgments on them according to specific taste cultures. In exploring how television studies has debated this issue of quality TV, we hope to suggest how this debate around quality functions within other "low" genres as well.

Jane Feuer's work on MTM Enterprises is probably the best-known discussion of what is considered quality TV. Feuer uses the MTM production company to chart one of the first developments of a particular house style and quality image of a television production company. Beginning with *The Mary Tyler Moore Show* (1970–77) and its many spin-offs, and then on to such critically acclaimed prime-time serial dramas as *Hill Street Blues* (1981–87) and *St. Elsewhere* (1982–88), MTM created an image for itself as the premier producer of quality television. While most MTM programs were not ratings toppers, they drew critical acclaim and "quality" audience demographics. MTM, and the writers and producers who came out of it, had such an impact on the television landscape and popular notions of "quality" TV that Feuer uses MTM's style to unpack television's current conception of quality.

One of the markers of quality Feuer discerns from her work on MTM is the stamp of a particular author or producer on a body of work. As she writes, "MTM's image as the quality producer serves to differentiate its programs from the anonymous flow of television's discourse and to classify its texts as a unified body of work."[1] John Caldwell describes how authorial recognition as an indicator of quality continues in the 1980s and 1990s with signature television producers, like Steven Bochco and Michael Mann, and the import of well-known film directors, including Steven Spielberg, Barry Levinson, and David Lynch.[2] Associating a television text with a particular author invokes the image of the artist, thus linking it to traditions of high art rather than a mass-produced commodity.

The mark of authorship is not uncommon in the world of American daytime soap operas. Soap producers are well known for their signature style and image associated with their particular soaps, establishing a sort of "house style."

Agnes Nixon is known for bringing controversial social issues to the forefront on daytime television in the 1970s with her creations *All My Children* (1970–) and *One Life to Live* (1968–). Husband and wife team William Bell and Lee Phillip Bell are known for their high production values, glamorous younger stars, and a focus on sexuality with their series *The Young and the Restless* (1973–) and later *The Bold and the Beautiful* (1987–). Irna Phillips stands as the mother of all U.S. daytime soap operas. Phillips created *Guiding Light* (1952–), *As the World Turns* (1956–), and *Another World* (1964–99) and is also credited with starting the careers of both Nixon and William Bell. Ellen Seiter's work on Irna Phillips traces Phillips's influence on the narrative structure, themes, and production structure of the soap opera genre as we know it.[3]

Big-hit prime-time soap producers like Aaron Spelling and Darren Starr are more widely recognized as major television authors, but their status as "artist" has been relatively low due to the low status of the genre. Spelling stated very explicitly in interviews in the 1970s that he considered television little more than "eye candy."[4] Darren Starr increased his status by moving from a prime-time soap, *Melrose Place* (1992–99), and then jumped much higher with his move to premium cable with *Sex in the City*, where the tawdry romances of soaps moved to more explicit discussions of sexuality, with the "quality" marker of an HBO production. The recent hit *The O.C.* actively promotes its creator, Josh Schwartz, as a young, hip antidote to the standard soap fare. As we discuss later, Schwartz is painted as a film school–trained "auteur" rather than the next Aaron Spelling. This very deliberate move to distinguish *The O.C.* with the mark of authorship brings the program into the realm of quality—or at least hipness—and distances it from the soap genre. The television industry has used assigning a particular author as a way to shift a program away from being categorized as a soap, but academic soap opera studies have neglected to recognize the influence of a specific producer as a way of bringing debates surrounding quality into the discussion of soaps.

Another marker of quality Feuer traces through MTM productions is their somewhat liberal-slanted politics. Unlike Norman Lear's more politically overt sitcoms, MTM's more subdued progressive slant, according to Feuer, is an appeal to capture both a mass audience and a narrower quality demographic: "[An MTM program] must appeal both to the 'quality' audience, a liberal, sophisticated group of upwardly mobile professionals; and it must capture a large segment of the mass audience as well . . . the quality audience is permitted to enjoy a form of television which is seen as more literate, more stylistically complex and more psychologically 'deep' than ordinary TV fare."[5] This appeal to a more "sophisticated," upwardly mobile audience signals quality TV's trade-off between mass appeal (high ratings) and quality demographics. A quality demographic is young, affluent viewers, with money to spend, and with the cultural capital that translates into recognition by industry tastemakers with Emmys and other prestige awards. The label "quality" indicates audiences that would not otherwise want to be associated with the debased television form or the audiences that regularly watch it: "The quality audience gets to separate itself from the mass audience and can watch TV without guilt."[6] Soap operas are an interesting exception in that they are associated with both liberal politics and a downmarket audience.

While quality TV is often defined by its appeal to a certain audience demographic, the audience itself can play an active role in defining taste codes and the image of quality. In her article "Fans as Tastemakers: Viewers for Quality Television," Sue Brower looks at the way the audience group Viewers for Quality Television (VQT) negotiates markers of quality to suit their own definitions of taste.[7] While the professional women of the VQT are applauded for their "socially conscious" tastemaking efforts (at least by the industry, if not by academics), active soap opera fans would never be considered a quality audience. Soap fans are often seen as lonely women who can't differentiate between fantasy and reality. Similarly to members of VQT, active soap fans also participate in letter-writing campaigns to change certain story lines or save a particular character or actor. Today working women and college students are just as likely to be soap fans as part of a quality audience. College students now make up one of soaps' largest audience demographics. Studies of fandom rarely intersect with debates around quality. Soap opera fans don't have the kind of perceived cultural capital necessary to be included in ideas of quality audiences.

For soap operas, the notion of quality is sometimes linked to global circulation and success. CBS's *The Bold and the Beautiful* is the most watched American soap around the world, broadcast in more than ninety countries. The huge viewership for *Dallas* (1978–91) and *Dynasty* (1981–89) around the globe disrupted received wisdom about the limited appeal of imported programming, and the success of these prime-time soaps played a key role in undermining public service broadcasting in Europe. Eventually, audiences tired of the over-the-top style of this generation of soap operas. More recently the somewhat greater realism of teen soaps such as the American *Dawson's Creek* (1998–2003) and the Australian *Neighbours* (1985–) has achieved significant success in the global TV market. If international success influences some of our definitions of quality, "low" genres, such as soaps, must be included in the discussion. In the contemporary television market, there is increasing competition with network soap operas from imported Spanish-language soaps, and telenovelas that acquire enormous audiences worldwide and are available through cable in most major urban markets in the United States.

Charlotte Brunsdon's work poses an interesting challenge to television scholars' usage of the term "quality." Although Brunsdon recognizes there are always issues of power at stake when making judgments of quality, she encourages her colleagues to resist the "abyss of relativism" and engage in debate to promote variety and diversity of both production and audiences.[8] There are indeed debates and measures of quality within the world of soap operas, even if those outside daytime television aren't looking. Certain soaps are perceived as more "realistic" and socially conscious; others have a distinctly camp sensibility with a good dose of satire, such as NBC's fantasy/supernatural soap, *Passions*. CBS soaps have higher production values and a richer look, as with *The Young and the Restless,* which has consistently topped the ratings for years. The markers of quality are measured and traded within the daytime production world, but academic work on soaps tends to lump them together as a single product. In her plea for a reconsideration of quality within television studies, Brunsdon argues that "the generic diversity of television must be taken into account in discussions of quality, but not in ways which makes quality 'genre-specific,' creating certain 'sink' or 'trash' genres of which demands are not made."[9] As we have argued, while many of the markers of quality apply to or at least intersect with the soap opera, the genre is rarely contemplated in those terms. The link between quality TV and soap operas may seem tenuous, but it offers an avenue for scholars to tackle recent changes in the genre.

Repurposing Soap Opera for Digital Cable

One way in which soaps are attempting to revitalize the genre and address the changing lifestyles of their audience is with the option of syndication, rarely used in the history of U.S. soaps. Similar to talk shows and game shows, daytime soap operas have been deemed unsuitable to replay in later broadcasts. This is partly a result of the low status of the soap opera as a trash genre, and of industry practices, which—for the practical reason of the sheer volume of programming hours—never conceived of the genre as exploitable for the "repurposing" that has been happening on the new cable network SoapNet since its premiere in January 2000. Although the genre has been popular since the early days of television, the actual narratives and performances have been a one-time-only broadcasting product. Lynn Spigel points out that "television even erases its own past; it selects only a few programs for syndication and leaves out countless others."[10] Until the debut of SoapNet, specific soap opera texts have suffered this kind of erasure from television history, but the possibility of syndication on channels like SoapNet may offer a new profitable prospect for the genre. Thus, we must also consider how the advent of the rerun of serial television may change the terms in which we have previously studied soap operas.

Until now the serial nature of the soap opera has marked it as unsuitable for profitable rebroadcasting on U.S. television. The advent of the ever-increasing number of cable outlets and continual narrowcasting to even smaller audiences has finally brought about the syndication of American soaps. Premiering in January 2000, the cable channel SoapNet now rebroadcasts daily episodes of currently running network daytime soaps and airs several canceled daytime and prime-time soaps. Attempting to address the changing lifestyles of soap viewers, the cable network airs prime-time same-day replays of current afternoon soaps. The Disney-owned cable channel reruns all the ABC-owned soaps, *General Hospital* (1963–), *One Life to Live,* and *All My Children,* and has recently added NBC's *Days of Our Lives* to its same-day rebroadcasting schedule. The channel also offers an afterlife to several beloved canceled soaps, including *Ryan's Hope* (1975–89) and *Another World.* Using distinctly campy marketing campaigns, SoapNet pitches its lineup of prime-time classics *Dynasty, Dallas,* and *Knots Landing* (1979–93) as "Dysfunctional Family Night.

SoapNet's marketing is able to repurpose the soap genre with a light-hearted, ironic spin, capitalizing on the extremes of the genre. The chan-

Premiering in January 2000, SoapNet rebroadcasts
daily episodes of currently running network daytime
soap operas, as well as recycling several canceled
daytime and prime-time soaps, such as *Dallas*.
Courtesy of SoapNet/Buena Vista Entertainment.

nel delights in playing up the genre's melodramatic excesses with holi-
day theme specials such as a Labor Day "Who's Your Daddy?" marathon, highlighting classic paternity plots with scenes of labor and delivery,
and a Halloween "Back from the Dead" marathon. With its tagline "The
new way to watch soaps," SoapNet targets working women and college
students as more sophisticated audiences with good senses of humor,
rather than the outdated idea of the domestic female daytime viewer.
Along with soap-centered talk shows and news specials, SoapNet re-
addresses loyal soap fans with a modern sensibility while capitalizing on
this relatively untouched commodity of soap opera reruns.

While broadcasting soap reruns is a relatively new phenomenon, for quite some time soap fans have enjoyed their own type of rerun through personal collections. Using their VCRs, many fans have compiled extensive archives of their favorite shows and story lines and trade or sell them to other fans online. When examining how the broadcast rerun will affect the terms in which soap operas are studied, we must also take into account these personal collections as used by fans to enjoy repeated viewing of particular soap moments. Recognizing the differences between repeated viewing of soaps through reruns and through personal collections will hopefully offer new insights into the particular pleasures of watching serial narratives.

Watching reruns—soap reruns in this case—constructs a very different mode of viewership than ordinary television watching. John Weispfenning's work on the cultural functions of reruns cites a uses and gratifications survey in which respondents report their motivations behind watching reruns: "They wanted to remember parts they had missed before or forgotten, they wanted to look for different things, and . . . they wanted to be reminded of the ending."[11] These descriptions may fit many of the reasons fans might want to watch their favorite soaps again. In "wanting to remember parts missed or forgotten," soap fans can attempt to fill in gaps of their own knowledge of soap histories by watching reruns. Knowledge of complex narrative histories of specific soaps functions as a marker of cultural capital within fan communities. Newer fans can revisit past story lines of a current character to gain greater understanding of motivations behind current plots and character actions, thus finding increased pleasure in both viewings. Older fans who viewed the reruns in the original broadcast are reminded of particular scenes and stories they previously enjoyed. In "wanting to look for different things" in reruns, fans may find that their attention has shifted to emphases on different characters or even different soaps. Watching soaps in reruns allows fans the opportunity to revisit story lines that they may not have paid much attention to during their original run, as determined by their current viewing habits and preferences.

Finally, "watching reruns to be reminded of the ending" presents an interesting issue when it comes to watching soap opera reruns. As discussed in previous work on soap operas, lack of closure is an important structural component of the soap opera form and of serial narratives in general. The narrative conflicts of the soap opera world never "end" in any permanent way. All romances are subject to upheaval, families are continually broken and reunited, and even death is a conditional state of being. Yet story lines and characters do come to at least conditional endings, mostly in ceremonial rituals like weddings, births, deaths, and so forth. These endings often function as the emotional apex of a story line and serve as a payoff for fans' patience through months and years of continual delay. In this way, fans can watch soap reruns to be reminded of one of these particular conditional endings in which they invested so much time during the original run. In fact, these types of episodes are some of the ones most collected by fans and highlighted by "official" soap opera archives and histories. The experience of revisiting these particularly emotional events can stand in for years of faithful viewing. While the availability of reruns will not likely alter the daily viewing of new episodes by current fans, being able to revisit one's own particular favorite moment allows the fan access to past emotional ties that were closed off when story lines ended in the first-run broadcast.

The idea of the historical specificity of particular soaps or soap opera narratives involves the text's historical context, the context of its original broadcast, and fan attachment to specific moments in a soap's narrative history. As with all reruns, broadcasting of soaps in rerun replaces the original historical contexts in which the programs were first aired, and therefore may produce a wildly different experience from the experiences of the original viewers. This process of rewatching or rereading particular television texts multiple times is common to most fan cultures. Many fans have their own videotape collections of their favorite series or episodes. These collections are another major form in which soap operas are rewatched by viewers. While both the broadcast rerun and the videotaped collection draw the soap opera text out of its "internal chronology" of the original broadcast, rewatching from a soap opera collection raises several new issues surrounding fans revisiting soap narratives.

In her book *On Longing: Narratives of the Miniature, the Gigantic, the Souvenir, the Collection,* Susan Stewart mentions some interesting points on the process of collecting that are relevant to the investigation of soap fans who save and rewatch tapes of specific soaps and story lines. Stewart describes the archetypal collection as "a world which is representative yet which erases its context or origin."[12] While doing so may seem at odds with the soap collector's pride in his or her personal knowledge of soap history, many collectors edit together specific story lines, removing the context of other stories occurring simultaneously within that particular show. This process of collecting and removing particular story lines from their original context allows the fan to tailor his or her own collection. Stewart sees this removal of the item from its original context as an important element of control in the collection process: "Once the object is completely severed from its origin, it is possible to generate a new series, to start again within a context that is framed by the selectivity of the collector."[13] This puts the emphasis on the collector's personal taste and immediate gratification rather than waiting through the constant delay and continual interruption offered by traditional broadcast soap viewing.

The recontextualizing of story lines into their own separate narratives also allows fans to subvert the continual lack of closure by seeing story lines through to their "conditional ending" or emotional peak in rewatching these condensed versions. Collectors replace production with consumption. Then, as they continue to consume objects, they eventually become the "producers" of a collection mirroring the self: "The self generates a fantasy in which it becomes producer of those objects, a producer by arrangement and manipulation."[14] This production of identity through the process of collecting signals the importance of personal taste and attachment to specific narratives within soaps. Soap fan collectors save and reedit individual soaps and stories. While some fans may have large daily archives of a particular soap, they still exercise a selection process in choosing one show over another. It should be remembered that before the relatively recent broadcast reruns of soaps, collectors were saving these texts from the abyss of nonsyndicated television history. James Clifford maintains that "collecting . . . implies a rescue of [a] phenomenon from inevitable historical decay or loss. The collection contains what 'deserves' to be kept, remembered, and treasured."[15] The choice of tapes from a particular soap or story line suggests a fan's personal emotional investment or taste preferences, thus reflecting his or her own sense of self.

This reflection of the self can also be seen in examining the phenomenon of watching "reruns-as-reruns," indicating that the viewer has previously seen the rerun in its original or another context. In her article "The Dislocation of Time: A Phenomenology of Television Reruns," Jenny Nelson asserts that this experience of watching reruns "contributes to the 'I' recognizing its own responsibility in creating such an interest. The person turns a critical eye on the past-seeing self."[16] The soap opera viewer may be able to engage in a nostalgic look at the self through rewatching soaps that held personal significance at some particular point in time. Nelson claims our fascination with the rerun lies in its connection to our personal history: "Where was I then? What was I like then? How was I situated and informed? These are the once-lived experiences that return to us through our own narration of a rerun."[17] While the collection may indicate a process of self-creation, the experience of rewatching the reruns that make up the collection may be a way in which the viewer reflects upon his or her own experience with those particular soap moments.

Watching any programming in rerun form is a distinctly different experience from first-time viewing, but especially so when it comes to the serial nature of soap operas. The syndication of soap operas offers a completely changed viewing context for new and old audiences. Moreover, it provides a newfound source of profits for producers and an alternative avenue for scholars to examine how fans interact with particular soap histories and how soap narratives live on in fan cultures.

Passions and the Supernatural Soap

One of the most important tactics for the survival of the soap opera genre is the ability to attract new, younger, and therefore more desirable audiences. Taking a cue from successful WB and Fox fantasy-based and science fiction–based dramas, the afternoon soaps have also attempted to capitalize on such elements with the introduction of a modern supernatural story line on the show *Passions*. Soaps have long been the home of the most far-fetched narratives, but *Passions* pushes the limits of even soap definitions of "realism," and "good taste" according to afternoon standards. Premiering on NBC in 1999, *Passions* took a calculated risk in trying to attract younger viewers by merging the typical soap opera format with a supernatural/fantasy twist. From its inception, the program's small New England town of Harmony included a three-hundred-year-old witch, Tabitha Lenox, who was burned at the stake by the town's colonial ancestors. Along with her sidekick, Timmy, a small doll she brought to life, Tabitha masqueraded as the town eccentric while trying to wreak havoc on the townspeople's emotional and spiritual lives. In *Passions,* the evolving soap opera format has taken a self-conscious turn, finally reveling in its own status as the lowest of the low in terms of television genres. This new format uses parody and camp to create a critical distance from the traditional soap opera format, assuring young audiences that this is definitely not their mothers' soap opera.

Not since *Dark Shadows'* (1966–71) run had daytime soaps attempted to captivate young viewers by mixing the soap opera genre with fantasy and gothic horror. Declining daytime viewership in the 1990s led soap producers to reconsider the supernatural as a possible lifeboat for sinking ratings. The return of the supernatural in soaps first occurred in 1994, when writer James Reilly devised a plan to save the daytime staple *Days of Our Lives* (1965–) from its ailing ratings position by introducing a supernatural story line, complete with a full-fledged satanic possession and low-budget special effects like glowing eyes and levitations. "The Desecrator," as the narrative is referred to on fan Web sites, follows the demonic possession of one of the show's primary female heroines, Dr. Marlena Evans, played by Deidre Hall. The story line was blasted by the mainstream press as "ludicrous even by soap opera standards";[18] one critic asserted the show had "ceased to be a soap opera and has become a live action cartoon instead."[19] Critics ridiculed the special effects as "unintentionally laughable" and critiqued the show's rampant misuse of Catholic doctrine.[20]

The borderline comedic nature of the special effects may at first seem prohibitively naive. The over-the-top use of bright yellow contact lenses and a gravelly voice of Satan dubbed over Hall's performances suggested, however, that the producers were well aware that these choices fell outside more "serious" depictions of the supernatural in film and television science fiction, falling into the realm of camp. So while there was a critical backlash against the supernatural story line of *Days of Our Lives,* large ratings increases and audience awards indicated that this unusual narrative was definitely piquing some viewers' interests.

Trying to find a solution for falling ratings of its other daytime soaps in 1999, NBC gave successful *Days of Our Lives* writer James E. Reilly a new soap with the intention of drawing a significantly younger audience. The all-important demographic for daytime soap operas is women from the ages of eighteen to forty-nine, a group that is seen as having the most purchasing power for the products of daytime sponsors. NBC's other soaps, *Another World* and *Sunset Beach* (1997–99), were coming in last with this core demographic, while the more outrageous story lines of *Days of Our Lives* usually earned that show a number one rating with eighteen- to thirty-five-year-olds.[21] Ratings for soap operas were at an all-time high in the 1970s and 1980s, but by the 1990s they had seen an extreme drop-off in target demographics, down 27 percent from 1994 to 2000.[22] Networks considered it essential to find new viewers among teens, the ideal age at which to create long-term fans.[23]

Reilly's outlandish story lines on *Passions* also attempted to tap into the growing popularity with youth audiences of other prime-time supernatural dramas, such as *Buffy the Vampire Slayer* (1997–2003) and

The X-Files (1993–2002). In its push to attract younger audiences, the show also undertook a series of cross-marketing schemes, including cosmetics featured on the show, sponsored by an online company complete with its own Web site,[24] along with a line of jewelry and clothing "inspired" by the show's characters.[25] While the use of cross-marketing strategies is slowly emerging in all the daytime soaps, with soap fan events at theme parks and the SoapNet cable channel, *Passions* seems particularly attuned to the need for ever-increasing visibility to attract younger female viewers.

Passions reflects a changing viewership with a radically different perspective from older audiences. *Passions* revises the conventions of a genre that was based largely on the importance of domestic life, family, and the housewife, allowing younger viewers to both critique and indulge in the guilty pleasures of these fantasies of romance and family. By adding a supernatural element, the show regularly presents a fanciful picture, with characters devoting their energy to personal and emotional issues. *Passions'* parodic use of fantasy implies that soap operas' absurd romances and adventures are just as unrealistic to the younger female viewer as the idea of witches and angels living next door. *Passions* asserts a preferred mass camp reading of the soap with an expectation that viewers are familiar with the conventions; it then utilizes supernatural story lines as a way of poking fun at the traditional disaster and disorder that typically occur in the more "realistic" world of the traditional soap. *Passions'* camp sensibility can serve as an intentional rebuttal to the outdated image of the traditional daytime audience, appealing especially to a younger viewership.

James Reilly's use of fantasy and parody proved successful once again in 2003, when he was brought back as the head writer on *Days of Our Lives* to save the show from falling ratings and threatened cancellation. Reilly resuscitated the show for a second time with his "Salem Stalker" plotline in which the show's heroine, Dr. Marlena Evans, became a serial killer and gruesomely murdered ten of the series' longtime characters. In typical Reilly fashion, it turned out that all the characters were actually alive and being held captive on a desert island. While Reilly's authorial style flies in the face of traditional soap story lines, his touch has proved successful at boosting ratings and attracting new viewers. The use of campy fantasy and horror may offend some older soap fans, but the ability to draw in younger viewers is critical for the survival of soaps themselves. In this willingness to spurn older women viewers, we can see the diminishing influence of the traditional sponsor. In the network era, the traditional nature of the soap opera was assured by sponsors, such as Procter and Gamble, that relied heavily on the soap opera to secure the hearts and minds of the elusive "household purchasing agent" (women aged eighteen to forty-nine). In the past, soap operas stood as a continual reminder of the long arm of the sponsor in proscribing the destiny of television genres and limiting the possibilities for generic change. That era of sponsor control may finally be coming to an end, freeing up producers to reinvent soap operas and regain cultural relevance. Turning the daytime diva into the daytime demon may soon become as much of a staple of soap opera narratives as amnesia or returning from a presumed death once was.

Hip and Humorous: *The O.C.*

Prime-time soap operas have differed from their daytime counterparts in their higher budgets and production values, their greater focus on male characters (from Rodney Harrington of *Peyton Place* [1964–69] to Blake Carrington of *Dynasty*), their injection of local color (Texas ranches on *Dallas,* scenes of Malibu on *Knots Landing*), and their more compressed story arcs. Teen prime-time soap operas such as *Melrose Place* and *Beverly Hills 90210* (1990–2000) enjoyed a strong run in the 1990s, after interest in shows such as *Dallas* and *Dynasty* waned. The latest incarnation of the prime-time soap opera is *The O.C.,* which premiered during the summer of 2003, when it was introduced as a limited episode series on Fox. *The O.C.,* which prospered once it gained a regular slot in the fall season, suggests new strategies for marketing soap operas to a younger audience, such as establishing an ironic distance from some of the trashier elements of daytime soaps. It achieves this not by aspiring to the status of a quality program (although the regular presence of film actors, location shooting, and controversial sexual content are reminiscent of contemporary elements of quality television) but by profiling the show's executive producer as a young, hip "auteur" and placing the two young male protagonists, Seth Cohen (Adam Brody) and Ryan Atwood (Benjamin McKenzie), at the center of the story, flush with their brooding masculinity and youthful escapades.

Josh Schwartz, the creator of *The O.C.,* was twenty-seven years old at the time of the program's premiere. He had left the University of Southern California film school before graduation when he was awarded a studio contract. His artistic integrity is emphasized in publicity materials for the series. Positioning Josh Schwartz as an auteur, *The O.C.* raises

Product placement and fashion magazine publicity are integral parts of *The O.C.* The young female lead, Mischa Barton, who plays Marissa Cooper, is regularly featured in this kind of publication modeling clothes and being interviewed about her favorite designers. Courtesy of Warner Brothers Television.

itself above the creative anonymity that pervades most soap opera production, emphasizing his background in film as well as television, his obsessive attention to every detail of the production, and his infusion of autobiographical material into the story line. Rather than a cliffhanger, the final episode of the 2004 season saw the two male heroes heading out of town, much along the lines of a road movie rather than a soap opera.

Outdoors locations instead of studio sets, male characters given prominence over female characters, irony over melodrama—these are elements that help *The O.C.* gain a degree of separation from its generic forebears. Schwartz carefully emphasizes the importance of comedy and deliberately references soap opera conventions in a sarcastic way. At a press conference hinting about what would happen in the fall season, he joked about the soap opera's reputation for killing off and reviving characters who prove popular with fans. Rather than treat the grandmother's cancer with the gravity normally reserved for middle-aged female characters—especially ailing ones—Schwartz quipped, "The nana really popped for people, and therefore I think it's safe to say the chemo's working."[26]

Publicity emphasizes Josh Schwartz's use of personal contacts to entice hip guest stars from the non–soap opera world to appear on the show. Paris Hilton, the star of her own reality show and a constant presence on celebrity gossip programs, did a cameo performance on *The O.C.* The young female lead, Mischa Barton, who plays the love interest for Ryan, is featured in fashion magazines and interviewed about her favorite designers. Chris Carmack, who plays Luke—Marissa's former boyfriend, and later her mother's lover—is a well-known Abercrombie and Fitch model. In general, product placement and fashion magazine publicity are integral parts of *The O.C.* scheme. Schwartz's hip, humorous approach is emphasized: all elements are relatively foreign to the classic version of the genre and its publicity arms such as *Soap Opera Digest*. As the *Los Angeles Times* television critic praised the program, "'The O.C.' is distinguished by its relentless determination to balance soap-opera trash with pop-culture smarts."[27]

From the perspective of generic convention, *The O.C.* deviates little from the classic formulas of soap opera. One family stands at the center of the story: an attractive professional couple (the woman is a real estate developer, the man an attorney) who live an enviable life of glamour and affluence in Newport Beach. Conflicts stem from their different backgrounds (East Coast vs. West Coast, Jewish vs. Protestant, liberal vs. conservative). Their romantic and sexy relationship is based on the cherished soap opera theory that opposites attract. The wife's father, stepmothers, best friends, tennis club pals, and former high school friends form the background for the middle-aged couple's conflicts. The couple have one teenage son, Seth, and take into their home a second "adopted" son—a troubled young man from the wrong side of the tracks (in this case, the city of Chino, California) whose past incessantly intrudes on the serene life of Newport.

These two young men figure prominently in the show. Schwartz likes to emphasize that his own life resembles that of the somewhat offbeat but highly popular character Seth Cohen (Adam Brody), and that he has infused many of his own fantasies into this character's sex life. Through the prominence of these two male characters, *The O.C.* disguises itself as a non-soap through frequent brushes with the police, near-constant fistfights, teenage sex, pregnancy, weapons, and gangs. (Referring to the second season, Schwartz commented: "We are going to slow down the storytelling. There won't necessarily have to be a brawl at every black-tie affair.")[28] Masculinity, violence, and troubled youth retain the focus of attention, even while the show displays the classic soap opera reliance on coincidence, love triangles, and the keeping of secrets. *The O.C.* has met with great success among male college students, who reportedly watch the show together in large groups of mostly men in dorms and fraternities.

Daytime soap operas typically take place in New England small towns, and even in these fictional locations the lack of racial and ethnic diversity often pushes the boundaries of plausibility. In *The O.C.*, the proximity of the U.S.–Mexican border is referred to only in the context of a place teens go for a wild weekend—visiting a sort of downmarket Las Vegas. The cliffhanger of the first summer season involved Marissa, drugged and drunk, lost and alone in a sinister Tijuana bar. Similarly, the demographic realities of Orange County itself are completely absent. (The nickname "O.C." is unknown to actual residents of the area.) The real Orange County features one of the highest percentages of immigrants, Vietnamese, Cambodians, and Latinos, and families living in poverty in the United States. Likewise, Anglo-Americans make up barely 50 percent of the population.[29] Schwartz's O.C. is all white, with the exception of one returning Latina character, Theresa, who signifies troubled elements from Ryan's past and is the sole repository of the other characters' liberal impulses and concerns for social justice. Thus, social problems (teen pregnancy, poverty, and domestic violence) are heaped on the show's single minority character in an overwhelmingly white and segregated world.

Theresa's narrative arc is worth investigating in some detail because it also marks a change from the soap opera's traditional embrace of women's issues. When Theresa arrives in Newport Beach, she is fleeing her Latino boyfriend, Eddie, who is portrayed as a sheer villain. He is a macho counterpart to Ryan's violence-prone but sensitive male character. While Marissa and Ryan are broken up, Ryan sleeps with Theresa. After Ryan reunites with Marissa, he learns that Theresa is being physically abused by Eddie. At this point, Sandy—Seth's father—provides legal advice to Theresa and contemplates driving out to Chino and trying to scare Eddie into leaving Theresa alone. When Ryan discovers the news, he starts off to beat up Eddie and is restrained only by Sandy's reminder that if he does so he will break probation and end up in juvenile hall again, which is where he was during the program's premiere episode. As a solution, they move Theresa into the Cohen pool house, where she can feel safe and live for free. With this issue still unresolved, Marissa learns that Theresa is pregnant, and the news soon spreads to Ryan, Seth, and his parents, Kirsten and Sandy.

Theresa's pregnancy functions primarily as a cliffhanger—featuring the question of which young man is the father, Eddie or Ryan? Ryan takes this opportunity to do the honorable and right thing by marrying Theresa, thus displaying his superior moral fiber and willingness to sacrifice his entire life in Newport to be a man. When Theresa decides to have an abortion, Kirsten reveals in a private conversation that she herself had an abortion as a teenager and always regretted it. Kirsten persuades Theresa to ignore the chasm of difference in wealth and opportunity between the two women, bypass "what makes sense," and have the baby. Thus, the cliffhanger at the season's ending has Ryan leaving town to return to Chino, work at a blue-collar job, drive a beat-up old car, and leave his fashion model girlfriend behind for Theresa. All the other characters are grief-stricken at the prospect of losing Ryan. The core Newport Beach community—all Anglo and all affluent—share the sense that Ryan's consignment to life in Chino is a tragedy.

While Theresa's story line lasted for only four episodes at the end of the first full season, these episodes suggest how carefully *The O.C.* centers on the feelings of its young male protagonists. Theresa's character enjoys little development and virtually no introspection—she is the pure melodramatic victim of circumstance. The fans' hearts and minds are with the core characters: the Cohens, Marissa, and Ryan. Theresa is little more than an obstacle to their happiness and a fleeting opportunity to evidence their heartfelt liberal sympathies. Moreover, Theresa's problems are never fully developed, which runs counter to the traditional soap opera's concern for social issues related to women. In fact, the episodes that included Theresa's story arcs are distinguished by a great deal of screwball comedy and sexual innuendo, involving a Vegas bachelor party with prostitutes and gambling, and a bachelorette party complete with male strippers and a drunken (female) brawl.[30] Overall, the abuse of Theresa functions exclusively to establish Eddie's villainy and provide a space for the male characters to consider an alternative course of action to violence.

As a new variation on the genre, *The O.C.* has little appeal to women viewers because there is so little critique of male behavior. Roles for female characters are similarly limited to their function as love interests for the young male leads. Josh Schwartz has revitalized the genre through his injection of screwball comedy and a witty, self-reflexive hero. Production budgets are high, and settings and themes lively and topical, but he has created a show more akin to the prerogatives of prime-time drama than afternoon soap operas.

In the end, the case studies of *Passions* and *The O.C.* illustrate how soap opera producers are struggling to reinvent the genre. *Passions* represents the move to inject the soap opera with a camp sensibility and mix it with horror and fantasy; *The O.C.* represents a strategy of distancing itself from the label of "soap" by adding an authorial stamp and centering the narrative on how its young male leads negotiate the demands of masculinity, instead of focusing on its female characters. These examples, along with the possibilities presented by a channel like Soap-Net, provide a glimpse into some of the radically different ways in which the soap opera is transforming. It remains to be seen how thoroughly these survival tactics will revitalize the genre, but early indications suggest that the soap opera has already achieved a certain degree of success in adapting to the tastes and demands of a younger, hip, and more urban audience.

Notes

1. Jane Feuer, "MTM Style," in *MTM: "Quality Television,"* ed. Jan Feuer, Paul Kerr, and Tise Vahimagi (London: BFI Publishing, 1984), 33.

2. John Caldwell, "Excessive Style: The Crisis of Network Television," in *Television: The Critical View,* ed. Horace Newcomb (New York: Oxford University Press, 2000), 659–62.

3. Ellen Seiter, "To Teach and to Sell: Irna Phillips and Her Sponsors, 1930–1955," *Journal of Film and Video* 40, no. 1 (1989): 2–15.

4. Ellen Seiter, "The Hegemony of Leisure: Aaron Spelling presents 'Hotel,'" in *Television and Its Audience: International Research Perspectives,* ed. Phillip Drummond (London: British Film Institute, 1986), 156–75.

5. Feuer, "MTM Style," 56.

6. Ibid.

7. Sue Brower, "Fans as Tastemakers: Viewers for Quality Television," in *The Adoring Audience: Fan Culture and Popular Media,* ed. Lisa A. Lewis (London: Routledge, 1992), 163–84.

8. Charlotte Brunsdon, "Problems with Quality," in *Screen Tastes: Soap Opera to Satellite Dishes* (London: Routledge, 1997).

9. Ibid., 134.

10. Lynn Spigel, "From the Dark Ages to the Golden Age: Women's Memories and Television Reruns," in *Welcome to the Dreamhouse: Popular Media and Postwar Suburbs* (Durham, N.C.: Duke University Press, 2001), 374.

11. Furno-Lamude and Anderson quoted in John Weispfenning, "Cultural Functions of Reruns: Time, Memory, and Television," *Journal of Communication* 53 (March 2003): 167.

12. Susan Stewart, *On Longing: Narratives of the Miniature, the Gigantic, the Souvenir, the Collection* (Baltimore: Johns Hopkins University Press, 1984), 152.

13. Ibid.

14. Ibid., 158.

15. James Clifford, *The Predicament of Culture: Twentieth-Century Ethnography, Literature and Art* (Cambridge, Mass.: Harvard University Press, 1988), 231.

16. Jenny Nelson, "The Dislocation of Time: A Phenomenology of Television Reruns," *Quarterly Review of Film and Video* 12, no. 3 (1990): 89.

17. Ibid., 90.

18. David Bianculli, "On 'Days,' Hall's Been to Hell—And Back?" *New York Daily News,* July 3, 1995, 58.

19. Nancy M. Reichardt, "'Days of Our Lives' Answers the Call,'" *Los Angeles Times,* February 5, 1995, TV Times 11.

20. Ibid.

21. Chuck Ross, "NBC Weighs Replacing Two Low Rated Soaps," *Advertising Age,* March 22, 1999, 3.

22. Lisa Leigh Parney and M. S. Mason, "Selling Soaps," *Christian Science Monitor,* July 7, 2000, Arts 13.

23. Ibid.

24. "Synergy Brands' BeautyBuys.com Will Sponsor NBC's Web Site for Its New Passions TV Soap," *Business Wire,* June 14, 1999.

25. Joe Flint, "NBC Internet to Sell Jewelry Inspired by Soap Opera," *Wall Street Journal,* December 8, 1999, B6.

26. Tom Jicha, "O.C. Faces Heavy Surf on Return," *Florida Sun-Sentinel,* July 22, 2004, E1.

27. John Horn, "He's 'O.C.'s' Fresh Breeze," *Los Angeles Times,* March 21, 2004, E30.

28. Jicha, "O.C. Faces Heavy Surf on Return," E1.

29. Peter Y. Hong, "The U.S. Census Data Reflects Southland's Highs, Lows," *Los Angeles Times,* June 5, 2002, B1.

30. We are referring here to episode 25 "The Shower," airdate April 21, 2004; episode 26 "The Strip," airdate April 28, 2004; and episode 27 "The Ties That Bind."

7 beyond genre

cable's impact on the talk show

Jeffrey P. Jones

Talk is, and always has been, central to television.[1] The talk show, a standardized yet malleable and recombinant format featured in every daypart of television programming, continues to reign as one of the most consistently popular programming genres on television. Indeed, the talk show's presence on television has only increased over the last decade due to the explosive growth of both syndicated and cable programming. Broadcast stations have gobbled up a variety of syndicated talk shows featuring the spectacle performance of personal, intimate relationships, a practice that has led to the displacement of soap operas as the dominant genre in afternoon programming. There has been no shortage of scholarly attention to this shift in industrial, textual, and audience practices related to afternoon talk shows.[2] What has been underanalyzed, however, is the concurrent role of cable television in reshaping and reconstituting the talk show genre. Although the 1990s witnessed the rapid expansion of cable networks—and, in turn, these programming entities' search for inexpensive original content that could provide brand distinctiveness (see Edgerton and Nicholas's chapter in this volume)—there has been relatively little critical examination of how the talk show has been part of that expansion and, in turn, how the talk show genre has changed as a result.

This chapter seeks to address that oversight, though not by surveying the array of talk formats that have appeared across the great diversity of new cable networks over the last decade. Instead, the emphasis here is on two landmark cable programs and a cable network, all developed in the early to mid-1990s, and all of which have had a significant impact on the talk genre in various ways. Their significance is not that they have simply introduced new talk programming formulas that have been replicated across the television landscape, but that in the process, each has also blurred and transformed preexisting generic boundaries. These influential programs and their respective networks include *Politically Incorrect* on Comedy Central (1993–96), the Fox News cable network, and *The Real World* (1992–) on MTV. It is important to note at the outset that this discussion does not treat *The Real World* as a talk show per se, for it fits more properly within the genre of reality programming (as examined by Ron Simon in this volume). Nevertheless, *The Real World* is examined here because it exemplifies the role of contemporary reality programming in blurring boundaries between the reality and talk genres and, in the process, actively challenges the conception of the talk show as a stable or even distinct genre.

The blurred generic boundaries produced by each of these programs are seen most clearly when employing the categories crafted by Robert Erler and Bernard Timberg in their taxonomy of talk on television: "entertainment talk" (such as *The Tonight Show* [1954–] and *The Jerry Springer Show* [1991–]), "news talk" (such as *Meet the Press* [1947–] and *Washington Week in Review* [1967–]), and "socially situated talk" (such as *Judge Judy* [1996–] and *Survivor* [2000–]).[3] Although considered by the industry and critics alike as an entertainment talk show, *Politically Incorrect* was instrumental in the blurring of boundaries between entertainment and news talk programming. It led the way for subsequent shows such as *Dennis Miller Live* (HBO, 1994–2002) and *The Daily Show* (Comedy Central, 1996–) to mix and blend the traditionally distinct talk show assemblage of celebrity talk, on the one hand, and serious-minded political talk by experts, on the other. In the process, *Politically Incorrect* challenged the status (if not the validity) of programs in both existing categories.

Similarly, Fox News has blurred the boundaries between news/information and advocacy/opinion. In the early 1980s, CNN altered the television landscape by offering extended news coverage around the clock, though sprinkled with intermittent public affairs talk programming to fill out the twenty-four-hour broadcast cycle. By the late 1990s, however, CNN's competitor, Fox News, had transformed television news as a genre entirely, elevating talk shows to the status of news and substituting interpretation for information, opinions for reporting. As the rat-

ings leader in cable news, Fox's stunning success with its overtly ideological programming has led all cable "news" outlets, including CNN,
MSNBC, and CNBC, to respond to the competition by moving away
from reporting (especially in prime-time hours) and, instead, featuring
more talk show programming than news broadcasts.[4]

Finally, MTV's success with the documentary-style, unscripted soap
opera *The Real World* laid the groundwork for much of the reality programming that has dominated entertainment television of late. These
shows blur the boundaries between public and private life, offering a
reconstitution of how lives will be played out on the public stage. Though
they borrow freely from other genres (such as the documentary, the
game show, the demonstration show, and the dating show), the primary
activity in many forms of reality programming is talk (whether through
dramatic conflicts, interviews, or confessionals). This can be seen, for
instance, in the discussions of aesthetic design on *Trading Spaces* (2000–),
the bickering between shop workers on *American Chopper* (2003–), or
the banal ruminations of the airheaded superstar Jessica Simpson on
Newlyweds: Nick & Jessica (2003–).

Although some readers may resist the connection between reality programming and the talk genre, much of the literature on both talk and
reality programming considers these as part of the same televisual phenomena.[5] Indeed, Erler and Timberg's category of "socially situated
talk" provides just such a designation for housing the disparate forms of
talk produced in reality programming.[6] And, as will be discussed later,
the popularity of reality talk is part and parcel of the larger cultural interest in "reality" entertainment that, as John Corner puts it, offers "more
relaxed, franker, and revelatory kinds of speech."[7]

The chapter begins by considering the industrial and cultural-political
environment from which these landmark cable programs and cable networks emerged in the 1990s, including how and why these factors helped
alter talk programming as a genre and continue to influence this programming today. I then move to a discussion of the ways in which reality programs such as *The Real World* recast intimate talk on television in
ways that resemble the talk show, yet compose a new form of serialized
talk. The chapter concludes by examining whether cable programming
has hence brought us to a place where the myriad forms of talk on television challenge the notion of "talk show as genre" *entirely*. I argue that
television talk is now beyond genre because contemporary cable programming actively works against any stable notion of what constitutes
talk as a distinctive category.[8]

Cable Talk Programming in the 1990s

The single most important issue facing the television industry in the 1990s was increased competition between the broadcast oligopoly and cable programmers. Cable television had already presented alternatives for viewers throughout the 1980s, but as more and more neighborhoods were wired for cable and the bandwidth capacity of cable operators increased, the cable programming side of the industry was poised for a rapid expansion of new networks and programming options. As one broadcasting executive argued in 1993, "It's not business as usual anymore. We've got to find ways to re-create this business so that it will survive into the next decade."[9] The competition to draw audiences away from their entrenched viewing habits with broadcast programming was exacerbated for cable programmers by a simultaneous battle between newer and more established cable programmers. New cable channels were desperate to create programming that would give them an identity with viewers and, in turn, increased cable system carriage. Established cable networks, on the other hand, were beginning to see their audience share shrink as a result of viewers having more choices from which to select. They also realized that their own product (for instance, music, sports, and news) was beginning to lose its novelty as a stand-alone programming format. This was exactly the situation faced by Comedy Central, a new cable network established in 1991, and MTV, created in 1981 but facing a declining audience share by the early 1990s.

Comedy Central was born of the merger between Time Warner's Comedy Channel and Viacom's HA! TV Comedy Network and immediately began to search for a formula that would make the network more than simply a location for stand-up comedy routines and sitcom reruns.[10] The network, therefore, needed programming that was distinctive and original, something that would define the channel in viewers' eyes. Original programming, such as sitcoms or dramedies, can be expensive to produce, while talk programming is famously not. The network, then, began a "quest to be more topical," as network executives put it, by mining news and other political events for their comic potential through various talking head or running commentary gags. After exploiting George H. W. Bush's State of the Union address and the political party conventions in 1992, the network adopted the slogan "Same World, Different Take" as a means of branding itself as a smart and savvy political animal—that is, a place to watch comedy with a purpose. It was with this thinking that the network purchased a new talk show called *Politi-*

cally Incorrect from Brillstein-Grey Entertainment and HBO Downtown Productions (a program that was the brainchild of stand-up comedian Bill Maher). This hybrid political-entertainment talk show, featuring Maher and four other "public persons" (television and movie actors, comedians, musicians, athletes, journalists, novelists, politicians, and lobbyists) in a roundtable format discussing politics, was an inexpensive acquisition that went on to become the network's flagship program before departing to network television (ABC) in early 1997. Comedy Central recognized the significance of this impending loss and thus created *The Daily Show* in 1996, another inexpensive political-entertainment talk show, as *Politically Incorrect*'s replacement (and new standard-bearer for the network).

If inexpensive talk-centered programming was popular enough to become the top-rated show on a comedy network, why not create a talk network itself composed of nothing more than such programming? This was the intent of several media corporations in the mid-1990s, including NBC (America's Talking), Multimedia/Gannett (The Talk Channel), and the Free Congress Foundation (National Empowerment Television). All these networks eventually failed, but NBC's efforts with America's Talking are worthy of consideration in light of what resulted. America's Talking was born on July 4, 1994, and was dedicated to all-talk programming (an effort to expand the limited talk television concept NBC was featuring on CNBC during prime-time hours). With talk radio's enormous popularity in mind, the network hired Roger Ailes, former Republican Party strategist and the executive producer of Rush Limbaugh's syndicated television program, to head both America's Talking and CNBC. As a result, Ailes brought the strategies he developed with Limbaugh to the new network, offering initial program lineups and an overall channel concept that mirrored the success Limbaugh was having with his "common man" persona and rage-against-the-system populism on talk radio.

As the Republican-based populist upsurge of the 1994 midterm congressional elections gave way to the reelection of Democratic president Bill Clinton in 1996, the belief that a television channel based solely on the all-talk format could be successful had proved unfounded. The network recognized this and received a transfusion of cash by joining forces with Microsoft to create the all-news channel MSNBC in 1996, which was designed to compete with CNN and the also newly founded Fox News. With this change, Roger Ailes departed America's Talking to become CEO at Fox News. Whereas Ailes previously failed to capitalize on his efforts to feature conservative and bombastic talk programming with both *Rush Limbaugh* (1992) and America's Talking, this formula finally proved successful by cloaking it under the mantle of news reporting and journalistic "objectivity" (branding his new network "Fair & Balanced," in contradistinction to his supposedly liberal competitor, CNN). The irony, of course, is that the network jumped to the lead of the cable *news* ratings pack by producing more *talk* programming than news reporting, yet using the label of "news" as a more acceptable paradigmatic framework. As ABC News president David Weston explains it, there are "powerful reasons for the embrace we're seeing of opinion journalism on TV. It's vivid. It's entertaining. And let's face it: It's less expensive."[11]

Beyond the search for inexpensive programming that the talk genre so easily provided, Weston's observation here leads to the second but related contextual feature of cable television programming in the mid-1990s—that is, style. John Thornton Caldwell argues that the competition between broadcast and cable networks also led to an intensive program of innovation and stylistic development. The new look, what he calls "televisuality," is an aesthetic tendency toward excessive style. "Television moved from a framework that approached broadcasting primarily as a form of word-based rhetoric and transmission," he argues, "to a visually based mythology, framework, and aesthetic based on extreme self-consciousness of style."[12] Style became the subject, the defining practice of television as a means of attaining a distinctive look in the battle for audience share. Excessive style, though, is more than simply a visual phenomenon. It becomes a means of developing a "look" by individualizing programs in viewers' minds via their distinctive appeal.

A driving force behind the need for this new exhibitionism was the changing relationship between audiences and the televisual product. "The individuation and semiotic heterogeneity evident in televisual excess," Caldwell argues, "means that such shows are from the start defined by, and pitched at, niche audiences who are flattered by claims of difference and distinction."[13] These new rules affect both viewers and industry, and the texts that exist between them. Viewers are positioned as savvy and self-conscious televisual consumers by the industry, while the texts "demand a more conscious form of viewer negotiation."[14] For both *Politically Incorrect* and Fox News, the distinctive look, unique style, and particular relationship with audiences exemplify this televisual imperative toward distinction—offering viewers something fresh, innovative, and, in the eyes of viewers and producers alike, more *real* than their generic cousins.

Politically Incorrect offered a format that blurred the boundaries between various entertainment and public affairs talk formulas. (Center) Host Bill Maher. Courtesy of *Politically Incorrect with Bill Maher.*

Politically Incorrect began as an effort to reintroduce meaningful group talk to television.[15] The producers believed that entertainment television was dominated by sterile, publicity-driven and scripted encounters between host and guests.[16] Likewise, a seemingly scripted language of insider politics dominated political talk television, mainly offered by pundits whom the average viewer cared little about and had a hard time identifying with. Hence, *Politically Incorrect* offered a talk format that challenged established conventions in traditional public affairs, late-night, and daytime talk shows. It differed from the traditional political talk show by offering a comedian as host and "star" of the show, a comedic monologue of political jokes, and guests who were not "political experts" but nevertheless talked about politics. Moreover, these participants performed in front of a live audience (which pundits rarely do), while mixing serious discussions with humorous asides. The program altered the late-night talk show by featuring a host with a defined political persona, focusing the discussions on serious political issues in a conflictual but entertaining manner, and by booking guests who were not appearing on the show simply to promote their own latest projects. Finally, *Politically Incorrect* altered the daytime talk show formats by dealing with social issues in specifically political ways, by offering guests the opportunity to talk to each other without having to talk through the host or to invited "experts," and by reducing the role of the studio audience to that of observers.

This stylistic blurring of boundaries between entertainment and public affairs talk seems even starker in other political-entertainment shows that followed in the footsteps of *Politically Incorrect*. Both *Dennis Miller Live* (which ran for nine years on HBO) and *The Daily Show* (also having run for nine years on Comedy Central) offer direct political humor and commentary in the first part of the program but then turn directly to a celebrity interview that may have nothing to do with politics in any way. This format, along with the type of humor that Maher, Miller, and Stewart offer, requires a level of both political *and* cultural sophistication from its viewers that the standard entertainment talk and pundit news shows do not. Returning to John Thornton Caldwell's argument about televisuality in post-network television production, these newer talk show texts "demand a more conscious form of viewer negotiation" and work to craft personal relationships with niche audiences who are flattered as savvy televisual consumers. These shows (including newer manifestations such as *Real Time with Bill Maher* on HBO [2003–] and *Dennis Miller* on CNBC [2004–5]) offer a distinctive look and style where viewers aren't asked to segregate their interests in politics from their concurrent interests in entertainment/celebrity culture. Instead, these interests are integrated and offered as seamless realms—the way they are generally perceived and engaged in life outside of television today.

Caldwell's argument regarding excessive style could not be more prescient when we consider Fox News and how it has transformed cable news as a genre. At its worst, the network has almost single-handedly transformed news into commentary; at its best, it has led the way in elevating opinioned talk to the status of factual reporting in the twenty-four-hour cable news market. At Fox, style and substance are one and the same, or at least are mutually reinforcing. Fox solicits viewers with a barrage of flamboyant graphics and video game–style sound effects that mark its distinctiveness and pronounce its extreme self-consciousness of style. The screen is filled with the fluid movement of bombastic sounds and spectacular images that simultaneously announce the type of content that will follow. The network's major stars themselves have moved

Style and substance often merge at Fox News, as in the network's many flag-waving visual effects. Courtesy of the Fox News Network.

fluidly between tabloid television (Bill O'Reilly), talk radio (Sean Hannity), and network news (Brit Hume) and intone a rhetoric that rarely deviates from overt partisanship and flag-waving patriotism. Indeed, the viewer is invited to participate in the network's unapologetically right-wing perspective, proclaiming both the viewer and the network as united in their rejection of the mainstream (read: liberal) news media and society.

This fluid movement also occurs between the network's news reporting and its commentary, muddling for the viewer any distinction between what the network itself might consider a news report and a talk show. The methods and tactics of interviewing guests on programs such as *Fox and Friends* (1998–), *Special Report with Brit Hume* (1996–), and *The Fox Report with Shepard Smith* (1996–) are indistinguishable from those that occur on *Hannity & Colmes* (1996–) and *The O'Reilly Factor* (1996–). John Corner reminds us that there is a distinction between an *information interview* employed in news reporting (designed to draw on expertise or direct knowledge) and the *viewpoint interview*

The overt partisanship and right-wing histrionics of Bill O'Reilly have singled him out as Fox News's biggest star. (Left to right) O'Reilly and former House Speaker Newt Gingrich. Courtesy of the FOX News Network.

(designed to be conflictual in nature and displaying high levels of tension and theatrics) that is often employed in talk shows.[17] This distinction is largely obliterated in Fox's approach to television news talk, however. The information interview seemingly takes place when the interviewee agrees with the ideological position of the network hosts, whereas the viewpoint interview style quickly appears when the speaker veers off the "proper" talking points or away from a right-leaning epistemology.[18]

In short, the excessive style of Fox News actively challenges the preexisting boundaries between dispassionate reporting and hyperbolic talk and opinion to the point where a program like *The Daily Show with Jon Stewart* can successfully craft a nightly parody of that style because it has become so commonplace across cable news channels. Certainly Fox takes this genre-bending approach much further than its competitors at CNN and MSNBC, but there is a bit of truth in the critique of CNN by Stewart when he says the person who supposedly checks facts for the network "is just the one going, 'You know what I heard?' That's what they should call CNN—'You Know What I Heard?' I don't even know if they've got an acronym for that."[19] Perhaps the greatest challenge to the distinction between news talk and opinion is that Fox generally refuses to admit it is merging these once distinct formats.[20] CNN, however, has recently signaled that the network now recognizes the distinction and will return to its old ways of presenting viewers with "information not opinion." "CNN is a different animal," says CNN's president, Jonathan Klein (formerly of CBS News). "We report the news. Fox talks about the news."[21] Or at least that is the approach CNN says it will now follow after having been passed by Fox News in the ratings war between the two networks.

The third contextual factor associated with the rise of *Politically Incorrect* and Fox News is the audience's desire for less mediated, more reality-centered experiences with television talk. This interest in "the real" can be seen at numerous junctures in television and in other media during the early to mid-1990s. The 1992 presidential campaign included numerous appearances by the candidates on entertainment talk shows such as *Larry King Live* (1985–), *The Arsenio Hall Show* (1989–94), and *Donahue* (1970–96). The popular success of these appearances signaled a public questioning of the legitimacy of traditional forums of political information and talk on television. These entertainment talk shows, which incorporated interaction between audiences and the candidates, allowed people to circumvent elite gatekeepers by directly addressing the candidates with questions that were more pertinent to their interests. Whereas the calculated, rehearsed, and manipulative rhetoric of political performance and spin had become an uncomfortable reality of political life by the early 1990s, these new forums for political talk seemingly offered a more genuine and accessible look at the candidates.

Similarly, several scholars have noted how syndicated afternoon talk shows, or audience participation programs, offered important opportunities for audiences to question what constituted "authority" and "expertise" in televised talk about issues of public concern, including questioning who has the right to speak and be heard about such issues. These authors point to the ways in which ordinary people are allowed to speak for themselves, basing their arguments on lived experience, not theoretical expertise.[22] Thus, viewers enjoyed seeing people like themselves who offered narratives grounded in real-life experiences and common sense. This type of programming fits into what Jon Dovey calls "first person media . . . subjective, autobiographical and confessional modes of expression."[23] This includes talk shows and other programming forms such as docudramas, reflexive documentaries (such as *Sherman's March* [1986] and *Roger and Me* [1989]), and "camcorder cults" that drove tabloid shows such as *Hard Copy* (1989–99) and *A Current Affair* (1986–96). And, of course, the mid-1990s were awash in the buzz over the interactive potential of the Internet and new communication technologies. No longer would viewers be passive consumers of information handed down from media corporations on high. The media consumer was about to be transformed into the "prosumer" (or so the rhetoric would have it), with the ability to produce and distribute his or her own information, unrestricted by traditional media gatekeepers.

It was in this environment of unmediated audience empowerment and populist skepticism of elite authority that talk radio hosts such as Rush Limbaugh roared their disapproval of the "liberal media" and lionized themselves as purveyors of the commonsense "truth" that mainstream media would deny their listeners. As we have seen, Fox News chief Roger Ailes adopted a similar populist mantra when he headed the talk television channel America's Talking, noting that his network was "trying to represent real people."[24] This mantra carried over to Fox News, whereby the network flattered its viewers as being able to discern the truth within its overly conservative reporting by using the slogan "We report, you decide." Fox, it seems, would report the "reality" that the liberal media would not entertain.

It was also in this environment of desiring something more "real" or truthful that *Politically Incorrect* was born. The show's creator and host, Bill Maher, was tired of the fakery associated with scripted late-night talk shows and hence argued upon the show's founding, "Talk shows had become boring, publicity-driven promotional shows with one guest at a time. They were missing the two biggest areas of humor: the connection of guests and controversial subjects."[25] He wanted to produce a show in which guests would interact with each other, and that interaction would be based on things in life that actually matter. This desire to create a more real and spontaneous conversation about controversial issues is, indeed, according to one study, what audiences say they liked about the show—that Maher and guests produced a political conversation that was more real than that offered by traditional, pundit-centered political talk shows.[26]

In sum, then, these shows exemplify the ways in which both the television industry and audiences have embraced programming that breaks down categorical structure and, in many ways, redefines the rules of acceptable talk. *Politically Incorrect* demonstrated that public affairs could be discussed in entertaining and pleasurable ways. Fox News asserts that talk about public events should include more ideologically committed opinions. In short, *Politically Incorrect* and Fox News are prime examples of how certain paradigmatic formulations of the talk genre have become destabilized and, indeed, work against the generic designation for all of television talk.

Television Talk and the Challenge of Reality Programming

Concurrent with the appearance of *Politically Incorrect* and Fox News was MTV's reality program *The Real World*. Like its cable brethren, it was the product of an intensified environment of competition for viewers, and the need to compete by offering low-cost original programming. In the early 1990s, for instance, the network began to realize that despite being seen as a cultural icon, a place that defined youth culture, it was nevertheless suffering from poor ratings. "We had influential content, influential music, things were changing, but we had low, low ratings," says former MTV president Judy McGrath.[27] As a result, MTV introduced *The Real World* in 1992, a distinctive program that became the network's top-rated weekly show two years later. The program is largely centered on unscripted talk and, hence, is produced at a fraction of the cost of other forms of original programming.[28]

As with *Politically Incorrect* and Fox News, MTV turned toward stylistic development and new relationships with audiences, in this instance, by embracing their desire for a more "realistic" unmediated experience. With this cinema verité form of programming, MTV's audiences were given a break from the highly stylized music video content that dominated most of the network's programming fare in the late 1980s and early 1990s. This distinctive form of programming offered audiences what seemingly was the "real world"—chaotic, unplanned, and unrestricted by the typical rules of bounded network fare. And although it would take several years for such programming to become the blockbuster phenomenon that would transform both network and cable entertainment programming, *The Real World* established the prototype for a form of reality talk programming that accentuated its accessibility and immediacy, its seemingly unperformative reality, and the centrality of intimate talk (evident in such later series as *The Surreal Life* [2003–],

The Osbournes [2002–5], *The Anna Nicole Show* [2002–], and *Newly-weds: Nick & Jessica,* among others).

The Real World was groundbreaking as a form of reality programming precisely because nothing really occurs on the show besides talk.[29] That is, there is nothing more essential to the show's drama than what the characters have to say to each other and to the audience as they explain their actions and thought processes by means of individual interviews. Whatever activities the characters engage in are nowhere near as important as what these characters talk about. Producer Mary-Ellis Bunim emphasized this kind of appeal early in *The Real World's* run when she said, "We want arguments. We want to see people from very different backgrounds come together, shout it out and work it out."[30] The reason, of course, is that Bunim realizes the powerful attraction audiences have to witnessing genuine discursive conflict and its resolution. This voyeuristic aspect of talk within reality programming leads John Corner to reflect on what he calls "overheard speech." As he argues, "The accessing of a space of action/speech which is marked as anterior to television's own spaces of performance or of intervention generates distinctive, revelatory qualities."[31] The overheard speech that constitutes reality programming, then, is talk that is quite distinct from the performance of political pundits on Fox, for instance, or even the seemingly more natural, though packaged and produced, talk provided by *Politically Incorrect.*

But the revelations of overheard speech do not simply come through the interpretive capacities of the viewer. Overheard speech is also accompanied by what amounts to a narration of the action that is produced through interviews with the characters. This is what Corner refers to as "experiential interviews," television talk that generates utterances grounded in personal identity and "a kind of remembering aloud."[32] These reflections allow the interview subject to share his or her thoughts and feelings about the interactions between characters that the viewer has just witnessed. Every interaction that is shown—however trivial—must be reflected upon, psychologized, and evaluated. Action and reflection and, in turn, revelation become one in the overall performance, for no action presented deserves to be seen if it cannot be talked about.

What is distinctive is that the talk produced can be quite similar to that elicited by Oprah, yet in reality programming, no interviewer is present on-screen. As such, the characters are seemingly communing with the viewers at home instead of offering a version of talk mediated by an interrogator. Each interviewee appeals to the viewer to adopt his or her explanation, interpretation, or judgment of the value and worth of the other characters. Far from simply being a fly on the wall (to reference the rhetoric of cinema verité programming), the viewer is positioned as the interviewer, the one who receives the intimations and is expected to respond to such revelations. The relationship to the talk show here is palpable.

In the end, however, this process of action, reflection, and revelation is quite different from the kind of talk offered by personal relationship programs such as *The Oprah Winfrey Show* (1996–). Though here, too, the personal and private is offered up for public consumption, the viewer of programs like Oprah's is primarily a witness to the hosts, guests, and audience members who act, speak, advise, and present their own conclusions about the world. Through the documentary-style interview and overheard talk on reality shows such as *The Real World*, however, the most important arbiter of meaning and judgment is the viewer. As Corner again notes, interview talk "will remain the communicative core around which a number of very different programme formats are organized, accessing the viewer to personally mediated knowledge and experience and providing kinds of talk forms which augment those of the professional broadcaster."[33] In that regard, reality shows both extend and broaden the range of television talk beyond that which existed on television only a decade ago, and in the process, they have blurred the boundaries between the talk and reality genres.

As noted earlier, it would be a mistake to suggest that reality shows *are* talk shows. Neither the multifarious and cross-generic texts themselves, nor the disparate industrial practices involved in their production, nor the varied audience relationships to such programming should lead to such an extreme conclusion. Yet we must nevertheless recognize the factors associated with reality programming that erode the privileged place of the traditional talk show as the central location for the display of talk on television today. Syndicated afternoon talk shows have exploited the audience's desire to overhear and vicariously participate in some of society's most intimate thoughts, behaviors, and experiences. In many instances, however, reality shows have now altered the circumstances and settings of such conversations and, in turn, the manner of the vicarious experience. *The Real World,* along with its numerous derivatives in cable and network programming, brings the conversation out from behind the desk and beyond the studio, and recasts such talk in a living room or bedroom. Viewers overhear intimate talk but are offered the additional opportunity to develop parasocial relationships (or what Horton and Wohl call "intimacy at a distance") with the characters who take part in this new form of serialized talk.[34]

Indeed, when examining central components of two different forms of talk shows—the parasocial relationships that audiences have with celebrity talk on entertainment shows and the enhanced level of intimacy in the talk of strangers on relationship shows—we can see how reality programs merge and blend these components into a successful variety of talk programming. The entertainment talk show offers a highly scripted version of slightly intimate talk between people (e.g., celebrities and host) with whom audiences feel they have a relationship. The afternoon talk show offers a somewhat less scripted version of much more intimate talk, though between people (beyond the host) for whom audiences generally have limited feelings. Reality shows, however, offer the highest level of unscripted intimate talk but simultaneously offer the opportunity for new parasocial relationships with these serialized characters.

Although the industrial recasting of intimate talk in the 1980s and 1990s retained the "talk show" designation, the recasting of intimate talk between ordinary people in reality programming has not received this label. The point here is less to make the case for the reality show as a talk show than it is to lead us to question whether talk programming can be contained within any generic boundaries when we witness such similarities in purpose and form. Perhaps this is even more the case when we recognize the similarities in industrial imperatives to produce inexpensive programming in both reality programming and traditional talk shows, in addition to the audience's desire to hear talk among diverse people across varied subjects in different situations (as with *Politically Incorrect* and Fox News).

Beyond Genre

When considering the plethora of talk programming (talk shows, news, and reality shows) that is now produced across cable, broadcast TV, and syndication, we should perhaps consider whether the designation of the "talk show" as a distinct genre is still a meaningful one. Compare, for instance, *Emeril Live* (1997–), the flagship cooking show on the Food Network, to *The Late Show with David Letterman* (1993–). The former, of course, is called a demonstration show, and the latter is called a talk show. Yet Emeril performs in front of a live audience, has a band, tells jokes, stands behind his version of a desk (countertop), interacts with the audience and band, and is the main element of the show's appeal as its star. Hence, does the fact that he talks about tuna tartare instead of Christy Turlington become the defining factor in how this show is conceived or categorized by the industry, audiences, or scholars? Other examples of TV talk provide the same dilemma. Is the confrontational give-and-take followed by publicly exacted shame produced on *Judge Judy* really that different from what occurs on *Maury Povich* (1992–)? Do the spectacle performances that constitute *The Jerry Springer Show* equate with the conventions of traditional talk shows, or should they instead lead us to see this program as simply another form of unscripted reality programming—complete with expert casting and anticipated physical encounters?

News, entertainment, public affairs, and reality talk all blend together in contemporary television programming. What are we to make of comedian Bill Maher and actor Ron Silver as the only guests appearing on CNN's *Wolf Blitzer Reports* (2000–) to "debate" the war in Iraq?[35] Is there really much difference between watching Jessica Simpson and her husband, Nick Lachey, talk about themselves on CNN's talk show *Larry King Live,* and the same verbal navel-gazing that occurs on their own MTV reality show, *Newlyweds: Nick & Jessica?* Is the cattily scripted talk on *The View* really that far removed from the cattily unscripted talk on *The Real World?* Is *The Daily Show* a talk show, a parody of news, or both? Finally, what sense do we make of the fact that the cable news network CNN International carries *The Daily Show* on its channels around the world? Are news talk, celebrity talk, and comedic parody talk all interchangeable? In today's TV environment, the answer is evidently yes.

To be sure, broadcasters, syndicators, and cable networks will continue to produce talk shows for every daypart that utilize the standardized codes and conventions that typically constitute a "talk show" in viewers' minds. These programs will be built around stars like Jimmy Kimmel, Ellen DeGeneres, and Tucker Carlson, and their talk will continue to be composed of the seemingly unscripted banter that is directed toward selling various kinds of commodities (such as cultural products, government policies, or the star system itself). Such programming is cheap to produce and has wide utility as a well-defined and popular style among its many fans.

Nevertheless, any conception of the "talk show" as a singular or even stable generic form should be reconsidered. Competition for viewers across the vast array of cable channels has led to stylistically creative yet inexpensive programming decisions that exploit different approaches to presenting televised talk. The boundaries of what constitutes various forms of talk as a genre have largely eroded, with cable TV leading the way in undermining this traditional form. Ultimately, if we are to define the talk show genre at all, its most salient characteristic is instability; it is a fluid form that begs, borrows, and steals from other genres and, conversely, can be borrowed from as well in order to catch the viewer's attention.

The popularity of this kind of programming should also lead us to consider that viewers, too, are complicit in this blurring of boundaries between talk that is private and public, serious and entertaining, informational and judgmental, pleasurable and unpleasurable, performative and "real," perhaps reflecting a postmodern sensibility or simply a reflection of how viewers have come to interact with television. TV talk is thus positioned beyond genre, where the competition brought on by an ever-expanding universe of cable programming has elevated displays of talk to a central place in several distinct programming formats. As a result, it simply may not make a lot of sense anymore to conceive of the TV talk show as being much different from other programming that features nonfictional talk.

Notes

1. As John Corner notes in his discussion of the role of talk on television, "It is through speech that television addresses its viewers and holds them in particular relations both to specific programmes and to channel and station identities. Talk thus generates the socio-communicative sphere within which television images operate." John Corner, *Critical Ideas in Television Studies* (New York: Oxford University Press, 1999), 37.

2. Jane M. Shattuc, *The Talking Cure: TV Talk Shows and Women* (New York: Routledge, 1997); Sonia Livingstone and Peter Lunt, *Talk on Television: Audience Participation and Public Debate* (London: Routledge, 1994); Joshua Gamson, *Freaks Talk Back: Tabloid Talk Shows and Sexual Nonconformity* (Chicago: University of Chicago Press, 1998); Laura Grindstaff, *The Money Shot: Trash, Class, and the Making of TV Talk Shows* (Chicago: University of Chicago Press, 2002); Kevin Glynn, *Tabloid Culture: Trash Taste, Popular Power, and the Transformation of American Television* (Durham, N.C.: Duke University Press, 2000); Patricia Priest, *Public Intimacies: Talk Show Participants and Tell-All TV* (Creskill, N.J.: Hampton, 1995); Vicki Abt and Leonard Mustazza, *Coming after Oprah: Cultural Fallout in the Age of the TV Talk Show* (Bowling Green, Ohio: Bowling Green State University Popular Press, 1997).

3. Robert J. Erler and Bernard M. Timberg, "A Taxonomy of Television Talk," in Bernard M. Timberg, *Television Talk: A History of the TV Talk Show* (Austin: University of Texas Press, 2002), 195–203.

4. For the typical weekday programming schedule in September 2002, CNN

aired talk shows from 2:00 P.M. to 5:00 A.M. (EST), Fox aired talk from 4:00 P.M. to 6:00 A.M., and MSNBC aired news only from 9:00 A.M. to 12:00 P.M. See Tim Rutten, "Talk Is Cheap, or at Least Cheaper Than Newscasts," *Los Angeles Times,* June 7, 2002, D2.

5. See, for instance, Corner, *Critical Ideas in Television Studies,* 38–44; Bernadette Casey, Neil Casey, Ben Calvert, Liam French, and Justin Lewis, *Television Studies: The Key Concepts* (New York: Routledge, 2002), 196–198; Arild Fetveit, "Reality TV in the Digital Era," in *The Television Studies Reader,* ed. Robert C. Allen and Annette Hill (New York: Routledge, 2004), 554n23; Erler and Timberg, "Taxonomy of Television Talk," 195–203.

6. Erler and Timberg, "Taxonomy of Television Talk," 201.

7. Corner, *Critical Ideas in Television Studies,* 38.

8. Writing in 1993, prior to the changes described here, talk show scholar Wayne Munson recognized this point by noting the genre's numerous recombinant features and postmodern qualities, but also in pointing out that the "genre" may not even be a single category capable of being contained in such a designation. Wayne Munson, *All Talk: The Talkshow in Media Culture* (Philadelphia: Temple University Press, 1993), 7.

9. Quoted in John Thornton Caldwell, *Televisuality: Style, Crisis and Authority in American Television* (New Brunswick, N.J.: Rutgers University Press, 1995), 292.

10. For a more thorough discussion of the formation of Comedy Central, see Jeffrey P. Jones, *Entertaining Politics: New Political Television and Civic Culture* (Lanham, Md.: Rowman and Littlefield, 2004), 64–66; Jeffrey P. Jones, "Comedy Central," in *The Encyclopedia of Television,* 2nd ed. (London: Taylor and Francis, 2004), vol. 1, 564–66.

11. Peter Johnson, "Will Fox News' Success Force Competitors to Take Sides?" *USA Today,* November 22, 2004, 3D.

12. Caldwell, *Televisuality,* 4.

13. Ibid., 251.

14. Ibid., 256.

15. The success of *Politically Incorrect* in this regard has led to a revival in group talk across a variety of channels and subjects, including *The View* (ABC), *The List* (VH1), *Tough Crowd* (Comedy Central), *The Best Damn Sports Show Period* (Fox Sports), *Around the Horn* (ESPN), and *Reliable Sources* (CNN).

16. For a more thorough account of the creation of *Politically Incorrect,* as well as the genre-busting characteristics of the program and others like it, see Jones, *Entertaining Politics,* 52–88.

17. Corner, *Critical Ideas in Television Studies,* 42–43.

18. Numerous examples of this contrasting style can be seen in the documentary *Outfoxed: Rupert Murdoch's War on Journalism,* dir. Robert Greenwald, 2004.

19. Theresa Bradley, "Solidly Stewart," at *ABCNews.com,* November 14, 2002.

20. For instance, Roger Ailes argues, "Presenting a point of view is not necessarily biased. Eliminating a point of view is biased." Jacques Steinberg, "Fox News, Media Elite," *New York Times,* November 8, 2004, C1.

21. One of Klein's first actions with the network was to cancel its long-running public affairs shoutfest, *Crossfire*. He noted that this move "toward reporting the day's events and not discussing them" would be the new approach at the network "unless the first batch of things we're trying to do don't turn out well." See Bill Carter, "CNN Will Cancel 'Crossfire' and Cut Ties to Commentator," *New York Times*, January 6, 2005, C5.

22. Paolo Carpignano, Robin Anderson, Stanley Aronowitz, and William DiFazio, "Chatter in the Age of Electronic Reproduction: Talk Television and the 'Public Mind,'" in *The Phantom Public Sphere*, ed. Bruce Robbins (Minneapolis: University of Minnesota Press, 1993), 93–120; Livingstone and Lunt, *Talk on Television*.

23. Jon Dovey, *Freakshow: First Person Media and Factual Television* (London: Pluto Press, 2000): 1.

24. Such rhetoric always begs the follow-up question, "As opposed to 'non-real' people?" See Rich Brown, "America's Talking Cable Channel Takes Off," *Broadcasting and Cable* 124 (July 4, 1994): 16.

25. Wayne Walley, "NCTA Surfer; Clashing Opinions Fuel 'Incorrect,'" *Electronic Media*, May 8, 1995, 39.

26. See Jones, *Entertaining Politics*, 161–86.

27. Alex Williams, "MTV's Real World," *New York*, December 9, 2002, at http://www.newyorkmetro.com.

28. As Doug Herzog, senior vice president for programming at MTV at the time, put it, "What 'Real World' costs to make per episode is less than Roseanne gets in pay per episode." Sid Smith, "MTV's Puckish, Camera-in-Your-Face 'Real World' Brings Down the House," *Salt Lake Tribune*, September 23, 1994, D6.

29. In this regard, *The Real World* contrasted with other reality shows of the time such as *Cops* or *Rescue 911*, where some sort of visual action was central to the overall narrative meaning and viewer appeal (such as watching police officers discover a suspect hiding in a garbage can, or the voyeuristic thrill of engaging in a police chase only to watch the villain crash and burn on a hairpin curve).

30. Smith, "MTV's Puckish," D6.

31. Corner, *Critical Ideas in Television Studies*, 44.

32. Ibid., 43.

33. Ibid., 44.

34. D. Horton and R. Wohl, "Mass Communication as Para-social Interaction: Observations on Intimacy at a Distance," *Psychiatry* 19 (1956): 215–29, reprinted in *Communication Studies*, 4th ed., ed. John Corner and J. Hawthorn (London: Arnold, 1993), 156–64.

35. *Wolf Blitzer Reports*, CNN, broadcast March 13, 2003. The "credentials" these two entertainers brought to this news channel's debate on whether the U.S. government should eschew further diplomacy and move ahead with its plans to invade Iraq are Maher's position as a liberal political talk show host and Silver's being a conservative actor on a popular political drama (*The West Wing*).

3 | new directions in television genres

8

the changing definition of reality television

Ron Simon

As philosopher Jean Baudrillard was interrogating the nature of reality in the eighties, a new form of television was attempting to integrate reality into escapist prime-time entertainment. Reality television has since become a dynamic and globally reaching form of programming, much to the consternation of critics and the many members of the creative television community. This new phenomenon not only challenged the future of production but also repositioned what had gone before in television history. Reality has always been an integral part of broadcasting, but its significance and influence have rarely been acknowledged. This new genre crystallized a stream of television that has run parallel to the fictional worlds and celebrity culture of Hollywood. As much as the audience has gazed at the Hollywood stars, the viewer has also taken pleasure in seeing an average Joe or Josephine on television.

Even in its current incarnation, reality television is a very malleable, fluid concept, not unlike the real as dissected by Baudrillard. TV reality has absorbed a multitude of other genres, including soap opera, adventure, and variety, while retaining some core identity. At its heart, reality refers, sometimes very tangentially, back to the commonplace world we experience and live in every day and especially how real people interact in undirected situations. This type of television wants to capture seemingly improvisatory events as they are happening, situations that are unfolding in front of the camera to which the producers and participants theoretically do not know the outcome. Reality television is thus defined in opposition to the dominant entertainment model of American entertainment, which has always been based on scripts and stars. But the messiness of ordinary life has always been difficult to fit into a box, especially a flat, one-dimensional screen. Raw footage, the purest form of documentary, has always been problematic; some other type of extra value has been thrown into the mix, from mood music to a celebrity narration. And how television reflects the concrete world has been conditioned by many factors: the technology of the time, the creative aspirations of the producer, and the expectations of the audience.

Early Searches for the Real in Nonfiction and Fiction

The beginnings of reality television emerged from the psychology department of Cornell University in the thirties. There a young research assistant, Allen Funt, became obsessed with the particularities of everyday life. He first tried to capture the quirkiness of the human voice on *Candid Microphone,* a radio series, but television proved to be more amenable to his congenial psychological experiments. Premiering in 1948 on ABC, his *Candid Camera* (1948–53, 1960–67, 1990, 1998–) became the first and longest-running reality-based series on television. The program was constructed around footage taken by a hidden camera of everyday people caught in unusual situations. Also serving as host, Funt devised short scenarios that captured not only what people said but also how they behaved nonverbally—their gestures, facial expressions, and unstated confusions. Hampered by technical and logistical difficulties, such contrived stunts as talking mailboxes appeared simple but took many hours to prepare and execute. In fact, fifty sequences were filmed for every five to make the program, certainly a harbinger of things to come in the reality genre.

In the premiere episode of *Candid Camera,* Funt proclaimed to his audience, "You are the star!" Aware that he was conferring celebrity status on his human guinea pigs, Funt was hoping for more than a pre-Warholian aura of fame. Instead, he envisioned his series as a Whitmanesque salute to the vitality of the American citizenry. Funt delighted when his outlandish situations and imposing authority figures were playfully resisted by the average citizen. He insisted that "we need to develop ways to teach our children to resist unjust or ridiculous authority." Later he would add the viewer-friendly signature line, "Smile, you're on *Candid Camera.*"

Psychologists were intrigued with the concept of putting ordinary people into unusual circumstances to see how they behaved; consequently, many created their own reality experiments on film as academic adaptations of *Candid Camera*. Many scientists accepted a hidden camera as a necessary means for probing the complex human interactions in modern society. As television scholar Anna McCarthy has discovered, Allen Funt directly inspired Dr. Stanley Milgram's study of obedience to authority.[1] Milgram, admiring Funt's blend of social science and entertainment, contrived an educational experiment in which one subject played a teacher and was asked to administer electric shocks to another to help this participant learn. Almost 70 percent of the teacher subjects requested the painful shock, urged on by a Funt-like authority.

For two decades the Milgram experiment, looking like a *Candid Camera* outtake, was cited to explain blind obedience, especially behavior during the Nazi regime in Germany and the atrocities in Vietnam. In the early seventies another scientist, Philip Zimbardo, also influenced by Funt's stunts, created a filmed scenario whereby half of a group became prisoners, the other half guards. Again, the authority group was not reluctant to administer severe punishment. Both Milgram and Zimbardo selected the most ordinary subjects to understand the social processes of obedience that possibly could lead to the execution of large-scale atrocities. These psychologists presaged a *Survivor*-type reality television that would conform to seventeenth-century philosopher Thomas Hobbes's view of existence: "In a pure state of nature—with no arts, letters, no society—the life of man is solitary, poor, nasty, brutish, and short." By the late 1970s, ethical guidelines discouraged the use of deception in psychological research; consequently, a Milgram-type study could not be carried out today. No such guidelines exist in reality television, as such postmodern hidden camera experiments as MTV's *Jackass* and *Punk'd* along with NBC's *Spy TV* have proved so well.

Candid Camera and other long-running contestant shows such as *Truth or Consequences* (1950–52, 1954–65, 1991–92) and *Beat the Clock* (1950–61, 1969–74, 1979–80) thrust the ordinary citizen into a preplanned event, thriving on spontaneous reactions. The emphasis was on the physical; the scripted world of live TV would define what everyday language in television, film, and theater should sound like. One fictional writer, Paddy Chayefsky, had a major impact on this incipient search for the real, pioneering a new type of intimate psychological drama for live television in the early fifties. He envisioned television as the medium uniquely suited to explore what he called "the marvelous world of the ordinary." Chayefsky wanted his dialogue to sound as if it had been wiretapped from real life. Instead of the poetic musings of a Tennessee

Williams or the didactic arguments of an Arthur Miller, Chayefsky created dialogue that reflected the rhythms of ordinary life: the repetitions and the non sequiturs. Director Steven Soderbergh, who has experimented with the reality genre in film and television, stated that "to create the sloppiness with which most of us speak actually takes real discipline." Chayefsky's signature drama, *Marty* (1953), the story of a lonely Bronx butcher who is being pressured by his family to marry, engaged the audience like no drama before and became the first television work to be adapted into a movie (in 1955). The success of both works spurred producers to search for real-life Martys for audience identification. Why pay writers to create authentic characters when they exist on every street corner?

The Manipulation of Reality: The Beginnings

The inclusion of regular people on quiz shows was usually a one-shot deal; the contestant was incorporated into the quiz narrative to briefly interact with the host, play the game, and make a quick exit to civilian life. Individuals were interchangeable, each signifying the unwashed mass out there in fifties TV land. After the success of *Marty*, two producers, Steve Carlin and Dan Enright, devised shows that would feature average Americans in regular, continuing roles. In fact, Carlin's description of his ideal candidate sounded very much like Rod Steiger's Marty: "We want personable, although not necessarily good looking, people. Nice people, intelligent people—people who look like your neighbors."[2] Carlin and Enright first experimented with children's shows, *Rootie Kazootie* (1950–54) and *Juvenile Jury* (1947–55), respectively. Most commentary on these shows, even today, describes these kid series as spontaneous and totally unpredictable, just like childhood itself. But having children in extended conversations proved problematic for the producers. *Juvenile Jury* was built around a panel of engaging youngsters who advised their peers on perplexing personal problems. Enright realized that there was no way that kids could give off-the-cuff answers amid the pressures of live television. The only way to give each of the kids a personality and keep the show moving was to massage reality and give all the questions and answers to the youngsters before the telecast.[3] *Juvenile Jury* appeared unpredictable because the youngsters could never entirely memorize the script. These shows seemed so pure that no questions of manipulation were raised during the quiz show investigation by the 1958 New York grand jury and the 1959 hearings of the House Subcommittee on Legislative Oversight.

These producers of children's shows made their prime-time debuts with big-money quiz shows, with emphasis on the contestants as stars. Carlin's *The $64,000 Question* (1955–58) and Enright's *Twenty-One* (1956–58) searched for average Americans demonstrating a sophisticated mastery of difficult subjects. This was more than just buying vowels in the *Wheel of Fortune* mode; almost all the questions involved the possession of erudite knowledge. The contestants appeared over the course of several weeks, developing cult followings; the winners emerged as exemplars of the abiding intelligence of the American people, a *Song of America* triumph following in the tradition of Whitman and Funt.

Early rehearsals proved that the games were too difficult for the contestants. The producers learned that if you posed random questions spontaneously to guests, you got not an entertaining show but, in the words of Enright, "dismal failure." The main revelation during pretesting was that showmanship and contestant control had to take precedence over honesty; champions over time had to be constructed. Enright found his Marty type in Herb Stempel, an ex-soldier studying at City College of New York. Stempel was recast as a penniless ex-GI struggling to make his way through college; in reality, Stempel's wife was well-off, and the couple never had problems with finances, facts hidden from the television audience. Stempel won a good deal of money as a continuing champion of *Twenty-One,* but nonetheless the audience did not identify with one of their own. Instead of a triumphant Everyman, he came off as a creepy nerd, a human computer. Laying down the foundation for many reality shows that followed, Enright looked for Stempel's opposite, a Jimmy Stewart persona, thus foregoing real life for the movies. He found Charles Van Doren, tall and handsome, a blue-blooded Ivy Leaguer as opposed to the stout, ethnic, untelegenic Stempel. But, like Stempel, Van Doren was given the answers, and his fall from grace doomed the first wave of reality shows.

Although the only concrete law broken by the contestants and the industry was perjury during the grand jury hearings, the networks canceled most of the live series that validated the everyday. Instead, the networks, working with the Hollywood studios, produced such generic filmed staples as the Western and the detective series that valorized escapism and the presence of alluring actors on a weekly basis. Producers never figured out how to present the everyday person in an ongoing narrative without manipulating the story. Except for *Candid Camera,* which held its own in a schedule filled with sixties fantasy, the "marvelous world of the ordinary" was banished from prime time, relegated to news and public affairs.

The Reality Documentary

At the same time live television was declining, a small group of filmmakers were grappling with the possibilities of a new technology, the lightweight, 16mm film camera. Instead of being bound in a studio, with this new camera filmmakers could go to places where they were normally denied access because of the bulkiness of 35mm equipment. Led by Robert Drew and inspired by Italian neorealism, this pioneering group devised an aesthetic on how to capture people and events as accurately as possible with a minimum of filmmaker interference or interpretation. The new ad hoc movement, called cinema verité, or direct cinema, was an attempt to strip away the accumulated conventions of traditional cinema in the hope of rediscovering the outer world.[4] The filmmakers wanted to break the barriers between the documentary subject and audience, basing their faith in unmanipulated reality. Anticipating the Dogme 95 movement that tried to redeem the portrayal of reality on film several decades later, Drew and others laid down several rules for documentary filmmakers to consider, their own vows of chastity.

First, the filmmakers should not use any extraneous audio, committing themselves to a total reliance on synchronous sound, avoiding any type of narration. The image should speak for itself, and filmmakers should relinquish the authority to tell you what to look for and what you have seen. Commentaries take away the surprise and often the discomfort of experiencing something new.

Second, cinema verité mandated that the filmmaker should not interfere in the filming of any event, being as inconspicuous as possible. The filmmaker should not influence what subjects say or suggest how to behave.

Finally, editing should not be used to present the filmmaker's perspective on the subject. Ideally, editing should represent as truly as possible what viewers would have experienced in sight and sound had they witnessed the situations depicted in the film.

A generation of documentary filmmakers would wrestle with these rules in trying to be true to the outside world. Television initially embraced the intimate detail and rough edges of this new vision, and Drew and his compatriots were commissioned for a series of documentaries. The defining film of this new movement was *Primary* (1960), a behind-the-scenes look at the Democratic race between Senators John Kennedy and Hubert Humphrey. With the sweeping freedom that the new light-weight equipment allowed, the program gave viewers a never-before-seen look at a political campaign, following candidates up close during an election and entering private spheres never before invaded by the camera. Besides following his technological mandates, Drew also wanted to catch his subjects in moments of decisive action. Consequently, the vérité filmmakers gravitated more toward artists and politicians than the ordinary Tom, Dick, and Harriet, using their cameras to explore unseen aspects of celebrity culture.

Although purists regarded this movement as a philosophical explora-tion of the real world, the general public grasped vérité filmmaking on simple physical terms: shaky, out-of-focus camerawork and grainy, black-and-white stock. But, ironically, it was a documentary revolution that could be done at home. In the late fifties Bell and Howell, one of the first spon-sors of Drew films, marketed 8mm equipment to the consumer. Ama-teurs could very easily mimic direct cinema stylistics in their own home movies. Thus began the first intersection between the professional world of reality filmmaking and private sphere of do-it-yourself recording.

An American Family

In the sixties some of the cinema verité filmmakers also investigated ordinary existence. David and Al Maysles took this new style of docu-mentary filmmaking to the large screen, with the theatrical *Salesman* (1969), an exploration of the tedious and conflicted world of Bible merchants; Fred Wiseman, funded by public television, interrogated such institutions as the educational system, the police force, and the military. The Maysles brothers and Wiseman did not act in strict accordance with the rules of direct cinema; in fact, they considered themselves documen-tary novelists. Their canvas was raw reality into which they molded their personal expressions of life with a shaky camera and black-and-white intensity. They all freely admitted that their fly-on-the-wall, objective documentaries were riddled with their subjective opinions, but without explicit narration, they also gave audiences the freedom to make up their own minds.

The most ambitious documentary employing many of the mandates of the cinema verité movement was *An American Family*, a twelve-part series that recorded the everyday lives of the Loud family from May 30 through December 31, 1971. Producer Craig Gilbert spent many months to find that one family in more than fifty million available in the early 1970s that would serve as the real-life counterpart of such idealized TV families as those on *Father Knows Best* and *The Donna Reed Show.* Pat and Bill Loud were a handsome, affluent couple with five children, living in Santa Barbara, California; they had the looks and personalities to be the leading characters in a documentary narrative. More than three hundred hours of their family life was shot on 16mm film, with the whole project taking a year to edit.

An American Family used an episodic, ensemble structure common to soap operas. Like the daytime serials, the series emphasized intimate daily life, focusing on multiple characters over plot. Although *An American Family* included various story lines, the dominant themes were the marital problems of Mr. and Mrs. Loud and the flamboyant lifestyle of the eldest son, Lance. Divorce was a novel topic for prime time, and few viewers had ever encountered an openly gay son. Although the opening credits suggested a guide on "how to read the family" (a family breaking down), the program included no expert commentary or interviews. Many reviewers criticized the Louds as affluent zombies, not worthy of any critical attention, but anthropologist Margaret Mead envisioned the series as a new and significant way in which people could look at life, by seeing the real lives of others interpreted by the television camera.

Other critics invoked Heisenberg's principle of indeterminacy—the mere fact of observation has an influence on the observed. Some attributed the parents' separation and Lance's homosexuality to the presence of the production crew. Whether the Louds signaled a breakdown in American society or a harbinger of things to come, *An American Family* opened up the institution of the family and issues of gender, sexuality, and interpersonal relationships for public discussion, becoming a touchstone for a new generation of documentary and reality producers in the nineties.

A New Wave of Reality Programming

In the 1980s "factual" television became an unexpected moneymaker. Continually dismissed as a fad by critics and the industry, the new genre kept mutating into something bigger and more profitable. The format took on many guises throughout the decade—infotainment, tabloid TV, crime-time television, trash TV, and on-scene television. These new per-

The 1973 PBS documentary *An American Family* used an episodic, ensemble structure common to soap operas in presenting an intimate portrait of the Loud family from Santa Barbara. (Left to right) The Louds—first row: Michelle, Pat, and Bill; second row: Kevin, Grant, Delilah, and Lance. Courtesy of Thirteen/WNET.

mutations were characterized by a hybrid of genres that were previously discrete, blurring the lines between documentary journalism and glitzy entertainment. The initial mix featured elements from mainstream television reporting, most notably the local style of electronic newsgathering (ENG), with comely correspondents providing on-the-spot coverage. Thus the first wave of reality television was actually inspired more by the conventions of the seventies newscasts than the actualities of the outer world.

From the 1970s on, executives used reality-type programming, noticeably cheaper than traditional Hollywood fare, to test the waters of new scheduling opportunities. The prime-time access rule opened up the early evening daypart to independent producers. One of the early successes was *PM Magazine* (1978–90), an initiative of local Westinghouse stations that served up a mix of human interest and celebrity stories. Following in the tradition of Charles Kuralt's *On the Road* segments for CBS and the offbeat pieces that ended local newscasts, *PM Magazine* prized unusual stories of the unsung characters populating the American vista. Small, portable minicameras allowed reporters to go deep into the heartland to discover uplifting triumphs of the can-do spirit. This search for the American Quirky quickly became prime-time fodder with the popularity of George Schlatter's *Real People* (1979–84), a humorous and often touching tribute to the everyday citizen, all the more unusual in the era of the melodramatic *Dallas* and *Dynasty*. But this "lighter side of the news" trend in programming became outlandish, with such *Real People* imitators as *That's Incredible* (1980–84, 1988–89) and *Those Amazing Animals* (1980–81) often resembling a carnival freak show in the ongoing quest for novelty.

Reality shows gained prominence in a televisual environment marked by the increasing financial tightening and labor turmoil of the late 1980s. Economically, the genre fit the demands of both producers and distributors seeking cost-efficient programming. This new breed of program did away with higher-priced stars and a union crew; a single host often accounted for the only talent payment. Costs could be cut dramatically: in the earlier nineties an average dramatic show cost $1 million; a newsmagazine show like *60 Minutes* came in at $600,000, and a week of reality newsmagazine came in under $400,000.

This latest incarnation of reality was much darker and more sinister than the endearing "human interest" mode, reflecting the harsher realities of President Reagan's America. Modeled on the flashy tabloid newspapers of Rupert Murdoch, such series as *A Current Affair* (1986–96) and *Hard Copy* (1989–99) trafficked in the sensational: gruesome murders, messy divorces, and celebrity wrongdoings. Producers often appropriated techniques from film noir, including cynical narration and evocative mood music, to further dramatize their excessive explorations of society's underbelly. The tabloid trend accentuated not everyday life but the disruptions of everyday life, especially crime and menace.

A subgenre flourished that focused solely on television's role as avenging angel to combat criminality. John Walsh, whose six-year-old son had been kidnapped and murdered, served as the host of the series that exemplified this new interactive model, *America's Most Wanted* (1988–). Employing stylized re-creations and eyewitness testimony, Walsh presented backstories of criminals currently on the loose. He urged his viewers to phone the show's hotline (1-800-CRIME-TV) to provide new leads for law enforcement officials. This new reality paradigm combined traditional public service concerns with dramatization informed by the fictive styles of Hollywood, a most uneasy alliance of news and artifice. *America's Most Wanted* was very cognizant of the new MTV age, awash in highly stylized segments full of quick cuts, music underscoring, and elaborate special effects; this reality presented as evidence required a great deal of massaging. Combating random assaults on orderly existence became the motif of two other long-running reality series: *Unsolved Mysteries* (1988–99), which encompassed everything from mysterious disappearances to UFO experiences, and *Rescue 911* (1989–96), which portrayed real-life responses to emergency calls. These law and rescue shows totally disregarded the older traditions of documentary, blurring reality and representation in a bouillabaisse of acting, interviews, simulations, and moral exhortations.

Video Vérité

For a generation that grew up with television, the video image connoted an up-close-and-personal immediacy, an unvarnished reality that was lost in the chemical processes of film. In the early seventies, video's instantaneous authenticity was embraced by a variety of young innovators: performance artists (Vito Acconci, Joan Jonas), collectives (TVTV, Ant Farm), and documentarians (Jon Alpert, Skip Blumberg). By the eighties, video had penetrated the home market, and such family gatherings as weddings and birthdays were preserved on tape. The refinement of home video equipment also gave the average citizen the potential power once granted only to the professional or reality journalist. Now instead of 8mm film, videotape signified the collision between the public and private spheres. Commercial television was quick to exploit the look of tape to signal both the brutalities and the pleasures of the external world. Production crews follow real-life policemen tracking low-life criminals in Fox's video voyeuristic series *Cops* (1989–). Shooting with a sometimes more than one hundred to one ratio, *Cops* mimics the conventional police drama while visiting the nocturnal underside of local law enforcement, chock-full of sleazy drug dealers and hardened officers. Often accused of being exploitative, *Cops* does keep faith with one tenet of cinema verité, the avoidance of narration, but the message of law and order is loud and clear.

Beginning as a special the same year that *Cops* commenced, *America's Funniest Home Videos* (1990–) reversed the flow of production, encouraging amateurs with camcorders to create humorous vignettes for broadcast. At its height of popularity, the series reportedly received more than two thousand video submissions a day. The videos were not served vérité; they were grouped thematically and further embellished with music, sound effects, and wisecracks. The particularities of everyday life were universalized with a laugh track and played for slapstick. *Funniest Home Videos* did signal the international ramifications of the reality movement. The series was based on a weekly variety series in Japan, *Fun with Ken and Kato Chan*, to which viewers mailed in video clips. The American version became such a popular success that its format rights sold throughout the world.

Realitas Personae

Charles Van Doren and the Louds were compelling figures from earlier reality eras. The new wave of reality programs in the eighties and early nineties were better at transmitting mood—from fear to funny—than characters. Whether in *Cops* or *Funniest Home Videos,* the emphasis was not on personality, except for the host; segments were manufactured with the same production values and intensity week in and week out, reality on an assembly line. A veteran soap writer, Mary-Ellis Bunim realized from her days on *As the World Turns* and *Santa Barbara* that viewers were addicted to individualized characters and provocative storytelling. With her partner Jonathan Murray, a veteran news producer, Bunim created a reality show, *The Real World* (1992–), with the allure of a socially conscious serial during the "I feel your pain" administration of Bill Clinton. *The Real World* threw together young adults from different backgrounds and lifestyles as roommates for several months. This weekly "hamsters in a box" scenario—part *American Family*, part psychological experiment—was set in an alien environment, a lavish, hip apartment wired with surveillance equipment. A wide range of social issues emerged from the daily interactions of the participants living in the televised fishbowl. During the New York episodes of the first season, racial conflicts within the group created dramatic tension; the second season's Los Angeles cast confronted sexual harassment within their own environs. The inclusion of outspoken AIDS activist Pedro Zamora, who has since died of the disease, in the 1994 San Francisco season provided MTV's young audience with an honest portrayal of the emotional distress caused by the virus. The best of *Real World* was often an indelicate balance between sexy glamour and gritty realism.

Bunim and Murray consciously skirted many of the cinema verité mandates adhered to by *An American Family*. They created a very commercial product, with emotional hooks at every act break. They also developed the first-person confessional, reality TV's equivalent to the Shakespearean soliloquy. Viewers not only see the young people in an unscripted interaction but also immediately afterward hear each of them talking individually about that experience in an interview taped separately by the producers. This reaction is given equal weight to the motivating action; in such montage, deed and reflection are one. These video diaries help to propel the narrative, elevating an ordinary event into a privileged moment of thought and insight, with some pettiness thrown in. The private confessional has been adapted by most subsequent series, with reality participants now extremely adept at "Oprah speak," expressing their inner feelings at a moment's notice.

Most producers wholeheartedly agree with *The Real World*'s golden rule: casting is the most crucial element to the success of a reality series. In fact, reality producers refer to their cast as characters, not real people. Before selecting a participant, *The Real World* spends three months with an individual, interviewing him or her numerous times, as well as following the prospect with cameras for several days. While creating *Survivor* (2000–), Mark Burnett typecast his castaways in the most general terms: Gay Man, Wild Woman, Single Mom, and Yuppie. Later he refined his categories to include reality types that help to create a socially volatile mix on TV: Everybody's Friend, the Redneck, the Slacker, and the Victim. Burnett and his staff have always had a huge pool of contestants from which to choose: for their initial season they were deluged with more than six thousand videotaped applications, from which they interviewed six hundred people. Reality producers do everything possible to blueprint contestant interaction before the actual taping to plan against the inchoate inertia of daily life. To see if their social engineering works, producers, whether on location or at headquarters, usually in Los Angeles, stay in continual communication with the director and crew to spot and develop story lines. This active engagement with the narrative can very easily slip over to staging scenes and preplanning dramatic arcs, a fact that participants have been reluctant to discuss for fear of legal reprisal.

The reality science experiment with human hamsters has played out in a variety of artificially constructed environments, all equipped with countless microphones and cameras. The most successful reality shows have incorporated game show strategies, especially a contest with an ultimate winner, all of which help to propel the narrative to a definitive conclusion. *Survivor* isolates sixteen men and women on a desert island, separated into two tribes. For thirty-nine days the castaways fend for themselves—including building shelters and finding food—and compete in challenges that bring immunity from being voted off the island. The games within the ultimate game give a linear structure to the individual episodes, but the audience pleasure comes from seeing how the contestants survive each other: the negotiation between building alliances and selfishly looking out for oneself. *Survivor* consciously plays off its mythic underpinnings: it is *Robinson Crusoe* meets *Gilligan's Island* meets *Ten Little Indians* meets *Lord of the Flies* meets Charles Darwin, a veritable collision of high and low cultures.

A British television producer, Charlie Parsons, developed the *Survivor* concept originally for Swedish television. Titled *Expedition: Robinson*, the series became a *succès de scandale* after one of its participants committed suicide (now reality contestants are required to undergo psychological testing before being selected). A former British army Special Services member and producer of Discovery Channel's *Eco Challenge*, Burnett negotiated to buy the American and Canadian rights from Parsons and sold his weekly version, which appropriated elements from cultural anthropology and religious ritual, to CBS as a summer replacement series. Burnett approached the production process as a military operation. More than twenty camera people and thirteen editors work full-time during the production of *Survivor*. For a single forty-two-minute episode, three hundred hours are taped, the equivalent of all the shooting on *An American Family*. This is certainly not old-school cin-

Debuting as a summer replacement in 2000, *Survivor* combined Darwin and *Gilligan's Island* to become the most successful reality franchise on American television. (Left to right) Contestants Richard Hatch and Rudy Boesch. Courtesy of CBS Television.

ema verité, where you film as much as you can and then selectively edit. In the end, Burnett has stated that *Survivor* is 80 percent documentary and 20 percent drama, each episode replete with cliffhanging hooks and misleading teases.

Over a thirty-month period, John de Mol of Endemol Entertainment developed the reality series with an Orwellian resonance, *Big Brother*, for Dutch television. Premiering in 1999, the series captured international attention and has since been licensed to eighteen countries. The American version (2000–) initially locked ten strangers into a specially designed home built on CBS network facilities. This artificial home is equipped with twenty-eight cameras and sixty microphones to spy on everything that transpires, from bathroom arguments to romantic encounters. Unlike *The Real World* and *Survivor*, which switch locations each season, *Big Brother* has used the same modular living quarters for each contest. *Big Brother* is also the one reality program scheduled as a soap opera. During the inaugural year, episodes were broadcast up to five times a week. The series has undergone many refinements over four years, but it still plays at least three times a week, a chance for viewers to identify with the psychological rigors of the games, as well as pinpoint the causes of the participants' jealousies, frustrations, and rivalries. Each week one of the contestants is voted out of the house, and those proceedings have always been telecast live. One of the defining values of the reality show has been its immediacy, a seemingly present-tense quality to the narrative. Although viewers know that even an episode of *Survivor* has been taped months earlier, the pleasure is still based on the unpredictability of the outcome.

The pleasure of any story, real or fictional, is trying to guess the outcome. Mark Burnett has stated, "You cannot predict how human beings will react in a strange, unfamiliar situation plus unfamiliar harsh environment." Mary Beth Haralovich and Michael Trosset have studied the uncertainties and role of chance in *Survivor* and discovered that there are twenty-one trillion permutations in predicting the exact order in which the sixteen castaways will be voted off.[5] The show helps to manage these endless possibilities by having everything occur in three-day cycles, culminating in a ritualistic challenge and tribal council. *Big Brother* has also evolved into a standardized format: live eviction and head of household competition on Thursday, nominations for eviction on Saturday, and "power of veto" competition on Tuesday. But many reality shows are also constructed so that the audience, especially the young demographic, can go beyond the television experience. Because *Big*

Brother operates almost in real time, passionate fans are urged to subscribe to the video streams on the Web site and view the activity in the house live 24/7. According to Ernest Mathijs and Janet Jones, these multiple uses of media and technological breakthroughs call "into question the singular states of the *Big Brother* television text."[6] Reality shows have been quick to exploit the latest in new technology as promotional tools to transform viewers into Internet-savvy fans who become part of an online community, purchasing merchandise and chatting about the latest episode. In fact, Henry Jenkins of Massachusetts Institute of Technology labels reality TV the "killer app" of a media convergence that is both grassroots and corporate driven.

If the first wave of reality shows focused on crime and violence, the second wave, debuting in the new century, concentrated on what was once hidden on American mainstream television: sex. While there was always the possibility of a romantic fling on *Survivor* and *Big Brother,* a new breed of reality was built exclusively on sexual voyeurism. But this is a TV reality sort of voyeurism: millions of people watch on TV a group of ordinary people who know they will eventually be watched on TV. These sensational reality shows were constructed as racy hothouses where contestants had little concern about the outside world—no telephones, newspapers, radio, or television—only the possibility of sexual tension. Commodifying the Prince Charming fairy tale, *The Bachelor* (2002–) gathered a hunky group of men vying for the romantic attention of a single babe over a period of fantasy dates. *The Bachelorette* (2003–) inverted the formula, placing the burden of choice on the female, while *Joe Millionaire* (2003–) parodied this video quest for love and money by having a hot bachelor pretend that he had inherited $50 million.

Several reality shows have tested the limits of decency, but their offensiveness has not affected the ratings or put this subgenre in jeopardy. *Temptation Island* (2001–2), a salacious hybrid of *The Love Boat* and *Fantasy Island,* sent unmarried couples to a tropical paradise to test their loyalty in the company of swinging strangers. In years past, *Who Wants to Marry a Multi-Millionaire?* (2000) might have sunk the whole genre, prompting a congressional investigation. The wealthy man, Rick Rockwell, sought by fifty attractive women, turned out to be a total fraud. Not only had a restraining order been filed against him, but also Rockwell's wealth was vastly overstated. These hedonistic reality shows have simultaneously validated and mocked the mythology of romance and chivalry, suitable programming for a generation that has grown up on pop culture irony.

Signature Series and Singular Placements

In less than ten years the reality genre has journeyed from prime-time access and fringe filler to signature programming around which the brand of a network can be built. Several cable networks have transformed their core identity via one successful reality series. A simple premise of two sets of neighbors redoing a room in each other's house with the aid of a professional designer and carpenter resulted in the brand-defining hit *Trading Spaces* (2000–) for the cable channel TLC. *Trading Spaces* has often ranked as the highest-rated program on basic cable and spun off two series (*Trading Spaces: Family* and *Trading Spaces for Kids*), as well as sold a slew of ancillary products. Bravo was a cable channel for the arts until the makeover tsunami known as *Queer Eye for the Straight Guy* (2003–), in which five gay experts in design and fashion changed the look and lifestyle of an average Joe. Instead of a stodgy network continually rerunning *Inside the Actors Studio,* Bravo was redefined as a metropolitan oasis for the fashionably hip. ABC revitalized the entire Disney corporation with the phenomenal success of *Who Wants to Be a Millionaire* (1999–2002), hosted by the irrepressible Regis Philbin. *Millionaire* was a high-tech update of *The $64,000 Question* with flashing strobes and a dark, cavernous set, intersecting with the reality movement by putting the contestant in a pressurized "hot seat." Searching for that one common viewer with uncommon knowledge, Regis encouraged audience interactivity, inviting his audience to try out by calling a toll-free number. Disney gambled on the popularity of *Millionaire* by programming the show up to five nights a week. For two seasons *Millionaire* dominated the Nielsen ratings, bringing a wide array of demographic groups under the network tent, just as if it were 1955 all over again. But, as quickly, overexposure killed one of the most popular series in the history of network television. In this instance T. S. Eliot was right; "human kind can not bear too much reality."

Reality television presents a model for twenty-first-century television that simultaneously looks back and forward in an age of media convergence. Commercial television began with advertisers as a programming force, and it was not uncommon for such stars as Jack Benny and Milton Berle to integrate their sponsor's product into the show. In an age of fast-forwarding through commercials, reality television has nurtured this softer sell, the art of product placement. Products are often positioned as prizes or special comforts for contestants to fight over. In a game of deprivation, snacks like Doritos become fetishistic objects of power for

Survivor players. Contestants in *Big Brother 4*, cut off from society and culture, reveled in a surprise musical performance by Sheryl Crow, whose new CD was also being marketed to the larger audience. Few commercials could market such longing for a product, despite the narrative absurdity of junk food in the jungle and a pop star in an Orwellian elimination match. On the first season of *The Apprentice* (2004–), contests revolved around such novelty items as lemonade and rickshaws; in the show's highly profitable second season, Trump's tycoon wannabes interacted with Mattel's toys and Procter and Gamble's Crest toothpaste. *American Idol* (2002–), a talent contest constructed as an interactive experience, conceptualized its young audience as a focus group that ultimately would anoint a new superstar and then serve as its fan base. The fans are shamelessly urged to buy the CDs and attend the tours of the performers in whom they have invested so much time and energy.

Americans may not be able to quote the Bible and Shakespeare as they once did, but almost everyone can identify Andy Warhol's famous prediction that everyone will be famous for fifteen minutes. Warhol's comment on the evanescence of fame has become the abiding truth of the reality television movement. Few participants have been able to sustain a career after their brush with reality. Except for Richard Hatch, the winners of *Survivor* and *Big Brother* do not come quickly to mind, even though they appeared on numerous morning and late-night shows after their coronation. Most people would need a lifeline to recall the first big winner of *Who Wants to Be a Millionaire* (Internal Revenue Service worker John Carpenter). Perhaps that is why *TV Guide* and *Entertainment Weekly* feature whatever-happened-to articles about last year's victors. Even the celebrated winners of *American Idol* contests—Kelly Clarkson, Ruben Studdard, Fantasia Barrino, and Carrie Underwood—all of whom had instant hit records, have had trouble fitting into contemporary entertainment formats, especially those of radio.

Ironically, the most famous and recognizable reality show participants are those who were famous before; they now are using the genre recombinantly to redefine themselves. Ozzy Osbourne resuscitated his career as the "Prince of Darkness" playing himself as a bumbling, bleeping dad in *The Osbournes* (2002–5), a reality comedy that invited comparisons to a sitcom from another era, *The Adventures of Ozzie & Harriet*. Notorious for a sex video, heiress Paris Hilton legitimized herself as a scrappy Beverly Hills sashimi out of water in *The Simple Life,* a reality updating of the rustic comedy *Green Acres*. Because of *The Apprentice,*

Donald Trump's image has evolved from rapacious entrepreneur to nice-guy mentor, simply by firing people on air. Unlike his melodramatic counterparts, J. R. Ewing of *Dallas* and Blake Carrington of *Dynasty*, Trump, with the same lavish lifestyle and oversized ego, became more likable the more he was on reality television. As Trump has stated, "People are able to see me in action. They hear my voice and see my eyes. There's nothing I can hide. That's me. Television brings out your flaws, your weaknesses, your strengths, and your truths. The audience either likes you or it doesn't. Obviously, the audience likes me."[7]

What Hath Reality TV Wrought?

Reality television has been among the most debated genres in television. Many critics see it as a debasement of traditional values, a blurring of categories once kept separate and sacrosanct: documentary and entertainment, nonfiction and fiction, the private and the public, culture and commerce. Like television itself once was, reality has been blamed for the dumbing down of the American public; former NBC news president Reuven Frank labels the trend as "shrewd and cynical formulas that manipulate the least admirable traits of the public." Some left-wing commentators have blasted the genre as a reflection of the conservative arrogance and business orientation of the Bush administration. Writing in *Harper's*, Francine Prose listed the themes of reality television that corresponded with those of the Republican Party: "flinty individualism, the vision of a zero-sum society in which no one can win unless someone else loses, the conviction that altruism and compassion are signs of folly and weakness, the exaltation of solitary striving above the illusory benefits of cooperative mutual aid, the belief that certain circumstances justify secrecy and deception, [and] the invocation of a reviled common enemy to solidify group loyalty."[8]

But other intellectuals have given critical legitimacy to the burgeoning genre. Scholar Julia Kristeva defended *Loft Story*, the French version of *Big Brother*, as a new space for communication that replaces the vanishing family, church, and grandmother. Speaking of the British version, scholar Jonathan Bignell theorized that "*Big Brother* showed society to itself, largely unconsciously by putting key aspects of contemporary ideology on display."[9] Certainly, following in the tradition of *An American Family*, reality programming is negotiating, subtextually at least, with such issues as sexuality, class, and power in the twenty-first century. Every week, it seems, one artificial environment of reality is coming to grips with misunderstandings between blacks and whites, questions of what it means to be gay, or accusations of being white trash. To perk up ratings, producers actively engage in hot-button issues. The third season of *The Apprentice* offered its own vision of class warfare, dividing its contestants into "Street Smarts" (no college education) and "Book Smarts" (degree laden).

Reality TV could also be posited as the first postmodern genre, where nothing—identity, lifestyle, or relationships—is fixed; everything is a construct ripe for radical transformation. In this new mediated world, life is malleable, always in need of a perpetual makeover. From the English homes of *Changing Rooms* (1996–2004) to the widely different American marriages of ABC's *Wife Swap* (2004–) and Fox's *Trading Spouses* (2004–), traditional cornerstones such as self, family, and home seem outdated; every aspect of life is now a work in progress. Reality television has seemingly merged the tenets of postmodern theory with the demands of postindustrial capitalism.

Reality television is also gaining legitimacy in the Hollywood community, where a war once raged between scripted and unscripted television. The Directors Guild of America (DGA) formed the Reality Television Committee in 2003 to encourage flexibility in the staffing of DGA members on reality shows, emphasizing the logistical and visual complexity of the genre. The *DGA Magazine* noted that the director of the extreme stunt show *Fear Factor* (2001–) applies cinematic techniques he culled from James Cameron and John Woo movies to make the series viscerally compelling.[10] In 2003 the Emmy Awards included a Reality-Competition Program category, which quickly became one of the highlights of the evening. The globe-trotting scavenger hunt *The Amazing Race* (2001–), produced with a glitzy intensity by movie mogul Jerry Bruckheimer, received the Emmy Award for the first two years, much to the visible consternation of Donald Trump in 2004, who reverted to his unlikable self.

The portability and miniaturization of the TV camera has made the reality show almost inevitable. The camera can now pry into any space, public or private. But to capture the human reality has always been problematic; from *Candid Camera* to *Survivor*, much footage has always been needed for a single lifelike scene. But no matter how contrived and manipulated the reality shows have become, at the heart of the phenomenon, borne out by countless Web sites and Internet discussions, is the audience's pleasure in identifying with one of its own, an everyday person grasping at a brief moment of TV fame. More than any other television genre, reality television constructs its casts to appeal to many different demographic, ethnic, and regional groups, all informed by the Warholian truth about fame. Perhaps the reality phenomenon signals a new audience investment in television. One traditional dichotomy has been obliterated: the separation of creating television and watching television. Viewers now can freely move between those two very different states. Futurists predict that everyone will be able to record on video every moment of his or her life on a portable iPod device because of the eventual cheapness and condensation of storage space. Reality TV is just the beginning, and Socrates will be momentarily updated: the untelevised life is not worth living.

Notes

1. For a fuller discussion of Allen Funt and Stanley Milgram, see Anna McCarthy's essay "'Stanley Milgram, Allen Funt, and Me': Cold War Social Science and the Roots of Reality TV," in *Reality TV: Remaking Television Culture,* ed. Susan Murray and Laurie Ouellette (New York: New York University Press, 2004), 19–39.

2. For a detailed discussion of the contestants sought by Steve Carlin and others, see Kent Anderson, *Television Fraud: The History and Implications of the Quiz Show Scandals* (Westport, Conn.: Greenwood Press, 1978), 12–14.

3. *Juvenile Jury* panelist Douglas Stuart, now a professor of political science, talked about his experiences during my presentation "The Changing Definition of 'Reality' on Television" at Dickinson College on October 2, 2002.

4. For a detailed discussion of the cinema verité movement, see Robert C. Allen and Douglas Gomery, *Film History: Theory and Practice* (New York: Knopf, 1985).

5. For a more detailed discussion of the role of chance in *Survivor,* see Mary Beth Haralovich and Michael Trosset's essay "'Expect the Unexpected': Narrative Pleasure and Uncertainty Due to Chance in *Survivor,*" in Murray and Ouellette, *Reality TV: Remaking Television Culture,* 75–96.

6. For a detailed examination of the *Big Brother* phenomenon, see Ernest Mathijs and Janet Jones, eds., Big Brother *International: Formats, Critics, and Publics* (London: Wallflower Press, 2004).

7. Donald J. Trump as told to Cal Fussman, "What It Feels Like to Be . . . Trump," *Esquire,* August 2004, 74.

8. Francine Prose, "Voting Democracy Off the Island: Reality TV and the Republican Ethos," *Harper's,* March 2004, 60.

9. Jonathan Bignell, *An Introduction to Television Studies* (New York: Routledge, 2004), 202.

10. Ray Richmond, "Directing for Reality TV," *DGA Magazine,* July 2004, 33.

9 | unreal tv

Rhonda Wilcox

> Buffy, I believe the subtext here is rapidly becoming text.
>
> —Buffy's mentor Giles, in *Buffy the Vampire Slayer*[1]

In the last decade of the twentieth and the first decade of the twenty-first century, series such as *Buffy the Vampire Slayer, The X-Files, Twin Peaks, Northern Exposure, Xena: Warrior Princess, Star Trek: The Next Generation, Lois and Clark, Nowhere Man, Roswell, Smallville,* and *Angel* have explored new genre territory. Earlier forms of the pattern appeared in the 1980s with *Max Headroom, Moonlighting,* and *Remington Steele.* These series, while practicing what *Buffy* creator Joss Whedon calls "emotional realism,"[2] also contain elements of the unreal, whether fantasy, science fiction, the supernatural, or the surreal (cf. literary magical realism). These unreal elements are used not merely for plot convenience or escapist action but to layer the series with symbolic depth: as in traditional literature,[3] symbols in these shows constitute a means of exploring themes not immediately apparent on the surface, in the plot and dialogue. The series also generally display self-awareness of textuality fueled by hybridization of genres (detective, horror, comedy, soap opera, etc.) and paralleled by an awareness of social influences.[4] The social issues are often represented symbolically (monsters such as *Twin Peaks'* BOB or *Buffy's* vampires). This symbolic representation and play of self-reference invoke active television viewing; in turn, these series are most likely to be associated with fan followings of great numbers and intensity.[5]

It is important to note that it is not the unreal elements themselves, but the way the series deals with them, that places a series in this genre. Not all science fiction series, for instance, fit into this category. A case in point: the Joss Whedon series *Firefly* (2002) is wonderfully realized science fiction, with well-developed characters, thoughtfully explored themes, exciting plots, and great visual appeal. It is not, however, Unreal TV. As Whedon has stated, it is not "metaphor" television. *Firefly* invites immersion in its world rather than consciousness of its created nature. Unreal TV engages the audience's awareness of the nature of the television creation.

But it should also be recognized that the aesthetic experience of Unreal TV is not a simple puncturing of the surface, a popping of the balloon of fiction. Instead, it involves the pleasure of a balancing of immersion and awareness. On the other side from *Firefly, The Simpsons* (1989–), a complex marvel of extratextual allusions and self-referential games, does not fit in the category of Unreal TV simply because, as a cartoon, it disallows such immersion. Similarly, *Monty Python's Flying Circus* invites viewers to play with various levels of reality (including the incorporation of cartoon) and bases its humor in detachment. However, comedy itself is not an automatic excluding factor, as *Buffy* and *Moonlighting* demonstrate. Again in contrast to *The Simpsons* and *Monty Python,* Unreal TV's potential for audience immersion comes in part because most of these series have a long-term narrative, whether it accrues incrementally (as with *Star Trek: The Next Generation*) or episode by episode (as with *Twin Peaks*).[6]

Because Unreal series present believable characters in emotionally dynamic relationships, it is possible to enjoy Coleridge's willing suspension of disbelief and at the same time to know (with an almost biblical entry into postlapsarian awareness, a loss of televisual innocence) the enjoyment of the construction of the text. The queering of reality, one might call it. So-called reality TV pretends to convey an unmanipulated record of the world (though many a viewer knows otherwise). Unreal TV is at once more modest and more artful in its recognition that it is text. Jim Collins argues for the importance of postmodernism in understanding the significance of shows like *Twin Peaks,* though he acknowledges "the divergent, often contradictory ways the term [postmodernism] has been employed." He notes the "hyperconsciousness" and the "tonal oscillation and generic amalgamation"[7] characteristic of many of these series. However, a viewer's recognition of the use of pervasive symbolism (typically modernist rather than postmodern) can also invoke consciousness of the text. And, in fact, many of these series use both

While practicing what creative producer Joss Whedon calls "emotional realism," *Buffy the Vampire Slayer* also contains elements of the unreal, whether fantasy, science fiction, the supernatural, or the surreal. (Left to right) Sarah Michelle Gellar as Buffy Summers and David Boreanaz as Angel. Courtesy of 20th Century Fox Television.

symbolism and self-reference as well as other means to consciousness of the text. John Fiske in *Television Culture* praises the fact that television viewers can see so many different meanings—can read the signs of television in so many different ways; polysemy is democratic, he suggests.[8] But Unreal TV viewers recognize that there are not just signs—or accidental leaks of meaning—but symbols and authorially purposeful play of thought in these series.

Interpreting symbols or contemplating self-reference—both involve active viewing. And, again, these series offer emotional connection to vivid, often mythic characters. It is therefore not surprising that many of these series have strong fan reactions. Of course, it might also be said that such series in any case require smart audiences, so that the active audience response is almost a given. *Moonlighting* was the subject of many a watercooler conversation. Even small Gordon College in Barnesville, Georgia (population six thousand), had a *Twin Peaks* viewing and analysis club. *The X-Files* became famous for its online X-philes discussion groups. *Northern Exposure* fans have an annual "Cicelian" meeting where copies of articles on the series are given away. One hardly needs to mention *Star Trek* conventions. *Buffy* has had not only fan conventions but full-fledged academic conferences devoted to it alone in three countries to date (England, Australia, and the United States). It could be argued that every fan fiction is an interpretation of a series,[9] and these series are preeminent among fan fiction (fanfiction.com listed more than fifteen thousand fan-authored short stories and novels on *Buffy* alone in 2003). Fans in all these contexts rejoice in the deeper meaning of the series and relish its discussion. With their balance between immersion and consciousness, Unreal TV series engage both feeling and thought.

Unreal TV series, through their construction, often confront issues of epistemology and related questions of identity. In fact, they engage the ancient theme of appearance versus reality in a world where more and more people recognize that social perceptions are constructed, and that what is shaped through the television box can be almost as limiting as Kantian forms of thought.[10]

In some cases the content of the series itself focuses on the media or more generally on the search for truth (or the question of whether truth is possible). Edison Carter/Max Headroom (like Kolchak before him) is a reporter, as are Lois and Clark and *Smallville*'s Chloe; Thomas Veil, the Nowhere Man, is a photojournalist. The second major profession representing the search for truth is that of detective: FBI agents Mulder and Scully, and *Twin Peaks'* Agent Cooper; Laura Holt and Remington Steele; Maddie Hayes and David Addison; Angel and the members of Angel Investigations. The *Star Trek* crews (especially *TNG*) and, arguably, Sam Beckett are more generally explorers. But the defining element in Unreal TV is that audiences participate in the search because meaning is conveyed through symbolism and self-conscious, often self-referential, form. The audience consciously collaborates in creating meaning. As Fiske and others note, the audience always participates in making meaning, but with Unreal TV both viewers and creators acknowledge and use that fact.

The themes to be derived from this operation (explored more specifically later in the chapter) are diverse in kind: worldly wise doubt and skepticism about the face that the world presents (*Max Headroom, The X-Files, Nowhere Man*) or a joyful sense of empowering play in recognizing (and, in a way, taking control of) the means of production (*Moonlighting, Northern Exposure, Buffy*).

Given that Unreal TV viewers are highly conscious of the series' construction (while still emotionally engaged with the content), it is not surprising that they are particularly aware of the role of the series' creators. Unreal TV tends to be auteur TV,[11] starting with the granddaddy of TV auteurs, Rod Serling. Joss Whedon of *Buffy* and *Angel;* Glenn Gordon Caron of *Moonlighting* (and, earlier, *Remington Steele*); J. Michael Straczynski of *Babylon 5;* of course, David Lynch and Mark Frost of *Twin Peaks;* Chris Carter of *The X-Files;* Joshua Brand and John Falsey, Columbia graduates like their Dr. Fleischman of *Northern Exposure;* and, not to be forgotten, Gene Roddenberry of *Star Trek*—these are among the names of television artists whose work is recognized by active viewers. As TV audiences become more and more sophisticated, and recording systems make re-viewing and locating episodes easier, TV creators can extend the collaborative exploration implicit in the emotional and formal challenges of Unreal TV.

The roots of the genre, however, go back to the 1950s. *The Twilight Zone* (1959–65) and *The George Burns and Gracie Allen Show* (1950–58) are both grandparents in the family of Unreal TV. It is well-known that Rod Serling used *The Twilight Zone* to teach social lessons through symbolism. "The Eye of the Beholder" warns against prejudice and judging by appearances; "Monsters Are Due on Maple Street" shows the effect of McCarthyist attitudes;[12] "After Hours" shows a young woman that she is no more than a mannequin. Race, politics, gender issues, and more are conveyed in Serling's symbolism. George Burns, on the other

Moonlighting has long been acknowledged for its formal experimentation and self-reflexivity, as in this dream sequence featuring Ray Charles and the Rayettes. (Left to right) Front row: Ray Charles and Bruce Willis as David Addison Jr.; second row: the Rayettes. Courtesy of ABC Circle Films.

hand, keeps company with Luigi Pirandello as he breaks the fourth wall to address the audience.[13] *Star Trek* (1966–69) and *The Avengers* (1966–69) can be seen as parents representing the symbolic and self-referential sides of the family. *Star Trek* was beloved by fans not just because of the pleasurable (if episodic) interplay of the characters but also because the show clearly conveyed symbolic meaning.[14] The bridge of the starship *Enterprise*—on which were to be found women, blacks, even, during the cold war, Russians—represented the integrated society we could achieve. Conflict was symbolically displaced onto battles with aliens, and the half-alien Spock was a constant (and popular) reminder of the need to accept the Other in ourselves.[15] *The Avengers,* on the other hand, played with reality. With a succession of female leads, it became most famous when starring Patrick Macnee and Diana Rigg as John Steed and Mrs. Emma Peel, the perfect exemplars of upper-class British civilization—and Mrs. Peel in particular the admired representative of the active, intelligent modern woman. Each week they triumphed; yet the presentation of their enterprises was so stylized and their opponents were often made so ludicrous[16] as to suggest that such success was indeed a fantasy of an earlier British social system.[17] A similar effect regarding the United States and the fantasy of the success of its agents could be seen in *The Man from U.N.C.L.E.* (1964–68). These series provided the pleasure of the triumph of the protagonists while at the same time seeming to wink at the audience with the realization that the world is not so simple, the battle not so easy. Their playfulness can be seen more clearly by contrast with the more realistic *Secret Agent* (1965–66), starring Patrick McGoohan, which, however, gave way to *The Prisoner* (1968–69), created, produced, and written by and starring McGoohan, a story of the Kafkaesque life into which a man is thrust when he wants out of the world of espionage.[18] *The Prisoner,* a memorable creation, is arguably too clearly allegorical to produce that double consciousness characteristic of Unreal TV. The Unreal TV experience involves both suspension in the fiction and realization of the fictional construct. It is debatable whether *The Prisoner* allows sophisticated viewers ever to escape the consciousness that they are watching an artifact of the imagination. However, whether or not it stands firmly within the genre, it can certainly be seen as an antecedent series (see, for example, *Nowhere Man,* discussed later).

The seventies had less to offer, but they did bring a crotchety uncle to the family with *Kolchak: The Night Stalker* (1974–75), starring Darren McGavin. McGavin's Kolchak was a crime reporter, and, as Brooks and Marsh say, "If he was sent to cover a crooked politician, he would find that the man had sold his soul to the Devil—literally"[19]—compare *Buffy the Vampire Slayer's* Mayor Wilkins. *The X-Files'* creator, Chris Carter, cited *Kolchak* as inspiration and had McGavin appear on his series. Kolchak had difficulty getting his stories into print, and like characters in *The X-Files,* he perceived media and governmental suppression of the truth, supporting viewers who questioned the constructed nature of public information. And like *The X-Files, Kolchak* used paranormal experiences to symbolize social issues—again, engaging active viewing.

In the 1980s, television producers crossed the detective show with romantic comedy to produce *Remington Steele* (1982–87) and *Moonlighting* (1985–89). The two were so clearly related that they were originally counterprogrammed, both being broadcast at 10:00 Tuesdays at the beginning of *Moonlighting*'s run. *Moonlighting* has long been acknowledged for its experimentation; little scholarly attention has been given to *Remington Steele*. Yet they are in some ways mirrors of each other in their textual playfulness. Each series links the finite mystery of a detective story with the infinite mystery of an unresolved relationship; both explore, in their different ways, the consciousness of illusion.[20]

In *Remington Steele,* Laura Holt has constructed an imaginary male boss, Remington Steele, in order to attract to her detective agency clients who might doubt the abilities of a woman. She has been hired to guard jewels that a mystery man is trying to steal for a foreign government. In a scene straight out of Hitchcock's *North by Northwest,* the mystery man answers a telephone page for the illusory Steele in order to escape pursuit by killers. Attracted to Laura, he proceeds to attempt to inhabit the role of Steele permanently. No one knows this Remington Steele's real past—and as the series evolves, we learn that even he does not know his real identity, and is (mythically enough) searching for his father. While Laura Holt, a math major (cf. Emma Peel) and a highly logical person, uses her detective training, Steele attempts to (and sometimes does) solve crimes by identifying the events of the episode with stories from old movies. But the movie references pervade the series in more than one way. They can be overt or covert. In "Steele Flying High," the characters compare the events to *The Maltese Falcon.* In "Thou Shalt Not Steele," on the other hand, a Mr. Gutman tells Steele, "Your foolishness has exhausted my patience"—but the connection to *The Maltese Falcon* is left to the audience to make; the film is never named in that episode. Similarly, "You're Steele the One for Me" opens with a Shinto shrine version of the funeral scene from *Charade.* Alert audience members can see that the parallel has been made, but the characters do not. However, the fact that the characters often *do* search for parallels to movie scenes means that the audience is more alert to them as well. And the whole series focuses on both Laura Holt and the mystery man dealing with the illusion of the nature of identity in the shape of "Remington

Steele." The second season's credit sequence illustrates the theme: Laura Holt is seated alone in a movie theater; in comes a man in a tux, her invention, "Remington Steele." They watch the screen, edged by red velvet curtains, observing as scenes from their own lives unreel in film. At the end, we see Steele without the draperies. He has become real. How real is he, though? A later episode is an extended dream sequence after Laura Holt is hit on the head; her hallucinations make clear her uncertainty about her partner. But how real is the identity any of us creates? We have watched the opening credits on-screen just as they have watched themselves; we are perhaps in their position in more ways than we realize. *Remington Steele's* play with identity, illusion, and reality is much more complex than is generally acknowledged.

One of the writers for *Remington Steele* is the man who created *Moonlighting,* Glenn Gordon Caron. Perhaps this accounts for the fact that the heroes of the two series are Addison and Steele—the names of the two authors of the pertinently titled eighteenth-century *Spectator* essays. *Moonlighting,* as many viewers remember, is a highly self-conscious series. While in *Remington Steele* the man was the good-looking front for the detective agency, in *Moonlighting* this is the woman's job (though she is also an active manager); photos of a younger Cybill Shepherd from her own modeling career form part of the text, complicating the nature of the representation.[21] The experienced detective Addison is in his own way a mythic figure, a trickster. The exuberance of Caron's/Bruce Willis's Addison was such that he broke not only social but also textual bonds: like George Burns, he directly addressed the audience. "They're gonna move us to cable," he warns with a smirk in "Portrait of Maddie." Other characters break the fourth wall, but Addison/Willis does so most often. The show became more and more overtly self-conscious. "The Straight Poop" is constructed around interviews by a real interviewer with not only cast members but others, such as an uncredited Pierce Brosnan from *Remington Steele,* saying that he and Maddie had almost worked together. "The Dream Sequence Always Rings Twice" sets up the characters to live through a film noir episode; it is introduced by Orson Welles warning the audience not to be surprised when their screen goes black and white twelve minutes into the episode. "Big Man on Mulberry Street" presents a musical dance sequence choreographed by Stanley Donen. Perhaps the single most famous episode is "Atomic Shakespeare," in which we see a dream version of *The Taming of the Shrew,* with Maddie as Kate and Dave as Petruchio. Occasionally the narrative per se finishes before the end of the episode, and we are addressed by the characters—Maddie and Dave talking, for instance, with the writers—as if they, and not Cybill Shepherd and Bruce Willis, incarnated the parts. Mr. Pirandello, here we come.

The artificiality of TV as a medium is represented very differently on *Max Headroom* (1987). The epistemological search here is headed not by a detective but by a crime reporter, Edison Carter. The series is memorably set "twenty minutes into the future," as the screen announces to us—and a dystopic future it is, with hordes of homeless, body banks where whole (and not-quite-dead) bodies can be bought or sold, and television networks that literally kill for ratings. Whereas *Remington Steele* uses film references, in *Max Headroom* the subject is TV. The heroic Edison risks his life for a story—but even the best-known reporter of the network is controlled and may be tossed away (in the pilot, he is dumped in a body bank) if he strays outside the prescribed lines. External visuals of the city and elements of the music evoke Ridley Scott's *Blade Runner* (1982). Edison Carter shares the blade runner's noir experience; the series also emulates the movie in its contemplation of the nature of identity, of the artificial and the real. Our point of view shifts from screen to screen—we see the standard omniscient narrator view of the series; we see an old woman's face distorted through Edison's television lens as he interviews her (and we later see her undistorted image as she manages the body bank); we and the newsroom "controller" see what Edison sees through his screen as he moves through the news site and the controller accesses banks of computers to advise him. Later we see the secret screens of the network executives, who observe from behind the television screen to see a viewer literally destroyed by watching what the executives have broadcast. Superfast commercial images, Blipverts, will detonate the head of a sedentary viewer: couch potatoes, be warned. It is when Edison learns of this and tries to break the story that he is endangered. Trying to escape from the thugs of his own corporation, Edison hits his head on the parking garage exit arm, marked to indicate its maximum headroom. In an attempt to discover how much the now unconscious Edison knows, the corporation's boy genius, Bryce, creates an artificial reconstruction of Edison's mind, which calls itself Max Headroom. Max, head and shoulders only, appears on the computer screen. He is perfectly willing to speak freely—too willing; of the network executives, he asks, "You mean you're the people who execute audiences?" Like the person from whom he is derived, Max strays outside the boundaries, escaping into computers all over the city. He seems to be in some ways an id version of Edison.

That the Max Headroom creation, originally placed in a story about the mental manipulation of TV commercials, was later widely used in a soft drink commercial campaign gives one pause. Edison is in some ways a cyborg; his camera and his computer input are parts of him that he plugs in and out of. When a careless "controller" cuts him off from his "feed," street toughs almost kill him. When Edison is cut off from the corporate teat, he is dead. A new, more intelligent controller (Amanda Pays) and others save him, but they have to bring him back inside the system to do so. Id-like Max is the only one who remains free, and it is a circumscribed freedom. The resolution seems right for the dark and yet nonetheless heroic and humorous presentation of the world in this series.

Cynicism had no place in the show that premiered later in the same year as *Max Headroom*—*Star Trek: The Next Generation* (1987–94). Fans had been waiting almost twenty years for the rebirth of *Star Trek*. Although the series did not hit its stride as quickly as *Max Headroom,* over the long run it did impressive work. Like the original *Star Trek, TNG* traded in the coin of symbolism. More than the original *Star Trek,* it also played with levels of reality. The symbolism continued the old themes of tolerance and exploration—and of accepting the Other: eight decades after the original, the bridge crew now included a Klingon.[22] A major symbol was the use of the android character Data to represent oppressed minorities.[23] In an echo of the Dred Scott case, he underwent a trial to determine, as Whoopi Goldberg's character, Guinan, pointed out, whether he should be considered "property"; and the android child Data created was, in effect, sold down the river. Data is just one example of the series' many symbols. An interesting addition to the *Star Trek* world was the holodeck, the holographic entertainment area. Through it, characters were enabled to explore other styles of drama—à la *Moonlighting*—as the captain pretended to be a Raymond Chandler–like detective, Data played Sherlock Holmes, or Will Riker, second in command, visited a Bourbon Street bar. The holodeck was, symbolically, a door into characters' subconscious. The series also used it to question characters' views of reality: in particular, there is a string of holodeck episodes in which several of the male characters are in effect taken to task for creating and desiring the twenty-fourth-century equivalent of balloon sex dolls, rather than the real women of the *Enterprise* ("11001001," "Booby Trap," "Hollow Pursuits").[24]

But there are even more complex and intriguing investigations of reality in *TNG*. Shakespearean actor Patrick Stewart, the new captain, was in the original 1977 cast of Tom Stoppard's *Every Good Boy Deserves*

Favour, a play in which audience members, like the characters, are sometimes unclear about whether the main character is or is not hallucinating. In 1993 Stewart arranged a touring production featuring *TNG* actors. *EGBDF* and the May 1993 episode "Frame of Mind," both featuring Jonathan Frakes (Riker) as a political prisoner in an insane asylum, repeatedly test reality. These two extratextually related productions—both of which would have been known to serious fans of the series—constitute an exceptionally complex intellectual creation.[25] This *Star Trek* was going where no series had gone before. Other *ST* series included social symbolism—the representation by *Star Trek: Deep Space Nine* (1993–99) of the Palestinians' troubles through the Bajorans, for instance, or in the Maquis of *Star Trek: Voyager* (1995–2001). But no later *ST* series surpassed the combination of symbolism and textual interplay to be found in *TNG*.

There has probably never been a stranger or more beautiful television series than David Lynch and Mark Frost's *Twin Peaks* (1990–91).[26] At first it seems intensely realistic, as we watch two parents painfully learn of the death of their daughter. But *Twin Peaks* is a mythic place, and it will be entered by a mythic hero—Agent Dale Cooper,[27] whose name suggests Fenimore Cooper and his descriptions of the wild American forests.[28] The town of Twin Peaks seems a place of old-fashioned values—everyone is shocked by the death of Laura Palmer—but it is on the border of "una selva oscura," Dante's dark wood in which we can so easily lose our way. It is the dark wood into which Hester Prynne strays with her lover; and in fact young Audrey Horne calls herself Hester Prynne when she crosses the border to try to discover Laura's killer. It would be very difficult to briefly express the combination of wholesomeness and peculiarity, of innocence and the recognition of perversion, that constitutes *Twin Peaks*. The entire series seems like a dream; "my dream is a code waiting to be broken," says Agent Cooper.

The opening credits, unlike those of most TV series, do not introduce us to the faces of the regulars; instead, we see the place, and iconic, symbolic images associated with it: the wheels of the sawmill machinery slowly grind and spark, like the wheels of fate. In Agent Cooper's dream, the dead girl (or is it just someone who looks like her?) whispers the name of her killer; neither he nor we can hear—nor did her friends and family really hear the troubled Laura when she was alive. The solemnity of the series is complicated with strange humor. One of the saddest moments is a distorted echo of Ophelia's funeral from *Hamlet:* at Laura's funeral, too, young men fight over her, and a man—her father—flings himself onto her coffin. But the next day the waitress Shelley, in the diner, brings two old men to loud laughter as she uses a napkin dispenser and the edge of her counter to demonstrate how the coffin mechanism jammed, moving up and down in a grotesque echo of a lovers' bouncing bed, as the grieving father held his daughter's coffin. Rewatching the scene after the discovery of the father's nature is an even stranger experience.[29] The series' own elements of soap opera are internally mocked by the *Invitation to Love* series watched by some of the characters—such as the waitress Shelley. And the mocking waitress is herself the victim of abuse. *Twin Peaks* spins viewers like the blades of the fan in Laura Palmer's dark stairwell. Its mixture of styles repeatedly startles the audience into awareness of it as a textual creation, but the mystery of Laura Palmer's murder is so captivating that the audience is never released from its power.

When *Northern Exposure* (1990–95) was first broadcast, it was often compared to *Twin Peaks*. Both were set in woodsy small towns populated by quirky characters and visited by a big-city outsider as central character—a character who, it was clear, would learn the value of woodsy ways. But *Twin Peaks* is in many ways tragic, while *Northern Exposure* is essentially a comedy—though, as with most of these series, they mix genres. Instead of a detective as a central character, *Northern Exposure* has a doctor. Dr. Joel Fleischman—or Flesh-man—needed to be taught the ways of the spirit.[30] His relationship with Maggie O'Connell is emblematic. He at first assumes she wants him (in fact, he originally mistakes her for a prostitute), but "In your dreams, Fleischman," she tells him repeatedly. He, she, and other characters learn about their spiritual natures through the symbols of their dreams. The series also plays textually self-conscious games—sometimes lighthearted ones, such as a scene in which characters snap their fingers to music from Agent Cooper's *Twin Peaks* dream. Sometimes the silliness has a sharp point: in one of Dr. Fleischman's dreams, he is surrounded by beautiful women gyrating to the music of a rock song—but when the music stops and the gyrations continue, the ridiculousness of his fantasy is exposed. The series as a whole includes many Jungian/Campbellian images, sometimes overtly commented on by the philosophical radio DJ Chris Stephens. Maggie even has an encounter with, it seems, a mythic master bear, a shape-changing figure of male power. Fleischman and O'Connell seem in many ways mythically oppositional—animus/anima, male/female, rational/passionate, city/country, Jewish/Christian, cautious/bold. But there is often a twist; for instance, in most myths the sky is father and the

Northern Exposure was a fanciful and self-aware dramedy set in Cicely, Alaska, a town full of lovable eccentrics. (Left to right) Janine Turner as Maggie O'Connell and Rob Morrow as Dr. Joel Fleischman. Courtesy of Universal TV.

earth is mother—but Maggie, the bush pilot, is the sky woman. Their relationship, a mixture of myth and soap opera, is symbolically central to the series, though other characters have their spiritual quests, too. But this is also a series about a place: Cicely, Alaska, is a small town that was founded by pure-natured and loving lesbians and is now populated by Thoreauvian individualists. The town itself symbolizes the liberal American desideratum.

A completely different view of the world can be found in *The X-Files* (1993–2002). While Dr. Joel Fleischman needed to learn to slow down, open his heart, and trust other people, the well-known motto of *The X-Files* is "Trust No One." If the town of Twin Peaks was full of secrets, it is now the body of FBI Agent Dana Scully[31] and the mind of Agent Fox Mulder that represent the mystery; her body and his mind have been tampered with by conspiratorial forces. But this is the late *X-Files*. In the early *X-Files*, Agent Scully and Agent Mulder were brilliant and active. Their open interchange of views was stimulating, especially given that Scully took the skeptical position traditionally associated with males, and Mulder was the believer. *Twin Peaks'* Cooper, who is willing to use a deductive method that came to him in a dream, is Mulder's direct predecessor—the man who recognizes the nonrational elements of life. When Scully asked (as she often did), "What do you think?" and Mulder answered, "I think I want to see what's in that cellar," we knew the cellar symbolized the hidden places they were willing to enter—whether the darkness of political conspiracies, the uncertainties of the paranormal, or the dimness of the subconscious. The quintessential *X-Files* image shows Scully and Mulder with their flashlights in the dark, looking for those answers that symbolized so much more than the solution to a case.[32]

In "One Breath," from the second season, Scully's mother recalls aloud a story of Scully's youth. There is a snake and a loss of innocence, but the Garden of Eden story is reversed: Scully tries to save the snake. Catholic though she is, the character does not accept the patriarchal story. At the end of the pilot episode, Scully and Mulder gaze at each other through a one-way mirror. He is in the interrogation room with someone who may be an alien abductee, while she (originally sent to observe Mulder) is in the observation room with the company men, the men in suits; through the glass, darkly, Mulder and Scully look each other in the eye. That one of those suits is the show's chief villain, the cigarette-smoking man, is part of the symbolism. It is only too appropriate that the man who runs a government conspiracy should indulge in tobacco, the harmfulness of which was hidden for years by cigarette companies. Or consider the fate of a woman who sells out to the suits in order to advance her career: by the end of the episode, she has been transformed into a puddle of goo. In the first years of the series, symbolism was dominant. In later years, metatextual episodes became more prevalent—episodes like "Postmodern Prometheus" (a play on *Frankenstein*'s subtitle), loved by some fans and hated by others. The best representative of the latter type was perhaps writer Darin Morgan's "Jose Chung's *From Outer Space*," about the construction of a best seller telling the story of an abduction with *Rashomon*-style variations in viewpoint. The ultimate resolution is irresolute, as was typical of many of the best episodes of *The X-Files;* the longing for closure, narrative or epistemological, is not to be answered. What the truth is we cannot know. *The X-Files,* most fans agree, stayed on the air too long. There were factual contradictions in the increasingly byzantine story line; long past the point of logic, Scully questioned what she had experienced; and David Duchovny's Fox Mulder left the series. But at its height, *The X-Files* presented a powerfully emotional story enriched by culturally resonant symbols. How, indeed, do we deal with the alien?

The X-Files was a cult favorite that advised its viewers to "trust no one." At its height, the series presented a powerfully emotional story line enriched by culturally resonant symbols. (Left to right) Gillian Anderson as Dana Scully and David Duchovny as Fox Mulder. Courtesy of David Gray/Fox Broadcasting.

The darkness of the alien within was rarely touched on in *Lois and Clark: The New Adventures of Superman* (1993–98). Clark Kent, Superman, was indeed an alien, but he was completely benign. Series creator Deborah Joy Levine chose an interesting path with her villain, however; she made the traditionally bald Lex Luthor a devilishly attractive tycoon. And by the end of the first season she had made clear that her Lex Luthor was a Lucifer figure, the appropriate opponent for the "god in a cape" ("Witness").[33] From the start of the series, Lex had spoken of the importance of taking the high ground, and at season's end Lucifer had his fall—metaphorically as the character was arrested; literally, as he intentionally (like his angelic counterpart) plunged from the skyscraper site of what was to have been his wedding to Lois. The series also, like *Remington Steele* before it, purposefully explored the idea of role playing, particularly in terms of relationships between men and women. "We all wear disguises—don't you?" says Lois to the unnecessarily bespectacled Clark in the appropriately titled "I'm Looking Through You." The series played with self-reference, too. "He comes from Smallville," complains Lois in the pilot; "I couldn't *make* that name up." After a supposed Lois and Clark wedding episode in which the wedding did not transpire, the real wedding episode was titled "Swear to God, This Time We're Not Kidding." Though the series weakened as Levine's input was lessened, it is (again like *Remington Steele*) underestimated in terms of the grace and thoughtfulness of its early episodes. The dance of metaphor and language reflect the dance of the couple's relationship.

Babylon 5 (1994–98) is best known as a "saga"—a full-length, complex story of a microcosmic space station (named in the title) written by J. Michael Straczynski. Often compared to Russian novels such as *War and Peace, B5* is not at first glance a candidate for categorization as Unreal TV. But its space station represents the interaction of difference—like a messier (and much bigger) bridge of the *Enterprise.* Minbari/ human Delenn, like Spock, explores the alien within. And, as Petra Kuppers argues in *Cult Television,* the active relationship between JMS (Straczynski's online signature) and fans illuminates self-reference in the text. Thus, in the episode "View from the Gallery," two dockworkers hold, in effect, the position of viewers as they comment on the characters during their workday (a pattern *Buffy* later uses as well).[34] All these series are most fully visible to those who know the whole text, and that is perhaps more important for *B5* than for any other series but *Buffy.*

Nowhere Man (1995–96) does not tend toward self-referential remarks and is not peppered with symbols, but its overall premise is unquestionably symbolic: the search for identity. Fans of the series from the start compared it to *The Prisoner.* Its protagonist and only regular character was given the symbolic name of Thomas Veil, and he did spend his life trying to pierce the veils of illusion. In the first episode, audiences saw photojournalist Veil become the victim of an elaborate conspiracy. He had taken a photograph of four hanged men, and apparently it conveyed dangerous information. Emerging from a restaurant men's room, he finds his wife has disappeared and all record of his life has been erased. The conspiracy elements resonated with the audience during this time of *The X-Files;* in fact, the show was scored by *X-Files* composer Mark Snow. Like Dr. Richard Kimble in *The Fugitive,* Veil wandered from place to place, but his world was much darker and more nightmarish. He questioned—especially at the end—even his own understanding of self. The character balances on the edge between symbol and person.

Nowhere Man is different from *Quantum Leap* (1989–93), another series in which the protagonist in a sense loses himself. In *Quantum Leap,* the central character is named for the famous absurdist playwright

Samuel Beckett, and Dr. Sam Beckett's situation does have absurdist elements. A physicist (among other things), he has discovered how to travel in time—but is bouncing uncontrollably from within one human to another. He experiences the world as a black man during segregation, as a pregnant woman, as a rape victim; clearly the central metaphor is to see the world from another's eyes.[35] Though Sam initiated the leaping, he does not control the way it proceeds. In effect, as his holographic companion, Al, tells him, when Sam corrects a wrong, God sends him on to the next job, the next person to aid. In the end (to the fury of many a "Leaper" fan), Sam chooses selflessness and never returns home. In the same subcategory one might place *John Doe* (2002–3), in which a man found literally adrift, at sea, is discovered to have an almost un-limited, cyborg-like memory of facts—though he cannot remember his own past: modern life is often filled with a jumble of facts and no real sense of reality. In terms of Unreal TV, these three are all borderline series, each based on the search for identity but without a pervasive use of other symbols or self-reference.

Xena: Warrior Princess (1995–2000) at first glance seems strictly fan-tasy. Strong, dark warrior woman Xena is accompanied on her picaresque journeys by small, blonde Gabrielle. Xena hobnobs with the likes of Hercules (the show is a spin-off from *Hercules: The Legendary Journeys* [1994–99]), Ares, and Aphrodite. But the show was, as many fans soon discovered, clearly self-conscious in its playful anachronisms and queer text clues. Many fans have expressed pleasure in the double entendres and intimate scenes that hint at a sexual relationship between Xena and Gabrielle without making it overt. It is not simply the possibility of lesbian relationship but the textual tease that gives pleasure as well. The series' self-consciousness can be seen in other ways, too: like *Moonlight-ing* (and later *Buffy*), it experiments with formal variations, most nota-bly in "Bitter Suite," a punningly titled operatic musical episode in which Xena and Gabrielle sing out their painful differences with each other.[36]

Buffy the Vampire Slayer (1997–2003), like *Xena*, features a strong female hero and a highly developed formal consciousness. The balance between immersion and self-consciousness is exquisitely maintained in *Buffy*. Buffy, a California teen whom we meet when she is sixteen, moves to adulthood in the series' seven seasons. Her character follows the pat-tern of the hero's journey so well described by Joseph Campbell, and in that sense the central character is herself symbolic.[37] Even an ordinary-seeming teen fights a heroic struggle every day. Furthermore, Buffy (as creator Whedon made very clear) represented every woman who stands up for herself—the repudiation of the victimized female of standard horror. Campbell might have been surprised to see the hero's journey taken by a feminist character over the course of seven years. Another large symbolic pattern especially focused on in the early years is that adults often do not recognize the monsters teens are facing.[38] The daring language used by the characters in *Buffy*, often commented on in the press, represents both the characters' willingness to be different, to break rules, and the communication divide with adults.[39] As for the monsters facing teens, specific symbols invest specific episodes: Internet predators are actual demons ("I Robot, You Jane"); a high school clique is a pack of hyenas ("The Pack"); and a girl finds that after she sleeps with a guy he turns into a monster ("Innocence"). The show never discursively preaches; fans enjoyed seeing the ideas embedded in symbolic relationships. Intratextual references through the course of the series—for example, dreams that predict events to occur years and seasons later—enrich the narrative, as do many intertextual references (a standard device of Unreal series such as *B5* and *TNG*) to sources as various as Shakespeare, Arthur Miller, Ingmar Bergman, and Stan Lee's *Spider-Man*. The show occasionally uses direct self-reference, but more notably displays its self-consciousness through formal experimentation— a mostly silent episode ("Hush"); an all-dream episode including Greek poetry, in Greek, and dream variations on *Apocalypse Now* ("Restless"); and, like *Moonlighting* and *Xena*, a musical episode—in this case, a full-fledged musical (in a sixty-eight-minute initial broadcast) composed by Whedon and performed by the regular cast with one Broadway guest (Hinton Battle).[40] The experiments are always vessels for the emotions of the characters. Thus, for *Buffy*, analysis of form leads to understanding of feeling.[41]

Angel (1999–2004), a *Buffy* spin-off, continued the symbolic exploration of meaning from a largely male-centered perspective—but challenging the traditional male stance, as *Buffy* challenged the female.[42] During the first season, when both series were on the same network, they were run back-to-back. Other shows with spin-offs had arranged character crossovers before, but when *Buffy* and *Angel* did crossovers, they were broadcasting something very like two-hour movies. Angel, a vampire with a soul, had loved Buffy, but the perfect joy of their first (and, depending on your interpretation, only) lovemaking results in the activation of a clause of a gypsy curse: Angel keeps his soul only so long as it torments him for his past deeds. Faust-like, he is damned if he ever reaches satisfaction, if he ever stops questing. Accompanying him on his quest (and in a paranormal detective agency) are, among others, *Buffy* expatriates ex–rich bitch Cordelia and (after the death of the half-demon Doyle) the failed demon hunter Wesley and, by the end of the first season, street vampire fighter Gunn, one of the rare African Americans in these series, which usually treat race symbolically. With fewer formal experiments than *Buffy*, *Angel* is almost as symbolically redolent—and within a darker context often recognized as vampire noir.[43]

Roswell (1999–2002), while it had even less of *Buffy*'s formal experimentation, did begin with a thoroughgoing use of symbolism. Though its symbolism was not as wide-ranging as that of some other series, it was an intense representation of a coming-of-age story and of sexual awakening. Telepathic connection and physical healing link the two central teens, the journal-keeping science student and occasional narrator Liz and the secretly alien (read: every teen feels like the different one) Max. Widely referred to in the press as a *Romeo and Juliet* story, the series even made use of a balcony for Liz, and the weaker second season explored *Hamlet* imagery with Max as an undecided prince denied his alien throne. Curiously, *Roswell* has something in common with *Twin Peaks:* though it certainly does not have the earlier series' sophistication of tonal variation or visual and musical stylistic interplay, both seem to wind through their central symbolic quests in sixteen or seventeen episodes. In episode 17 of *Twin Peaks,* Agent Cooper solves Laura Palmer's murder and leads her father toward the light; in episode 16 of *Roswell,* Liz and Max reach an illuminating symbolic sexual culmination in the desert dark and return hand in hand to face their parents in the morning—defying the *Romeo and Juliet* analogy. *The X-Files'* director of photography John Bartley, who worked on *Roswell* for its first season, sometimes made fading into the blinding light of the desert as visually emblematic of the quest for knowledge as he had *The X-Files'* searching in the dark.

Smallville (2001–), like *Buffy* (for its first five years), *Angel,* and *Roswell* (for its first two years), was a WB Network series. This series certainly played with intertextual references, particularly drawing on the rich lineage of Superman. Smallville's Mayor Siegel, for instance, recalls Jerry Siegel, Superman's cocreator. But like most other such WB series, this show's main unreal emphasis was symbolism. Early promotional ads featured Clark, red *S* on his chest, hanging from a cross in a cornfield; Remy Zero sings, "Somebody save me," in the theme song, and Clark is marked as a savior/Christ figure who would suffer for others. Metaphor is rampant, particularly in the early episodes. A hot-tempered football coach literally sends out flames in "Hot-Head"; an old man who wants to recapture his youth literally rejuvenates (and wastes life again) in "Hourglass"; a stressed student aiming for a scholarship literally clones himself to cover his schedule in "Dichotic." In "Rosetta," a noteworthy instance of intertextuality occurs when Christopher Reeve, star of several Superman movies, plays a scientist who advises Clark about his future. The recently deceased Reeve sounds a note against "Superman" hubris in the intertextual subtext.

By the time this book reaches print, there will surely be more such shows, but the ones discussed in this chapter are among the most notable examples of a category that seems to have successfully established itself—and that seems likely to continue. As the series discussed here indicate, Unreal TV includes some remarkable work. This genre, at its best, has produced some of the most inventive and culturally rich programs over the last generation.

Notes

1. David Greenwalt and Joss Whedon, "Ted," season 2, episode 11, *Buffy the Vampire Slayer.*

2. Rhonda V. Wilcox and David Lavery, introduction, *Fighting the Forces: What's at Stake in* Buffy the Vampire Slayer (Lanham, Md.: Rowman and Littlefield, 2002), xxiv.

3. M. Keith Booker argues for considering four of the series discussed in this chapter (*The Twilight Zone, The Prisoner, Twin Peaks,* and *The X-Files*) as comparable to literature in *Strange TV: Innovative Television Series from "The Twilight Zone" to "The X-Files"* (Westport, Conn.: Greenwood Press, 2002), 2. He also discusses the series' "inherent intertextuality" (15) and postmodernism. See also Collins, note 7.

4. For an extended discussion of self-referentiality, see Michael Dunne, *Metapop: Self-Referentiality in Contemporary American Popular Culture* (Jackson: University Press of Mississippi, 1992); he includes an analysis of *Moonlighting*, 37–47. Robert J. Thompson, in his list of defining characteristics of "quality television," includes "memory" (narrative continuity), genre mixing, "literary and writer-based" work, "self-conscious[ness]," and a tendency toward the socially "controversial," in *Television's Second Golden Age: From "Hill Street Blues" to "ER"* (New York: Continuum, 1996), 14–15. On the application of these elements of Thompson's list, see also Wilcox and Lavery, introduction, xxi–xxiv.

5. For an analysis of fan responses that also includes discussion of characteristics of the text, see Sara Gwenllian-Jones and Roberta E. Pearson, eds., *Cult Television* (Minneapolis: University of Minnesota Press, 2004), with essays on *The Avengers, Babylon 5, Buffy the Vampire Slayer, Star Trek: The Next Generation,* and *The X-Files.* For some of the other notable discussions of fan reactions to Unreal

TV series, see also Camille Bacon-Smith, *Enterprising Women: Television Fandom and the Creation of Popular Myth* (Philadelphia: University of Pennsylvania Press, 1992), on *Star Trek;* Henry Jenkins, *Textual Poachers: Television Fans and Participatory Culture* (New York: Routledge, 1992), also on *Star Trek;* David Lavery, "Introduction: The Semiotics of Cobbler: *Twin Peaks'* Interpretive Community," in *Full of Secrets: Critical Approaches to "Twin Peaks,"* ed. David Lavery (Detroit, Mich.: Wayne State University Press, 1995), 1–21; Henry Jenkins, "'Do You Enjoy Making the Rest of Us Feel Stupid?': alt.tv.twinpeaks, The Trickster Author, and Viewer Mastery," also in *Full of Secrets,* 51–69; Jimmie L. Reeves, Mark C. Rodgers, and Michael Epstein, "Rewriting Popularity: The Cult Files," in *"Deny All Knowledge": Reading "The X-Files,"* ed. David Lavery, Angela Hague, and Marla Cartwright (Syracuse, N.Y.: Syracuse University Press, 1996), 22–35; Amanda Zweerink and Sarah N. Gatson, "www.buffy.com: Cliques, Boundaries, and Hierarchies in an Internet Community," in *Fighting the Forces: What's at Stake in* Buffy the Vampire Slayer, ed. Rhonda V. Wilcox and David Lavery (Lanham, Md.: Rowman and Littlefield, 2002), 239–50. There are many more such studies. For an analysis of the analyses (with a focus on *Star Trek* and *The X-Files*), see Matt Hills, *Fan Cultures* (London: Routledge, 2002).

6. On narrative, see Gwenllian-Jones and Pearson, introduction, xi–xii.

7. Jim Collins, "Postmodernism and Television," in *Channels of Discourse, Reassembled: Television and Contemporary Criticism,* 2nd ed., ed. Robert C. Allen (Chapel Hill: University of North Carolina Press, 1992), 327, 333, 347. On postmodernism and television, see also Booker, *Strange TV,* 22–48, and Douglas Kellner, "*The X-Files* and the Aesthetics and Politics of Postmodern Pop," *Journal of Aesthetics and Art Criticism* 57, no. 2 (1999): 161–75.

8. John Fiske, *Television Culture* (London: Routledge, 1987).

9. Useful discussions of the interpretive implications of fanfic are offered by Helen Caudill, "Tall, Dark and Dangerous: Xena, the Quest, and the Wielding of Sexual Violence in *Xena* On-Line Fan Fiction," in *Athena's Daughters: Television's New Women Warriors,* ed. Frances Early and Kathleen Kennedy (Syracuse, N.Y.: Syracuse University Press, 2003), 27–39, and Kristina Busse, "Crossing the Final Taboo: Family, Sexuality, and Incest in Buffyverse Fan Fiction," in Wilcox and Lavery, *Fighting the Forces,* 207–17.

10. Kant posited that minds can perceive only what they are, in effect, constructed to perceive. There is thus a parallel between the limitations of perception caused by the physical limits of the medium of television (the box) and the limits created by the guiding views constructed by enculturation. However, Kant referred to what he argued was an essential of epistemology, whereas the other limits mentioned here are in part subject to change potentially resulting from the self-consciousness of the percipient. See Immanuel Kant, *Critique of Pure Reason,* trans. J. M. D. Meiklejohn (London: Colonial Press, 1900), 21–23.

11. On the debate regarding the possibility of auteurism in television, see Hills, *Fan Culture,* 131–34.

12. Peter Wolfe, *In the Zone: The Twilight World of Rod Serling* (Bowling Green, Ohio: Bowling Green State University Popular Press, 1997), 11, 128–29.

13. Though she references Tom Stoppard rather than Pirandello, the point about the series' self-referentiality is made by Joann Gardner, "Self-Referentiality in Art: A Look at Three Television Situation Comedies of the 1950s," *Studies in Popular Culture* 11, no. 1 (1988): 35–43.

14. An early analysis of the symbolism of *Star Trek* can be found in Karin Blair, *Meaning in "Star Trek"* (New York: Warner, 1977).

15. Harvey R. Greenberg focuses on the significance for adolescents of grappling with a changing self-image via the symbol of the half-alien character in "In Search of Spock: A Psychoanalytic Inquiry," *Journal of Popular Film and Television* 12 (1984): 52–65.

16. On the stylization of the protagonists and antagonists, see Mark O'Day, "Of Leather Suits and Kinky Boots: *The Avengers,* Style, and Popular Culture," in *Action TV: Tough-Guys, Smooth Operators, and Foxy Chicks,* ed. Bill Osgerby and Anna Gough-Yates (London: Routledge, 2001), 221–28, 233.

17. For a Marxist interpretation, see David Buxton, *From "The Avengers" to "Miami Vice": Form and Ideology in Television Series* (Manchester: Manchester University Press, 1990), 90.

18. A good, relatively short analysis of multiple symbols in *The Prisoner* can be found in Booker, *Strange TV,* 71–96.

19. *The Complete Directory to Prime Time Network and Cable TV Shows 1946–Present,* 8th ed. (New York: Ballantine, 2003), 647.

20. On *Moonlighting*'s intertextuality, self-referentiality, hybridity, and fan reception, see J. P. Williams, "The Mystique of *Moonlighting:* When You Care Enough to Watch the Very Best," *Journal of Popular Film and Television* 16 (1988): 90–99. On *Remington Steele*'s self-referentiality, see Jane Feuer, "The MTM Style," in *MTM "Quality" Television,* ed. Jane Feuer, Paul Kerr, and Tise Vahimagi (London: British Film Institute, 1984), 48–50. On the self-referentiality of both series, see Rhonda V. Wilcox, "TV and the Curriculum: Contemporary Television as Valid Undergraduate Course Material," *Humanities in the South* 70 (Fall 1989): 6–8, 12.

21. On this particular type of intertextuality, see Hilary Radner, *Shopping Around: Feminine Culture and the Pursuit of Pleasure* (New York: Routledge, 1995), 52–65.

22. See Leah R. Vande Berg, "Worf as Metonymic Signifier of Racial, Cultural, and National Differences," in *Fantasy Girls: Gender in the New Universe of Science Fiction and Fantasy Television,* ed. Elyce Rae Helford (Lanham, Md.: Rowman and Littlefield, 2000), 51–68.

23. See Rhonda V. Wilcox, "Dating Data: Miscegenation in *Star Trek: The Next Generation,*" in Helford, *Fantasy Girls,* 69–92.

24. See Rhonda V. Wilcox, "Shifting Roles and Synthetic Women in *Star Trek: The Next Generation,*" *Studies in Popular Culture* 13, no. 2 (1991): 53–65.

25. Rhonda V. Wilcox, "Shakespeare, Stoppard, *Star Trek:* Bending the Fourth Wall" (paper presented at the Popular Culture Association in the South Conference, October 7–9, 1999, Roanoke, Virginia).

26. Fan-scholars (as Matt Hills would term them) Craig Miller and John Thorne

have for a decade published *Wrapped in Plastic,* a serious magazine devoted to *Twin Peaks.*

27. The special nature of the searcher who fully inhabits his body is discussed by Martha Nochimson, "Desire under the Douglas Firs: Entering the Body of Reality in *Twin Peaks,*" in Lavery, *Full of Secrets,* 144–59.

28. On *Twin Peaks'* intertextuality and particularly its literary allusions, see Rhonda V. Wilcox, "Beyond the Borders: Living on (the) Edge in *Twin Peaks,*" *Wrapped in Plastic* 17 (1995): 20–25.

29. On the nature of the father, doubling, and the abuse symbolism of BOB, see Diane Stevenson, "Family Romance, Family Violence, and the Fantastic in *Twin Peaks,*" in Lavery, *Full of Secrets,* 70–81.

30. Rhonda V. Wilcox, "'In Your Dreams, Fleischman': Dr. Flesh and the Dream of the Spirit in *Northern Exposure,*" *Studies in Popular Culture* 15, no. 2 (Spring 1993): 1–13.

31. See Linda Badley, "The Rebirth of the Clinic," in Lavery, Hague, and Cartwright, *"Deny All Knowledge,"* 148–167.

32. Rhonda Wilcox and J. P. Williams, "'What Do You Think?': *The X-Files,* Liminality, and Gender Pleasure," in Lavery, Hague, and Cartwright, *"Deny All Knowledge,"* 99–120.

33. Rhonda V. Wilcox, "Lois's Locks: Trust and Representation in *Lois and Clark: The New Adventures of Superman,*" in Helford, *Fantasy Girls,* 96.

34. Petra Kuppers, "Quality Science Fiction: *Babylon 5*'s Metatextual Universe," in Gwenllian-Jones and Pearson, *Cult Television,* 46–55.

35. J. P. Williams discusses the unreal element of Sam's/actor Scott Bakula's cross-dressing in scenes in which he plays women in "Biology and Destiny: The Dynamics of Gender Crossing in *Quantum Leap,*" *Women's Studies in Communication* 19 (Fall 1996): 273–90.

36. For a discussion of *Xena* as queer text in general and of "Bitter Suite" in particular, see Elyce Rae Helford, "Feminism, Queer Studies, and the Sexual Politics of *Xena: Warrior Princess,*" in Helford, *Fantasy Girls,* 135–62.

37. On Buffy and the monomyth, see Laurel Bowman, "Buffy the Vampire Slayer: The Greek Hero Revisited," home page, 2002, October 12, 2002, http://web.uvic.ca/~lbowman/buffy/buffythehero.html; Nancy Holder, "Slayers of the Last Arc," in *Seven Seasons of "Buffy": Science Fiction and Fantasy Writers Discuss Their Favorite Television Show,* ed. Glenn Yeffeth (Dallas: Benbella, 2003), 195–205; Rhonda V. Wilcox, "'Who Died and Made Her the Boss?' Patterns of Mortality in *Buffy,*" in Wilcox and Lavery, *Fighting the Forces,* 6–7, 16–17; and Wilcox, "'Pain as Bright as Steel': The Monomyth and Light as Pain in *Buffy the Vampire Slayer*" (keynote lecture at Blood, Text, and Fears: Reading around *Buffy the Vampire Slayer,* an International Conference, October 19–20, 2002, University of East Anglia, Norwich); Rhonda Wilcox, *Why Buffy Matters: The Art of* Buffy the Vampire Slayer (London: Tauris, 2005), chap. 2.

38. Rhonda V. Wilcox, "'There Will Never Be a "Very Special" *Buffy*': Buffy and the Monsters of Teen Life," *Journal of Popular Film and Television* 27, no. 2

(Summer 1999): 16–23; republished in *Slayage: The Online International Journal of Buffy Studies* 2 (March 2001), www.slayage.tv.

39. On this element of *Buffy*'s language, see ibid., 23–24, and Michael Adams, *Slayer Slang: A "Buffy the Vampire Slayer" Lexicon* (Oxford: Oxford University Press, 2003), 113–25.

40. On the self-referentiality of "Restless," see David Lavery, "Afterword: The Genius of Joss Whedon," in Wilcox and Lavery, *Fighting the Forces,* 251–55. On "Hush," "Restless," and "Once More, with Feeling," see chapters 9, 10, and 12 of Wilcox, *Why Buffy Matters.*

41. Many are among those Matt Hills calls scholar-fans. In addition to the collections edited by Kaveney, Wilcox and Lavery, Yeffeth, and Early and Kennedy (which also covers *Xena* and others), there is James B. South, ed., *"Buffy the Vampire Slayer" and Philosophy: Fear and Trembling in Sunnydale,* Popular Culture and Philosophy 4 (Chicago: Open Court, 2003). In addition to the linguistic analysis by Adams, there are two serious religious/ethical studies: Jana Riess, *What Would Buffy Do? The Vampire Slayer as Spiritual Guide* (San Francisco: Jossey-Bass, 2004), and Gregory Stevenson, *Televised Morality: The Case of "Buffy the Vampire Slayer"* (Lanham, Md.: Hamilton Books, 2003). Other book-length studies are current and forthcoming, including Wilcox, *Why Buffy Matters.* The plethora of *Buffy* studies is best to be discovered by consulting the online refereed quarterly (edited by Lavery and Wilcox) *Slayage: An Online International Journal of Buffy Studies* (www.slayage.tv), with its news announcements on conferences and publications and its link to Derik Badman's academic *Buffy* bibliography.

42. Stacey Abbott, introduction, *Reading "Angel": The Spinoff with a Soul,* ed. Stacey Abbott (London: Tauris, 2005).

43. See Stacey Abbott, "Walking the Fine Line between Angel and Angelus," *Slayage: The Online International Journal of Buffy Studies* 9 (August 2003).

10 | HBO's approach to generic transformation

Al Auster

Back in the mid-1990s, the major television networks thought of getting together and forming a "committee on Emmy fairness."[1] The purpose of this committee was to somehow curb the number of Emmys being awarded each year to Home Box Office (HBO), the cable television network. That committee, which never got off the ground, would stand even less of a chance of success these days. For example, in 2004 HBO received 124 Emmy nominations, with its closest competitor, NBC-TV, receiving 64. HBO's 124 nominations were more than those of CBS, ABC, and Fox networks combined. Indeed, it was the fourth straight year that HBO led all networks in Emmy nominations. Emmy Award nominations and Awards are not the only sign of HBO's running away from the competition. In 2004, two of its most successful series, *Sex and the City* and *The Sopranos*, scored network-sized audiences for their finales, with 12.5 million and 10.5 million viewers, respectively (this for a cable network with 28 million subscribers, which is only one-third the size of the potential audience of the broadcast networks).

This is a far cry from the network that started its history in 1972 with bicycling programming including polka contests and the film version of Ken Kesey's *Sometimes a Great Notion*. HBO came of age perhaps with its 1975 satellite broadcast of the celebrated "Thrilla from Manila," a heavyweight championship bout between Muhammad Ali and Joe Frazier. Indeed, to those familiar with film history, HBO's spectacular rise is somewhat reminiscent of the emergence of two fly-speck studios during Hollywood's classic period: Columbia, riding the talents of Frank Capra, and of course Disney, vaulting to eminence on the strength of its little mouse. But there is more than just symbolism attached to this comparison, since HBO actually functions more like a studio than a network.

Among the factors that are the current basis of this system are the 28 million subscribers paying anywhere from $6.95 to $12.95 per month to receive the cable network. This subscriber base frees the network from being beholden to advertisers and sponsors who might otherwise try to influence programming. A second important factor is the fact that HBO is a cable network and thus is free to present nudity and obscenity. Equally important is the fact that HBO is freed from the public service requirements of broadcast TV networks and thus needn't maintain expensive news operations with low profit margins.

Less obvious but no less significant is the consistency of HBO's management teams. While other networks have changed managements as frequently as NFL teams do, HBO has been headed from the early eighties through the present by just three CEOs: Michael Fuchs, Jeff Bewkes, and currently Chris Albrecht, each serving as mentor to the other. This has permitted HBO to move in new directions while maintaining certain core strategies. Thus, Jeff Bewkes changed the direction of HBO from wholesale reliance on Hollywood films and made-for-TV films to the development of miniseries and dramatic series. More recently, HBO has capitalized on new revenue streams such as the sale of DVDs of its most popular series and a movement in the direction of network syndication, with an airbrushed version of *Sex and the City* as its first offering.

All these factors have contributed to HBO's success and made it a magnet for talented producers, directors, and writers. These creative people have been drawn to HBO not only by its freedom from interference by sponsors, or the ability to present material that includes obscenity and nudity, but also by the fact that HBO supports its programs with generous funding. One episode of *The Sopranos,* for example, costs approximately $3 million to produce. Just as significant as the money that HBO will pour into a series is the fact that the network will allow a series to find an audience, and will not cancel a series (as the broadcast networks do) if it doesn't immediately gain decent ratings. As a result, HBO has become the standard of quality in contemporary American television. As one foreign observer has commented, "Almost all the must-see shows are made by one channel."[2]

The Documentaries

While being quick to exploit new possibilities and new directions, HBO has maintained a steadfast commitment to certain basic counter-programming strategies. Long before HBO came on the scene, the networks had deserted documentary production, and the only game in town for documentaries was PBS. There is no doubt that with the programming of documentaries by Ken Burns and Fred Wiseman, as well as the continuing documentary series such as *Frontline, Nova, POV,* and *Independent Lens,* PBS certainly attempted to meet the challenge. However, once HBO came on the scene with its annual budget of $20 million for documentaries and under the leadership of Sheila Nevins, its vice president for original programming, no other network could match HBO's achievement in documentaries. Indeed, at the 2003 Academy Awards, three HBO-funded documentaries (*Capturing the Friedmans, My Architect,* and *Balseros*) were among those nominated for the Oscar.

Nevins, who has described her taste as "Chekhovian," goes on to add, "I believe it's dark and raining outside almost all the time and that sex is a big laugh and we're too serious about what's fun and we're not honest enough about what's sad."[3] She has, in recent years, emerged as the patron saint of documentaries. Nevertheless, one wondered at the outset which direction HBO documentaries might take, since so many of them involved sex, prompting some to parody HBO's slogan, "It's not TV, it's HBO," with the line "It's not TV, it's porn."

Perhaps in keeping with Nevins's notion that sex is a big laugh, HBO developed documentary series such as *Real Sex, G-String Divas,* and *Taxicab Confessions.* If your taste ran to nonfiction films featuring transvestites describing the first time they had sex with a man, and hidden cameras showing a man and woman making love in the back of a taxicab, these were the documentary shows for you. The salaciousness of these series hasn't embarrassed Nevins at all. As a matter of fact, she's made the claim that these series laid the groundwork for the freedom enjoyed by *Sex and the City.*[4] It hardly seems necessary for Nevins to defend herself, however, what with a matchless record of ten Oscars, forty-three Emmys, seventeen Peabodys, and a roster of brilliant documentaries that includes, among others, *Dear America: Letters Home from Vietnam, King Gimp,* and *Spellbound.*

Not content to rest on its laurels and in keeping with Nevins's credo about honesty in the face of sadness, HBO has also created the series *America Undercover* with films such as *Just Melvin, Just Evil,* about a family of child molesters, and *Soldiers in the Army of God,* which deals with antiabortionists who did not shrink from violence. Nor did the Nevins documentary unit hesitate to do a documentary about a subject that one might suspect had been done to death called *Monica in Black and White,* featuring Monica Lewinsky. HBO's willingness to depict the good, the bad, and the raunchy has contributed to an enhanced profile for the TV documentary, as well as helping the genre achieve both popular success and critical acclaim.

The Made-for-Television Movies

Even though documentaries have come to be a symbol of HBO's successful transition from merely replaying Hollywood theatrical films to acting as a production company in its own right, narrative films remain the backbone of HBO's schedule. Of course it was soon evident to HBO that it could not rely on the Hollywood studios' rather limited output as the sole source of scheduling once it began to have competition from other premium channels such as Showtime. Thus, in 1983 HBO began producing its own made-for-TV movies. At first, these films were a rather timid mixture starring old Hollywood icons such as Elizabeth Taylor, James Stewart, and Bette Davis. The sole exception that year, which gave an inkling of what HBO's films were to become, was *The Terry Fox Story.* The film deals with Terry Fox, an athletic Vancouver boy who, as a result of bone cancer, had his leg amputated, becoming a national hero when he succeeded in a cross-Canada marathon to raise money for the Canadian Cancer Society. The narrative could have easily degenerated into a tear-jerking, "how sweet are the uses of adversity" film. What saved it, and was suggestive of what the future might hold, was the fact that Terry Fox (Eric Fryer) was a jerk. Needless to say, portraying Fox as a cranky, unlikable cancer victim was a departure from both the expected and the norm. And so was telling the story of someone most Americans had probably never heard of.

A few seasons later, another sign that HBO films weren't going to offer the usual run-of-the-mill features was the network's risky decision to produce a biopic of Edward R. Murrow. Aside from the fact that even before his death Murrow was conceived of as the patron saint of broadcast journalism, there was television's reluctance ever to take a serious or critical look at its own history (no network, oddly enough, including CBS, had ever attempted to do a Murrow biopic). But potentially even more troublesome were Murrow's former colleagues, William S. Paley,

Dr. Frank Stanton, and Fred Friendly, who were still alive at the time of production and were proven veterans at protecting the Murrow legend as well as their own reputations. Suffice it to say that HBO's *Murrow* (1986) was a way of tweaking the networks and at the same time compelling them to take notice of HBO's films.

Following *Murrow,* HBO launched a stream of biopics that would have been the envy of Jack Warner and Darryl F. Zanuck. These included *Mandela* (1987), *Stalin* (1992), *Citizen Cohn* (1992), *Truman* (1995), *Gotti* (1996), *Winchell* (1998), and *Lansky* (1998). One of them, *Truman,* which won an Emmy, was faithfully produced from David McCullough's 1992 Pulitzer Prize–winning biography and was especially refreshing in our era of political spin, triangulation, and soft money, in that it depicted the career of a politician (portrayed by Gary Sinise) whose decision making relied on nothing more statistically sophisticated than his own sense of right and wrong. Of course, the way to undo the credibility of any biopic is excessive reverence. And while HBO biopics did not always succeed in avoiding this flaw, its strategy for maintaining its productions' legitimacy was to produce as many films about sinners as it did about saints. Thus, HBO's list of biopics included a rogues' gallery, which ranged from the practically demonic *Stalin,* to the merely villainous *Gotti* and *Lansky,* to the morally ambiguous *Winchell,* to the comically duplicitous *Don King: Only in America* (1998).

It was HBO's biopic *The Josephine Baker Story* (1991), however, that landed the network its first Emmy for a made-for-TV movie. The film starring Lynn Whitfield made excellent use of some of cable's advantages, such as the option for on-screen nudity. Thus HBO's version could portray quite literally the life of the Saint Louis washerwoman's daughter who became an international star by dancing nude at the Folies-Bergère in her famous *danse sauvage.* The film also reveals the racism that followed Baker when she returned to the United States, when, even though a major star of the Ziegfeld Follies, she was not permitted to stay at any of the major hotels in New York. It also chronicles her role in the French resistance during the German occupation of France in World War II and the McCarthyite charges of communist sympathies leveled against her during the fifties.

More than garnering the first in a long line of gold statuettes, *The Josephine Baker Story* inspired HBO to develop a series of films that dealt with the history, lives, and problems of marginal and oppressed groups. Among the most prominent of these were stories of African Americans: *The Tuskegee Airmen* (1995) dealt with black World War II aviators who fought a two-front war against both fascism and homegrown racial prejudice; *Miss Evers' Boys* (1997), the tragic story of the Tuskegee syphilis experiment; the Emmy Award–winning *A Lesson before Dying* (2001), about a black death row convict; and, most recently, the Emmy-winning *Something the Lord Made* (2004), the story of Vivien Thomas, a black medical technician who engaged in pioneering research on open-heart surgery.

HBO films also explored the issue of AIDS: *And the Band Played On* (1992), an adaptation of Randy Shilts's history of the early years of the disease, and *Gia* (1998), the story of the lesbian supermodel who died of AIDS. Its 1996 production *If These Walls Could Talk* was a triptych of tales about abortion, starring Demi Moore, Sissy Spacek, and Cher, which still retains the record as the highest-rated of all HBO films.

In recent years, HBO has confined itself to producing between eight and twelve films per year. What have increasingly replaced the old biopics are films with historical narratives. *The Gathering Storm,* made in 2000 and starring Albert Finney and Vanessa Redgrave as Winston and Clementine Churchill, focused on Churchill's years in the political wilderness prior to World War II, and won the Golden Globe for best made-for-TV movie. Also in 2004, HBO produced *Iron Jawed Angels,* starring Hillary Swank, which was the story of the American suffragist movement up to the point when women gained the right to vote.

Another trend in HBO's films has been productions that adapt scripts that initially were produced in the theater. These HBO films are practically a roster of Pulitzer Prize winners for drama, including *Wit* in 1999 and *Dinner with Friends* in 2000. Aside from their winning the Pulitzer, these two films share another eminent link—both were directed by celebrated film and stage director Mike Nichols. Ultimately, it was working on these two small films for HBO that convinced Nichols and HBO to collaborate on the greater task of bringing Tony Kushner's 1993 Pulitzer Prize–winning epic *Angels in America* to the screen. This $66 million, two-part production more than anything was a symbol of HBO films' coming-of-age. Kushner himself commented on this when he told the *New York Times,* "If it had been a major studio, it would have been immediately tortured to death. There's no way anyone could have signed off on a six hour movie."[5] Kushner's use of the AIDS crisis to explore the American body politic and psyche since World War II was an amazing theatrical accomplishment, for which HBO won a record-breaking eleven Emmy Awards.

It was obvious that HBO films, some made for less than $3 million (the sum some Hollywood films now budget for their caterers), were a force to be reckoned with, even by first-run theaters. As a result, in another break from their traditional pattern, some HBO-funded films appear in theaters before being shown on the network, and even compete at worldwide festivals. *American Splendor* (2003), the story of the real Harvey Pekar, who was the basis of the cult comic book character, won the Grand Jury Prize at the Sundance Film Festival, and *Elephant* (2003), Gus Van Sant's film that dealt with a Columbine-like school massacre, won the Palme d'Or at the Cannes Film Festival.

Clearly, HBO's contribution to the genre of the made-for-television movie has been to take it to new levels of sophistication. Not only have they awakened public interest in historically important figures such as Truman, Stalin, and Churchill, as well as previously neglected moments in African American and women's history, but HBO films have shown a willingness to produce films about riskier topics. Furthermore, with its growing roster of Pulitzer Prize–winning dramas, HBO has staked out a place for itself as the venue for quality made-for-television movies. Indeed, by producing films that have initially appeared in theaters and at film festivals, it has begun to eliminate the distinction between made-for-television movies and theatrical films.

The Sitcoms

HBO's success with films and documentaries obviously inspired the network, albeit tentatively, to try to make its mark in the sitcom genre, which was to some extent a truer test of HBO's coming-of-age, since from the very beginning of television, situation comedies have been the backbone of the networks' prime-time schedules. Indeed, series like *I Love Lucy* (1951–57), *The Mary Tyler Moore Show* (1970–77), *All in the Family* (1971–79), and so many others were some of the broadcast networks' proudest achievements. However, the network sitcom had fallen upon leaner days, and with rare exceptions the genre had fallen into one of its fallow periods. None, even the most popular of the network sitcoms, even came close to exerting the kind of creative influence and ratings dominance once exerted by sitcoms such as *The Cosby Show* (1984–92) and *Roseanne* (1988–97). Indeed, as popular shows such as *Friends* (1994–2004) faded from the scene and others such as *Everybody Loves Raymond* (1996–) and *Will and Grace* (1998–) were nearing the same fate, and with nothing on the horizon to equal their popularity, Cassandras were predicting the eventual disappearance of sitcom fare from network schedules. Ultimately this is what made HBO's sitcoms so welcome, since they had a freshness that gave the genre a creative charge, resulting, of course, in numerous network and cable imitations.

HBO's approach to the sitcom was, however, rather tentative at first. The first comedy series that the network undertook was the political satire *Tanner '88* (1988). However, *Tanner's* pedigree was of the highest order, being the brainchild of Garry Trudeau of *Doonesbury* fame and directed by Robert Altman. Tanner was a Zelig-like candidate who followed in the footsteps of the major candidates and whose presence revealed the farcical elements of our political process. However, more than just a clever send-up of American political culture, it was the first sign that HBO was about to challenge network television on its home turf. It was, as television historian Robert J. Thompson called it, "the first real shot across the bow."[6] *Dream On* (1990–96), the follow-up to *Tanner '88*, was neither as funny nor as inventive. As a matter of fact, the only things that really distinguished it from its network counterparts were the full frontal nudity and the ingenious use of old film clips (the hero, the divorced semi-schlemiel Martin Tupper [Brian Benben], book editor, sees them in his fantasies). It was also the first production effort of Kevin Bright, Marta Kaufman, and David Crane, who went on to produce the mega network hit *Friends*.

In contrast to *Dream On* and *Tanner '88*, *The Larry Sanders Show*, starring Garry Shandling, was a brilliant program that garnered instantaneous praise and a cultlike following. In the years it was on the air (1992–98), Larry, his unctuous sidekick, Hank (Jeffrey Tambor), and his often brutal producer, Artie (Rip Torn), ran roughshod over television's obsessions with wealth, sex, celebrity, and ratings. Hardly anything about television escaped the show's skewer. In one episode, Larry and his staff are discussing an upcoming show at the same time they're watching the O. J. Simpson trial when Larry is reminded that he once turned O. J. down for a spot on the show. In his defense Larry moans, "Who knew he was going to get this *hot*."

No sooner had *The Larry Sanders Show* finished its run than another HBO sitcom took the public by storm. The four single heroines of *Sex and the City* (1998–2004)—Carrie Bradshaw (Sarah Jessica Parker), Samantha Jones (Kim Cattrall), Charlotte York (Kristin Davis), and Miranda Hobbes (Cynthia Nixon)—sit around talking dirty and comparing their sexual exploits, as well as the size, girth, and even taste of their male (and in some cases female) partners, as they yearn for Mr. Right or, in Carrie's case, "Big" (Chris Noth). What made *Sex and the*

The four heroines of HBO's *Sex and the City* discussed their sexual lives with openness and obvious relish, but the program also conveyed a palpable sense of urban loneliness. (Left to right) Cynthia Nixon as Miranda Hobbes, Kim Cattrall as Samantha Jones, Kristin Davis as Charlotte York, and Sarah Jessica Parker as Carrie Bradshaw. Courtesy of HBO Productions.

City such a hit on HBO was the candid way these women spoke about sex, and the obvious relish with which they approached their sex lives. In a way, *Sex and the City*'s approach to women's sexuality and sexuality in general was enormously refreshing on television. What also made the comedy original was its take on urban loneliness. Granted, of course, that "The City" part of *Sex and the City* was a narrow swath of Manhattan stretching from SoHo to the Upper East and Upper West Sides, with some detours to the Hamptons, and the women in the sitcom were all white, Anglo-Saxon, and—with the exception of Charlotte after her conversion to Judaism—Protestant, what each of the women in the sitcom wanted despite all their heavy breathing references was "Mr. Right." Thus, the series' finale, which found all our heroines in the arms of loving relationships, was the kind of consummation anyone would want from what, despite all its dirty talk, was a romantic comedy.

Not a romantic comedy at all, and more in the line of *The Larry Sanders Show,* is the HBO series *Curb Your Enthusiasm* (2000–). To get a sense of *Curb Your Enthusiasm,* imagine, if you were ever a fan of *Seinfeld,* George Costanza (Jason Alexander) with an income of approximately $80 million a year and a beautiful, practically saintly spouse, and you get a picture of the character of Larry David on the series. Larry David, the alter ego of Larry David, the former coproducer of *Seinfeld,* is a curmudgeon whose tone deafness to even the most common forms of civility gets him into one difficult situation after another. In one situation, Larry's comment to a lesbian couple who are about to adopt a Chinese baby that they should name the baby Tang (after all, it is the name of a soft drink) sends the couple ballistic. In another episode Larry gets upset when he finds that his order of kung pao shrimp, which had been mistakenly sent to a friend's house, is missing a couple of shrimp. He of course accuses the friend of eating his shrimp—effectively sealing the end of their friendship.

Larry's friends on the show, which include featured roles by celebrities like Ted Danson, Michael York, Martin Scorsese, Ben Stiller, David Schwimmer, Mel Brooks, and others, form a hilarious comedy backdrop to Larry's cranky antics. However, it is the core cast of Jeff Garlin, Larry's manager, who usually plays Oliver Hardy to Larry's Stan Laurel; comedians Richard Thomas and Shelly Berman, as Larry's neurotic doppelgänger buddy and his father, respectively; and Cheryl Hines as Larry's patient wife, Cheryl, who supply most of the often improvised comic situations and dialogue. *Curb Your Enthusiasm* has already garnered a great deal of praise. Alessandra Stanley of the *New York Times* went so

With largely improvised dialogue, HBO's *Curb Your Enthusiasm* featured creator Larry David as a curmudgeon whose tone deafness to even the most basic forms of civility gets him into one difficult situation after another. (Left to right) Jeff Garlin as Jeff Greene and Larry David as himself. Courtesy of HBO Productions.

far as to place Larry David's character in the pantheon of TV curmudgeons, a notable list that includes such icons as Ralph Kramden and Archie Bunker.[7] It is another in the list of HBO sitcoms that have allowed HBO to take an honored place as a creative force in the most hallowed of all television genres.

However, not to be outdone by the networks, where the number of failed sitcoms is legion, HBO also had a considerable number of failures in this genre. No one will lament the passing of *The Mind of the Married Man* (2001), an opposite-sex version of *Sex and the City*. And no one seems to have seen any virtues in *Arli$$* (1996–2002), which nonetheless managed to survive on HBO for eight seasons, more than either *Sex and the City* or *The Larry Sanders Show,* and routinely got 3 percent ratings, which in cable terms put it in the same league as the World Wrestling Federation. Perhaps what made *Arli$$* so popular (except with critics) in our sports-obsessed society is that it was a wonderful send-up of the whole culture of celebrity, money, and hype that surrounds sports. Only Arliss Michaels (Robert Wuhl) could say without embarrassment to a club owner, "$750,000? Oh, come on, the guy's gotta eat."

At its best, HBO was pushing the sitcom genre radically forward. Nowhere else on television could one find sitcoms so frank about men's and women's sexuality. Nowhere else could one find situation comedies that were as incisive about that bit of showbiz testosterone called "talk shows," the Oz-like world of the sports agent, or the follies of our political culture. To their credit, HBO sitcoms such as *The Larry Sanders Show, Sex and the City,* and *Curb Your Enthusiasm* could take a place of honor shared by the best of previous sitcoms such as *The Mary Tyler Moore Show, All in the Family,* and *Seinfeld.* Indeed, on HBO the sitcom genre was what it was at its best, a true comedy of American manners.

The Miniseries

For the most part, the miniseries genre, which had provided many brilliant television moments, such as *Rich Man, Poor Man* (1976), *Roots* (1977), and *Holocaust* (1978), had, with rare exceptions, been abandoned in favor of less costly programming. But HBO, once again freed from the constraints of network television concerning nudity and the use of language, became a magnet for talented producers. A major breakthrough for these miniseries occurred in 1998 when Tom Hanks and Ron Howard produced the Emmy Award–winning miniseries *From the Earth to the Moon.* In tracing the *Apollo* program from its beginnings to the terse comment that "the *Eagle* has landed," Hanks and Howard presented a stirring docudrama of the moon landing.

Hanks followed this up on HBO in 2001 by collaborating with Steven Spielberg on another magnificent American achievement of the twentieth century: the World War II campaigns of American GIs. Using Stephen Ambrose's best-selling book *Band of Brothers* as their basis, Hanks and Spielberg produced a ten-part, $125 million Emmy-winning miniseries that told the story of Easy Company of the 101st Airborne Division starting from its training in Georgia through the end of the war. Each episode was complete with the opening comments of the actual soldiers who took part in these events. *Band of Brothers* went on to depict the bonding among these men who were to go through the enormous physical and emotional trials of war.

In addition, the series shows in meticulous detail the D-day landings, the Battle of the Bulge, the discovery and liberation of the concentration camps, and the final defeat of Germany. It presents a vivid cast of characters such as Lieutenant, later Major, Richard Winters (Damien Lewis), whose tactical skill and consideration for the lives and welfare of his men earn "the band's" eternal gratitude and respect. Another very interesting character is Captain Lewis Nixon (Ron Livingston), Winter's second in command, who is as emotional and self-destructive as the latter is calm and stoical.

The Dramatic Series

In the late nineties, the major networks' dramatic series had settled, with rare exceptions, into a routine of family-cop-doc-lawyer shows. Indeed, one of the most successful of these dramatic series, *Law & Order* (1990–), was a combination of the cop-lawyer genre. Occasionally a series such as the political drama *The West Wing* (1999–) or the supernatural series *Buffy the Vampire Slayer* (1997–2003) broke from this mold. However, by and large network programmers stayed within the safe confines of these franchise dramas. A major contribution of HBO was to move the dramatic series into new realms of experience, and even to resurrect older forms of the dramatic series genre, such as the Western, which ever since the demise of *Gunsmoke* had ceased to be a factor in the television dramatic series genre.

A fine example of how this worked was the first HBO dramatic series, *Oz* (1997–2003). Tom Fontana, who had previously produced *St. Elsewhere* and *Homicide,* was tempted by the network's offer of no restrictions on language and content to create *Oz. Oz* was the kind of series no network would even consider doing. Indeed, it made Fontana's previous network series, the grittily realistic police drama *Homicide,* look like *Little House on the Prairie. Oz,* the nickname for Oswald State Penitentiary, is a maximum-security prison in an unnamed state. It is a seething cauldron of society's psychopaths, misfits, and criminals, a place where a cannibalistic prisoner (he ate only his mother—he was saving his father in the freezer for Thanksgiving) is one of the more mellow inmates.

Oz is a place that would fit neatly into Thomas Hobbes's description of life as "nasty, brutish, and short," the special emphasis being on short, since so many of the episodes had a relentless savagery. It is a place where men and women are routinely murdered or brutally raped. However, *Oz* also presents some interesting depictions of prison life that are usually missing in prison films, and certainly would have been anathema to the major networks. *Oz* is unusually candid about prison homosexuality and presents it in all its variations, from prison rape to homosexual affairs that are emotionally supportive and truly affectionate relationships. *Oz* also presents the difficulties involved in any kind of rehabilitation. Despite an experimental cell block known as "Em City" under the leadership of Tim McManus (Terry Kinney), a progressive administrator, where inmates can wear street clothes instead of prison uniforms, live in glass modules instead of prison cells, have ample opportunities for continuing education, and elect democratic inmate councils, prisoners continue to use drugs (which seem to be as plentiful in prison as on any street corner in the inner city) and to murder each other at an alarming rate.

Oz's gritty, hard-edged representation of prison life was a welcome portrait of another side of criminal life in America. For all the cop shows such as *NYPD Blue, Law & Order,* and *CSI* that portray criminals being apprehended, none ever deals with what life is like behind bars. And with America's prison population now reaching almost gulag proportions, *Oz*'s determination to be candid about prison conditions was to be applauded. So, too, was its creation of a gallery of acidly etched continuing characters such as Vern Shillinger (J. K. Simmons), the leader of the prison's Aryan Nation; Kareem Said (Eammon Walker), the imam of the prison's Muslims; Father Ray Mukada (B. D. Wong), the prison's Catholic chaplain; and Tobias Beecher (Lee Tergesen), a yuppie lawyer sentenced to hard time for vehicular homicide, who became a prime example of how prison life can brutalize anyone.

Though *Oz*—most likely because of its relentlessly downbeat quality—never achieved the success of HBO's dramatic series such as *The Sopranos,* it nevertheless was something of a template for future HBO programs. And it showed that the maverick network would not hesitate to produce even the most risky of creative conceptions (with little interference for the creative personnel who would get involved). Obviously, not every HBO dramatic series enjoyed equal success. For example, *The Wire,* a series that is just entering its fourth season on HBO, is rarely mentioned in the same breath as such HBO dramatic series as *The Sopranos* and *Six Feet Under.* However, it has its share of enthusiastic fans. Written by David Simon, whose previous work on *Homicide* and *The Corner* had garnered him the title the "Balzac of post-industrial Maryland,"[8] it is a story of a motley group of misfit cops who in a myriad of sometimes hard-to-follow subplots tackle political and labor union corruption, dope dealing, and their own frequent tendency to screw up.

Other HBO miniseries, like the overhyped *K Street* (2003), a production of George Clooney and Steven Soderbergh, never lived up to their promise. The contrast in *K Street* between real political players and activists like James Carville and his wife, Mary Matalin, politicians like

Howard Dean and Senators Rick Santorum and Orrin Hatch, and journalists such as Joe Klein and Howard Kurtz, and fictional members of
the Carville-Matalin nonpartisan lobbying firm, which was supposed to
mix reality, fiction, and hyperreality, was confusing and essentially un-
dramatic. Indeed, it became nothing more than Carville, Matalin, and
their presumed office of fictional high-powered nonpartisan lobbyists
spinning and maneuvering to get op-ed pieces in print and their clients
on TV talk shows.

Similarly, *Carnivale* (2003–5), HBO's twelve-part dramatic series, with
its combination of dustbowl grit in the form of the mysterious two-bit
carny strip show where the escaped chain gang prisoner Ben Hawkins
(Nick Stahl) finds refuge, and the over-the-top apocalyptic menace in the
form of Brother Justin (Clancy Brown), never seemed to connect with a
large audience. Indeed, for some it was a pale reflection of HBO's previous effort at the gothic and supernatural, *Tales from the Crypt* (1989–96),
which often featured major actors (Tim Curry, William Hickey) and in
some cases, such as the Emmy Award–winning episode "You Murder-
ers," experimented with interesting formal devices such as digitally inserting cameos of Alfred Hitchcock and Humphrey Bogart.

Another new HBO continuing dramatic series, which the network
hopes might be a successor to *The Sopranos,* is David Milch's foul-
mouthed Jacobean Western *Deadwood* (2004–), which mixes historical
characters such as Wild Bill Hickok and Calamity Jane with fictional
ones such as the aptly named Al Swearengen. Needless to say, a moment
in the series' first season, when Swearengen (played by the brilliant English actor Ian McShane) launches into a memory-laced, obscenity-laden
soliloquy à la Molly Bloom as he is engaged in a sex act, marks it as a
program that might become one of HBO's more popular new dramatic
series.

The Sopranos and Six Feet Under

Two of HBO's dramatic series have gone beyond mere audience favorites. Take, for example, the *New York Times* critic Stephen Holden's
comment that *The Sopranos* "just may be the greatest work of American
popular culture of the last quarter century,"[9] or *New York Sun* critic
David Blum's declaration that *Six Feet Under* "now ranks alongside 'The
Sopranos' as one of the great family dramas of our time."[10] While these
hosannas may to some extent be taken as critical hyperbole, there is no

Hailed by the *New York Times* as possibly "the greatest work of American popular culture of the last quarter century," HBO's *The Sopranos* has become the kind of rich, sprawling narrative that was once the province of the nineteenth-century novel. (Left to right) Joe Pantoliano as Ralph Cifaretto, Steve Van Zandt as Silvio Dante, James Gandolfini as Tony Soprano, and Tony Sirico as Paulie "Walnuts" Gaultiere. Courtesy of HBO Productions.

question that these series have transcended mere popularity and entered the pop culture pantheon.

Whether or not *The Sopranos* ultimately continues this level of critical acclaim, it is a series about gangsters and as such fits neatly into popular culture critic Robert Warshow's famous dictum that "the gangster is lonely and melancholy, and can give the impression of a profound worldly wisdom."[11] That sense of profound melancholy indeed surrounds Tony Soprano (James Gandolfini), the head of a New Jersey Mafia family. However, though the world of Tony Soprano contains more than its share of criminality and the multiple "whackings" that have become a necessity in any narrative about the Mafia, its main attraction is that it also places Tony in the complex web of a problematic marriage, the complexities of parenthood, and caring for aging and infirm parents and relatives that many of us face. It also takes Tony and puts him on the couch, which one would hardly expect of a Mafia don, and, in the process of exploring his psyche, gives a rare glimpse, for television or film, of the real dynamics of psychotherapy. As a result, *The Sopranos* has become the kind of rich, sprawling narrative that was once the province of the nineteenth-century novel.

Also among the rewards of *The Sopranos* is watching a wonderful set of actors. First and foremost of these is James Gandolfini, playing the bearlike, charismatic Mafioso don Tony Soprano, who can alternately be seductive, crude, charming, murderous, and filled with remorse as well as almost crippling neurotic symptoms. Also apropos of Warshow's famous comment, Tony can give off not just a sense of melancholy, for his failures as a husband, father, and gang leader, but a feeling of entropy, because he senses that somehow history has passed him by, or, as Tony puts it, "I feel like I've come in at the end. Like I missed the best bits."

Every bit as tough as Tony is his wife, Carmela, played by the brilliant Edie Falco. Carmela and Tony's marriage has long ago reverted to low-intensity combat. Nonetheless, there is no trifling with Carmela. There is no nonsense when it comes to protecting her home or her children, and when Tony's obsessive infidelities become too much for her to bear, she doesn't hesitate to throw him out of the house and sue for divorce. However, the religious, bourgeois Carmela made a Faustian bargain when she married Tony, and even though she surrounds herself with all the symbols of an upper-middle-class suburban lifestyle, she is morally conflicted because the true economic, emotional center of that life will always be tainted.

Despite all its elements of the contemporary world such as suburban life, psychoanalysis, and strong women, *The Sopranos* is still essentially a gangster story. And, as Warshow told us, the gangster is essentially a lonely, doomed, and tragic figure. Consequently, the sixth season, which its creator David Chase has promised us for 2006, can no more avert its tragic denouement of either death or imprisonment than the Greek tragedies could. Nonetheless, *The Sopranos* underscores the relevance of the genre and HBO's vision in allowing Chase to produce the series, which, however subsequent generations judge it, will still be, to quote James Cagney in *White Heat* (1949), "top of the world."

In contrast to *The Sopranos,* where a tragic denouement is to be expected, HBO's other miniseries, *Six Feet Under,* usually begins each episode with a death that is sometimes tragically, but oftentimes comically, portrayed. *Six Feet Under* is the brainchild of Alan Ball, who won an Academy Award for his *American Beauty* (1999), in which the protagonist (Kevin Spacey) begins the film by announcing, "In less than a year I'll be dead. In a way I'm dead already." Ball seemed the perfect candidate to create a series that was equal parts Jessica Mitford and Evelyn Waugh.

Six Feet Under, though it didn't start out this way, became a more explicit version of the daytime soaps, with a compelling narrative and dynamic characters. These include the initially Peter-Pannish Nate (Peter Krause), who has matured into a guilt-ridden single father; his brother David (Michael C. Hall), who began the series as a closeted gay man and later became involved in a problematic relationship with an ex-cop, Keith (Matthew St. Patrick); and their sister Claire (Lauren Ambrose), who, as she seeks a creative vocation, seems to wind up looking for love in all the wrong places. Presiding over this dysfunctional family is their widowed mother Ruth (Francis Conroy), whose neat bun makes her look like Whistler's mother, but who is nonetheless a matriarch still in search of an identity.

These main characters are complemented by a host of subsidiary characters, who in the course of four seasons become major ones themselves: Brenda, played by the excellent Australian actress Rachel Griffiths, as Nate's on-again, off-again lover, and Frederico Diaz (Freddy Rodríguez), who begins as an employee in the Fisher family mortuary and later becomes a partner, and has some serious marital problems of his own. Equally interesting is the murdered Lisa (Lili Taylor) as Nate's extremely New Age wife and the mother of their daughter, Maya, as well as the often-married academic geologist George (James Cromwell), the most recent addition to the family, who becomes Ruth's second husband. In addition, the series can alternate between black comedy, such as when one corpse winds up with a missing foot, or one of Claire's ne'er-do-well boyfriends laces some marijuana with embalming fluid, and moments of chilling, almost film noir quality, such as an episode in which David and his hearse are carjacked by a sadistic thug. These qualities, plus what one critic has called its "visually ravishing" style,[12] prevented the series from lapsing into some kind of *Addams Family* melodrama. As a matter of fact, it was these elements that kept the large and loyal following, whom some began referring to as "Deadheads,"[13] waiting with anticipation for the beginning of each new season of *Six Feet Under.*

Indeed, despite long hiatuses (sometimes lasting more than a year in the case of *The Sopranos*) and blatant efforts by the broadcast networks to imitate the formula with series such as *Kingpin* (NBC) and *Line of Fire* (ABC), the HBO miniseries have been met by overwhelming audience response when they have returned to the air. The reason for this can't only be the fact that the HBO miniseries permit the kind of language and nudity that the networks aren't allowed to duplicate. The reason may also have to do with the risks that HBO has taken to produce what on the surface might seem dramatic series with marginal characters and situations, strong writing, and indelible characters and the actors who create them. Almost as formidable, and what is new in the television dramatic series genre, is the fact that each season has a narrative closure that permits it to be seen individually. Indeed, the series' release on VHS tapes and DVDs has made them accessible to larger and larger audiences.

Whither HBO?

The popularity of dramatic series such as *The Sopranos* and *Six Feet Under* has created certain downsides for HBO. On an economic level there is the matter of churn—a situation that occurs when you have millions of people who subscribe for these series and then drop the network as soon as their run is over. And with *The Sopranos* soon to enter its sixth and perhaps penultimate season, finding replacements for series like *The Sopranos* (unless David Chase can be persuaded to keep the series going) and *Six Feet Under* is imperative.

By the same token, HBO has cut back on the number of made-for-television movies and has revised its role as almost the sole venue for movies about racial and other minorities. Indeed, the network that once gave us *The Tuskegee Airmen* and *The Josephine Baker Story* no longer seems to be interested in these stories. Perhaps this has happened as HBO has begun to turn to making films that will also appear in theaters, and the fear is that there is less of a crossover audience for films about, for example, African American history.

Similarly, with *Sex and the City* gone, there is no longer any women's programming worth viewing on the network. It doesn't seem that *Entourage* (2004–), which is a merely a male version of *Sex and the City*, is likely to take up the slack. Consequently, if one were to create a wish list for HBO, one might include some more original series and women's programs, and additional made-for-television movies; most of all, one might eliminate the late-night porn in favor of some interesting late-night programming. *Da Ali G Show* and *Real Time with Bill Maher* are a good start.

Despite these shortcomings, there is no doubt that HBO is the most adventurous network on television. To accomplish this, HBO has made the most of its natural advantages over the broadcast networks. But the ability to show recent Hollywood features, the freedom to portray nudity and to include strong language, and its subscription funding don't adequately explain it. These are advantages that other cable networks enjoy, and those networks are not producing the kind of programming one finds on HBO.

To understand HBO's success, one must observe a system that has developed a strong counterprogramming strategy, created by a series of gifted executives (Fuchs, Bewkes, Nevins), that has filled the gaps that the other networks have left. Coupled with this is a willingness to take risks on series that on the surface might seem marginal. Finally, there is the self-assurance of a network that gives gifted producers, such as David Chase, Alan Ball, Darren Starr, and Larry David, to name a few, the space—and money—to create without interference.

In so doing, HBO has had a large impact on television genres. Television documentaries have been freed from their primary tethering to public policy and historical issues. The distinction between the made-for-television movie and the theatrical film has begun to disappear. HBO has also inspired the sitcom to resume its role as a comic commentary on contemporary American manners and culture. Finally, the HBO dramatic series has become a form wherein each season can be enjoyed and judged as an individual unit. Therefore, there seems little doubt that along with dominating the Emmy Awards each year, HBO will continue to be the venue where the must-see shows will be found. In view of this, the other networks may have to resurrect the idea of a "committee on Emmy fairness."

Notes

1. Bill Carter, "The Miramax of the Emmys," *New York Times,* September 14, 2003, 24.

2. Grace Bradberry, "Swearing, Sex, and Brilliance," *Observer,* October 20, 2002, 8.

3. Julie Salamon, "Nevins Rules," *New York Times Magazine,* March 3, 2002, 66–69.

4. Diane Werts, "It's Not Just about Sex," *New York Newsday,* March 11, 2001, 55.

5. Jesse McKinley, "Red Carpet Days for HBO Films," *New York Times,* February 26, 2004, E1, 6.

6. Quoted in David Bianculli, "It's HBO and It's Tough," *New York Daily News,* February 8, 2002, 33.

7. Alessandra Stanley, "Sexy Women Out, Cantankerous Guys In," *New York Times,* January 2, 2004, E1.

8. A. O. Scott, "Working the Beat," *New York Times Magazine,* July 20, 2003, 7–8.

9. Quoted in Bradberry, "Swearing, Sex, and Brilliance," 8.

10. David Blum, "'Six Feet Under' Finds Its Footing," *New York Sun,* February 28, 2003, 15.

11. Robert Warshow, *The Immediate Experience* (New York: Anchor Books, 1964), 42.

12. Joy Press, "Exquisite Corpses," *Village Voice,* March 19–25, 2003, 55.

13. Marvin Kitman, "Digging Up New Love for 'Under,'" *New York Newsday,* July 28, 2002, D58.

11 | "i want my niche tv"

genre as a networking strategy in the digital era

Gary R. Edgerton and Kyle Nicholas

Something altogether new and different is happening to television genres in the ever-expanding multichannel universe of the digital era. When viewers currently flip through their channel lineups, they see all sorts of networks based on traditional story forms (the Biography Channel, Comedy Central, the History Channel); narrative genres that were previously popular on radio and in the movies (SoapNet, Westerns, Sci Fi Channel); formats that harken back to the earliest days of television (news, sports, children's programming); webs devoted to specific demographic groups (Lifetime, BET [Black Entertainment Television], Galavision); and even services designed to offer helpful advice about a wide range of lifestyle choices and activities (HGTV [Home and Garden Television], Travel Channel, Food Network). Never before has TV networking been so intimately linked to the process of genre formation, subject to the delicate negotiation that occurs between the industry and its business and creative personnel, the programming they produce, and the consumptive and identity-building behavior of audiences that network executives carefully target.

The recent proliferation of television networks spiked to 339 in 2003, up from 170 in 1998 (and substantially higher than the 74 in 1990 and 28 in 1980).[1] The identifiable turning point was the passage of the Telecommunications Act of 1996 that accelerated the ongoing trends toward an ever-greater consolidation of ownership across the various mass media, as well as an increasing convergence of technologies and content resulting from the emerging digital revolution. Cable and satellite TV

247

have together led the way in this transition, as 85 percent of the nation's 108 million households (as of February 2004) now subscribe to either cable (68 percent) or DTH/direct-to-home satellite TV (17 percent).[2] Moreover, prime-time viewing of cable (48 percent of the audience) finally surpassed the numbers achieved by the traditional broadcast networks (46.6 percent) in 2002, and cable's comparative popularity increased even further (50.3 percent versus 44.8 percent) in 2003.[3]

Three overlapping delivery systems—broadcasting, cable, and satellite TV—distinguish television networking. Six multimedia transnational corporations actually own a majority of the most important network properties across all three of these industrial sectors. The six major broadcast networks (ABC, CBS, NBC, Fox, WB, and UPN) are currently subsidiaries of only five mega media conglomerates: Disney is the parent of ABC; Viacom, of CBS and UPN; General Electric, of NBC; News Corporation, of Fox; and Time Warner, of WB. In addition, seventeen of the top twenty cable networks are either completely owned or co-owned by four of the five aforementioned transnational corporations: Disney has ESPN, A&E, Lifetime, ABC Family Channel, ESPN2, and the History Channel; Viacom has Nickelodeon, Spike TV, MTV, and VH1; General Electric has USA Network, A&E, CNBC, and the History Channel; and Time Warner has TNT, CNN, TBS, and CNN Headline News. The fifth mega media conglomerate, Rupert Murdoch's News Corporation, purchased DirecTV in December 2003, thus taking over America's largest satellite TV company in one bold stroke.

Corresponding to this unprecedented rise in numbers and consolidation in networking, television's newest business model no longer favors the six major broadcast networks. In contrast, cable channels target smaller niche audiences, program and promote their brand identities to viewers all year long, and aggressively cater 24/7 to consumer needs across a wide array of programming choices that usually begin on television but then extend quickly throughout a variety of related media, especially on network Web sites. Branding—which refers to defining and reinforcing a network's identity—has become the all-important strategy as the TV environment becomes increasingly cluttered with dozens of marginal channels. Brand recognition, in turn, has emerged as the most valuable form of currency as programming content is now widely adapted to other print, audio, video, and Web-based technologies to be marketed to network consumers.

Cable, in particular, has enjoyed success in competing for audiences with the six broadcast networks precisely because it utilizes genre as a tactic to differentiate itself, rather than as a means of minimizing risk by assuring product standardization. According to television scholar Michael Curtin, genres have customarily followed "a familiar cycle in the history of broadcast programming [of] innovation, imitation, [and] saturation."[4] Genre critic Jason Mittell further relates "how the classic network system used formulas, recombinant innovations and program cloning to try to appeal to viewers through a strategy of 'least objectionable programming' that remains important to this day."[5] Prior to the current digital era, television production practices encouraged modest innovation in the execution of well-known programming formulas, leading to a recognizable and simultaneous rise-and-fall cycle of popular genres across all the major broadcast networks. This pattern was widely evident beginning with the emergence of the three-network oligopoly in the 1950s and continued unabated through the rise of cable television during the 1970s and 1980s.

In *Inside Prime Time* (1983), media sociologist Todd Gitlin calls television's style of invention "recombinant," employing a biological metaphor that is fully consistent with the taxonomic nature of traditional genre criticism. Gitlin argues that "if clones are the lowest forms of imitation, recombinants of elements from proven successes are the most interesting" (citing the then critical hit *Hill Street Blues* as a prime example of recombination, being an amalgam of the crime show, the documentary, the soap opera, and the sitcom).[6] Most interestingly, Gitlin claimed that the "era of recombinatory excess" finds its most fundamental expression in the business of television, rather than what appears on the screen, asserting that "recombinant style shapes not only the marketing of new toothpastes but the marketing of high as well as popular culture."[7]

What Gitlin's prescient observation anticipates is the accelerated convergence of advertising and entertainment that is now endemic in the digital era. More than anything else, this widespread move toward recombining, repositioning, and repurposing previously successful television formulas is what the current explosion in networking is all about. "There's nothing that delivers eyeballs like networks—nothing," notes reality mogul Mark Burnett (CBS's *Survivor,* NBC's *The Apprentice*), "so one of the solutions [for the networks] is smarter marketing integration."[8] Since the 1980s, genres have actually grown far more useful to the TV industry as marketing devices than as production strategies. They have become starting points from which to imagine whole new television services more so than innovative series (although any start-up

Hill Street Blues is a prime example of recombination, being an amalgam of the crime show, the documentary, the soap opera, and the situation comedy. Daniel J. Travanti as Captain Frank Furillo. Courtesy of the National Broadcasting Company.

network eventually needs to produce its own original programming as well, if it hopes to stay competitive after the initial novelty of a new channel wears off).

TV genres are currently an essential part of the brave new world of branded entertainment. Within the parlance of the television business, genres were first used as utility brands. For example, CNN was founded in 1980 as the all-news channel. The problem with utility branding is that this kind of marketing is literally too generic and therefore too easily copied. Turner Broadcasting and the entire industry soon learned that, in 1983, when Westinghouse and ABC started the short-lived Satellite News Channel (SNC), followed in 1996 by MSNBC and Fox News. "Utility brands offer a functional relationship to the viewer with the promise of providing useful information," explains Steven Schiffman, executive vice president of marketing for the Weather Channel; "the problem, though, is that a competitor can always come along who is even more useful."[9]

Instead, TV genres are now employed as points of departure in fashioning a network's identity brand. Unlike utility branding, this more sophisticated type of branding is designed to tap into what a target audience really cares about, thus forging an emotional bond that reaches well beyond any content category. To take the case of news again, CNN has become the hard news cable network ("breaking news first") from a distinctly middle-of-the-road perspective, while Fox News has clearly established itself as the conservative alternative (delivering the so-called fair and balanced approach). In contrast, MSNBC has proved far less successful in crafting its own unique identity, with a lineup composed mostly of talk and softer news (shifting branding claims from "MSNBC: The Whole Picture" to "The Best News on Cable" to now "America's NewsChannel" in the hope of eventually finding its special niche). "Identity brands have an 'emotive' relationship to the viewer," continues Schiffman. "They offer the 'promise of an experience' and a feeling, and they inspire loyalty in the face of competition."[10]

Successful networking today aims at intensifying the connection between a channel and its target audience. High branding (which is a concept that is quickly becoming part of television's popular discourse) does not just mean network logo, tagline, or program recognition, but implies a strong relational bonding between a channel and its viewership. "Brands have begun taking the position that the viewer must really invite you in," asserts Jak Severson, CEO of Madison Road Entertainment (an independent television production studio), "which means it can't be about advertising as much as it has to be about entertaining."[11] From the perspective of TV networking, then, branding operates much as the critical concept of a "supertext" functioned for genre theorists a generation ago. As John Cawelti recounts, "The supertext [genre] claims to be an abstract of the most significant characteristics or family resemblances among many particular texts."[12] It functioned as an idealized focal point around which analysts envisioned the working parameters of a genre. Similarly, network executives strive to make their brands synonymous with the genre they are specializing in, so that the "channel's spin" becomes the most influential determinant in television genre development these days, more so than any aesthetic or narrative innovations.

A TV genre today is therefore subject to the ongoing demands of branding a network. It is a shorthand tactic by which network programmers build a target audience; and since the endgame of networking is first and foremost attracting and holding a specific viewership, the conventions of any television genre are readily stretched, recombined, and repurposed with that goal firmly in mind. Genres have also become virtually interchangeable with the highest-profile network brands. For example, Keleman Associates of New York City won the 2000 Research Case Study Award of the Cable and Telecommunications Association for Marketing (CTAM) for its ESPN-funded study, "Television Network Branding in the Multichannel Universe." Keleman reported that viewers "identified powerful network brands within specific genres" for each of the eight programming categories under consideration: for survey respondents, ESPN meant television sports, "Discovery (science/nature), HBO (TV movies), The History Channel (history-documentary), NBC (general entertainment), CNN (news/information), HGTV (how-to/do it yourself) and A&E (cultural/arts)."[13]

Global branding is now becoming the norm in TV networking. The top 10 percent of all television channels are currently busy establishing a reach that travels well beyond their countries of origin. When viewers worldwide watch TV, they generally disregard the distinctions between service promos, shows, and ads; consequently, successful branding is as dependent on network-defining promotional tactics (logos, interstitials, vignettes) as it is on popular programming. Executives and producers alike use genres strategically to inspire every kind of content that goes out through cable lines or over the air. Television genres are accordingly far more elastic, improvisational, and recombinant than they've ever been. Two cases in point are the A&E Television Networks (AETN) and the Scripps Networks. These examples are particularly instructive because they run the gamut of corporate size and income in networking but still reflect basically the same types of branding patterns. AETN is co-owned by two major media conglomerates (Disney/ABC and General Electric/NBC Universal) and a mini-major corporation (Hearst) with combined revenues of $57.3 billion in 2003, while the Scripps channels are held solely by one mini-major (E. W. Scripps) with annual earnings totaling $1.5 billion in comparison.[14]

Branding Genres

AETN is a joint venture shared by Disney/ABC (37.5 percent), the Hearst Corporation (37.5 percent), and General Electric/NBC Universal (25 percent). Founded in 1984, AETN is the parent corporation of A&E (88 million subscriber households), the Biography Channel (23 million), the History Channel (86 million), and the History Channel International (38 million). The combined reach of AETN in 2004 was 235 million homes, telecasting in twenty languages across seventy countries. In addition, television services such as the four networks that constitute AETN typically identify their target audiences by demographic makeup (with A&E, for instance, it is upscale women aged twenty-five to fifty-four), lifestyle characteristics (AETN features viewers who are interested in arts and culture as a pastime), and what TV executives call "passion or touch points" (where channels establish as close a relationship as possible with viewers and build brand loyalty over time). In general, passion or touch points entail nurturing one or more signature programs (usually "original" series), extending the brand beyond television into a number of transmedia ventures (such as related Web sites, home video/DVDs, print), expanding the reach of the original brand—the foundational network—into one or more spin-off channels, and constantly working to keep the network brand in tune with the needs and desires of its niche target audience.

A&E's signature program is *Biography* (1987–), which averages a nightly viewership of nearly three million, spawning videotapes, DVDs, a magazine called *Biography* with a readership of two million, and the Biography Channel (a spin-off network inaugurated in 1998). The *Biography* franchise celebrated its fifteenth anniversary with its one thousandth episode in 2002. AETN first employed A&E and the *Biography* series to establish its brand ("the art of biography, drama, and documentary") before attempting any offshoot services. A&E is thus a prime example of a foundational network (which is loosely defined as a channel having reached the threshold of eighty million subscribers). A&E next spawned the spin-off network the History Channel in 1995, specifically earmarking men aged twenty-five to fifty-four, who had remained until then an untapped segment of AETN's target constituency. "The History Channel [soon became] the fastest growing cable network ever" on both the domestic and international fronts.[15] The reason for this record-setting rise was that history proved to be a reliable television genre for attracting male viewers on a regular basis (along with news

THE HISTORY CHANNEL

DAYTIME PROGRAMS

A new journey into the past begins every day. The History Channel proves that there's more to stimulating daytime TV than soaps and talk shows. Tune in and enhance the quality of your daytime viewing.

HISTORY THEATER:

If all the world's a stage, history is its theatre. This show features outstanding theatrical presentations, from both the U.S. and England, set in historic periods. Presented in the form of multi-episode series, it's a new way to watch compelling stories unfold day after day while you enjoy quality television.

HIGH POINTS IN HISTORY:

A virtual anthology of historical documentaries, *High Points* offers a wide range of perspectives on greatness. Shows that cover some of the most important events and people from the past, and that take viewers back to the places and the moments that still stand out for the way they've shaped who we are today.

THE REAL WEST:

Buffalo Bill, General Custer, Dodge City. Now there is an entire series devoted to exploring some of America's most enduring myths and legends. *The Real West* covers some of the subjects Americans love best in an enlightening and entertaining way, like cowboys, outlaw gangs and boom towns. It provides unusual close-ups, not just of the best known stories, but of fascinating sidelights, such as Wild West Shows, Wild, Wild Woman and the Texas Rangers.

YEAR BY YEAR:

YEAR BY YEAR travels back in time to chronicle the events that stand out and define some of history's most interesting years. Each episode is focused on a single year, and combines documentary newsreels and historic footage so that you'll experience it, not just as it looks to us today, but how it was seen and reported by the people at the time.

The History Channel became the fastest-growing cable network ever by promising its target audience "All of History, All in One Place." Courtesy of A&E Television Networks.

and sports programming). As a result, the History Channel quickly transformed into a foundational network in its own right, prompting the launch of the History Channel International in 1998.

Most significantly, TV genres are now stretched to conform to their respective network brands. Together the History Channel and the History Channel International provide an ideal case study of how this typically happens in three important ways. First, genre content is localized to appeal to a rapidly increasing array of racial, ethnic, and international constituencies in the move to globalize a network brand. For instance, the History Channel International "adapted programs to local needs, using dubbing or perhaps adding a new host" for any new affiliated region that chose to accept its signal. As the coverage of the History Channel International grew dramatically from 1998 through 2003, network executives also made a concerted effort to enter into a series of "joint ventures . . . acquir[ing] locally produced programs" from participating nations to "fill out the rest" of its twenty-four-hour, seven-day-a-week schedule.[16] This careful attention to the expectations and desires of its rapidly expanding audience base also facilitated a quick and ready infusion of alternative styles and perspectives into the history genre from television producers on continents as widely diverse in cultural orientation as Europe, South America, Asia, and Australia.

Second, TV genres are typically subject to the same kind of stylistic influences that are affecting the rest of television at any given time (whether or not these content changes make sense in regard to the integrity or credibility of the form). For example, the History Channel has been as susceptible to the "*Survivor* aftereffect" as any other network brand or genre. A recent instance of "reality history" is *Extreme History with Roger Daltry,* which debuted on the History Channel in the fall of 2003. This half-hour series capitalizes on the strategy of marketing history alongside rock and roll by the casting of a well-known pop star as the show's featured host. A network press release even describes "Roger Daltry, [the] lead singer of the legendary rock band The Who, . . . [as] an avid history buff, [who] goes on location to demonstrate the challenge of surviving history's epic adventures, explorations, and battles."[17] Episodes include Daltry scaling the Montana Rockies like Lewis and Clark in 1805; driving steers through the Chisholm Trail of Texas and Oklahoma; and shooting the Colorado rapids in a wooden rowboat as John Wesley Powell did in 1869. Daltry's exploits as a celebrity surrogate reenacting a prefabricated historical narrative epitomize the History Channel's branding claim that it is the niche network "Where the

Past Comes Alive." Reality histories such as *Extreme History with Roger Daltry* also illustrate the ongoing negotiation between popular programming trends, branding imperatives, and generic change that is always a part of producing historical programming (or any other genre) on TV.

Third, network branding also sets in motion many of the transmedia and extratextual transformations that occur in television genres today. For instance, audiences of the History Channel and the History Channel International are provided with many interactive opportunities on the Web sites of these two networks (see HistoryChannel.com and HistoryInternational.com), such as researching additional information about programs and the specific topics they raise; relaunching related video clips; checking out upcoming TV listings; playing history-related games; participating in online discussion groups about the network or specific series; downloading free classroom lesson plans; visiting the History Channel Store to browse literally thousands of ancillary products (such as DVDs, videotapes, books, apparel, toys, posters, calendars, home decor, and unique gifts); or even taking tours (entitled "Lewis & Clark Trail," "Civil War Trail," "D-Day and the Battle of the Bulge") with other History Channel viewers. The bottom line in branding is that it always aims to shift the emphasis in genre construction and reception from program viewing to some kind of consumptive activity.

Nowhere is this trend toward generic transformation across multiple media more evident than on the task-oriented formats of the four Scripps networks—HGTV (Home & Garden Television), Food Network, DIY (Do-It-Yourself) Network, and Fine Living. Despite being the twenty-fifth-largest media group in the United States, E. W. Scripps is modest in size and scope (twenty-one daily newspapers and ten TV stations along with its cable networks) when compared with the 2003 combined holdings of AETN's co-owners (twenty-four broadcast and cable networks, ten television production studios and sixty-three TV stations, five radio networks and seventy-five stations, two movie studios and a theater chain, e-businesses and publications, newspapers, magazines, book publishing, music recording and publishing companies, sports teams, theme parks and resorts, restaurants, and retail outlets).[18] E. W. Scripps's legacy is built solidly on the Cincinnati-based Scripps Howard newspaper chain, even though its four cable channels have recently emerged as the most profitable part of this mini-major's business portfolio.

In a move designed to diversify into cable, E. W. Scripps purchased Cinetel Productions, an independent television studio in Knoxville, Tennessee, in early 1994.[19] On December 30 of that year, Scripps introduced HGTV into 6.5 million homes and forty-four markets, targeting an adult audience (which skewed female) aged twenty-five to fifty-four. HGTV found a ready niche by pioneering the lifestyle-oriented do-it-yourself home improvement genre with programming organized across five overlapping categories (decorating, gardening, remodeling, at home, and crafts). In 1997, Scripps bought a controlling interest in the Food Network from the A. H. Belo Corporation, another owner of newspaper and broadcast properties, while concurrently expanding the reach of HGTV into Europe, Japan, Australia, and the Philippines. Scripps then spun off DIY from HGTV in 1999 as a simultaneous on-air/online channel providing more in-depth tips and step-by-step instructions on domestic repair.[20] Fine Living soon followed in 2002 as an upscale extension of HGTV specializing in adventure and travel advice, household upgrades, and consumer reports on higher-end products and luxury items.

E. W. Scripps's two foundational networks—HGTV (84 million) and the Food Network (83 million)—are now well established and among the fastest-growing channels in the television industry, while DIY (23 million) and Fine Living (19 million) are holding their own as up-and-coming spin-off networks. Programmers at HGTV and the Food Network, specifically, jump-started their respective services with signature programs (such as HGTV's *Room by Room* and the Food Network's *How to Boil Water*) that emphasized self-improvement lessons filtered through a traditional makeover story line. Moreover, the Beta Research Corporation's annually conducted "brand identity" survey ranked HGTV ninth and the Food Network tenth as most "family-oriented" among all broadcast, cable, and satellite TV networks in 2004, whereas the Food Network was first and HGTV second "in terms of having well-liked hosts and personalities."[21] This last designation, in particular, underscores the host-driven relational nature of much of the programming produced by Scripps. Many of HGTV's original homegrown personalities are still popular and on the air, including Carol Duvall, Joe Ruggiero, and Kitty Bartholomew, and the Food Network has built its cooking shows around approximately three dozen celebrity chefs starting in 1994 with its first breakout star, Emeril Lagasse.

HGTV programming telecast from twenty-three different countries in 2004 (with programs such as *The World's Most Beautiful Homes*), while the Food Network is similarly global in orientation with such series as the cult favorite *Iron Chef* ("*Ultimate Fighting Champion* meets Julia Child"), which is a recombinant cooking-comedy-game show originating in Japan. HGTV.com is also one of the online industry's fastest-growing destinations, with more than three million different visitors each month from around the world. Likewise, the international fan base of the Food Network includes four million unique users of FoodNetwork.com on a yearly basis. As is the case with the History Channel (HistoryChannel.com), the interactive posture taken by the target audiences of the Scripps Networks illustrates the sea change in TV reception patterns over the last fifteen years. "The average television household [in January 2003] has 89 channels at its disposal, up from 33 in 1990," according to Nielsen Media Research.[22] Nevertheless, individual audience members typically "devote most of their viewing to about eight channels."[23] Today TV fans are far more committed to their own networks of choice than ever before and are far more willing to extend their television watching into program-related activities on the Web sites of their favorite networks. The online communities now flourishing around HistoryChannel.com and HGTV.com provide two representative examples of how TV viewers market specific programs among themselves, participate in a whole host of old and new consumptive practices that are easily accessed on network Web sites and, more specifically, contribute to the shaping of the History Channel and HGTV brands (along with the television genres that initially inspired them).

Consuming Genres

Networks now employ online discussion boards as a common passion point strategy for creating an even stronger and more long-lasting connection with their respective target audiences. Although smaller in number than a channel's aggregate viewership, daily participation on HistoryChannel.com and HGTV.com, for instance, regularly totals in the tens of thousands of loyal fans across all the various categories and subtopics of conversation. Participants use these discussion boards to engage in interactive text-based dialogues with other like-minded network devotees. Viewers who are both more comfortable with using online media and personally engaged with what they've just seen on TV utilize HistoryChannel.com and HGTV.com to express their likes and dislikes about their preferred channels, while an even greater number of "lurkers" simply "listen in." Overall, these online conversations offer a privileged view into how participants make sense of network programming, reinforce or challenge each other's understanding of shows and hosts, and integrate the channel's generic content into their daily lives.

More specifically, the History Channel's discussion boards are organized into eight overlapping categories ("Polls," "Wars," "The World," "Religious History," "Educators' Forum," "Sports History," "Veterans' Forum," and "On TV"). These groupings provide simple and easily recognizable links from which to access broadly defined agenda items, even as viewers generate their own subtopics within each of these general areas. On a typical day, for example, "Wars" is usually the most popular category, averaging 190,000 separate posts over 15,000 different discussion threads; in contrast, "Educators' Forum" is the least active section, with 2,500 posts over 375 threads. Perhaps the most important grouping for our purposes is the third largest, "On TV," where participants consider the merits of individual shows, establish their own expertise in comparison to other viewers, exchange information about programming and network plans, and recommend the pros and cons of ancillary products that are available for purchase at the "official store" of the History Channel. All told, "On TV" averages more than 11,000 posts and 2,250 various discussion threads each day.

Two of the most identifiable characteristics of HistoryChannel.com participants are their inclinations to argue among themselves about story details and to debate the historical accuracy of programming, probably reflecting the male-oriented communication style of the network's target audience and how seriously these fans take their interest in the past. HistoryChannel.com discussions tend to be highly opinionated, dense in structure, and comparatively weighty in tone. A case in point is the remarks surrounding the November 21, 2003, airing of episode 9 of *The Men Who Killed Kennedy*, entitled "The Guilty Men," on the eve of the fortieth anniversary of the assassination of JFK. Among other claims, this program suggests that Lyndon Baines Johnson was complicit in the shooting of Kennedy, which set off a firestorm of controversy beyond the History Channel and HistoryChannel.com—including public protests by Gerald Ford and former Johnson aides Bill Moyers and Jack Valenti (then president of the Motion Picture Association of America). Network executives eventually issued a formal apology in April 2004 and permanently shelved *The Men Who Killed Kennedy* from any future telecasts. Fan reaction to the show and the subsequent imbroglio was similarly heated. Typical postings included one by Duncan Ross, who started the thread with a rare signed post:

> **dross7677:** It is a sad day when one of my favorite stations airs a program which simply appeals to a fringe segment, has no basis in fact, and is an ethical disgrace. I am speaking, of course, of your program with

respect to Lyndon Johnson as the murderer of JFK. . . . From now on, I will question anything I see on your channel.

Squatch: You obviously watched the show, therefore the History Channel accomplished their mission objective. No sense in telling/suggesting/implying someone they can't say or air something in America—It's their God given/Constitutional Right. I was entertained which is the root objective of the ENTERTAINMENT industry.

Xman: Is this JFK presentation supposed to be entertainment or factual reporting? It's the goofiest thing I've seen in a long time. And we wonder how normally rational people can be taken in by e-mail scams, fortune tellers, and the many get-rich schemes!

Duffyduz: Boy, and I use that term purposefully, do you need to get caught up on this cou de' etau [*sic*]. Either you didn't live through it, or you choose to bury your head in the sand. . . . "Duh, everything looks okay from here." These researchers are after the TRUTH about one of America's darkest day[s]. . . . "Boy," open your mind, and look at what we—the people that have been paying attention for forty years—know about this. . . . Think for yourself

In general, HistoryChannel.com postings include many personal opinions and interpretations, which is common for most network discussion boards. One distinguishing feature of this particular newsgroup, however, is the frequent allusion to other, related communication examples, suggesting a relatively high degree of media literacy among HistoryChannel.com participants. For instance:

Sydneysider: I've just looked at the PBS website connected with the Frontline program "Who was Oswald?" and I must say it is complete and utter garbage: http://www.pbs.org/wgbh/pages/frontline/shows/oswald/.

LimeyLouie: I was watching the news (CNN I think) and they reported that an independent council [*sic*] concluded that there was more than one gunman in the Kennedy assassination. It was a quick story and not many details were given out about the story. So I kept tuning into other news sources in hopes of getting more details about it. Nothing else was reported anywhere on any news shows and/or channels. I went on Anomalies.net and posted a topic to see if anyone else had heard about this report. I got an interesting reply. A person sent me a link to his/her ftp site and told me to download the Zapruder film and examine it closely.

Lancelot128: Can you believe that Court TV had the gall to say the

Warren Commission Report was all true, that there was no conspiracy. I cannot believe they said that! Court TV must be in someone's pocket!!! Wonder who??? . . . And now Court TV has taken down their comment site. LOL [laugh out loud].

K_pede1120: Tonight on 20/20 they claim, that they will reveal who fired the fatal shot. Should be interesting after watching all the JFK murder theories on the History Channel all week.

Dsomer996: *Capital Gang* on CNN Sucks! Dear CNN Capital Gang, After hearing you're [*sic*] broadcast tonight (which by the way, I never watch you controlled corporate media gangs), I was outraged to hear you putting down the History Channel.

Timestwo: Peter Jennings Special on ABC. I am embarrassed for ABC because of their poor display of journalism last night. As an American, I feel victimized by whomever is behind this blatant cover up.

Thomascrown: First why do we listen to Peter Jennings/Why do we watch . . . Listen up America. We as Americans should weed out those Anti-Americans and stop buying their products/movies/books/TV. If you're as Anti-American as Peter Jennings, please leave America. Yes there are major problems in the good 'o USA but it's the best and for my money so is The History Channel.

Sydneysider: If you want to know more about the Kennedy assassination than what the corporate media wants you to know, a really good place to start with is www.blackopradio.com.

"Sydneysider" is an active participant on HistoryChannel.com who often posts hyperlinks to related Web sites. Linking broadens the online deliberations by sharing new resources, but it also widens the topical universe to the point where discussions can appear to be expanding exponentially. In a lively and diverse thread, such as the one involving *The Men Who Killed Kennedy*, conversations can sometimes splinter and reconstitute just as rapidly as contributors draw new and unexpected connections. Comments also overlap, and themes can stop abruptly in one post, only to start again in a later e-mail message. One leitmotif of HistoryChannel.com participants' postings is their expressed desire to go beyond television watching to actually taking some kind of action, usually exploring some historical site or becoming more civically involved as in the "What Can I Do?" thread that followed the initial discussion of the JFK documentary.

Joly: This morning I called my representative and congresswoman asking for action and explanations. I ordered 3 copies of The Men Who

Killed Kennedy to pass on to friends and ask them to view and pass on to others. Next I will sign the petition [to support an inquiry]. KEEP IT GOING.

Keeper7: All it takes to reopen this investigation is *one person* with integrity and backbone in the government. There is just too much information available to allow this cover-up to continue. . . . All it takes is one person in the right position to pursue this. We can win!!!

BFranklin: I would be honored to take part. . . . Quite frankly, this whole situation has me so sad and pissed off that I am VERY tempted to proclaim to my government that I refuse to vote until this is cleared.

Wasitworthit: How can we get the American People to wake up and reclaim our rights as our founding fathers expected us to. Especially with our distrust of the government. I feel that the only way this can be possible, is that every member of the military from past wars, present, and future STAND UP and demand that the vault in the basement of the CIA where all the truth is held be opened to the public.

These brief representative postings indicate a few of the signposts around which the History Channel's target audience becomes emotionally engaged on a deep personal level with this specific network brand. History really does matter to these participants, who are overwhelmingly male (the highest concentration of any cable network), upscale and thus preoccupied with the "quality" and "credibility" of programming (among the top five channels for men making more than $75,000 a year), proactive in their lifestyle choices ("deep coverage" in opinion leaders and "business decision makers"), and generally conservative in political views and values.[24] Fans of the History Channel and the HistoryChannel.com are also technophiles committed to such prime-time series as *Modern Marvels* (1995–), *Tactical to Practical* (2003–), and *Tech Effect* (2004–). They join discussion boards that are situated on a regally colored crimson-and-gold visual field dominated by flashing program promotions, channel guides, calendars, video archives, and of course product advertisements. While some newsgroup participants clearly bore in on specific threads (such as the aforementioned postings on *The Men Who Killed Kennedy*), others surf the site, visiting one conversation after another in a more casual manner. HistoryChannel.com fans are free to comment on whatever discussions most attract them, and they lose themselves in whatever threads happen to catch their eyes at the moment. In the end, the History Channel delivers successfully on its promise to provide a combined televisual and virtual experience, "Where the Past Comes Alive," to its loyal target audience.

HGTV.com likewise fits into its own special niche by catering to the unique passion points of its particular fan base. In contrast to the densely threaded discussions found at HistoryChannel.com, the more female-oriented HGTV.com specializes in short, congenial posts that put a premium on the parasocial relationships among discussion board contributors, as well as between these Web site visitors and the numerous hosts that HGTV features. For example, HGTV.com fans frequently comment on hosts' appearances, various aspects of their personalities, and the quality of their on-air performances. Sometimes they even speculate about the personal lives of their favorite network stars, occasionally letting their passions boil over, as in the following thread devoted to the prospects of a "Calendar of the Guys of HGTV":

> **TheresaJohnson:** Nothing wrong with classy/sexy men with tools in the work setting. I'm asking cause I'd buy it. Has anyone asked the guys . . . Do the guys even know each other . . . that would be cool a group shot and then individuals get a month . . . Rick Spence [*Curb Appeal,* 1994–] and Hunky Paul [Paul James, *Gardening by the Yard,* 1996–] for June and July hot weather pic. Now that's a gift for Christmas. p.s can I come to the photo shoot?

> **Oomphgrrl:** Hmmmn. that could get really scary! Matt Fox [*Room by Room,* 1994–] in speedos? Michael Payne [*Designing for the Sexes,* 1998–] shirtless? Charles Burbridge [*Design on a Dime,* 2003–] on a leopard skin rug?

> **CurbAppealFan:** If that's what you're interested in, check out Rick's website and the music video section. He's got a video where he's in typical carpenter attire (or musician attire)—white T-shirt, faded jeans. The video moves really fast and has a lot of other people in it, but you would probably like what you'd see. I like the music as well. It's at http://www.funkyfresh.com/video/velvetelvis.wmv.

The discussion boards on HGTV.com are divided into six general categories averaging nearly one hundred thousand unique fan visits per day in 2004. Five of these hyperlinks correspond directly to the handful of programming areas featured on the television network ("Decorating," "Gardening," "Remodeling," "At Home," and "Crafts"). A sixth and final catchall category ("Fan Favorites") provides an alternative option for participants to express their likes and dislikes about this specific channel and its corresponding Web site. According to its promotional materials, "HGTV is the only network that provides viewers with an inside look at the emotional center of life—the home." Cultivating an intimate sense of place within an atmosphere of belonging is the ultimate passion point for this particular target audience. Hard-core fans and new initiates are joined together in the "HGTV family." It is the number one cable network for women aged twenty-five to fifty-four, working women over the age of eighteen making $75,000 a year or more, and all Americans who own their own home.[25] HGTV audience members integrate the network and HGTV.com into their lives in much the same way as they position television sets within their decor; they recognize that their TVs are indispensable to them, while also feeling self-conscious sometimes about the amount of time they spend watching as well as the reasons why:

LaDonnaRenee: Am I the only one? I don't watch a movie or TV commercial without noticing the background. I mostly notice kitchens and bathrooms. It may take me time to really understand what the commercial is actually about I am so busy gathering details from the room. The one that I especially like lately is the Lysterine [*sic*] mouthwash commercial where the whole family hides in cabinets and on the pot rack when the mom takes the mouthwash out of the grocery bag. That is a very nice kitchen.

Frazzled: I too will notice the surroundings and many times not even see the product. I watched *The Osbornes* [*sic*] on MTV the first time out of curiosity, after that—a few more times (muted I might add) to see that gorgeous house. What a surprise!

theOracle: My favorite is the scary movie that had lattice bathroom wallpaper—even on the ceiling. I was wondering—how do you paper a ceiling? Why would you, unless it was small?

Frazzled: Papering ceilings is done a lot in Victorian homes, and it can be quite the process.

theOracle: Victorians covered a lot of things because they didn't clean much, and heating was a sooty business. Spring cleaning was a big affair because that was often the only time rugs were beaten and walls were washed. Ceilings, too.

On the one hand, HGTV.com participants contribute to discussion boards to extend their knowledge and improve their skills. They regularly pick up tips, exchange product recommendations, and post photographs of their own creations. On the other hand, they also log on to share friendly conversations with other "how-to" aficionadas. They seek and give affirmation to each other along with the occasional advice, creating a pervasive sense of warmth and inclusion that only takes a backseat in those periodic posts where fans complain among themselves and to HGTV executives about something they might not especially like. For instance:

Pinktulips: I hate those before and after landscaping shows, as well as the "cover-your-eyes" surprise versions. Where I live PBS is offering a better selection of gardening shows than HGTV. They peaked at about 4 yrs. and then they must have changed managers because then the "me too" garbage started . . . I guess the programmers must think our intelligence level is under the table somewhere.

Intgrtyhon: HGTV used to be my favorite network. Now I only watch a handful of shows.

Supergirlsmom: Well, I guess that just leaves us with "TV," which all HGTV is anymore. There is very little information given. It's all about entertainment now. LEARNING about decorating seems to have taken a backseat to the "Oh my Gosh" factor. Perhaps there is a reason for it?

What underlies these specific objections is the recent decision by HGTV programmers and producers to shift the network's emphasis away from a sole reliance on expert information and practical advice to more story-driven, lifestyle-oriented narratives. This modification is meant to expand the channel's reach far beyond its 2004 prime-time average of slightly more than 650,000 TV households per evening. HGTV is attempting to strike a balance between its do-it-yourself signature approach and the kinds of tried-and-true melodramatic formulas that are likely to result in an even larger core audience over time. In turn, network executives monitor as much as possible the pace of generic change by paying close attention to both quantitative data provided by the Nielsen Television Index (NTI; ratings, shares, demographics) and Nielsen/Netratings (unique visitors, demographics, page views, time-spent information) and the qualitative feedback they gather from their Web site discussion boards like the examples reproduced here. The challenge for HGTV's decision makers is to facilitate this programming transition in such a way and at such a pace as not to alienate their loyal fan base while still attracting tens of thousands of new viewers and online participants each month. This transformation in generic content is not an easy task and requires close coordination among the kinds of choices that are available at HGTV and HGTV.com and the needs and desires of this narrowly targeted though ever-widening audience.

Like the History Channel and all the other successful foundational networks today, HGTV produces "a great commercial environment" that engulfs its viewers in personally engaging and entertaining generic content shaped by a strong and easily recognizable brand name. Fans of the network respond quickly to the intimate and soothing color scheme of HGTV.com that is consciously designed to evoke home and hearth (mint green on burnished red with sky blue highlights speckled with white puffy clouds). No wonder HGTV ranks number one among all channel/Web site tandems in the trust that its target audience places in the items it advertises, and number two in its audience's willingness to follow through and purchase these products and services.[26] Moreover, online chatting has emerged as the most direct way yet for Web site participants to express their preferences and negotiate an increasingly individualistic relationship with their networks of choice. All told, television genre construction has extended its reach into cyberspace, where conversations swirl amid programming, advertisements, and the watchful eyes of network executives who work feverishly to keep their core fans satisfied while concurrently enticing as many new consumers as possible to sample their branded content. TV genre formation thus comes full circle as an institutional process (from networking to branding to consuming) being renewed time and again in the digital era.

Notes

1. Michael McCarthy, "TV Watchers Can Tune in to Wider Selection of Channels," *USA Today,* April 12, 2004, 2B.

2. A. C. Nielsen Media Research.

3. Allison Romano, "Cable's Big Piece of the Pie," *Broadcasting and Cable,* December 30, 2002, 8; McCarthy, "TV Watchers Can Tune in to Wider Selection of Channels."

4. Michael Curtin, *Redeeming the Wasteland: Television Documentary and Cold War Politics* (New Brunswick, N.J.: Rutgers University Press, 1995), 248.

5. Jason Mittell, "Genre Cycles: Innovation, Imitation, Saturation," in *The Television History Book,* ed. Michele Hilmes (London: British Film Institute, 2003), 48.

6. Todd Gitlin, *Inside Prime Time* (New York: Pantheon, 1983), 75, 273–324.

7. Ibid., 79.

8. Sara Jacobs, "Branded Entertainment," *Hollywood Reporter,* May 4, 2004, http://209.11.49.186/thr/television/feature_display.jsp?vnucontent_id=1000502256.

9. Louis Chunovic, "Topic of Branding Is Red-Hot at CTAM," *Television Week,* July 30, 2001, http://www.tvweek.com/advertise/073001ctam.html.

10. Ibid.

11. Jacobs, "Branded Entertainment."

12. John G. Cawelti, "The Question of Popular Genres Revisited," in *In the Eye of the Beholder: Critical Perspectives of Popular Film and Television,* ed. Gary R. Edgerton, Michael T. Marsden, and Jack Nachbar (Bowling Green, Ohio: Bowling Green State University Press, 1997), 68.

13. ESPN, "ESPN Research Study Honored by CTAM: Network Branding Survey Singled Out as Top Case Study of the Year," press release, March 14, 2000, http://www.sportsticker.com/ESPNtoday/2000/mar_00/CTAMAward.htm.

14. Kim McAvoy, "Special Report: The B&C 25 Media Groups," *Broadcasting and Cable,* May 12, 2003, 12.

15. "Making History with History," *Reveries,* March 2001, http://www.reveries.com/reverb/media/scheff.

16. "The History Channel: Making the Past Come Alive," *Video Age International* 17, no. 4 (March–April 1997): 22–23.

17. The History Channel, "*Extreme History with Roger Daltry:* Surviving history's epic challenges . . . one day at a time," press release, July 14, 2003.

18. McAvoy, "Special Report," 12, 14.

19. The E. W. Scripps Corporation, "Our History," 2003, http://www.scripps.com/corporateoverview/history/index.shtml.

20. Home & Garden Television, "Background Information on HGTV," press release, September 16, 2002, http://www.hgtv.com/hgtv/about_us/article/0,1783,HGTV_3080_1420294,00.html.

21. Mike Reynolds, "Study: Several Cable Nets Are 'Family-Oriented,'" *Multichannel News,* April 14, 2004, 16; Jim Forkan, "Fox News Scores Branding Points," *Multichannel News,* April 22, 2002, 12.

22. Jim Rutenberg, "Few Viewers Object as Unbleeped Words Spread on Network TV," *New York Times,* January 25, 2003, 7B.

23. Geraldine Fabrikant, "Need ESPN but Not MTV? Some Push for That Option," *New York Times,* May 31, 2004, 6C.

24. "The History Channel: Viewer Profile," *Advertising Age* (2003 Cable Guide), http://www.adage.com/cableguide/25.html.

25. "HGTV/Home & Garden Television: Viewer Profile," *Advertising Age* (2003 Cable Guide), http://www.adage.com/cableguide/24.html.

26. Ibid.

4 | television genres in global perspective

12 globalization and the generic transformation of telenovelas

Timothy Havens

Latin American telenovelas have become a lightning rod of debate for scholars of television globalization. Some insist that these long-form melodramas, which often top the ratings throughout Latin America and may last more than two hundred episodes, put the lie to theories of media imperialism because the distinctly non-Western genre has found favor with viewers worldwide. International sales of the genre were estimated at $300 million in 2002, and telenovelas have appeared in hundreds of markets worldwide, supposedly demonstrating that the imperialist aims of large Western conglomerates do not drive international television flows.[1] Meanwhile, detractors of the genre see it as largely derivative of Western televisual forms and argue that, despite the inclusion of superficial Latin American cultural elements, the overriding ideologies of telenovelas encourage rampant consumerism and political conservatism. Moreover, they argue, the telenovela has lost most of its local cultural flavor as the genre's international sales have increased. The level of scholarly disagreement over the telenovela has led one set of authors to label it "the international telenovela debate."[2]

The purpose of this chapter is not to adjudicate the scholarly debates surrounding the ideological impact of telenovelas. Others have already shown that much of the disagreement on these matters stems from different levels of analytic focus among scholars.[3] Rather, I want to suggest that conventional discussions of telenovelas, as instances of *either* local autonomy *or* global homogenization, obscure more nuanced analyses of the variety of institutional roles that globally popular genres such as the telenovela play in today's international television programming business. I will argue that the era of global commercial television has sped the pace of change for genres such as the telenovela that seem uniquely suited to global program trade, as these genres split, merge, and transform due to the multiple duties they perform in settings around the globe and the constant search for new ways to target increasingly differentiated, multinational audience segments. Our theories about the impact of globalization on a genre such as the telenovela remain crude in television studies, typically assuming that globalization leads to homogenization. On the contrary, the case of the telenovela demonstrates that increased generic transformation and experimentation is a far more likely outcome of globalization.

The Telenovela: Its History and Importance

Radionovelas, the immediate progenitor of contemporary telenovelas, developed in Cuba in the 1940s as local formats of U.S. radio soap operas. The first radionovela to make the leap to television was *El Derecho de Nacer* (The Right to Be Born), which became so popular on radio that it was formatted for television in various nations across Latin America. After moving to television, the genre became known as the telenovela and spread with alacrity throughout Latin America. Today, most nations from Mexico to Chile produce domestic telenovelas.[4]

Unlike their northern cousins, telenovelas have distinct beginnings, middles, and ends, though a single telenovela can last as long as a year. Beginning in the 1960s and 1970s, telenovelas moved from daytime slots to prime time, where they were used to target a broad, mass audience.[5] Jesús Martín-Barbero identifies two main types of telenovelas: The first, which grew from Cuban radionovelas, concentrates on family intrigue and archetypal rivalries among family members or different families. The second originated with the 1968 Brazilian telenovela *Beto Rockefeller* and addresses contemporary social conflicts rather than familial ones. In both subgenres, the narrative gets its force from lovers who are separated by rival families or different socioeconomic backgrounds, and both trace the heroines' efforts to overcome the obstacles to true love. This theme of love conquering all is the basis of the classic telenovela, also known as the "telenovela rosa," or "pink telenovela."[6]

In spite of the fact that radionovelas and telenovelas spread across Latin America through the efforts of transnational broadcasting corporations from the United States, Cuba, Mexico, and Brazil, the genre took on unique characteristics in most nations. Mexican telenovelas have tended to favor the family-based telenovela rosa, though more recently major telenovela producers have used other subgenres to target different audiences. Brazilian telenovelas, meanwhile, focus more on social themes and have traditionally made more use of location shooting. They also have a reputation for having the highest production values in the genre. Venezuelan telenovelas, too, make extensive use of location shots and are known for featuring "steamy" love scenes, while Columbian telenovelas highlight local political issues such as kidnapping and violent crime.[7]

Beginning in the 1970s, the popularity of the telenovela across Latin America captured the imagination of media scholars, who argued that the genre encouraged dependency on the United States, especially through its portrayal of rampant consumerism. As another example of the Western and northern effort to cement the inferior economic position of Latin America in a world system dominated by the United States, telenovelas were thought to contain hidden messages of consumerism that diverted Latin American audiences from larger questions of social change.[8]

During the 1980s and 1990s, led by a shift toward reception study and recognition of the growing international trade in telenovelas from Mexico and Brazil, several authors began to comment on the resilience of local televisual forms and even discuss the "reverse cultural imperialism" evident in telenovela sales to the U.S. and European markets. One set of researchers began to chart the genre's international circulation and ask why the genre continued to flourish and even gain international audiences in a global media environment dominated by transnational corporations that supposedly were intent on spreading Western consumerism worldwide. Joseph Straubhaar, for instance, attributed the international trade in telenovelas to product life cycle, a general international business theory stating that all internationally traded commodities move from being produced in their nation of origin and sold abroad to being produced abroad and sold to their nation of origin. Another set of researchers, including Jesús Martín-Barbero and Ana M. Lopez, explored the reception of telenovelas, especially among minority groups throughout Latin America and the United States. Frequently focusing on the tensions between the urban and the rural, modernity and tradition, and communal integration and fragmentation, these scholars have developed an impressive body of research that offers one of the most convincing and sustained critiques of American media imperialism theories.[9]

At the same time, critics of the telenovela have remained equally vo-

cal. These researchers tend to question the significance of global telenovela flows or the impact of globalization on the genre's local cultural
specificity. Biltereyst and Meers analyze the flow of telenovelas from
Latin America to Europe during the 1990s, demonstrating the decreas-
ing reliance on imported telenovelas by most European nations as local
production companies have increased their capacities. At the same time,
competition from global media conglomerates in domestic markets across
Latin America has eroded the popularity of telenovelas there. This state
of affairs leads the authors to argue that the international telenovela
phenomenon, around which so much of the debate about globalization
has centered, may be in decline.[10] Meanwhile, countless researchers have
suggested that international sales of the telenovela have depleted the
genre's locally relevant content. In fact, we see an emergent, if only
tacitly acknowledged, theory about the impact of globalization on local
television content, which can perhaps best be described as an inverse
relationship between international syndication and cultural specificity:
as international sales increase, cultural specificity decreases. The Latin
American telenovela is offered up as the quintessential example of a programming genre that seems to have gone through an inevitable evolution in a world of global commercial media, from domestic cultural
relevance to transnational commercialist schlock. Even Martín-Barbero,
one of the earliest and staunchest defenders of the genre, believes that
"production for a global market implies the generalization of narrative
models and the thinning out of cultural characteristics."[11]

The scholarly debate over telenovelas has been stymied by an under-
developed sense of genre and generic change. Jason Mittell has argued
that television genres are textual categories constituted by various social
groups, including audiences, critics, and industry professionals.[12] Research to date has focused on the definition, interpretation, and evaluation of telenovelas among audiences,[13] but it has not examined the ways
in which industry professionals understand the genre and its significance.
This chapter attempts to correct this oversight by looking at how industry personnel use telenovelas to fill specific institutional needs, which is
necessary to understand the recent transformations of the genre and
their significance, as generic change "is a cultural process enacted by
industry personnel."[14] My analysis draws on Daniel Mato's observation
that changes in the transnational production of telenovelas in recent
years have led not to textual homogenization but rather to a simultaneous move toward standardization *and* differentiation within the genre,
such as the erasure of local dialects alongside the growth in nationally

distinct subgenres.[15] My argument expands Mato's insight beyond the immediate surroundings of Miami to consider the impact that international trade has had on the genre in general. Ultimately, I argue that the concept of genre is an inherently unstable category, incapable of answering debates about cultural homogenization, imperialism, and survival in a global television world. Rather, cultural integrity and homogenization are two extremes between which generic change oscillates depending on prevalent social, economic, and institutional conditions.

From Latin America to Europe: International Telenovela Sales, 1950–1990s

International trade in telenovelas goes back to the 1950s, when, following a path similar to that of radionovelas, Cuban companies sold scripts and production expertise to broadcasters throughout Latin America.[16] In 1959 Mexico began exporting finished telenovelas to the United States and Latin America after Telesistema Mexicano (TSM), one of the largest broadcasters and producers of the time, acquired a videotape machine. With the creation of the Spanish International Network in 1961, targeting the Spanish-speaking market in the United States, TSM had a steady buyer for its videotaped telenovelas. In addition to imported telenovelas from Mexico, local versions of the genre spread to Brazil, Venezuela, and many other Latin American nations. By 1976, the national Mexican broadcasting monopoly Televisa, which had incorporated TSM years earlier, exported twelve thousand hours of programming, mostly telenovelas.[17] Televisa remains the most prolific exporter of telenovelas, boasting a catalog of nearly sixty thousand hours of telenovelas and international sales revenues of $153 million in 2002.[18]

Brazilian telenovelas were slower to find their way into international waters because they were produced in Portuguese rather than Spanish and therefore lacked a natural market in the surrounding "geolinguistic region."[19] Brazil had sporadic telenovela exports throughout the 1960s, but its international activities began in earnest in 1975, when TV Globo sold a telenovela to Portugal. Two years later the Globo telenovela *Gabriela* became the first Brazilian hit in Portugal. By the early 1980s, *Escrava Isaura* (Isaura the Slave Girl), which was destined to become Globo's most successful telenovela abroad, began airing in Italy and France, and eventually spread throughout Western and Eastern Europe and Asia. Since the mid-1980s, Brazilian telenovelas have done remarkably well in international circles. TV Globo is by far the dominant telenovela exporter in Brazil, posting sales to more than seventy nations totaling $31 million in 1996.[20]

International telenovela trade really began to take off in the late 1980s, and the genre's international popularity soared in the 1990s, only to level off since 2000. As with much of the rest of international television trade, the surge in popularity of Latin American telenovelas owes largely to the expansion of television channels and programming schedules in the wake of worldwide deregulation and privatization of the airwaves in the 1980s, particularly in Western Europe. During this period, countless new commercial television channels began operating, and existing networks expanded their broadcasting hours. *Screen Digest* reported in 1992 that 75 percent of new European channels used imported programming to fill at least half of their schedules.[21] Telenovelas offered cheap, long-running programs that could fill airtime and, when they did draw a following, held a committed audience for a lengthy period of time.

The opening of international markets for telenovela sales spurred exports of the genre in Venezuela and Colombia, as well as in the larger Mexican and Brazilian markets. Coral Pictures sold the first Venezuelan telenovela to Spain in 1991, and its main domestic competitor, Venevision, quickly followed suit.[22] In 1996, the dominant Venezuelan producer, Venevision, exported telenovelas to thirty foreign markets, earning $20 million in sales.[23] Tepuy, a Spanish distributor, built its business around representing Colombian telenovelas to international buyers beginning in 1991.[24] Private broadcaster RCN in 2002 had enormous success internationally with the telenovela *Yo Soy Betty la Fea* (I Am Ugly Betty).[25] In addition to these "major" telenovela studios, a number of "independents" have cropped up since the late nineties; these typically are based in Miami and predominantly target the U.S. Latino audience. *Variety* estimated in 1999 that more than twenty companies were involved in international telenovela sales.[26]

The telenovela's international success led to aesthetic changes in the genre that reflected the growing importance of European and U.S. markets, although those changes were minimal through the late 1990s. Ana Lopez claims that efforts to appeal to U.S. viewers led Mexican producers to include U.S. Latinos and their concerns in telenovelas beginning in the 1980s. Mexican and Brazilian telenovelas decreased their use of on-location footage for more "universal" domestic settings that foreign viewers supposedly identify with better.[27] In the 1990s, actors in Argentine telenovelas altered their accents so that they could be more easily accepted in other Latin American markets. Mexican and Venezu-

Brazilian distributor Globo TV International markets its telenovelas as local cultural products throughout the world, as in this advertisement directed at Italian programmers and audiences. Courtesy of Globo TV International.

Globo TV International specializes in "Emotions without Frontiers," targeting the Russian market with this specific advertisement. Courtesy of Globo TV International.

elan telenovelas began using pan–Latin American stars to help smooth intracontinental acceptance of their programming, as well as to target the multiethnic Latino audience in the United States.[28] In 2002, the trade journal *Channel 21* noted several changes in the telenovela to better suit it for international markets, including shortening the length of each series, as the unpredictability of imported program performance makes most buyers unwilling to make long-term series commitments. Where international sales had become particularly lucrative and common, such as in Spain, telenovela producers had taken to writing in "vacations" for characters to those locations in an effort to connect more with foreign viewers. Finally, some of the domestic political elements of telenovelas were removed because it was thought that international viewers might find them off-putting, although Colombian telenovelas maintained a good deal of local political references.[29]

According to Daniel Mato, the absence of significant changes in the genre through the 1990s due to international syndication owes to the fact that the domestic market in each nation remained primary for two important reasons. First, domestic advertising sales were far more lucrative than international sales revenues, which accounted for between 2.5 and 8 percent of revenues earned by the main broadcasters of telenovelas in 1997.[30] Perhaps more important, domestic performance remains the main selling point for any television series on the international market because strong domestic ratings are frequently a prerequisite for securing a program's international sale. In addition, the scheduling of telenovelas abroad made for relatively low prices in most nations because they were placed in daytime hours that drew audience segments with minimal purchasing power. In Hungary, for instance, daytime hours when telenovelas were broadcast in the late 1990s accounted for less than 10 percent of total advertising revenues, while prime-time accounted for 80 percent.[31] Since the late 1990s, however, increased competition on the international sales markets, combined with the segmentation of the domestic audience in Latin America, has led to a growth in telenovela subgenres that are used to court a variety of audience segments both at home and abroad. These institutional changes have driven much of the innovation in the genre in recent years.

From Europe to Asia: 1995–2004

While changes to the telenovela were fairly minimal until the late 1990s, more recently, the economics, markets, and aesthetics of internationally traded telenovelas have changed rapidly. Contemporary subgenres include not only the telenovela rosa and various national subtypes but also children's, youth, and erotic telenovelas. In addition, the genre has combined with animation, reality shows, and other melodramatic forms. At present, the telenovela is in a state of extreme flux, owing to the genre's unique capacity to transcend cultural boundaries and the ways in which the concept of genre has become an institutional tool for linking transnational audience niches.

The primary international markets for telenovela sales have shifted significantly since 2000, as some regions of the world have turned away from the genre and others have warmed to it. Biltereyst and Meers find in their analysis of telenovela purchasing in Europe that the flow of telenovelas to broadcasters in northern and northwestern Europe, which typically pay the highest prices for programming in the region, has dried up. Meanwhile, even traditionally strong markets like Italy and Spain have diminished their reliance on the genre. In Spain, the television production industry experienced significant consolidation in 2002 and now lies mostly in the hands of six or seven main players. Increased competition for audiences has forced imported telenovelas out of prime time, which now relies mostly on locally produced Spanish telenovelas. Mexican-based Televisa, the main producer of Spanish-language telenovelas, had coproduction arrangements and investments in the Spanish market, but it capitulated to the powerful Spanish conglomerates and sold its stakes in 2002. The increased use of domestic programming by broadcasters across Europe, combined with increased competition for every segment of the audience during every daypart, has led European broadcasters to move away from imported telenovelas, which had been used as filler for unimportant time slots.

Central Europe became a major market for telenovelas in the midnineties, as formerly state-run networks across the region were privatized, new terrestrial, cable, and satellite channels were added, and public broadcasters began to rely more on Western imports. However, since 2000, sales to east-central European television channels have generally declined, partly because the libraries of the channels have filled up with telenovelas, and partly because of programming changes at the region's television channels. In 2000, a Hungarian television buyer at a general entertainment terrestrial channel estimated that, in terms of hours of programming, Latin American telenovelas constituted about one-third of her imports. By 2003, that channel had almost entirely stopped buying telenovelas. According to a buyer at a rival channel, the audience had grown tired of telenovelas and now embraced U.S.-produced fantasy series such as *Xena: Warrior Princess.*[32]

East and Southeast Asia, on the other hand, particularly Indonesia, the Philippines, and Malaysia, have seen a boom in telenovela exports since the late 1990s, with distributors reporting significant potential in Vietnam, Singapore, Thailand, and Korea. The major independent telenovela producers, including Coral, Telefe, Promark, and Comarex, estimate that as much as 35 percent of their international telenovela sales in 2003 came from Asian markets, and this sector is expected to grow to as much as 50 percent over the next several years.[33]

What impact the shift from east-central Europe to East and Southeast Asia as the main markets will have on the production of the genre is unpredictable. Apparently, like their European counterparts, Asian buyers prefer shorter-form telenovelas. Already, the Middle East has appeared as a vacation spot for telenovela characters, and it seems likely that resort areas in Asia will begin to appear as well. Regarding substantive changes in content, some international television professionals believe that a growing divide was developing among east-central European and Latin American viewers, with the former preferring "classic" telenovelas and the latter preferring more topical, modern themes. In fact, a shift in domestic Latin American production toward more topical themes may be partly responsible for the genre's decline in east-central Europe. At present, it seems as though Asian buyers are more accepting of the contemporary telenovelas.

A more profound market shift has been the growing importance of the U.S. telenovela market. As suggested above, the U.S. market has always been a prime target for telenovela distributors, but since the 1990s, the importance of U.S. Latino audiences has grown markedly, a fact underscored by NBC's purchase of the second-rated Spanish-language U.S. broadcaster, Telemundo, in 2002. That year, the U.S. Latino advertising market was estimated at two-thirds the size of the advertising market in the whole of Latin America.[34] Since 2002, most of the major Latin American telenovela producers have signed multiyear output deals with U.S. networks that give the networks a steady stream of programming, and give producers guaranteed revenue.[35] At the same time, Miami, Florida, has emerged as a center for independent telenovela producers, most of whom target the U.S. Latino audience. The U.S. broadcasting market has also witnessed an explosion of new Latino-oriented television channels since 2000, including nineteen new channels in 2004 and thirteen new channels in 2003.[36] In 2001, the National

Association of Television Programming Executives, the largest syndication marketplace in the United States, featured a panel on the growing Latino market during its annual sales fair.

Mato in 2002 identified a number of aesthetic changes in the genre that have accompanied the shift to producing in Miami, including a tendency to use a multinational Latino cast to target Latinos from various national origins, and the use of locations shots in Miami that appeal to an increasingly important Miami audience. These changes also help facilitate exports to Latin American markets for a variety of reasons. First, pan-Latin cable and satellite channels prefer the multinational casts, which make the programming more attractive in the multiple markets they serve. Second, Miami has become the "promised land" for many Latin Americans, and stories set in Miami appeal to their aspirations and fantasies. "Miami has an iconographic image, which is very attractive from a distributor's perspective," according to Marcos Santana, president of Tepuy International.[37] Third, as with any television program produced in the United States, the made-in-America stamp adds an atmosphere of quality and universality to the programs for international buyers. That is, among international television merchants, there exists a belief that U.S. series are more acceptable to international audiences, and programming that can claim U.S. origins benefits from this perception.

Comparing the impact of the U.S. and Spanish markets for telenovelas on the worldwide production of the genre, we can see that the relative positions of the trading partner in the world economy determine the influence that the import market will have on an indigenous genre when it travels abroad. While Spanish and southern European markets did lead some telenovelas to feature on-location shooting in these countries, the practice was limited and short-lived. However, in the more lucrative U.S. market, the trend toward producing in Miami for the U.S. Latino audience has led to more widespread and profound influences.

The changing tides of telenovela exports, from Western and Eastern Europe to Asia and the United States, demonstrate how such internationally popular genres are influenced by a host of worldwide economic and cultural conditions. Not only do economic and business changes among the main trading partners alter the genre, but regional and global programming trends also carry genres in and out of favor. For instance, the telenovela trend in east-central Europe began in such markets as the Czech Republic, Poland, and Russia. Based on the success of the genre in these markets, buyers in Hungary, Romania, and Slovenia began to purchase and schedule telenovelas, and the trend later spread to Bosnia and the

Balkans. Since 2001, however, the excitement has subsided, and programmers have moved on in search of the next newest trend.

The Changing Fate of Telenovelas in Latin America

While changes in other parts of the world have had their impact on the telenovela genre, multichannel competition, audience fragmentation, skyrocketing production costs, and economic instability across Latin America have also profoundly reshaped the genre in recent years, leading to an increasingly fragmented genre crosscut by numerous subgenres, and the decline of the genre's importance across the region. Some observers view the changing fortunes of telenovelas in Latin America as evidence of a new wave of U.S. media imperialism, as media conglomerates move into the region's multichannel pay television markets with popular U.S. genres. However, the genre's transformation owes rather to its versatility and the variety of roles that a global genre such as the telenovela is made to play in today's international program markets.

The changing international markets for telenovelas have led to a leveling off in growth rates for foreign sales revenues since 2000, even as foreign revenues have come to represent a larger share of telenovela producers' revenues due to the complete stagnation of the genre in advertising income generated by the genre in Latin America. Between 1996 and 2003, domestic advertising revenues generated by Latin American telenovelas remained stagnant at $1.6 billion, while foreign sales revenues grew from $200 million to $341 million. International sales at Televisa increased from about 5 percent of total revenues in 1996 to about 7 percent in 2002.[38] At the same time, the number of distributors selling internationally grew fivefold between the midnineties and 2002, and prices in many markets are off. "Russia was paying $1,200 per hour, now they're paying $800; Indonesia was paying up to $1,200, now it's $700," according to Germán Pérez Nahím, the former head of Venevision who currently heads SkyQuest, an independent producer and sales representative for America TV in Peru.[39] These lower prices mean that to maintain overall foreign sales revenues, distributors must increase the number of markets where they sell their programming. Consequently, in the early years of the twenty-first century, we have seen a boom in industry organizations and conferences devoted to the international expansion of the telenovela.[40]

Competition among telenovelas at home and abroad has driven up production costs, as producers use more stars, better writers, more exotic locations, and flashier postproduction techniques to differentiate their programming. In addition to the spike in the number of telenovela distributors operating in Latin America, competition from multichannel television and economic instability since the late 1990s have driven up production costs for telenovelas, as more and more distributors compete for increasingly fragmented audiences and shrinking advertising revenues. According to industry estimates, Latin America is the world's largest growth area for multichannel television services, with subscriber growth estimated to rise 150 percent between 1995 and 2005, and regional advertising revenues projected to reach $1 billion by 2010. The actual numbers have fallen well below these estimates, however, and subscription channels in Brazil accounted for only 1.7 percent of total advertising spent in the first half of 2001, compared with 55 percent for free television.[41] Still, though the loss of revenues at the large broadcasters has been small, it has not been insignificant. In addition, Latin American markets have experienced back-to-back economic crises, the first in the late 1990s stemming from the Asian economic crisis, and the second from the Argentine and Brazilian crises of 2002. These factors have conspired to drive up production costs for telenovelas. In Brazil between 1989 and 1995, production costs ballooned from $35,000 to $100,000 per episode. Likewise, the main Venezuelan telenovela exporter, Venevision, paid as much as $135,000 per episode in 1996. In 2000, Mexican telenovelas ran as much as $100,000 per episode.[42]

Latin American producers have taken four different approaches to dealing with the increased competition among telenovelas: they have focused on opening up other markets; developed coproduction arrangements and telenovela formats, where producers sell the skeleton of a series, including scripts, to local producers who remake the program with local actors; segmented the audience for telenovelas at home and abroad; and tried to expand their libraries beyond the telenovela genre.[43] Although none of these trends are completely new, each of them has taken on greater importance since 2002 due to changes outlined earlier in this chapter.

The telenovela rosa remains the dominant form of the telenovela in Mexico, and the classic Brazilian telenovela also continues to generate large audiences. *Terra Nostra*, the first historical Brazilian telenovela in decades, outperformed any contemporaneous telenovela in the domestic market and also sold to more than seventy countries abroad.[44] However, in addition to these classical subgenres, telenovela producers, including the major producers, have developed a growing number of new subgenres for different audience niches. Since 2003, telenovelas have been used to target children, teens, and adults separately and have incorporated reality shows, animation, and eroticism. Increased action sequences and topical themes such as drug addiction and AIDS have come to dominate teen-oriented telenovelas, which frequently feature pop stars and music video scenes. Children's telenovelas mix the melodramatic format with animation. And adult telenovelas, in particular Playboy International coproductions, have become popular with audiences in Latin America and beyond.[45] In the 2002 season, Televisa married the telenovela with the reality genre when it sponsored a reality-show vote-off contest to pick the actors for a forthcoming telenovela. According to Eugenio Lopez Negrete, the director general of Televisa International, "Telenovelas are becoming more audience-participative. With *Who is Salome?* the audience does not really know which of the three boys the lead character looks after is her real son and the viewer can be involved by voting [for] which of the three children it should be on the Internet or by calling."[46] In addition to helping channels compete for audience niches in the domestic market, these new subgenres can be sold or formatted abroad for similar audience niches. Thus, rather than addressing an undifferentiated, domestic audience, the newer forms address transnational audience niches.

Telenovela coproductions, which have become increasingly common, involve producers from different nations working together on a single series, which may be released in both markets, sold internationally, or remain primarily in one of the partner's markets. Explaining many trends in telenovelas, including coproduction, José Escalante, vice president and general manager of Coral International, a Miami-based producer-distributor, commented, "Traditional Latin producers have been improving the quality of their productions and they are investing larger amounts of money in these productions. Secondly, newcomers have bloomed in the distribution business, and countries that were not known for their telenovelas have started to produce excellent programming. And producers worldwide have started to produce and/or co-produce formats from other countries."[47] All the major telenovela producers have signed coproduction deals with U.S. companies since 2002, in an effort to increase domestically produced programming for U.S. Latino audiences. In addition, coproductions of telenovelas have occurred across Europe, Asia, the Middle East, and Latin America. "Even though we have an interest in co-producing in several genres," says José Antonio Espinal, director of Venevision International, "we are focusing on an area where we have a well-established expertise: the telenovela."[48]

Formatting of telenovelas, which entails buying the scripts, promotional materials, graphics, and so forth, of an already-produced series and creating a local version, has become more common since 2000. In an interview in 2001, Antonio Paez, vice president of Televisa International, told the international television trade journal *Channel 21* that he expected formatting to become a major revenue stream in the near future, a sentiment echoed by his colleagues across the region.[49] The hit Colombian telenovela *Yo Soy Betty la Fea* has been formatted in several markets, including India and Indonesia, while the Argentine youth-oriented *Chiquititas* has been reformatted in the United States and Portugal.[50]

The impact of coproduction and formatting on genre practices is an open question. Formatting would seem to have less impact outside the domestic market where the format gets produced, because the original producer-distributor has little involvement once the format is sold. However, buyers frequently change important elements in formats, and the original producers follow those changes closely to see if they can be incorporated into the original format, as has been the case with *Big Brother*. Formats are nothing new, but they are increasingly common forms of transborder television flow that have not figured prominently enough in our theorizations of contemporary television genres.

Coproductions, on the other hand, are more likely to have influences on a genre in every partner's market, since the coproduction concept, where all partners retain the rights to distribute the final product in their home markets, is predicated on the idea that the final product will be a blend of the cultures involved. In fact, trade journal articles and surveys of coproducers have found that learning technical and cultural lessons from producers in different nations is a common motivation for the practice.[51] Some kinds of cultural dialogue and learning certainly must occur among coproducers. Unfortunately, scholarly literature on telenovela coproduction and formatting is nonexistent, trade journal reports are largely factual and spotty, and the literature on coproduction looks at motives and expected outcomes, rather than the intercultural interactions among partners. Nevertheless, we can witness the kinds of results that this form of cultural mixing might lead to in ABC's efforts to improve its youth demographics for its daytime soaps. ABC production crews spent several months in 2002 meeting with telenovela producers and observing their productions in an attempt to introduce shorter narrative arcs that are common in telenovelas, and the strategy has paid off in the ratings.[52]

In addition to the economic, institutional, and aesthetic changes in the genre that we have already seen, the position of the telenovela in Latin American TV schedules and distributors' libraries has changed. While the genre continues to dominate prime-time programming, and individual telenovelas often pull in impressive ratings, other genres have begun to encroach on the telenovela's dominance, particularly reality programs. Reality shows are generally cheaper to produce and have had some ratings success in the region. Moreover, reality shows have become the newest global trend in programming, and, like their counterparts everywhere, Latin American producers and distributors want to capitalize on that trend. In Mexico in 2002, for example, *La Academia,* a homegrown pop star reality show, ranked number one on second-place broadcaster TV Azteca. Although dominant Mexican network Televisa had only telenovelas among its top five broadcasts, an airing of the local version of *Big Brother* came in at sixth place.[53]

The changing fortunes of the telenovela in the domestic environment mean that distributors have acquired international rights to a wider variety of genres. Moreover, the uncertainties of the global telenovela market have spurred a desire among Latin American distributors to diversify their programming libraries, which since 2002 have included reality shows, comedies, dramas, and variety shows, in addition to telenovelas. In 2002, for example, Tepuy International, a Miami-based telenovela producer, brought a slate of sitcoms and series to an international market, along with its traditional menu of telenovelas. "This is the first attempt to break into the market with a product other than a telenovela," said company president Marcos Santana. "If we want to grow, we must incorporate other genres."[54] In 2003, Marcella Campos, head of contents and international development for the Argentina-based production house Promofilm, sounded a similar chord regarding Latin American reality shows. "The format market in Latin America has changed a great deal in the last two years," she said. "These countries started out being just buyers, but now they are not only starting to create but also exporting their creativity to the rest of the world."[55]

The changing fortunes of the telenovela genre in its primary domestic markets seem to add fuel to the argument that the globalization of Latin American markets has led to a decline in culturally relevant programming. However, the claim that telenovelas are indigenous while local versions of *Big Brother* are not seems highly suspect. Rather, what has happened is that producers and programmers have begun to think of audiences differently and now seek to provide relevant programming for certain attractive segments of the audience at certain times of the day with new programming innovations. These niches increasingly extend beyond the nation-state to encompass similar audience segments around the world. Global genres such as the telenovela are key to cobbling together these far-flung audience niches.

Conclusion: Globalization and Generic Transformation

The institutional and aesthetic changes in the telenovela traced in this chapter unquestionably relate to larger economic and cultural processes of media globalization, as both Latin American conglomerates and audiences have become more integrated into a system of commercial media dominated by multinational corporations based in the United States and Europe. Certainly, broadcasters and producers in these richer nations have a greater impact on transforming the genre than those in economically less powerful nations, but to reduce these changes to a simple dichotomy of homogenization versus localization misrepresents the complexity of the interactions among global institutions, texts, and audiences. The telenovela has become more, not less, differentiated as the genre has had to fulfill a variety of roles for broadcasters around the world. Encompassing reality telenovelas, erotic telenovelas, animated telenovelas, and youth telenovelas, the genre offers multiple ways for broadcasters around the world to connect with increasingly differentiated audience segments, at the same time that direct sales, formatting, and coproductions offer a variety of costs and arrangements among buyers and sellers that can be tailored to the economic capacities and business priorities of different importers.

Rather than ask whether globalization leads to homogenization, we need to theorize the various strategies of standardization and differentiation that characterize global commercial television's treatment of genres and audiences. Genres offer television broadcasters a simple and fairly reliable way to connect with their audiences; they boil down the potentially infinite number of ways that television culture might appeal to viewers to a small and manageable size. Therefore, we need to ask several questions about the institutionalization of genres in a global media environment: Which genres are used to target which audiences? Why are certain genres used instead of others? How are undifferentiated audiences segmented, and why are they segmented in certain ways and not others? To what extent does the availability of certain genres drive the segmentation of audiences? Only by asking such questions can we begin to understand why certain genres seem to have global appeal. For instance, several broadcasters in a variety of markets around the world have identified a nine- to fourteen-year-old "tweenage" audience that supposedly has different tastes than older or younger children, and this process has led to the global popularity of Japanese anime as a genre capable of reaching that demographic.

Thus far, scholars of telenovelas, regardless of their theoretical orientation, have tended to assume that something universal in the genre explains its appeal, whether that universal element is crass consumer culture, the struggle between the modern and the traditional, or a melodramatic sensibility among the world's viewers. This examination of the global telenovela business has revealed that, while these reasons may have some validity when discussing audience responses, the main explanation for the global popularity of the genre is that it filled particular institutional needs at a moment when television sales and acquisitions businesses were looking to international sources. Telenovelas offered a cost-effective way to draw in substantial, but relatively unimportant, audience segments to daytime and afternoon time slots; their global popularity offers evidence of how an internationalized programming business leads programmers everywhere to think in similar ways about audiences' preferences and genres. By conceptualizing diverse audiences around the world as composed of the same segments that can be targeted with similar programming, producers and programmers have created the business conditions necessary for global genres to circulate. As business conditions continue to change, genres such as the telenovela that are called upon to fulfill multiple functions in diverse markets around the world will continue to splinter and blur into more and more subgenres at a faster and faster pace.

Notes

1. "To Russia . . . and Bosnia . . . and Latvia, with Love: Latin America's Quintessential Cultural Product—the TV Melodrama—Sees a Storyline Abroad," *Latin Trade* 11, no. 7 (2003): 28.

2. Daniël Biltereyst and Philippe Meers, "The International Telenovela Debate and the Contra-Flow Argument: A Reappraisal," *Media, Culture and Society* 22, no. 4 (2000): 393–413.

3. Ibid.

4. Gerardo Michelin, "Telenovelas in East Euro Comeback," *Channel 21*, July 17, 2003, http://www.c21media.net (accessed February 15, 2004); Andrew Paxman, "Roots of Form Trace to Cuba," *Variety*, October 7, 1996, 61.

5. Ana M. Lopez, "Our Welcomed Guests: Telenovelas in Latin America," in

To Be Continued: Soap Operas around the World, ed. Robert C. Allen (London: Routledge, 1995), 259.

6. Jesús Martín-Barbero, "Memory and Form in the Latin American Soap Opera," in Allen, *To Be Continued,* 279–80.

7. Daniel Mato, "Miami in the Transnationalization of the Telenovela Industry: On Territoriality and Globalization," *Journal of Latin American Cultural Studies* 11, no. 2 (2002): 195–212; Paxman, "Roots of Form Trace to Cuba."

8. This history of the scholarly response to telenovelas draws on Lopez, "Our Welcomed Guests."

9. Ibid.; Ana M. Lopez, "The Melodrama in Latin America: Films, Telenovelas, and the Currency of a Popular Form," *Wide Angle* 7, no. 1 (1985): 4–13; Jesús Martín-Barbero, "Matrices Culturales de las Telenovelas," *Estudios Sobre Las Culturas Contemporaneas* 2 (1988): 137–63; Jesús Martin-Barbero and Sonia Muñoz, *Televisión y Melodrama* (Bogotá, Colombia: Tercer Mundo Editores, 1992); Joseph Straubhaar, "Asymmetrical Interdependence and Cultural Proximity," *Critical Studies in Mass Communication* 8, no. 1 (1991): 39–59.

10. Biltereyst and Meers, "International Telenovela Debate."

11. Martín-Barbero, "Memory and Form in the Latin American Soap Opera."

12. Jason Mittell, "A Cultural Approach to Television Genre Theory," *Cinema Journal* 40, no. 3 (2001): 3–24.

13. See, for instance, Vivian Barrera and Denise D. Bielby, "Faces, Places, and Other Familiar Things: The Cultural Experience of Telenovela Viewing among Latinos in the United States," *Journal of Popular Culture* 34, no. 1 (2001): 1–18; Antonio C. La Pastina, "Product Placement in Brazilian Prime Time Television: The Case of the Reception of a Telenovela," *Journal of Broadcasting and Electronic Media* 45, no. 4 (2001): 541–57; Vicki Mayer, "Living Telenovelas/ Telenovelizing Life: Mexican American Girls' Identities and Transnational Telenovelas," *Journal of Communication* 53, no. 3 (2003): 479–95; Diana I. Rios, "U.S. Latino Audiences of 'Telenovelas,'" *Journal of Latinos and Education* 2, no. 1 (2003): 59–65.

14. Mittell, "Cultural Approach to Television Genre Theory," 7.

15. Mato, "Miami in the Transnationalization of the Telenovela Industry."

16. Joseph D. Straubhaar and Gloria Viscasillas, "The Reception of Telenovelas and Other Latin American Genres in the Regional Market: The Case of the Dominican Republic," *Studies in Latin American Popular Culture* 10 (1991): 191–215.

17. Elizabeth Fox, *Latin American Broadcasting* (Luton, UK: University of Luton Press, 1997), 50.

18. Mary Sutter, "Mexican Sidekick: Grupo Televisa Fights Typecast as Supporting Actor in the Growing U.S. Hispanic Market," *Latin Trade* 10, no. 7 (2002): 48–51.

19. The term comes from John Sinclair, *Latin American Television: A Global View* (Oxford and New York: Oxford University Press, 1999). He writes that a geolinguistic region "is defined not just by its geographical contours, but also in a virtual sense, by commonalities of language and culture" (1).

20. Mac Margolis, "Soaps Clean Up," *Latin Trade* 5, no. 4 (1997): 46; Sinclair, *Latin American Television*.

21. "Transformation Scene in World Television," *Screen Digest*, February 1992, 40.

22. Sinclair, *Latin American Television*, 84.

23. Margolis, "Soaps Clean Up."

24. Olimpia Del Boccio, "Tepuy, a Sign of Confidence," *Television Latin America*, May 1, 2001, 52.

25. Kate Burnett, "Happy Endings: Asia's Position on the Telenovela Distribution Roster Is Rising," *Television Asia*, October 2002, 52.

26. Andrew Paxman, "Novela Excess Puts Distribs in Distress," *Variety*, May 3, 1999, 74.

27. Lopez, "Our Welcomed Guests," 265.

28. Mato, "Miami in the Transnationalization of the Telenovela Industry."

29. Fiona Fraser, "21-on-21: Novela Revolution," *Channel 21*, July 1, 2002, http://www.c21media.net (accessed March 25, 2004).

30. These numbers must be taken with a grain of salt, since they refer to the percentage of *total* revenues from all business operations represented by foreign telenovela sales, not just the percentage of revenues from telenovelas that is attributable to foreign sales.

31. Agnes Koperveisz, head of research for TV2, Hungary, interview by author, Budapest, Hungary, November 2002.

32. Edina Balogh, acquisitions assistant for RTL-Klub, Hungary, interview by author, Budapest, Hungary, September 2002; Agnes Havas, acquisitions director, TV2, Hungary, interviews by author, Budapest, Hungary, July 2001, August 2002.

33. "As the Story Goes," *Television Asia*, January 2003, SS2; "The Asian Story," *Television Asia*, January 2003, SS9.

34. Kris Sofley, "Seducing the Hispanic Dollar," *Channel 21*, February 19, 2002, http://www.c21media.net (accessed January 11, 2004).

35. Mary Sutter, "Latin Lingo Linkups Linger," *Variety*, January 14, 2002, 14.

36. Christina Hoag, "Hispanic Television Networks Booming," *Miami Herald*, January 10, 2005.

37. Mary Sutter, "Se Habla Telenovelas," *Variety*, April 19, 2004, A1.

38. Mato, "Miami in the Transnationalization of the Telenovela Industry"; Sutter, "Mexican Sidekick."

39. Paxman, "Roots of Form Trace to Cuba."

40. Maria Esposito, "Telenovela Association for Lat-Am Producers," *Channel 21*, November 20, 2003, http://www.c21media.net (accessed May 22, 2004); "To Russia."

41. Carolina Fresard Alvarez, "Weathering the Storm," *Television Latin America* 3, no. 9 (2001): 44; Anna Marie de la Fuente, "National Subscriptions," *TV World*, May 1997, 43–44.

42. "A Brighter Vision," *Television Business International*, January 1997, 32; Thomas Catan and Raymond Colitt, "Brazil Seeks to Calm Fears over Economic

Crisis: Argentina Wants US Action to Prevent Neighbor's Problems Affecting Region," *Financial Times,* June 24, 2002; de la Fuente, "National Subscriptions"; Elizabeth Guider and Eileen Tasca, "Pearson TV Looks South," *Variety,* May 22, 2000, 1; Paxman, "Roots of Form Trace to Cuba."

43. Fraser, "21-on-21."

44. Marcelo Cajueiro, "Globo Preps 'Terra' Sequel," *Variety,* November 30, 2001, 32.

45. Fraser, "21-on-21."

46. Ibid.

47. Melissa Herman, "Forever Young," *Television Asia,* January 2002.

48. Tim Avis, "Hispanic TV—The Fine Art of Partnership," *Channel 21,* March 15, 2001, http://www.c21media.net (accessed January 10, 2005).

49. Ibid.

50. Ibid.; Burnett, "Happy Endings"; Ritesh Gupta, "How Betty Met Jassi," *Television Asia,* December 2003, 56.

51. Colin Hoskins, Stuart McFadyen, Adam Finn, and Anne Jackel, "Film and Television Co-Production: Evidence from Canadian-European Experience," *European Journal of Communication* 10, no. 2 (1995): 221–43.

52. Pamela Paul, "Soap Operas Battle the Suds," *American Demographics* 24, no. 1 (2002): 26.

53. Simeon Tegel, "Nonfiction a Hit with Top Mexican Nets," *Variety,* January 20, 2003, 34.

54. "Latin American TV Heads Want to Extend Programming Beyond Telenovelas," *Miami Herald,* March 17, 2002.

55. Gerardo Michelin, "Promofilm Leads Format Push in Latin America," *Channel 21,* February 3, 2003, http://www.c21media.net (accessed January 11, 2005).

13 from kung fu to imperial court

chinese historical drama

Michael Curtin

After festering for more than forty years, tensions between the People's Republic of China (PRC) and Taiwan escalated dramatically during the 1990s as the island began to move toward democratic reform, which in turn paved the way for the election of successive presidential administrations that have inched inexorably toward independence. Such aspirations for independence have enraged leaders in Beijing, who have been threatening to invade across the Straits for more than a decade, claiming that Taiwan is little more than a renegade province. Throughout this turbulent decade, leaders of the PRC have been pressing the Taiwanese to "reintegrate" with the motherland along the same lines as Hong Kong and Macau, which are now Special Administrative Regions (SAR) of China. Yet Taiwanese resistance to this proposal stems in part from Beijing's persistent meddling in the political affairs of Hong Kong since the 1997 handover. Perhaps more significantly, however, many Taiwanese fear integration with a country that is remarkably different from their own island society.

After decades of martial law, Taiwan now guarantees its citizens free expression and full voting rights, making it the first Chinese society in history to offer such political freedoms. The population is well educated and prosperous by global standards, and is dramatically more so by comparison to its mainland neighbor. Perhaps most notably for the purposes of this chapter, Taiwan has one of the most commercial and competitive television industries in the world, whereas *all* broadcasting stations in the PRC are owned and controlled by the government. If one were to imagine a coproduction arrangement for a prime-time drama series, it would seem highly improbable to pair up broadcasters from both sides of the Taiwan Straits. Yet, ironically, throughout this era of ominous political tension, such partnerships have flourished for Chinese historical drama, one of the most durable and marketable genres in Asian television.[1]

Just as intriguing are the reasons behind these unlikely collaborations. Provincial and municipal stations in mainland China turn to Taiwanese producers because unlike CCTV—the central television network based in Beijing—they are often running on tight budgets and must compete not only with the national network but also with dozens of stations now available on cable TV systems in major cities throughout China. This competition among stations is furthermore animated by diminishing support from government sources and an increasing reliance on advertising revenues to support station operations and personnel. Therefore, in an attempt to develop quality dramas that will fare well with viewers and advertisers, station managers turn to overseas partners with extensive financial and creative resources. Such collaboration not only enhances their pool of resources but also allows mainland stations to retain distribution rights for the PRC, which means, for example, that a provincial station in northern China can turn around and sell the coproduced series to channels and cable services in other parts of the mainland.

As for Taiwanese broadcasters, they too are driven to collaborate because of intense competitive pressure, which is a dramatic turnaround from the martial law era of cozy government oligopoly that prevailed for more than thirty years. From a three-channel economy in 1994, Taiwan has grown to become one of the world's most competitive cable markets, delivering more than one hundred channels to 81 percent of the population.[2] Government-sanctioned television stations that once dominated the airwaves must now struggle for audience attention, employing serial drama as one of the key weapons in their prime-time arsenal. Interestingly, however, these stations can no longer afford to mount lavish historical dramas on their own and therefore must find partners to help defray production costs. It would be untenable for them to turn to competitors in their own market and so, despite the bellicose rhetoric on both sides, many television executives quietly go about the business of cross-Straits production by focusing on the historical drama and conjuring up narratives that perform consistently well in their respective countries, as well as among Chinese audiences around the world.

The study of such a phenomenon invites us to consider the factors that have made the historical drama an especially viable candidate for such collaborations and therefore moves us into the realm of genre studies. Although this field of inquiry first emerged among literary critics who tended to focus on ideal types of narrative, John Cawelti began to deviate from this tendency as he took up the study of mass-market fiction, ranging from pulp novels to filmed Westerns.[3] Cawelti sought to shift attention from abstract conceptions of genre to a more careful consideration of genres' cultural function in modern societies. This approach was further elaborated by television scholars such as Horace Newcomb and David Marc, who pointed to the ways in which genres rehearse and reflect upon key social and cultural concerns of their eras.[4] Subsequently, Robert Allen and Janice Radway sought to demonstrate intersections between industrial strategies and interpretive communities, suggesting that genres both set boundaries for interpretation and open up possibilities for transgressive readings of popular texts.[5] Similar trajectories of research have taken place among film scholars over the past forty years, but David Bordwell has cautioned that reflections on the cultural significance of genre should be tempered by careful consideration of the pragmatic and sometimes serendipitous choices that professionals confront during the creative process.[6] Very briefly, then, one could argue that scholars have developed three approaches to the study of genre: cultural, industrial, and interpretive. This chapter employs cultural and industrial approaches to the study of Chinese historical drama in an attempt to explain the curious cross-Straits collaborations in popular television. It focuses on the Taiwanese side of the equation and suggests a number of factors that have influenced the development of the Chinese historical drama, among them economic globalization, political liberalization, a proliferation of media resources, and the end of the cold war. It furthermore demonstrates the ways in which polysemic qualities are crafted into these programs as part of a very self-conscious industrial strategy.

After Martial Law

If one were to name the media mogul who shaped the early years of Taiwanese television, it would not be an owner, entrepreneur, or media manager. Instead, it would be Chiang Kai-shek, who dominated almost every aspect of social life in Taiwan from the early 1950s to the 1970s. Prior to Chiang's arrival in 1949, many Taiwanese were hoping that the island would be granted independence after fifty years of Japanese colonial rule. Instead, U.S. leaders prodded the United Nations to turn the island over to the retreating Nationalist army, which was fleeing the advancing Communist forces on the mainland. Installing his regime in the former Japanese colonial capital of Taipei, Chiang was accompanied by soldiers and bureaucrats who took control of the state apparatus and established their Nationalist Party (known as the Kuomintang, or KMT) as the island's only viable political organization. Local Taiwanese administrators, intellectuals, and businesspeople were shouldered aside as Republic of China (ROC) officials doled out jobs, subsidies, and political favors to exiles from the mainland. Clustered in the northern part of the island around Taipei, the generation of mainland exiles came to be known as *waishengren* (people born outside). Yet, ironically, it was the Taiwanese who found themselves living as outsiders on their own island. The regime callously slaughtered its opponents, imposed martial law for more than three decades, and engaged in a thorough program of ideological indoctrination centered upon Chiang's claim that the ROC was the only legitimate representative of Chinese people. The regime dismissively treated Taiwan like a minor province, as little more than a temporary haven until the Nationalists could reclaim control of the mainland.

Yet for all its nefarious activities, Chiang's government also realized that it needed to cultivate the island population if it was to muster a new generation of soldiers for its future military campaigns. Consequently, universal education was instituted, and children began each school day singing songs glorifying President Chiang and spent much of their time studying the history, culture, and geography of mainland China, while learning little about their own island society. Mandarin became the language of instruction, governance, and big business, despite the fact that few Taiwanese could speak it fluently. Overall, the ideology of the regime was a mixture of sinophilia, virulent anti-Communism, and KMT republicanism. Schools, newspapers, and movies were all closely monitored, and when television arrived in the 1960s, it too was fashioned as an ideological tool of the state. Broadcasting exclusively in Mandarin, one station was controlled by the military (China Television System, CTS), another by the provincial government (Taiwan Television, TTV), and the third by the KMT (China Television, CTV).

Although Chiang ruled with a heavy hand, the regime found itself constrained by a number of factors. First of all, the Nationalist government needed to appear strong enough to defend itself from invasion by the PRC, requiring rapid modernization of the economy and the military, which in turn necessitated mobilization of the local population and support from the United States. In order to appeal for American allegiance, the regime fashioned itself as the democratic alternative to Communism, even if in fact it was thoroughly corrupt and autocratic. U.S. aid throughout the 1960s and 1970s helped to spur industrialization and rising standards of living, but when American support began to waver, beginning with Richard Nixon's trip to Beijing in 1972, the KMT found itself searching for new allies around the globe, and reform elements within the KMT began to press for further democratization. Chiang Kai-shek's death in 1975 and the ascendancy of his son as president marked a watershed in ROC politics; under pressure from local activists and critics, the government slowly began to expand opportunities for Taiwanese participation in politics and administration. This process culminated in the lifting of martial law in 1987, the emergence of the Democratic Progressive Party (DPP) as a legitimate opposition party, and the election of native-born Lee Teng-hui as president in 1988. It also sparked a cautious movement toward media liberalization, with television serving as one of the last vestiges of KMT hegemony.

A Changing TV Industry

Wholly owned by the Kuomintang, CTV was both lucrative and influential for more than three decades, but during the 1990s, as martial law began to wither and new media outlets began to flourish, party leaders reluctantly decided to release their grip on the station for a number of reasons. First of all, reformers within the KMT believed the commercial objectives of the station would best be realized by breaking explicit ties to the party. Second, as competition from cable television intensified, financial planners reasoned it was best to put the station up for a public stock offering sooner rather than later. Finally, some party leaders feared that, should the KMT lose control of the legislature, the station might be seized by the opposition DPP or rendered worthless by government regulatory action.

Consequently, in the mid-1990s, CTV's board of directors began looking for a savvy manager who could lead the company through a delicate period of transition as it prepared for a public stock offering. The transition would demand a sea change in corporate culture, asking staff members—many of them lifetime employees who were accustomed to the station's oligopoly status—to address changing conditions in the marketplace and to become more responsive to viewers and stockholders rather than party insiders. In 1996, the board settled on Su Ming

Cheng, a former television news professional and cabinet official who had at various points in her career worked closely with two of the leading reform politicians within the KMT, Lee Teng-hui and James Soong. Cheng moved swiftly to prepare CTV for an initial public offering by spinning off nine subsidiaries and establishing ten joint venture companies in such areas as computer graphics, digital gaming, and telecommunications. Now known as the CTV Media Group, it is headquartered in Nankang, a manufacturing district on the eastern outskirts of Taipei.

On the eleventh floor of the CTV complex, the expansive picture windows in Cheng's office provide an arresting view of Mount Chihsing, a four-thousand-foot peak that rises dramatically above the Taipei basin. An ikebana-inspired floral arrangement in one corner adds a splash of color, and a Chinese calligraphy brush painting smartly contrasts with the teak wall paneling, but overall the decor is modern and corporate. Conspicuously absent are any traces of CTV's connections to the ruling party or the government. No pictures of KMT leaders or even Chiang Kai-shek hang on the wall. Dressed in a smart black suit, Cheng has a ready smile and telegenic appearance that recall her prior career as an evening news anchor. Yet these days industry professionals are more likely to comment on her managerial performance at CTV, a company often referred to as the "brightest of the terrestrials." Cheng's diversification strategy has in fact worked well, with more than half of the company's profits now coming from nonbroadcast revenues.

From the outset, Cheng believed that TV ad sales in Taiwan could not keep up with the rapidly rising costs of program production, especially since advertising dollars are now spread among more than one hundred cable channels rather than the original three terrestrials. Indeed, between 1998 and 2000, ad revenues at CTV plummeted from US$147 million to $113 million, dropping some 23 percent.[7] In the face of such decline, Cheng contends that the company must diversify and globalize if it is to sustain profitability. The organizing principle behind this strategy is to reposition the CTV as a multimedia content provider with a strong focus on Chinese language and culture. "We're talking about transforming Chinese culture into something modern that can be accepted by the whole world," she says.[8] No longer a propaganda tool, CTV fashions products to suit diverse audiences: mass and niche, domestic and foreign. Moreover, CTV is moving beyond television to embrace new technologies and related media enterprises, such as video games and Internet services. Yet the core identity of the company revolves around its distinctive association with Chinese arts and culture.

"Whether fortunately or unfortunately, we were ruled by Chiang Kai-shek," says Cheng, "and at that time everybody thought that we were the rightful heirs to Chinese culture." Cheng compares ROC's sino-centric heritage to the disruptive turmoil of the Cultural Revolution in the PRC or the colonial experiences of Hong Kong, Macau, and Singapore. In her estimation, only Taiwanese stations like CTV can tap their deep connections to Chinese arts and culture to produce captivating media products in contemporary Chinese vernacular.

According to Cheng, "A modern language is something that can be accepted worldwide." It maintains its distinctive cultural traces and yet at the same time is capable of addressing audiences that come from a variety of backgrounds, especially young audiences. "Last night at the movies," she explains, "I saw the trailer for an animated mainland movie, called *Lotus Lantern*. You can really see the difference between it and Disney's *Mulan*. You look at it and you can immediately tell: no, it's just too Chinese. Not only too Chinese for Taiwan, but too Chinese for Hong Kong and a lot of other places. It's just too *old*." Interestingly, this conversation was taking place only a month before the July 2000 premiere of *Crouching Tiger, Hidden Dragon*, a film that succeeded precisely because its Taiwanese director, Ang Lee, was able to make a film that paid homage to romantic dramas and swordplay films of the past, while also producing a very contemporary transnational blockbuster using global talent and resources. Likewise, Cheng believes that CTV could be at the center of content development for a global market, providing financing and organizing resources on a regional basis.

Among the genres that seem especially ripe for transnational, multimedia development, prime-time drama is perhaps the most important form of core content that the station produces. Traditionally, 8:00 P.M. dramas have been a keystone of the evening TV schedule, forming a bridge between the nightly news and variety programs. A strong drama series not only attracts an audience but also helps to hold the audience throughout prime time. Moreover, since dramatic series are usually telecast five nights a week over a period of eight or more weeks, they also serve as an important promotional vehicle for the terrestrial stations. By comparison, cable channels in Taiwan find it difficult to finance original drama series, so they usually purchase dramas from foreign suppliers or they rerun series that were originally broadcast on their terrestrial competitors. When cable stations do venture into the realm of original prime-time drama, they usually produce low-budget studio series with Taiwanese dialogue and contemporary themes that resonate with island audiences

Huan Zhu Ge Ge is one of the longest-running and most popular
Chinese historical dramas, especially among young viewers, who are
prime users of ancillary products and services spun off from such
programming. (Left to right) Zi Wei and Mu Sha. Courtesy of
Hunan TV.

and are rarely exported. The terrestrial stations therefore distinguish
themselves by mounting lavish historical dramas, but interestingly, they
too have found it increasingly difficult to finance the programs and so
they must look for coproduction partners overseas, especially in mainland China. Moreover, they must, from the very outset of the production process, take into consideration overseas distribution of each series.
Consequently, the competitive economics of the *local* market are now
driving CTV and the other terrestrials toward *transnational* coproduction
and distribution.

In the spring of 2000, Su Ming Cheng was quite proud that CTV
dramas were playing in prime time on the leading terrestrial stations in
Hong Kong and the PRC. She was also delighted that the preceding year,
Huan Zhu Ge Ge (Princess Huan Zhu), another CTV coproduction, scored
record audiences throughout Greater China, especially among young viewers whom Cheng sees as prime users of ancillary products and services
spun off by such programming. "With all of our dramas we now target
young audiences and we try to develop computer software to go with
them," enthuses Cheng. "We have a joint venture with Soft China, the

biggest video game company in Taiwan, so now every one of our evening dramas is aimed at audiences who might be interested in these games."

Of the terrestrial stations, CTV has moved most aggressively to reposition itself in a changing media universe. It was able to do this because the station was "privately" owned and operated by the ruling KMT rather than by the government. By comparison, efforts to reform the other broadcast stations, CTS and TTV, present a far more complicated set of issues because both are government owned, and therefore any decision to reorganize them must be vetted by the legislature, a process that is sure to be fraught with political conflict and maneuver. Nevertheless, all three stations feel the pressure to reform as the competitive crush from cable TV continues to drive down advertising revenues and stimulate the search for new ways to attract audiences. The extent to which CTV can realize its ambitions as a transnational, multimedia enterprise with a contemporary Chinese identity is still up in the air, but the institutional dynamics provide a good example of the macropolitical and economic pressures that are driving Taiwanese broadcasters to seek coproduction agreements with stations in the PRC. At the level of program production, creative personnel look especially to historical drama as one of the few genres that can succeed as a transnational series.

Producing Historical Drama

During the late 1990s, TTV's Eric Yang emerged as one of the most successful young producers of television drama, scoring six hit series over the course of two years. His achievements were all the more remarkable because TTV, Taiwan's first television broadcaster, was in a downward spiral, especially with its eight o'clock dramas, which were then drawing ratings in the 2 to 3 range, a little less than half that of the other terrestrial stations. In 1999, Yang spectacularly reversed that trend with a series that more than tripled the station's ratings. Entitled *First Lady and the Officer*, it's the story of a Chinese general during the Qing dynasty who serves as the first imperial governor of Taiwan and marries a strong-willed young woman from the island. The story premise was gimmicky but also rich with possibility, explains Yang, since "this was the first time that China ruled Taiwan and he was the first governor, but at home it's a different story: he seems to have all this power, but he's scared of his wife. It's a story about their marriage but it's also a story about different kinds of power."[9] As with many Chinese TV dramas, the series refracts contemporary concerns through the prism of historical narrative, setting the story more than three hundred years in the past but fashioning a drama that is remarkably contemporary. At the time of its broadcast, identity issues were the subject of widespread discussion in Taiwan, as was deliberation over cross-Straits relations with China. Interestingly, mainland audiences were likewise intrigued by the series, since at the time the Beijing government was avidly promoting a policy of reunification that would bring Hong Kong, Macau, and Taiwan back to the motherland.

Yang furthermore explains that the couple's ongoing attempts to sustain domestic harmony are also complicated by a shrewd narrative device in which the first lady speaks in her native Taiwanese and the governor (a mainland actor) speaks in Mandarin. As in real life, one's expressive abilities in a native tongue surpass those of one's second language. The series invokes this device to subtly suggest the difficulties of communication between mainlander and Taiwanese, as well as to highlight distinctions between imperial culture and a local culture. Although this contrivance resonates with contemporary concerns over relations with the mainland, it also evokes memories of Chiang's occupation and sinification of Taiwan during his reign. Issues of difference—played out at the levels of language, culture, and gender—are therefore the central narrative concern, made all the more intriguing because the first lady is portrayed as a match for her husband in many ways, perhaps implying an equal status between Taiwan and the PRC or between native Taiwanese and *waishengren* or between contemporary men and women.

Although Yang acknowledges that the series' premise was formulated to attract coproduction partners in the PRC, another rationale for this cross-cultural drama grew out of his calculation of TTV's problems in the Taiwan market. At the time, he recalls, "Our ratings were low, even for a terrestrial, and it had been two years since TTV had the number one prime-time drama. *First Lady* was only my second series [as executive producer], but I was convinced that the reason we were failing was because too many people in the business still see Taiwan from a Taipei perspective and they forget the rest of the island." As noted earlier, *waishengren* tended to settle in the northern part of Taiwan, near the capital of Taipei, and consequently the area became dominated by the Mandarin language and a sino-centric worldview. The Taiwanese language (the Minnan variety of Chinese) continues to be widely used in the southern and central parts of the island, even by those who have been educated in Mandarin. Therefore, Yang's linguistic device was fashioned to appeal to viewers outside the northern metropolitan region; he also aimed his promotional efforts at southern and central cities, such as Kaohsiung and Taichung, buying radio spots and newspaper ads and staging promotional events with the leading actors. His strategy paid off handsomely. "The series before *First Lady* had a 2 rating," he explains, "but our first episode got an 8 and it went up to a 10.4 rating overall, and in central Taiwan we got a 14 rating, which is very high these days."

During one of our interview sessions, Yang and I met at the Living Bar in Taipei, a Japanese-owned, Western-style restaurant set on a quiet lane just behind the major department stores that line Chung Hsiao Road. It was a cool, rainy February evening, and Yang arrived in a navy peacoat, with a Nike knapsack casually slung over his shoulder. Tall, slender, and thirty-something, Yang spoke energetically, describing the mechanics of drama production in Taiwan. At the outset, his station's programming department develops a story line and makes initial casting decisions either alone or in consultation with an independent producer. The station then provides a financial commitment to the independent producer in exchange for territorial rights to Taiwan and overseas markets, such as Malaysia, Indonesia, and Korea. Taiwanese stations usually provide most of the financial resources for such series, for example, US$1.4 million for the first forty episodes of *First Lady*. With this agreement in hand, the producer then shops the concept around to provincial and municipal TV stations in the PRC. Most of these stations tend to be cash poor, but they are attractive partners because they can provide facilities, services, labor, and shooting locations that would otherwise be very expensive or, in the case of locations, unavailable in Taiwan. Historical settings and stunning terrain are two of the key attractions that mainland partners bring to the table. Moreover, labor and technical costs in the PRC are significantly lower than they are in Taiwan. In exchange for these services, the mainland coproduction partner secures series rights for the PRC. In addition to broadcasting the series on the local airwaves, the PRC partner will market it to other provincial and municipal broadcasters around the country. In the end, partners on both sides of the Straits gain broadcast rights to a much higher-quality product through a cross-Straits coproduction agreement.

Although most deals follow this well-established pattern, the negotiations are very fluid. For example, the Taiwan station may decide to limit its financial commitment to the series by bidding only for the island rights, requiring the producer to find another investor who is interested in picking up the international distribution market. Likewise, the mainland partner might provide only studio time in exchange for rights to transmission on its own station, leaving the rest of the PRC markets in the hands of the producer, who must then line up a distributor for the remaining territories. Overall, the Taiwan station usually plays a substantial role in financing and creative development, essentially acting as executive producer, while the mainland partner is most actively involved in staging and shooting the production. The independent producer is responsible for putting together the overall package, negotiating territorial rights, and hiring appropriate talent. Obviously, stars from each market enhance the appeal of a series, but producers also try to select appropriate writers, directors, and videographers from each territory. For example, mainland scriptwriters are widely revered for the depth of their historical knowledge and for the intricate plotting of their scripts, while many Taiwanese television executives express exasperation at the paucity of such talent in their own market. On the other hand, mainland writers and actors are also known to write and perform in a plodding style that doesn't appeal to the tastes of viewers in Taiwan, Hong Kong, and overseas markets. As a result, Taiwanese writers are often hired to generate snappier dialogue and wordplay. They are also considered especially adept at romantic plotlines, whereas mainland writers are considered best at imperial court dramas.

Each partner shares significant responsibilities and takes calculated risks, but none is more vulnerable than the independent producer whose very survival may rest on the success of a particular series. Profit margins are often thin, and losses can be substantial, but successful producers generally make money by developing strong reputations that can be parlayed into long-term contracts with stations in the PRC, Taiwan, and Hong Kong. A well-established producer, such as Yi Ren Media, can increase its profits by extending the run of a series (economies of scale) and by negotiating performance bonuses with stations. It can also negotiate for a share of the income derived from syndication. This combination of strategies can prove quite lucrative, as with the series *Princess Huan Zhu,* which performed well among Chinese viewers in markets around the globe, allowing Yi Ren Media to bid for much higher fees when it extended the series after the first forty episodes. Despite such successes, however, many production companies in Taipei live on the edge, moving from project to project, sometimes using income from a new project to pay off past debts and assuming new debts to keep a current series running. Staffing is kept lean to control overhead costs, and so the production team for each new series needs to be assembled from scratch.

Historical Drama in Social Context

Taiwan's independent producers are especially interested in historical dramas because these programs are durable performers in syndication markets throughout Greater China. Although contemporary dramas often attract higher ratings in local and national markets, historical dramas are easier to sell transnationally because they are less controversial and less culturally specific. "That's why so many prime-time dramas are set in the Qing dynasty," says Yang. Among Chinese audiences around the world, "there's no conflict over that part of history, but after the Qing dynasty, each government has a different interpretation of history." These ideological differences are compounded by other differences as well, notes Yang: "The closer you get to our time, the more likely you are to notice cultural differences. Taipei's lifestyle is different from Hong Kong's lifestyle and also different from the mainland." Historical dramas successfully negotiate such differences because they take contemporary concerns and displace them to a mythical past that is open to interpretation from a variety of perspectives. Moreover, the programs are attractive to audiences in rural as well as urban areas, and their appeal tends to cut across class boundaries as well. The use of historical characters and settings furthermore lends legitimacy to the series, making them appear educational in the eyes of many parents. And although critics regularly question the accuracy of such programs, audiences nevertheless draw lessons that they assume to be based on characters and events from China's past. In a broader sense, the shows allow viewers to rehearse their thoughts regarding what it means to be Chinese.

The historical drama genre can be divided into two main categories: one is the palace drama, which focuses on the political and personal intrigues within a specific dynasty; the other is the martial arts genre, where legendary figures do battle on behalf of a particular group or a set of moral principles. Palace dramas can be made more cost-efficient by restricting their focus to inner chambers of the court, or, more ambitiously, they can be ratcheted up to a grand scale, featuring dramatic location shots, action sequences, and large casts. Yet—not unlike Hollywood dramas such as *Dallas* (1978–91) and *Dynasty* (1981–89)—the defining feature of these series is the core relationships among family members in a powerful clan.[10] *Princess Huan Zhu* and *First Lady* fall into this category, since both focus on familial and romantic relationships as they play out within the context of imperial households. Yet interestingly, both proved exceptionally popular because they dwelled

Historical dramas are easier to sell transnationally because they are less controversial and less culturally specific. (Left to right) Qing Ar and Xiao Yan Zi in *Huan Zhu Ge Ge 3*. Courtesy of Hunan TV.

on the romantic fortunes of young women who seem to be exploring the nature of feminine power and identity, themes that clearly resonate with young female viewers today. *Yongzheng Dynasty* is an example of another type of palace drama that offers an elaborate tale of a strong and righteous young heir who rises to power amid the corruption and intrigues of the imperial court. The heir's struggles with bureaucracy are as much a study of statecraft as they are of family politics.

Palace dramas draw from a wealth of historical, operatic, and literary sources, yet they also tap the traditions of Chinese cinema, where such stories flourished, especially during the 1960s. Li Hanxiang, a leading director of the palace-chamber (*gongwei*) dramas for the Shaw Brothers Studio, argues that *gongwei* faded from popularity because they were costly to produce.[11] As the major Chinese film studios shuttered their operations, the output of the genre plummeted on the silver screen. Li makes no mention of television, yet it is interesting to note that Shaw Brothers moved most of its production capacity to television where, in the 1970s, it began to produce *gongwei* for the small screen, as did television stations in Taiwan and Singapore. Television producers with experience learned to scale *gongwei* series to budgets small and large, producing a steady stream of historical dramas from the 1980s up to the present day. Indeed, it may be the accessibility of *gongwei* TV series that has made them less attractive to cinema audiences over the past two decades.[12]

Equally popular on the small screen is the martial arts genre (*wushu*), which subdivides into kung fu and sword-fighting (*wuxia*) dramas. The latter revolve around a group of warriors, or sometimes a single warrior and his comrade, who for some reason have fallen upon hard times: the lord to whom they have pledged their allegiance has been slain, corrupt officials have taken control of the government, or they have been exiled after an invasion by outsiders. They are now "rebels without a cause" living on the margins of society, but they remain pure of heart and bound by deep ties of honor and brotherhood. The action is usually set in the distant past, reaching back as early as the seventh-century Tang dynasty. Members of the group often have quirky personality traits or fighting styles, but all are exceptionally dedicated warriors. A crisis inevitably emerges when a band of warriors or the common people of the land are suffering from the iniquities of a system ruled by evil others. They pledge themselves to battle for righteousness against enormous odds, and they often prevail after protracted and bloody fighting, thereby restoring the legitimate ruler to the throne and/or peace to the community.

The other subgenre, kung fu, focuses on characters who represent a particular fighting style, but, more important, they represent a worldview that is associated with their school of kung fu, organized under the leadership of a revered master. Kung fu heroes generally tread the path of ascetic restraint but invariably find themselves pulled into a conflict on behalf of an oppressed community. Despite their efforts to resolve problems peacefully, they ultimately are left with no alternative to physical force, allowing them to exhibit their well-honed skills while subduing the forces of evil and restoring community harmony. Sometimes these stories involve conflicts between kung fu schools, but keeping with the formula, one school is generally cast as an evil aggressor and the other as a more humble and righteous ensemble under the leadership of a benevolent master. Although kung fu stories can be set in the distant past, many of them take place during the late Qing dynasty or the early twentieth century, at times when traditional Chinese values were threatened by corrupt rulers or foreign invaders. Legendary kung fu masters usually practice traditional arts, medicine, or philosophy and may also possess mystical powers, since they must overcome spectacular odds in the pursuit of justice.

The formula for the martial arts drama is in some ways similar to the Hollywood Western during its halcyon days, when it provided a pretext for reflections on the relationship between tradition and modernity. But, as John Cawelti suggests, one of the signal characteristics of such fiction was its attempt to appeal to diverse audiences in a modernizing society by situating the action in an abstract diegetic world. The "Wild West" provided such a tableau, since it was far from the experience of most audience members. Moreover, he argues, Westerns needed to resemble games in the clarity of their rules and the patterns of action: "This game-like aspect of the formula permits anyone who knows the 'rules'—and in our culture children are instructed in the rules of the Western from a very early age—to enjoy and appreciate the fine points of play, as well as to experience the sense of ego-enhancement that comes when 'our side' wins."[13] Martial arts dramas are, like Westerns, rule-bound stories with clearly defined opposing players, a sequence of moves that must happen in a particular order, and an abstract social structure and physical landscape upon which the game is played out. The "game" is one that draws upon Chinese legend, novels, and opera from the past, as well as today's thriving mass-fiction industry, whose authors have refashioned these stories with a more contemporary inflection.

Eric Yang points out that in Taiwan a substantial audience can readily be tapped for martial arts dramas because a large reading public is already sold on the genre. The programs perform particularly well during school vacations, when teenage boys—a core audience—gravitate to them, especially if they are based on stories by popular novelists, such as Jin Yong, Liang Yuzi, or Gu Long. "According to my research," notes Yang, "any [martial arts] drama gets at least a 4 rating, so it's a guarantee of basic survival because students like to watch them and older male viewers in general are attracted to them." Yang says that most of the kung fu series he produced pulled ratings in the 5 to 9 range, making them impressive performers among their peers. They also prove effective as counterprogramming against another popular genre, the contemporary family saga, which tends to draw women and older viewers during the heart of prime time.

Audiences and Identity

As mentioned previously, historical dramas succeed on both sides of the Straits because they are seen as noncontroversial, even though they may in fact raise very relevant issues in an allegorical fashion. In 1999,

Yongzheng Dynasty drew fans throughout Greater China and was reportedly a favorite of PRC premier Zhu Rongji and Taiwanese president Lee Teng-hui, making it one of the few things that the two could agree on. Both reportedly admired the lead character because he was able to make difficult policy decisions without being swayed by flattery, familial pressure, or personal gain. Indeed, both Zhu and Lee are widely seen as leaders who have weathered adversity because of their political principles. Yet their principles and their political circumstances vary dramatically, with one battling an entrenched government bureaucracy in hopes of modernizing mainland society and the other struggling to sustain the independence of modern Taiwan in the face of exorbitant pressure for reunification with the PRC. Though regular adversaries over a number of explosive political issues, both leaders were captivated by the televised tales of politics and power offered up by daily episodes of *Yongzheng Dynasty*.

On the other hand, TV dramas with contemporary settings don't enjoy the polysemic range of interpretation that is characteristic of their historical counterparts. Rather than fantasizing about a vague yesteryear, audiences for contemporary dramas tend to be quite sensitive to the social differences they discern in the characters, narrative, and mise-en-scène of contemporary series. For example, when viewers watch a domestic scene, most seem to feel that the setting should be furnished in keeping with what they understand to be contemporary design. Likewise, clothing, autos, and consumer goods all should resonate with their immediate experience. "Since 1949," observes Yang, "Taiwanese people have had a very different lifestyle [from their counterparts in the PRC]: different celebrities, different novels, different authors." Consequently, contemporary mainland TV dramas don't fare especially well in Taiwan. "When I was in China recently," recalls Yang, "I watched a drama with beautiful scenery and good-looking actors (two of them from Taiwan), but it didn't look Taiwanese. The dress style was not very chic and the lifestyle didn't seem familiar." Executives from other Taiwanese TV companies agree, one suggesting that different consumer behaviors and fashion trends are quick to register with viewers. "The actors [in mainland dramas] are very label conscious, and they tend to flaunt expensive jewelry," one executive observes, "but they aren't the labels or the kinds of jewelry that are popular now" in Taiwan. Ironically, adds Yang, Taiwanese viewers are often more comfortable with contemporary *Japanese* dramas than they are with dramas shot in Beijing. "When we see a Japanese drama, we see very similar lifestyles," he says, an assessment widely shared among programming executives in Taipei who compete ferociously for the rights to Japanese series that feature contemporary themes and settings, as well as glamorous pop stars playing the lead roles.[14]

In post–martial law Taiwan, as islanders search for a distinctive identity, they look back to Chinese legend, they reflect upon Taiwanese customs, and they consider continuing ties to Japanese culture. These distinctive cultural coordinates make it difficult for contemporary dramas from the PRC to penetrate the television market in Taiwan. Likewise, Taiwanese producers believe it would be difficult for them to crack mainland markets with contemporary dramas of their own, and so they gravitate to the historical drama.[15] The economics of the market furthermore encourage such transnational coproductions, since costs continue to rise during an era of increasing competition and audience fragmentation. For example, TTV prime-time dramas are produced for $30,000 to $40,000 per episode. During the 8:00 P.M. telecast, advertising for a successful series is sold for $6,000 per minute, running up to ten minutes of advertising per hour. At the very most, TTV is taking in $60,000 per hour and spending as much as $40,000 on production costs alone.[16] Given the additional infrastructure, marketing, and personnel costs, profit margins are slim. Without coproduction opportunities and overseas distribution revenues, it is difficult for a drama series to turn a profit. Given the competitive dynamics of the market, terrestrial broadcasters and only the wealthiest cable channels venture into the realm of drama production. Among these producers, some focus on low-budget domestic dramas, while others tend to migrate toward historical serials and mainland coproduction agreements.

Conclusion

David Bordwell has observed, "It is always tempting to explain genre development as a reflection of social trends, but we get more pertinent and proximate explanations if we also consider the filmmaking practice and the genre's specific tradition."[17] As Bordwell suggests, and as we have seen in this chapter, antecedent traditions in related art forms often set the terms for genres as they migrate from one medium to another, and then one sees artists within the new medium experimenting with a genre and testing those innovations on audiences and other directors. Accordingly, Bordwell sees media professionals as working within sets of conventions and then experimenting in dialogue with other creative personnel. One producer might, for instance, introduce a *detective* plotline into a palace drama that, if successful with audiences, would invite imitation from other producers, thereby creating a generic cycle. This would in turn invite further innovation, as another producer then pushes the cycle in a new direction by introducing a *female* detective into the imperial court plotline. Genre pictures, according to Bordwell, not only speak to audiences but also converse among themselves, and their cycles of innovation are as much a conversation among practitioners as they are a reflection of the culture at large.

Bordwell's analysis conforms well to the foregoing assessment of the Chinese historical drama, although larger social and cultural forces do in fact influence a genre's development, as well. So long as we are cautious to avoid a simple "reflection" theory of culture, we can delineate some of the ways in which social forces register at the level of textual production and distribution. For example, post–martial law liberalization of media in Taiwan has spurred a dramatic multiplication of media channels, creating an intensely competitive environment that encourages broadcasters to seek alliances outside the island in order to respond to local market pressures. With the end of the cold war and the increasing liberalization of transnational trade, it becomes possible—indeed, necessary—for broadcasters to seek alliances on the mainland, despite the intense ideological struggles between leaders on either side of the Straits. This engenders the production of polysemic texts set in an abstract diegetic world where pertinent concerns are nevertheless raised for contemporary viewers. Most centrally these historical dramas address such issues as corruption, tradition, gender, and identity. Indeed, one of the most pervasive concerns of these transnational texts is to reflect upon the meaning of Chineseness in a rapidly changing modern world.

In other words, an industrial *and* cultural approach reveals how television personnel operate in dialogue with other craftspeople and within the context of larger social and historical forces. Such an approach draws from one of the key insights in Stuart Hall's "encoding/decoding" model.[18] Most commonly, scholars place emphasis on Hall's discussion of complex patterns of audience interpretation, while overlooking the equally important argument about the multiple ways in which message production—or "encoding"—is shaped by historical forces, industry practices, and feedback from audiences. By replacing the word "message" with "genre," we can move toward a dynamic model of genre development that takes into account influences that are both micro and macro. Moreover, such an approach would acknowledge structural forces, while also characterizing creative labor as both practical and interpretive. Television producers, according to Newcomb and Hirsch, are "cultural *bricoleurs,* seeking and creating new meaning in the combination of cultural elements with embedded significance. They respond to real events, changes in social structure and organization, and to shifts in attitude and value. They also respond to technological shifts, the coming of cable or the use of videotape recorders. . . . At each step of [the creative] process they function as cultural interpreters," and their texts participate in a broader cultural forum.[19]

Chinese historical drama is best understood as a stylized genre in which contrived roles and events provide a pretext for reflection upon the usefulness of myth and legend for a modern world. Such dramas are putatively about the past, but they are also about contemporary concerns, such as cross-Straits tensions between Taiwan and the mainland. To allegorically situate such tensions within the intimacy of a Qing dynasty household—where language, culture, politics, and gender clash— is as much a pragmatic textual gimmick aimed at responding to the exigencies of the industry as it is an interpretation of themes broadly circulating in the culture at large.

Notes

Thanks to the Taiwan National Endowment for Culture and Art and the U.S. Fulbright Commission for providing research support during the 1999–2000 academic year. I furthermore want to express my appreciation to colleagues at the Institute of Ethnology, Academia Sinica, and the Foundation for Scholarly Exchange who graciously hosted my sabbatical in Taipei and to colleagues and students in the School of Journalism and Mass Communication at the Chinese University of Hong Kong, where I served as a visiting professor during the 1996–97 academic year.

1. This chapter uses the term "genre" primarily as an industrial category. That is, the historical drama refers to a category of texts that feature similar thematic concerns, as well as similar conditions of production, distribution, and exhibition.

2. TV International, *Asia Pacific TV,* 8th ed. (London: Informa Media Group), 2003, 203.

3. John G. Cawelti, *The Six-Gun Mystique* (Bowling Green, Ohio: Bowling Green University Popular Press, 1971).

4. Horace Newcomb, *TV: The Most Popular Art* (Garden City, N.Y.: Anchor Press, 1975); and David Marc, *Demographic Vistas: Television in American Culture* (Philadelphia: University of Pennsylvania Press, 1984).

5. Robert C. Allen, *Speaking of Soap Operas* (Chapel Hill: University of North Carolina Press, 1985); Janice Radway, *Reading the Romance: Women, Patriarchy, and Popular Literature* (Chapel Hill: University of North Carolina Press, 1984).

6. David Bordwell, *Planet Hong Kong: Popular Cinema and the Art of Entertainment* (Cambridge, Mass.: Harvard University Press, 2000).

7. This trend continued the following year, with revenues falling to $88 million, a decline of 40 percent in three years. Informa Media, *TV International: Asia Pacific TV*, 7th ed. (London: Informa Media Group, 2002), 249.

8. Su Ming Cheng, interviews by author, March 13 and 22, 2000. Also note that much of the information in this chapter is a composite derived from in-depth interviews with media professionals in Taiwan during the spring of 2000.

9. Eric Yang, interviews by author, February 23 and June 27, 2000.

10. Note also the comparison to European soap operas in Tamar Liebes and Sonia Livingstone, *European Journal of Communication* 13 (1998): 147–80.

11. Cited in Bordwell, *Planet Hong Kong*, 150.

12. Of course, cinematic palace dramas did not disappear, but in the *commercial* Chinese film industry, their popularity declined considerably.

13. Cawelti, *Six-Gun Mystique*, 71.

14. For more about the popularity of so-called idol dramas in Taiwan, see Koichi Iwabuchi, *Recentering Globalization: Popular Culture and Japanese Transnationalism* (Durham, N.C.: Duke University Press, 2002).

15. Although cultural differences may limit the attractiveness of Taiwanese contemporary dramas among PRC audiences, a more difficult challenge is posed by import restrictions. Government officials tend to frown on imported programming from the "renegade province" of Taiwan. Yet some recent series, such as *Meteor Garden*, have proved popular, even though distribution is uncertain and audiences are most likely to view the series through pirated video.

16. Yang, interview.

17. Bordwell, *Planet Hong Kong*, 153.

18. Stuart Hall, "Encoding/Decoding," in *Culture, Media, Language*, ed. Stuart Hall et al. (London: Hutchinson, 1980), 128–40.

19. Horace Newcomb and Paul Hirsch, "Television as a Cultural Forum," in *Television: The Critical View*, 5th ed., ed. Horace Newcomb (New York: Oxford University Press, 1994), 505.

14 | innovation, imitation, and hybridity in indian television

Shanti Kumar

A genre is usually defined as a category of programming that shares a set of codes and conventions such as program length, setting, characters, plot, social values, and ideologies. Although such generalized definitions are useful to begin with, they are rather inadequate to describe the specificity of a particular genre, or to address the many similarities across genres.[1] The question of genre definition is further complicated in postcolonial contexts such as India, where the history of colonialism and the contemporary trends of globalization disrupt neat categories and traditional distinctions. A key problem that confronts television programmers, academic scholars, and media critics alike is that there are no easy markers to define a show as "Indian" given the flexible capitalist structures of the global media industries and the hybrid cultural tastes of the viewers at home.

Some media scholars, such as Keval J. Kumar, have addressed the problem by simply defining "Indian" genres as television shows based on Hindu mythological epics, such as *Ramayan* and *Mahabharat,* and film-based shows featuring song-and-dance sequences from Hindi cinema, such as *Chayageet, Chitrahaar,* and *Antakshari.*[2] Since most of the satellite television networks in India have now produced their own versions of Hindu epics and film-based shows in many regional languages, mythological epics and song-and-dance rotations are considered to be not only indigenous genres but also pan-Indian genres. By this definition, all other programming genres such as the sitcom, the soap opera, the police drama, the medical drama, the game show, and the reality TV show are not "Indian." Instead, Indian versions of these genres, which are indigenously produced in English, Hindi, and other regional languages, are seen as cheap imitations of "Western" television shows. According to this view, what makes a television genre "Indian" is not just the physical location of its production but also the certain sense of authenticity based on hegemonic notions of national identity and essentialist ideals of cultural history.

An alternative view, embraced by many programmers and network executives in India, suggests that the growing competition among domestic and foreign television networks since 1991 has stimulated indigenous production in a variety of genres such as daytime soaps, late-night talk shows, and reality TV shows, to name a few. Although some Indian soaps, talk shows, or reality shows may have started as copies or clones of American programs, industry experts argue that the intense competition in the television industry has forced both domestic and foreign networks to "Indianize" these global genres to better connect with their viewers' cultural tastes and linguistic affinities.

Anand Mahendroo, the managing director of Advance Entertainment Network, believes that any genre can work in India if it can "touch the hearts of the audiences."[3] For Mahendroo, the key to successful television programming is "getting the right mix." A good example of a television show that has the right mix, Mahendroo argues, is *Kaun Banega Crorepati* (*KBC*)—the Indian version of the internationally syndicated game show *Who Wants to Be a Millionaire.*[4] The reasons for *KBC*'s unprecedented popularity cannot be understood in terms of an appeal to an essentialist notion of Hindu culture or a state-sponsored definition of Indian nationalism. Rather, *KBC* established its "Indian" credentials by imitating an internationally successful game show and innovating just enough to make it appear sufficiently distinct from all the other shows in that genre. In other words, a television genre is not inherently "Indian" by definition, but it can attain that status through a process of hybridization and succeed when a television network is able to provide the "right mix" of innovation and imitation in its programming and scheduling strategies.

In *The Television Genre Book*, Steve Neale points to the centrality of hybridity in underscoring what he calls "the multidimensional nature of genre itself."[5] According to Neale, several factors contribute to the multidimensionality of genres. One factor that has been rather underplayed is "the degree of hybridity and overlap among and between genres" (such as the "comedy drama" genre in film, theater, radio, and television or the "news" genre in newspapers, magazines, radio, and television).[6] Also underplayed, Neale argues, is "the degree to which texts of all kinds necessarily 'participate' in genre" and "the extent to which they are likely to participate in more than one genre at once."[7] Given the variety of genres, their diverse meanings within and across media, and their many uses for academics, critics, audiences, and the television industry, Graeme Turner proposes that we approach the question of definition by thinking about the uses and limitations of genre as a meaningful category for its many constituents.[8]

For those who study or watch television, Turner argues, genre functions as a "means of managing TV's notorious extensiveness as a cultural form by breaking it up into more discrete or comprehensible segments."[9] For those involved in the programming of television, on the other hand, genre serves as a useful device "in the definition of a project by mapping its relation to other, similar texts." Pointing to the crucial role that programming and scheduling strategies play in the definition of a genre, Turner argues that academics need to pay more attention to the work of the programmer. He writes,

> The component that is often left out of the conventional media industry/text/audience triangle is the programmer or the scheduler: the person who places the programme within a channel or a network schedule. There has been very little academic attention paid to the work of the programmer, but it would seem logical to assume that their practices— and thus TV schedules—are influenced by their understanding of genre. One would imagine that an understanding of the pattern of differences and similarities that help define the individual programme must be built into the strategic structuring of a schedule that will match the competition and maximize the audience capture.[10]

Understanding the differences and similarities within and across genres in television's daily schedules is a rather complicated and multidimensional task. Therefore, what Turner describes as the "work of the programmer" must be understood in terms of the multiple roles that scheduling executives, producers, scriptwriters, editors, technicians, and actors play together in creating a television show based on their collective understanding of genre as a mediating mechanism to "match the competition and maximize the audience capture."[11]

In this chapter, I critically evaluate the multidimensional work of the programmer in creating a common understanding of television genres by invoking the figure of the *sutradhar* usually found in classical and folk theater in India. The term *sutradhar* literally translates as "the one who holds the threads." In classical Sanskrit theater, the *sutradhar* is a central figure who combines various generic elements to create a coherent narrative by acting as a producer, a narrator, a director, and even a manipulator of the performance.

The work of programming in the television industry that Turner refers to in the previously cited passage is, of course, more differentiated in its character than the work of the *sutradhar* in classical or folk theaters. For instance, the roles and responsibilities of key players in the creative processes of production and direction or the commercial processes of marketing and distribution are dispersed across many different departments within a television network. However, in order to explicate the multidimensionality of genre in television, I find it useful to articulate the many roles played by actors, producers, directors, and network executives in the work of programming through the composite figure of a *sutradhar* who mediates industry practices and audience expectations by being both within the text as a performer and beyond it as a programmer. In other words, work of the *sutradhar* in the text and on the stage (or as an on-screen performer in television) represents a key moment of articulation in the work of programming as it brings audiences face-to-face with the net result of the work that actors, producers, directors, scriptwriters, and network executives do behind the stage in theater—or offscreen in television.

Indian theater encompasses a great deal of linguistic, cultural, and regional diversity, and folk traditions such as the *Bhavai* in Gujarat, *Burra Katha* in Andhra Pradesh, *Jatra* in Bengal, *Nautanki* in Uttar Pradesh, *Tamasha* in Maharashtra, *Terukuttu* in Tamil Nadu, and *Yakshagana* in Karnataka have all borrowed from the classical conventions of Sanskrit theater. In these different versions of Indian theater, the *sutradhar* deals with a variety of subject matters in a performance and always connects the themes to contemporary concerns.

The task of the *sutradhar* is often so complex in these performances that a sidekick called the *vidushak* is introduced onto the stage. The *vidushak*'s role is akin to that of a clown or a jester. Using exaggerated gestures, excessive makeup, and crude humor, the *vidushak* can take liberties with narrative themes, social issues, and generic conventions in ways that the more serious *sutradhar* cannot. For instance, in some stage versions of the *Mahabharat* in folk theater, the performance introduces a *vidushak* to provide humorous commentary, although literary versions of the epic do not allow for such interventions by a comic figure. In a similar vein, I seek to introduce the figures of the *sutradhar* and the *vidushak* to intervene in debates over genre in Indian television, even though academic conventions in literary theory and in film and television studies have not considered the multiple roles played by the programmer as central to the task of defining genres.

Indian Mythologies

Although television was introduced into India in 1959, for almost two decades the government used the national network, Doordarshan, as an instrument of social change and produced programs that focused on issues like national integration, agricultural development, literacy, education, health, and family welfare. Things began to change during the 1980s, however, starting with the broadcast of the Asian Games, which were held in New Delhi in 1982. For reasons of national prestige, among others, the government of India rapidly transformed Doordarshan's outdated technical infrastructure to provide color transmission of the Asian Games to audiences within and beyond the country.

Following the successful transmission of the Asian Games, Doordarshan slowly moved away from its exclusive focus on educational programming and began experimenting with entertainment programming that was also seen as being socially responsible in the Indian context. On July 7, 1984, Doordarshan began broadcasting *Hum Log* (We the People), a part-educational and part-entertainment television serial that was based on a communication strategy designed by Miguel Sabido in Mexico to produce telenovelas for social change and national development. As Arvind Singhal and Everett M. Rogers argue, "*Hum Log* was an attempt to blend Doordarshan's stated objectives of providing entertainment to its audience, while promoting, within the limits of a dominant patriarchal system, such educational issues as family planning, equal status for women, and family harmony."[12]

The story of *Hum Log* revolves around the everyday activities of a North Indian joint family, with each episode focusing on the triumphs and tribulations of one or more of the nine central cast members portraying characters across three generations. Although everyday conflicts and tensions in relationships between parents and children, grandparents and grandchildren, siblings and cousins provided the necessary elements to serialize the episodic narrative, nationalist issues of patriotic pride, family planning, gender relations, and communal harmony also became central to the definition of *Hum Log* as the story of an "Indian" family.

The unprecedented success of *Hum Log* paved the way for other "socially conscious" soaps like *Buniyad* (The Foundation) and commercially sponsored sitcoms like *Yeh Jo Hai Zindagi* (That's Life). While the introduction of *Hum Log* and *Buniyad* in the mid-1980s established the "soap opera" genre as entertainment-educational programming, and *Yeh Jo Hai Zindagi* paved the way for other commercially sponsored sitcoms on Doordarshan, the telecast of *Ramayan* in 1987–88 transformed the age-old mythological epic into a hybrid television genre that was part religious, part social, part dramatic, and part soap-operatic. Even before the euphoria over the successful telecast of *Ramayan* had subsided, Doordarshan began airing a serialized version of another great Hindu epic, *Mahabharat.*

When it was first broadcast by Doordarshan in installments between 1989 and 1990, *Mahabharat* outscored even the astronomical viewership figures attained by the *Ramayan* serial that it had replaced in the "prime-time religion" hour on Sunday mornings. *Mahabharat* was reportedly seen with ritual regularity by more than 90 percent of all Indian television homes, transcending boundaries of religion, caste, class, language, region, and political allegiance. As in the case of *Ramayan,* weekly household routines were reportedly organized around the Sunday telecast, and family TV sets often became the sites of community viewing. In *Politics after Television,* Arvind Rajagopal ascribes the phenomenal success of *Ramayan* and *Mahabharat* to the creative ways in which the producers of these television epics were able to redefine the mythological genre as "*dharmic* serials."[13] Commenting on the "aura of spiritual sanctity" underlying the description of a television genre as a *dharmic* serial, Rajagopal writes, "'Dharmic' in this context refers to matters of religious or spiritual, and 'serial' is of course a neologism, referring to a periodical issue, in this case of a weekly television program lasting anywhere from thirteen weeks (the typical length of a Doordarshan serial) to two years or more. As a *dharmic* form, the Ramayan serial drew from and appealed to long-standing traditions of attendance at religious story-tellings, *kathas,* which could draw daily audiences running into the thousands for months together."[14]

By appealing to the viewer's familiarity with the traditional genre of *kathas* in classical and folk theaters, the producers of *Mahabharat* and *Ramayan* strategically invoked the figure of the *sutradhar* to articulate the epic's "aura of spiritual sanctity" to the more commercial concerns of the work of television programming. The narrative terrain of *Mahabharat* was so vast and diverse in the many tellings of the epic in folk theater and literature that the producers of the television version used a figure no less than Time itself to play the role of the *sutradhar*. At the beginning of every episode of the television *Mahabharat*, Time is anthropomorphized as the figure of a sage who sits against a cosmic backdrop of stars and planets, superimposed by a slowly turning wheel signifying eternal movements of the universe. In the first episode of the series, Time appears as the *sutradhar* to introduce the great diversity of plots, characters, settings, and social values that can be found through the course of the epic. Cautioning against readings of *Mahabharat* as the story of a great battle between warring cousins called Kauravas and Pandavas, Time invites the viewer to take a journey further into the past to find the true origins of the great Indian epic. Claiming to have been a witness to the beginning of the story, Time speaks of an era when the noble king Bharta ruled over a vast empire stretching from the oceans in the south to the Himalayas in the north. Performing the *sutradhar's* function of connecting the new with the old, Time reminds the viewers that the name of the modern Indian nation-state in Hindi, Bharatvarsha, is derived from this originary kingdom of the Bharata clan in the *Mahabharat* epic.

Not surprisingly, the producers of *Ramayan* also used the figure of a *sutradhar* to situate the television serial in a long tradition of epic narratives over several centuries and across many cultures in the world. To take on this onerous task of creating a coherent narrative based on the many popular tellings of the epic, the producers of *Ramayan* cast Ashok Kumar, the venerated Hindi film star of yesteryear, as the *sutradhar* of the television series. Appearing at the beginning of the *Ramayan* serial, Ashok Kumar invites the viewer to situate the television epic in the historical legacy of the many Ramayans that came before in literature, theater, drama, and cinema in a variety of languages not only across the geographic borders of India but also beyond its shores in faraway places such as Thailand, Russia, Germany, and England. Describing the story of Ramayan as a morality tale for all ages, Ashok Kumar thus situates the television serial in a long tradition of the mythological epic even as he volunteers to serve as the *sutradhar* for a new televisual genre that is part mythological and part contemporary for viewers in the Indian context.

Fans of Indian television in the 1980s recognized Ashok Kumar not only as a famous movie star but also as the *sutradhar* of the popular television serial *Hum Log* (1984), which predated both *Ramayan* and *Mahabharat* on Doordarshan by a good four to five years. Acting as the *sutradhar* for the many plots and subplots in *Hum Log*, Ashok Kumar—

Fans of Indian television recognized Ashok Kumar not only as a famous movie star but also as the *sutradhar* of the popular television serial *Hum Log* (We the People) in 1984. Courtesy of Doordarshan.

lovingly called "Dadda" as a mark of respect for his status as a grandfather (or an older brother in Bengali) in the Indian film industry—regularly appeared at the beginning and the end of each episode to summarize the central themes of the twenty-two-minute narrative. In his commentary, Ashok Kumar addressed the narrative conflicts and moral dilemmas of *Hum Log* in terms of their relevance for a typical Indian family that is caught between the cultural tensions of tradition and modernity in everyday life. At the end of his one-minute monologue, Ashok Kumar left the story in tantalizing suspense, with an invitation to the viewer to find out what happened next in the story by tuning in to the next episode of *Hum Log*.

Over the course of the 156 episodes of *Hum Log* in 1984–85, as Ashok Kumar signed off each episode by translating the show's title into a different Indian language, his one-minute summary came to symbolize the programming agenda of *Hum Log*'s producers, who had learned the art of making "socially conscious" soap operas from producers of telenovelas in Mexico and Brazil. In the process they had also learned to creatively "Indianize" the genre by borrowing the figure of the *sutradhar* from the narrative traditions of classical Sanskrit theater and regional folk forms in India. The introduction of Ashok Kumar in *Hum Log,* his reappearance in *Ramayan,* and the recurring role of Time in *Mahabharat* underscore some of the creative ways in which the figure of the *sutradhar* was used to mediate within and across old and new genres, and thus aid the work of programming in Indian television during the 1980s.

The Making of Generation [V]

In his book *Monopoly Television,* Jack Banks defines the American MTV as the prototype against which all other MTVs around the world must be evaluated.[15] Although Banks acknowledges that there are variations among MTVs in different parts of the world, he argues that American MTV has provided the basic formats for the globalization of music television as a whole. In other words, if a music video produced in India, China, or Indonesia does not imitate some or all the elements found in American MTV formats, its membership in the music video genre remains suspect at best. Moreover, American MTV remains the originary point of reference even when the taxonomy of music television genres is loosened a bit to include "hybrid" versions in the global context—such as the ones seen in top-ten rotations on MTV Asia, MTV Europe, and MTV India. Although many top-ten rotations on Indian television have been rarely dominated by American artists or music videos since the mid-1990s, the taxonomy of American MTV, according to Banks's argument, remains a crucial marker for defining genre consistency in music television.

However, the myth of an MTV-dominated world was shattered in May 1994, when a pan-Asian music television channel called Channel [V] began programming into India as part of Rupert Murdoch's Star TV network. Channel [V] came into being after MTV left the Star TV platform due to contractual disputes with Murdoch over programming and scheduling strategies in the Asia Pacific region. In its efforts to sustain its brand identity as an Indian music network, Channel [V] established production facilities in major cities like Delhi and Bombay. Although created in Indian production centers, the programming genres on Channel [V] seemed at first glance to be derived from MTV's globally familiar production techniques based on vérité camera work, cacophonous editing style, provocative animation, and top-ten video rotations. However, to this vulgar appropriation of MTV formats, Channel [V] creatively added iconographic elements of Bollywood musicals,

Straddling two cultures with ease, Ruby Bhatia, a former Miss India-Canada from Toronto, was India's first VJ on a music television channel. Courtesy of Channel [V].

as well as the self-deprecating humor and slapstick comedy that are hallmarks of Indian cinema. Channel [V] thus promoted the rise of a new satellite channel, casually mixing East and West in what one might refer to as television's first "masala" music service.[16]

Key features of the Channel [V] "masala mix" included creatively designed movie and music tie-in shows featuring film snippets and music, introduced by glamorous Indian and Anglo-Indian VJs with shows named after them. Ruby Bhatia, a former Miss India-Canada from Toronto, was India's first VJ on a music television channel. In 1994, when the executive producer and the creative director of Channel [V] "were searching for the face and personality" of their new music television network, "Ruby, straddling two cultures with ease, gave the channel a whole new identity."[17] As the face of a new network trying to Indianize the music television genre in the 1990s, Ruby's role was not unlike the role of the *sutradhar* played by Ashok Kumar to introduce new serials like *Hum Log* and *Ramayan* to an earlier generation of viewers in the 1980s.

Speaking neither in English nor in Hindi, but in both, Ruby provided "Hinglish" commentaries on music videos from a wide variety of genres in her top-ten countdown shows; she also hosted special events on Channel [V] to introduce domestic and international pop artists to the young viewer in India. One of Ruby's early roles as a *sutradhar* to help young Indian viewers connect with the world of music television was as the host of *The Great Indian Manovigyanik Show*, which loosely translates as The Great Indian Psychoanalytic Show. Describing the show as an "interview program with a difference," a Channel [V] publicity brochure explains, "Hosted by *Ruby*, The GREAT INDIAN MANOVIGYANIK SHOW, also known as THE M'Escos GIM SHOW, is a programme full of surprises as mystery celebrities present a selection of their favorite Hindi and international songs from the location of their choice especially chosen to give the viewer clues as to who might be presenting the programme."[18]

For instance, in an episode of the *Manovigyanik Show* featuring Indian pop star Alisha Chinai after the pathbreaking success of her music video "Made in India," Ruby opened the show with the following remarks: "Well, it's time for another *Mescos Great Indian Manovigyanik Show*. And we have somebody for you on our show today . . . who calls herself a 'rebellious schizophrenic.' Hmm . . . Something worth *manovigyankially* analyzing."[19]

Even a brief glimpse at the interview transcript reveals how seemingly at home Alisha, Ruby, and the sponsors (Mescos) of *The Great Indian Manovigyanik Show* are in their hybrid articulations of cultural identity and difference in the larger context of postcolonial discourse. Right from the initial setting, the show reveals Ruby as a cosmopolitan Indian woman who is as comfortable with her anglicized accent and modern attire as she is in conducting her interview from what looks like a stereotypically Indian palace from a bygone era. In this televisual re-creation of tradition and modernity, Ruby and Alisha deftly articulate their hybrid "Indianness" throughout the entire interview as they move back and forth between Hindi and English and speak in that uniquely Indian language that audiences have come to know as "Hinglish."[20] Take, for instance, the Hinglish sentence Ruby constructs at the beginning of the show to introduce Alisha to the audiences of Channel [V]: "We have somebody for you on our show today, *jisne apne* career *ki shuruat ki hai* with a commercial for a toothpaste" (she began her career with a commercial for a toothpaste).

In sharp contrast to Ruby's role as a Hinglish *sutradhar* who enthralled viewers with her ability to Indianize English and Anglicize Hindi in the same sentence, Channel [V] introduced an irreverent *vidushak* named Udham Singh in the role of a rustic VJ who provided scathing critiques of Indian and international music videos in a chaste North Indian dialect of Haryanvi. Hailing Udham Singh as the ultimate antidote to Western cultural imperialism, *Connect Magazine* in its May 1998 issue proclaimed, "As the world turns, as boundaries diminish, as the west falls in love with the east all in the name of marketing, there is one man who is giving new meaning to the phrase, global villager. Behold citizens of Earth, for in your midst resides a being who holds the key to forming a true brotherhood of man. His name is Udham Singh. Udham says it all—chaos, disorder, the Big Bang, upsetting the apple cart. . . . And if you want to flip him away like another TV channel, do so at your own peril."[21]

The man behind the rise of the global villager Udham Singh is a city dweller named Munish Makhija who dropped out of law school in Delhi to enter the world of television production. The legend of Udham Singh begins with the elections in 1997, when Channel [V] was looking for an actor to play a Jat election officer from the village of Meham in Haryana whose role was to persuade viewers to vote for the music channel's Viewers' Choice Awards. As a member of the production team that went to Meham, Makhija goofed around the sets by taking the mike into the crowd and speaking to people in chaste Haryanvi. Seeing how amused the crowds were with Makhija's act, Channel [V] producers stopped looking for their man from Meham and signed Makhija instead. When Makhija appeared in a promotional video for the Viewers' Choice Awards on Channel [V], the response from viewers was overwhelmingly positive, and Udham Singh became the star attraction of the awards show. The rest, as they say, is history.[22]

By the summer of 1997, Udham Singh had his own video countdown show, aptly called the *Udham Singh Show*. Seated on a traditional *khat* (or country cot) and armed only with a *lath* (or a barge pole), Udham Singh shared his unique perspective on everything from music videos to problems of everyday life: "Bhayo, laife main aage badhana hai to 82 (eighty-two) chahiya" (brother, if you want to get ahead in life you need an attitude).[23]

As fans and critics quickly realized, it was quite impossible to translate the *Udham Singh Show* into what *Connect Magazine* calls "the civilized languages of the West." The untranslatable language of Udham Singh not only helped Channel [V] to create the ultimate antidote to fears of Western imperialism but also provided an ideal foil to the hybrid

Hinglish language used by the more urbane VJs like Ruby. In doing so, Udham Singh performed the role of the irreverent *vidushak* by taking liberties with the language, narrative themes, social issues, and generic conventions of music television in ways that VJs like Ruby could not in their conventional role of the *sutradhar*.

Another irreverent and parodic countdown show on Channel [V] was *Videocon Flashback*, which played old Hindi film songs dating back to the sixties and seventies, adding catchy dialogues mimicked by the popular VJ Javed Jafferi. Performing the role of the *sutradhar* in one instance, and the role of the *vidushak* in another, Jafferi was instrumental in rekindling young viewers' interest in old Hindi film songs by giving them a new ironic, hip factor. Since the early success of Ruby Bhatia, Udham Singh, and Javed Jafferi, other VJs on Channel [V] and MTV have followed similar strategies of creative recombination of old and new genres in music television.

Recognizing the growing popularity of VJs among young television viewers in India, MTV launched a national contest called *MTV V.J. Hunt* in 1997 to recruit viewers as VJs to host new top-ten countdown programs on the network. *V.J. Hunt* was part of MTV's strategy to launch a new generation of VJs—such as Nikhil Chinappa, Cyrus "the Virus" Broacha, Cyrus Sahukar, Shehnaz Tresurywalla, and Malika Arora, to name a few. By using the VJs to host newer shows like *MTV Whatever Things, Love Line, Kya Bolti Tu,* and *Hero Honda Roadies,* MTV has created a formidable programming schedule to lure the lucrative youth market away from Channel [V].[24] VJ Cyrus Sahukar, who hosted *MTV Roadies,* one of the first reality shows on MTV, was re-signed to host the second season of the show, *MTV Roadies 2,* in 2004. Discussing the role of the VJ as the anchor of the *Roadies* reality show, reviewers at Indiantelevision.com opined,

> While the first edition tailed four boys and three girls on bikes across 4000 kms., discovering the essence of India—from the sands of Chennai to the high ranges of Chali—over 40 days, this time on the journey charted out will be from Kolkata right up to Wagah border and for 35 days. Incidentally, both the format and the sponsor—Hero Honda—are the same. The lesson that has been drawn from the last year's mistake is the change in the language. The anchor, a.k.a, "sutradhar" MTV VJ Cyrus Sahukar, will be spouting Hindi, and ditto for the essence of the show, which will be decidedly Indian.[25]

Even advertisers tried to piggyback on the popularity of VJs among young adults. Cadbury Dairy Milk hired MTV VJ Cyrus Broacha in

Franchised in more than thirty countries under an agreement with the London-based Celador Productions, *Who Wants to Be a Millionaire* became an instant runaway hit in India as *Kaun Banega Crorepati* beginning in 2000. (Left to right) An unnamed contestant and host Amitabh Bachchan. Courtesy of Star Plus Channel.

1998 to play the role of a *sutradhar* for a series of commercials—which were aired over several years—with a catchy slogan: *Khane Ka Bahana* (An Excuse to Eat). Explaining the reason for using a VJ to anchor the ad campaign, N. Shatrujeet of agencyfaqs! writes, "In 1998, when Cadbury India realized that many Indian adults—especially from the lower SECs [socioeconomic classes]—still sought a rational justification for eating chocolates, it launched the 'khaane ka bahaana' campaign, with Cyrus in a 'sutradhar' sort of role."[26]

As the advertising and programming strategies of Channel [V], MTV, and other music channels indicate, the figure of the VJ led to the creation of a new generation of *sutradhars* and *vidushaks* who serve to mediate the conventions of old and new genres as a way to help young Indian viewers deal with complex issues of nationalism, regionalism, and globalization in the world of music television.

Who Wants to Be a *Crorepati*?

In 2000, when Star Plus Channel launched *Kaun Banega Crorepati* (*KBC*), the Indian version of *Who Wants to Be a Millionaire*, the show quickly became the biggest hit on Indian television. Hosted by the

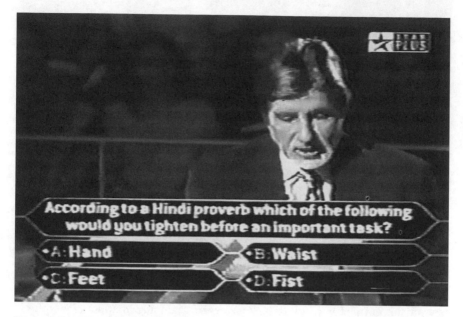

According to a Hindi proverb which of the following would you tighten before an important task?

•A: Hand   •B: Waist
•C: Feet   •D: Fist

Hosted by the megastar of Hindi cinema Amitabh Bachchan, *Kaun Banega Crorepati* captured the imagination of television audiences throughout India in a manner not seen since the serialization of *Ramayan* and *Mahabharat* on Doordarshan during the late 1980s. Courtesy of Star Plus Channel.

megastar of Hindi cinema Amitabh Bachchan, the show *KBC* produced catchphrases, such as "lock kiya jaye," "computer-ji," "pucca," and "fifty-fifty," that became popular parlance in India. At first glance, *KBC* may seem very similar to the many versions of *Who Wants to Be a Millionaire* produced in more than thirty countries under a franchise agreement with the London-based Celador Productions, which produced the first version in Britain. The title of the Russian version of the show translates into English as "Oh! Lucky Man," while the Spanish version premiered with the title "50 for 15" (which referred to the 50 million pesetas that the winner of fifteen questions would take home as the grand prize).[27] In the Indian version, *crorepati* refers to the contestant who can win the ultimate prize of Rs. 1 crore (approximately US$220,000).

As with all the international versions of the *Millionaire* show, the producers of *KBC* were contractually obligated to reproduce, down to the exact detail, the trademark title design, the show's sets, music, and question format, and the qualification process, all of which are laid out in a 169-page document created by Celador Productions.[28] The studio setting for *KBC* consists of the standard blue background, while the foreground is well lit to bring into focus an elevated stage with two seats in the middle for the host and the contestant, and a computer placed next to the host. The studio audience is seated around the stage, with the family members of the contestants seated prominently in the first few rows. The studio audience contributes to the pace and tone of the show by applauding for the correct answer and observing in hushed silence as the stakes get higher for the contestants. The camera work, editing, lighting, and music also contribute to the heightened sense of suspense and relief in relation to the highs and lows of each contestant's fortunes. The host plays an important role in creating and maintaining the ebb and flow of suspense and relief through the show, putting the contestants at ease with small talk at the beginning, reminding them of the rising stakes as the show goes along, and nudging them to consider the use of lifelines for the more difficult questions. A quick conversation with the family members in the studio audiences, or an occasional joke at the expense of the contestant in the hot seat, a polite hello to the friend who calls in to help the contestant in a pickle, and a sense of empathy with the winners and losers alike all help to personalize the host and make a connection with both the studio audiences and the television audiences.

In other words, the program format and the studio settings created for *KBC* are almost identical to all the other international versions of the *Millionaire* show. During the 2000–2001 season, however, when the program was telecast four days a week at 9:00 P.M. on Star Plus Channel, the show captured viewers' imagination in a manner not seen in Indian television since the serialization of *Ramayan* and *Mahabharat* on Doordarshan in the late 1980s. Initially, the ratings for *KBC* were stratospheric, with the first season enjoying a TRP rating of 14 (while most other shows on cable were struggling in the single digits). Although *KBC*'s TRP rating fell to 10.2 in the following year, viewer interest remained very high, and Star TV continued to receive around two hundred thousand calls a day from potential contestants.[29] Fans of the show who could not, or did not want to, get on the show were just as eager to share a seat next to the Big B (as Amitabh Bachchan is popularly known in India). Vandana Puri, the principal of a high school in Delhi, describes the excitement surrounding the viewing experience as follows: "Nine P.M.! All of us sit glued to the Star TV network. Hushed silence. Anyone who makes a wisecrack is snubbed with hostile glances. Each family member is ready with the answer before the guy on the hot seat can reply. KBC has indeed cast a magic spell on the Indian viewers.

It owes its spectacular success not to the intellectual class but to the common man. The questions asked are not really difficult. All you need is a little bit of common sense and use of the elimination process to reach at the correct option."[30]

To get every common man, woman, and child to play along, Star TV quickly followed up on the initial launch of *KBC* with a celebrity version featuring Indian film stars, and a junior version for kids, also hosted by Amitabh Bachchan. Sponsors of the show also began cashing in on the popularity of *KBC*. Bajaj Auto Limited, one of the associate sponsors of *KBC*, launched a major promotional campaign in December 2000 called "Bajaj Crorepati Hungama." Outlining the rationale behind sponsoring *KBC*, R. L. Ravichandran, Bajaj Auto vice president for business and product development, explained, "As the programme [*KBC*] is primarily targeted at families, we did not want to miss this great opportunity to attain high visibility for our range."[31]

Britannia Industries Limited (BIL), another major sponsor of *KBC*, launched a novel campaign to promote its Milkman brand of products, such as biscuits, chocolates, cold coffee, flavored milk, and lassi. From October 3, 2000, to January 3, 2001, consumers were invited to collect BIL wrappers worth Rs. 100 and exchange them for a "win-a-prize scratch card." One of the big prizes on the scratch card was the opportunity to participate in the *KBC* show on Star Plus.[32] Other advertisers were also quick to jump onto the *KBC* bandwagon. Virat Pressure Cookers, for instance, launched its own version of a national contest, called *Kaun Banega Cookerpati?* (Who Wants to Win a Cooker?). Readers were asked to submit a slogan for the company, and the winner could claim a five-liter Virat pressure cooker as a prize.[33]

Not everyone, of course, was caught up in the euphoria over *KBC*. In an online discussion group on *KBC* at mouthshut.com, a couple of irritated reviewers tried to explain to an overwhelming majority of fans that the show was just a cheap imitation of a foreign program. A posting by "Amrita" reads, "Before I start my review, let me educate the members here that KBC is an exact copy of [the] American show Who Wants to be a Millionaire." Another posting by "Sujay Marthi" is even more scathing: "What is it about this pack of new-age foreign-trained producers of TV serials/programmes that makes me think that they've all worked as stable hands before? The similarities in the two fields are too glaring to miss."[34]

For the die-hard fans of *KBC*, however, the criticism that the show is "an exact copy" of *Millionaire* seems to be of little concern, as the following posting by "dhrumil 83" on mouthshut.com reveals: "KAUN

BANEGA CROREPATI might have had been copied from 'WHO WANTS TO BE A MILLIONAIRE.' But to tell you the truth the copied version is better than the original one. SIMPLE ANSWER—It has AMITABH BACHAN [sic] in it. He is the one the greatest."[35]

Although some of reasons for *KBC*'s success may have to do with the trademarked presentation and packaging of the *Millionaire* franchise around the world, it would be difficult to ignore the role that Amitabh Bachchan plays as the *sutradhar* in making the show more appealing to Indian television viewers. In one of the more astute analyses of the *Crorepati* narratives, Shiv Visvanathan points to Amitabh's uncanny ability to create "human interest" encounters with the show's participants, in spite of his status as a living legend in Indian cinema.[36] As Visvanathan puts it, "Amitabh's style is to underplay himself but the legend is all there. His dress is low-key, and it does not distract. . . . If there is a touch of colour, it is the tie. Sartorially perfect and easy. The computer is pervasive in the background. But Amitabh humanises it, subliminally indicating that it is a new kind of guidebook, an electronic tutorial college, a giant collection of quizzes."[37]

Amitabh's uncanny ability to make a personal connection with the average television viewer cannot be understood by simply comparing his role as the host of *KBC* with the performance of other hosts of the *Millionaire* show, such as Regis Philbin in the United States. Given Amitabh's status as the undisputed megastar of Hindi cinema, we must recognize that his performance as the host of *KBC* is akin to the role of a *sutradhar* who skillfully connects cultural texts with audiences by drawing upon their common understanding of the codes and conventions of old and new genres.

Following Amitabh's success as the *sutradhar* of *KBC* on Star TV, a variety of game shows and reality shows on competing networks featured other famous movie stars from the Hindi film industry. To get a share of the advertising pie in the 9:00 P.M. prime-time slot that was all but owned by *KBC* on Star Plus, Zee TV began airing its own game show called *Sawaal Dus Crore Ka* (A Question of Ten Crores), with the noted character actor Anupam Kher in the host seat. Although Zee TV had upped the prize money stake by ten times over what Star TV offered contestants on *KBC*, the ratings for *Sawaal Dus Crore Ka* remained poor. Anupam Kher was soon replaced by the well-known heroine Manisha Koirala, but the show failed to take off. Over at SaBe TV, a new game show called *Jab Khelo Sab Khelo* (When You Play, We All Play) was launched during the daytime, with the popular television personality

Shekar Suman at the helm. Sony TV introduced its own game show called *Jeeto Chappar Phaad Ke,* with superstar Govinda threatening to give Amitabh Bachchan and *KBC* a run for the advertising money.

In 2002, Sony TV quickly followed up on the success of *Jeeto Chappar Phaad Ke* with a reality/game show hybrid called *Kahin naa Kahin Koi Hai* (Someone, Somewhere) featuring Madhuri Dixit—the number one heroine in Hindi cinema during the 1990s. Known as *K3H* for short, the show took the traditional concept of arranged marriages into television land by bringing together young men and women, along with their families, and helping them find a life partner over a span of four episodes. Previewing the opening episodes of *K3H* for the popular film magazine *Screen,* Chaya Unnikrishnan predicted (correctly) that it would be a big hit for Sony TV.[38] As Unnikrishnan put it, "Besides the unique concept of the show, the other ace up its sleeve is the anchor, the gorgeous Madhuri. Unassuming, friendly and full of warmth, Madhuri comes across as a gracious hostess and not the superstar that she is. Right from the way she introduces the girl, her teasing banter with the to-be bride and groom to the dignified manner in which she chats with the elders. Madhuri's body language is that of a helpful, non-intrusive *sutradhar.* All her efforts are towards creating a high comfort level for the participants."[39]

I have chosen to focus on Amitabh Bachchan's role as the *sutradhar* of *KBC* not because I believe that *KBC* is the most "Indian" game show on television. Clearly, other game shows like *Jeeto Chappar Phaad Ke,* with Govinda, and reality shows like *K3H,* with Madhuri Dixit playing the role of the *sutradhar,* are equally, if not more, "Indian" in their format, content, and character. Rather, I focus on *KBC* because it appears to be an extreme illustration of the commonly held view that internationally syndicated game shows and reality TV shows in India are cheap, vulgar imitations of popular American television genres. Yet, when we look closely at Amitabh Bachchan's role as the *sutradhar* and his creative enlisting of "computer-jis" as the *vidushak,* it quickly becomes clear why many Indian viewers did not see *KBC* as merely a copy of a globally successful franchise, even though many viewers were well aware of the existence of other versions of the *Millionaire* show around the world.

Conclusion

In this chapter, I have attempted to articulate the definition of genres to the work of programming in the television industry as a way to move the academic debate in television studies away from rigid taxonomies of indigenous versus foreign shows, or global versus local formats. Beginning in the early 1980s, programmers in the Indian television industry used the figure of the *sutradhar* to articulate the production practices of the new television genres of mythological epics and social dramas to more traditional media such as classical and folk theater. I have focused on the interplay between generic innovation and imitation in Indian music television by critically evaluating the roles of VJs as *sutradhars* and *vidushaks* in popularizing the music video genre as the hosts of top-ten rotation programs.

I contend that the VJs in music television have become very popular in recent years due to their ability to perform the *sutradhar* and *vidushak* functions for young viewers by connecting age-old musical traditions to newer genres such as top-ten countdowns of film songs and music videos. Finally, I have discussed how the figures of the *sutradhar* and *vidushak* enable hybrid articulations of "Indianness" in the internationally syndicated game show *Kaun Banega Crorepati*. In describing the work of programming in terms of the mediating function of the *sutradhar* and the *vidushak* in mythological epics, top-ten music rotations, and the internationally syndicated game show genre, I have argued for the need to recognize the industrial and cultural contexts in which television genres are produced, reproduced, and consumed in India today.

Notes

1. For an extended discussion of the uses and limitations of genre as a category of programming in television, see Robert C. Allen, "Bursting Bubbles: 'Soap Opera,' Audiences and the Limits of Genre," in *Remote Control: Television, Audiences and Cultural Power*, ed. Ellen Seiter, Hans Borchers, Gabriele Kreutzner, and Eva-Maria Warth (London: Routledge, 1989); Glen Creeber, ed., *The Television Genre Book* (London: BFI Publishing, 2001); Jane Feuer, "Genre and Television," in *Channels of Discourse Reassembled: Television and Contemporary Criticism*, ed. Robert C. Allen (London: Routledge, 1992); Brian Rose, ed., *TV Genres: A Handbook and Reference Guide* (Westport, Conn.: Greenwood Press, 1985).

2. "Transnational Broadcasting in Asia. An Online Discussion with Philip Kitley, Keval Kumar, Brian Shoesmith, Amos Owen Thomas and Tony Wilson," *TBS Journal*, no. 2 (Spring 1999), http://www.tbsjournal.com/Archives/Spring99/Symposium2/symposium2.html.

3. "I Believe That Every Genre Can Work, Says Producer Director Anand Mahendroo," Indiantelevision.com, March 12, 2003, http://www.indiantelevision.com/ficci/y2k3/mahendroo.htm.

4. Ibid.

5. Steve Neale, "Studying Genre," in Creeber, *Television Genre Book*, 2.

6. Ibid.

7. Ibid.

8. Graeme Turner, "The Uses and Limitations of Genre," in Creeber, *Television Genre Book*, 4–5.

9. Ibid., 5.

10. Ibid.

11. Ibid.

12. Arvind Singhal and Everett M. Rogers, "The *Hum Log* Story in India," in *Entertainment-Education: A Communication Strategy for Social Change* (Mahwah, N.J.: Erlbaum, 1990), 75.

13. Arvind Rajagopal, *Politics After Television: Hindu Nationalism and the Reshaping of the Public in India* (Cambridge: Cambridge University Press, 2001), 92.

14. Ibid.

15. Jack Banks, *Monopoly Television: MTV's Quest to Control the Music* (Boulder, Colo.: Westview Press, 1996).

16. Shanti Kumar and Michael Curtin, "'Made in India': In between Patriarchy and Music Television," *Television and New Media* 3, no. 4 (2002): 345–66.

17. "Channel [V] Southern Beam Programming," Channel [V] press release, May 1997.

18. Ibid.; emphasis in the original.

19. For a more detailed analysis of this show, see Kumar and Curtin, "'Made in India.'"

20. Ibid.

21. "The Name's Udham: Antidote to Western Cultural Imperialism," *Connect Magazine*, May 1998, www.connectmagazine.com/MAY1998/MayhtmlPgs/May98Udham.htm.

22. "A Fairy Tale Debut," *Tribune* (Chandigarth, India), September 6, 1998, www.tribuneindia.com/1998/98sep06/sunday/filmtv.htm.

23. Quoted in ibid.

24. For the growing competition among music television channels for the next big VJ, see Sabil Francis, "Music Channels Search for New Faces," agencyfaqs!, May 21, 2002, www.agencyfaqs.com/www1/news/stories/2002/05/21/4377.html. Also see Aparna Joshi, "Desperately Seeking That Magic Mix of Music and Moolah," Indiantelevision.com, July 15, 2002, www.indiantelevision.com/special/y2k2/musicstory/music.htm.

25. "MTV All Geared to Burn Some Rubber with 'Roadies 2,'" Indiantelevision.com, July 9, 2004, www.indiantelevision.com/headlines/y2k4/july/july56.html.

26. N. Shatrujeet, "Cadbury Dairy Milk: No More Excuses, Please," agencyfaqs!, April 1, 2002, www.agencyfaqs.com/news/stories/2002/04/01/4147.htm.

27. "Murdoch's Millionaire Fight," BBC News, September 21, 2000, news.bbc.co.uk/1/hi/entertainment/935526.stm.

28. Ibid.

29. "Survival of the Fittest," *India Today*, October 10, 2001, www.indiatoday.com/webexclusive/dispatch/20011010/dhawan.html.

30. Vandana Puri, "Sawal Hai—Chote Mian Ya Bade Mian?" *Meghadutam,* May 26, 2001, www.meghadutam.com/tdis.php.

31. Lalitha Srinivasan, "Will Kaun Banega Crorepati Bring a Windfall to Bajaj Auto?" *Financial Express,* July 18, 2000, www.financialexpress.com/fe/daily/ 20000718/efe18026.htm.

32. Reshma Gandhi, "Britannia to Piggy Back on KBC, Extend Milkman to Cold Coffee and Sweet Lassi," agencyfaqs!, October 18, 2001, www.agencyfaqs .com/www1/news/stories/2001/10/18/961.htm.

33. "Kaun Banega Cookerpati?" www.virat.8m.com/crorepati.

34. These postings are listed online at www.mouthshut.com/readproduct/ 925007365-1.html.

35. This posting is also listed online at www.mouthshut.com/readproduct/ 925007365–1.html.

36. Shiv Visvanathan, "The Crorepati Narratives," *Economic and Political Weekly,* August 26–September 2, 2000, www.epw.org.in.

37. Ibid.

38. Chaya Unnikrishnan, "Matchmaking on Air," *Screen,* August 2, 2002, www.screenindia.com/20020802/tvcov/html.

39. Ibid.

epilogue

reading tv genres

Brian G. Rose

The subject of television genres has been examined in a variety of ways over the last four decades. The earliest writings, from the 1960s, came from an environment that was just beginning to treat television and television programming with some degree of seriousness, instead of routinely condemning the medium for the dangers of its mass reach and lowest-common-denominator scheduling. The occasional articles that appeared in *Television Quarterly* or were collected in a few academic anthologies weren't overly concerned with detailed definitions of genre operations or cultural meaning. Instead, they tended to accept an economic notion of formula in which American television was, by necessity, made up of different types of programming in order to capture the changing tastes of the viewing public through the day and evening hours. The various types of fictional and nonfictional entertainment, inherited from film and radio, were accepted as a prerequisite of an expanding commercial medium.

Essays from this period tended to feature impressionistic definitions of individual formulas, sometimes flavored with a discussion of immediate predecessors (whether the novel, theater, or motion picture) and a brief survey of historical development. A typical example is a 1966 article by David Boroff entitled "Television and the Problem Play."[1] In contrast to most contemporary articles on TV drama, Boroff's approach was generally affirmative in tone as he traced the legacy of the theatrical "problem play" in series like *The Defenders* and *East Side/West Side*. His conception of TV formula, however, was rather loose and expansive, covering any one-hour, prime-time drama, whether it featured lawyers, doctors, or schoolteachers. Sheldon Leonard and Carl Reiner offered a more focused look at genre in their 1963 article "Comedy on Television: A Dialogue."[2] In a surprisingly serious discussion, the two veteran TV producers seek to define the rules of a successful sitcom, emphasizing the importance of performers and the overall style of the production company.

It wasn't until 1974 that a book-length study examining the variety of television genres appeared. Horace Newcomb's *TV: The Most Popular Art* set out to define an aesthetic for television using genre as one of his foundations.[3] To capture what was unique and distinctive about the medium, Newcomb turned to the concept of formula as charted by John Cawelti in his influential study *The Six-Gun Mystique*.[4] Cawelti's definition of formula as "a conventional system for structuring cultural products"[5] provided Newcomb with a way not only to organize the principal formats of television but also to analyze the nature of their durability and their continuing evolution.

TV: The Most Popular Art underscored the importance of TV genres by devoting separate chapters to situation and domestic comedies, the Western, mysteries, adventure shows, doctor and lawyer programs, soap operas, and nonfiction (news, sports, and documentaries). Each chapter offered a lively survey of how the various genres developed and described their principal conflicts, settings, characters, and social values. But Newcomb's primary concern was not simply to organize and categorize; instead, it was to use the notion of formula to build a case for television's original aesthetic qualities. He argued that innovative, socially aware programs like *Laugh-In, All in the Family,* and *The Prisoner* were illustrations of how "television can and does organize and arrange fictional material in forms of its own" without necessarily abandoning "the elements tried and proven in more formulaic presentation."[6] In the book's concluding chapter, Newcomb lays the groundwork for a TV aesthetic based on the medium's distinctive use of intimacy, continuity, and history in its genre programming.

Two years later, Newcomb edited *Television: The Critical View*—an Oxford University Press anthology that has been updated every five years or so (the sixth edition appeared in 2000).[7] This first edition was explicitly designed to foster a new climate of critical appreciation of the medium, emphasizing a broad-based humanistic approach. One of the unusual aspects of this collection is the surprisingly sophisticated writing on genres that Newcomb gathered from magazines like the *New*

Yorker and *Harper's*. At a time when television was generally regarded as a dangerous social influence or a purveyor of sordid schlock, Renata Adler's "Afternoon Television: Unhappiness Enough and Time,"[8] Michael Arlen's "The Media Dramas of Norman Lear,"[9] and Daniel Menaker's "Art and Artifice in Network News"[10] treat their respective formats of daytime dramas, socially aware situation comedies, and network newscasts with alert sympathy and insight. The essays by Carol Traynor Williams ("It's Not So Much, 'You've Come a Long Way, Baby'—as 'You're Gonna Make It After All'")[11] and James W. Chesebro and Caroline D. Hamsher ("Communication, Values, and Popular Television Series"),[12] both reprinted from the *Journal of Popular Film and Television*, reveal the two main tendencies in contemporary academic writing on TV genres: a detailed discussion of format development with a degree of cultural analysis (as Williams does with her historical overview of *The Mary Tyler Moore Show*) and a somewhat uneasy effort to apply a theoretical model drawn from traditional literary studies to television (which Chesebro and Hamsher attempt with their use of concepts drawn from Northrop Frye and Kenneth Burke to examine values in a variety of prime-time series).

Richard P. Adler's 1981 anthology *Understanding Television* also contained several essays that thoughtfully probed the meaning and history of individual genres.[13] Tania Modleski's "Search for Tomorrow in Today's Soap Operas" (originally published in 1979 in *Film Quarterly*)[14] helped initiate the serious study of daytime drama and ultimately formed a central chapter in her 1982 groundbreaking book, *Loving with a Vengeance: Mass-Produced Fantasies for Women*.[15] Modleski's views on how soap operas construct the female spectator as an "ideal mother" and the narrative and psychological significance of the form's constant commercial interruptions were provocative and enormously influential in the field of feminist media studies. David Thorburn's 1976 essay, "Television Melodrama,"[16] was, in its own way, of equal importance, forcefully arguing for a new aesthetic approach to prime-time melodrama, based on the medium's appetite for close-ups and the collective narrative memories of the mass TV audience. Arthur Hough's "Trials and Tribulations: Thirty Years of Sitcom"[17] was the first of what would be many attempts to chart the development of the situation comedy according to thematic time lines, such as the eras of the business sitcom from 1960 to 1965, the rural sitcom from 1960 to 1970, and the adventure sitcom from 1965 to 1970.

The early to mid-1980s marked an important transition period in TV genre studies, as media scholars, influenced by the growing interest in film genre, turned their attention to television. An example of this was E. Ann Kaplan's 1983 edited anthology *Regarding Television*.[18] Influenced by British approaches to television in *Screen* magazine and the writing of Raymond Williams (particularly his book *Television: Technology and Cultural Form*),[19] Kaplan's book brought together a number of stimulating essays investigating TV genres through the critical lenses of psychoanalysis, feminism, semiology, and structuralism. Robert Stam's "Television News and Its Spectator"[20] began with the basic premise that "television news is *pleasurable*"[21] and then proceeded to explore the narcissistic and voyeuristic tendencies of TV news viewers, the narrative codes of newscasts, and the Brechtian qualities of direct address embodied by anchor personalities. In her essay "Sport on Television: Replay and Display,"[22] Margaret Morse dissected the ways television has fundamentally altered the nature of sports, both in terms of economics and spectator perceptions, and how sports programming has led to a different construction of masculinity.

A large portion of Kaplan's anthology was devoted to daytime drama, signaling the increasing attention to the genre by feminist scholars. Tania Modleski examined how soap operas mirror the structure of female domestic life ("The Rhythms of Reception: Daytime Television and Women's Work");[23] Charlotte Brunsdon looked at the ways daytime TV constructs moral and cultural competencies in its viewers (*"Crossroads:* Notes on Soap Opera");[24] Sandy Flitterman provided a structuralist analysis of ads aired during soap operas ("The *Real* Soap Operas: TV Commercials");[25] and Robert C. Allen offered a sharp investigation of the various codes of the soap opera text ("On Reading Soaps: A Semiotic Primer").[26]

By the mid-1980s the multiplicity of TV genres was seen as one of the medium's primary characteristics and served as a central focus of numerous studies. Like Newcomb's *TV: The Most Popular Art,* Hal Himmelstein organized his 1984 book, *Television Myth and the American Mind,* into individual genre chapters that briefly examined historical antecedents, traced program development on television, and defined major conflicts and themes.[27] Taking his cue from approaches in contemporary film theory, Himmelstein looked at genres as specific social discourses "using a particular language to develop a secular mythology guided, often unconsciously, by our culture's dominant ideology."[28] Throughout the book, traditional formats like the sitcom, the melodrama, and the talk show were discussed not only in terms of their prevailing social myths but also in the various ways they typically evaded and simplified the pressing social concerns of the times in which they were created.

Two books appearing in 1985 also surveyed the variety of TV formulas but in more general, less overtly ideological, terms. The first books on television to feature the word "genre" in their titles, both *American Television Genres*,[29] by Stuart M. Kaminsky with Jeffrey H. Mahan, and *TV Genres*,[30] edited by Brian G. Rose, were broad overviews of the field, though with different methodological perspectives. A companion of sorts to Kaminsky's 1974 *American Film Genres*,[31] *American Television Genres* was primarily an introductory survey of genre study. Each individual genre chapter employed a different critical approach—quiz and game shows were examined in terms drawn from Northrop Frye's *Anatomy of Criticism*,[32] police shows were analyzed from a Proppian narrative framework, science fiction and horror were discussed from a Jungian perspective, and a Freudian approach was used for the detective formula. Nevertheless, in their introduction, the authors did make several assumptions about television and its genres. Similar to Hal Himmelstein, they viewed "the medium as a shared cultural experience in which important questions are mythically addressed and social tensions resolved,"[33] and believed formulas exist because the audience needs to instantly "understand the cultural context in which the information is given."[34] Though they stressed the importance of understanding the unique ways television presents genre in comparison to other media, they also maintained that "when we talk about the idea of genre, we assume that the categories already exist and that we know what they are."[35]

TV Genres offered a less theoretically driven and more comprehensive overview of nineteen leading formats, ranging from the Western to the made-for-TV movie, from docudramas to religious programming, and from educational and cultural shows to advertising. Each chapter followed the same structure: a general introduction, a section on historical development, a discussion of major themes and issues, a bibliographic survey, and a videography. In his introduction, editor Brian G. Rose proposed a largely economic approach, noting that television genres, "like radio genres, movie genres, or the genres of popular literature, are essentially commodities, manufactured for, and utterly dependent on, public consumption and support," and that "the formulas that have endured are those which manage to yield a regular profit for their producers."[36] Surveying the range of programming cycles from Westerns to socially aware comedies to prime-time continuing melodramas, he stressed the crucial role of network programming practices and production techniques and the ability of perennial formats to "develop and grow over time."[37] The future of genres, he felt, would be in their responsiveness to ever-shifting demographics and their continuing ability to "satisfy the changing demands and desires of advertisers and audiences."[38]

Perhaps the best summary of the varying contemporary approaches to genre can be found in Jane Feuer's 1987 essay "Genre Study."[39] After a shrewd discussion of the differences between genre analysis in literature and that in film and television, Feuer divided current critical views on popular genres into three main categories: the aesthetic ("attempts to define genre in terms of a system of conventions that permits artistic expression"),[40] the ritual ("genre as an exchange between industry and audience, an exchange through which a culture speaks to itself"),[41] and the ideological ("genre as an instrument of control").[42] She then applied these approaches to the situation comedy, revealing their individual strengths and their many weaknesses, particularly in terms of explaining genre evolution and the role of the audience. Comparing the more predictable rise and fall of film genres with the less clear-cut development patterns of television formats, she concluded with the observation that "genre theory as a whole might work better for film than for TV," since, as critics like Raymond Williams previously noted, "television programs do not operate as discrete texts to the same extent as movies; the property of 'flow' blends one program into another, and programs are regularly 'interrupted' by ads and promos."[43]

Feuer's conception of genre strategies was examined more closely in John Fiske's 1987 book *Television Culture*.[44] Fiske maintained that the principal weakness of the aesthetic approach was its strict reliance on a textual definition for genre "that rarely fits any specific instance."[45] He proposed instead that a "genre seen textually should be defined as a shifting provisional set of characteristics which is modified as each new example is produced."[46] For Fiske, the ritual and ideological approaches were more productive, since they permitted opportunities to analyze the interaction between network economics and the social and political interests of television viewers. Citing critics like Steve Neale and John Hartley, he argued that "genre is a means of constructing both the audience and the reading subject: its work in the economic domain is paralleled by its work in the domain of culture; that is, its work in influencing which meanings of a program are preferred by, or proferred to, which audiences."[47]

As interest in television genres grew during the 1980s, a number of book-length studies of individual formats began to appear. No genre attracted greater attention than soap operas—a fact that has remained true ever since. Spurred by the growth of feminist studies, several important titles were published within the first few years of the decade. The year 1982 saw the publication of Dorothy Hobson's *"Crossroads": The Drama of a Soap Opera* (a case study of the popular prime-time English serial)[48] and Tania Modleski's challenging analysis of victimized women in literature and daytime television, *Loving with a Vengeance*.[49] Muriel G. Cantor and Suzanne Pingree's sociological examination, *The Soap Opera*,[50] came out the following year. Then, in 1985, two classic studies were published. The first was Ien Ang's *Watching "Dallas": Soap Opera and the Melodramatic Imagination*,[51] a fascinating exploration of topics ranging from the ideology and pleasures of the serial form and its dominant mode of "emotional realism," to the worldwide phenomenon of *Dallas* and the meaning of its popularity for its largely female viewers. The second was Robert C. Allen's *Speaking of Soap Operas*,[52] a model of genre analysis that provided a thorough examination of soap opera semiotics, history, sociology, narrative practices, and audience reception.

During the next two decades, studies of soap operas from every perspective continued to appear. Some of the most notable included Martha Nochimson's psychoanalytic inquiry *No End to Her: Soap Opera and the Female Subject*;[53] Laura Stempel Mumford's *Love and Ideology in the Afternoon: Soap Opera, Women, and Television Genre*,[54] which examined narrative issues and family relationships; Dannielle Blumenthal's sociological study *Women and Soap Opera: A Cultural Feminist Perspective*;[55] Charlotte Brunsdon's history of feminist daytime drama criticism, *The Feminist, the Housewife, and the Soap Opera*;[56] and Nancy K. Baym's ethnographic portrait of an Internet soap chat group, *Tune In, Log On: Soaps, Fandom, and Online Community*.[57]

Situation comedy also proved to be popular with genre scholars. One of the first books to look closely at the format was David Grote's *The End of Comedy: The Sit-Com and the Comedic Tradition*,[58] which offered a disparaging view of television comedy in comparison with the classical theatrical traditions identified by Northrop Frye as "new comedy." David Marc's wittily written and passionately argued *Demographic Vistas: Television in American Culture* appeared a year later, in 1984, signaling a new style and approach to genre study.[59] Marc examined both prime-time and late-night comedy from a perspective that embraced historical scholarship, critical biography, and social analysis. In addition to providing provocative auteur portraits of Jackie Gleason and Paul Henning (the creator of *The Beverly Hillbillies*), Marc also traced the rise of self-reflexivity as one of American comedy's dominant modes of expression. Five years later, Marc wrote a more extended study of the form, *Comic Visions: Television Comedy and American Culture*,[60] which discussed the growth of television comedy, and its relationship to cultural and political trends, from the 1950s onward. (In keeping with their concerns with contemporary developments in television programming and industrial practices, both of Marc's books appeared in revised editions in the 1990s.)[61] Other important works on the genre of comedy included Jane Feuer, Paul Kerr, and Tise Vahimagi's valuable anthology *MTM "Quality Television,"*[62] which looked at the economics, style, and ideology of MTM Productions and its innovative situation comedies (and prime-time dramas); Ella Taylor's sociological analysis of domestic life in sitcoms over the last forty years, *Prime-Time Families: Television Culture in Post-war America*;[63] and Kathleen Rowe's feminist examination of disruptive comic figures, particularly Roseanne Barr, in *The Unruly Woman: Gender and the Genres of Laughter*.[64]

Over the last two decades, virtually every television genre has prompted significant full-length studies, from Westerns (J. Fred MacDonald's *Who Shot the Sheriff? The Rise and Fall of the Television Western*)[65] to feminist cop shows (Julie D'Acci's *Defining Women: Television and the Case of Cagney & Lacey*)[66] and from children's programming (Heather Hendershot's *Saturday Morning Censors: Television Regulation before the V-Chip*)[67] to quiz shows (Thomas DeLong's *Quiz Craze: America's Infatuation with the Radio and Television Game Show*).[68] While many of these books had their roots in historical issues or modern theory, genre publishing sometimes had its source in contemporary programming phenomena. Witness the flurry of books beginning in the mid-1990s responding to the rise of tabloid talk shows. The first to appear was Vicki Abt and Leonard Mustazza's *Coming after Oprah: Cultural Fallout in the Age of the TV Talk Show*,[69] which came out in 1997. Joshua Gamson's *Freaks Talk Back: Tabloid Talk Shows and Sexual Nonconformity*[70] was published a year later. This was followed by Kathleen S. Lowney's *Baring Our Souls: TV Talk Shows and the Religion of Recovery* (1999);[71] Laura Grindstaff's *The Money Shot: Taste, Class and the Making of TV Talk Shows* (2002);[72] and Julie Engel Manga's *Talking Trash: The Cultural Politics of Daytime TV Talk Shows* (2003).[73] Bernard Timberg's definitive study of the growth and impact of the entire talk show genre, *Television Talk: A History of the TV Talk Show*,[74] appeared in the midst of this onslaught in 2002.

The international aspect of TV genres has also been the subject of scholarly attention. Noteworthy books include John Tulloch's study of British and Australian television, *Television Drama: Agency, Audience, and Myth,*[75] James Chapman's *Saints and Avengers: British Adventures Series of the 1960s,*[76] Jeffrey S. Miller's *Something Completely Different: British Television and American Culture,*[77] Robert Allen's *To Be Continued ... Soap Operas around the World,*[78] and Lisa Parks and Shanti Kumar's *Planet TV: A Global Television Reader.*[79]

Investigations into film genre theory in the 1980s and 1990s by Steve Neale, Thomas Schatz, and Rick Altman led a number of media scholars to explore the diverse operations of genres in television. In his article "Flow, Genre, and the Television Text," Gregory Waller emphasized the role of intertextuality and generic overlap, and the inherent capacity of TV genres to grow and change, as of "central importance in any consideration of the aesthetic and ideological workings of contemporary American popular culture."[80] He also stressed the transmedia interrelationships of various TV genres—whether they be novelizations, movies made from TV series, or vice versa—as a way to see genre as a group of texts that "mean what they do in opposition to each other."[81]

John Corner, in a chapter in his book *Studying Media,* acknowledged that "genre is a principal factor in the directing of audience choice and of audience expectations," while worrying that "too little attention has been paid to how its specificities affect viewing behavior."[82] Hoping to counter an essentialist tendency he found common in most writing about TV genres, he emphasized a sociological mode of inquiry with a greater attention to audience studies. An excellent introduction to the range of contemporary perspectives on genre can be found in Glen Creeber's 2001 anthology, *The Television Genre Book.*[83] Creeber assembled more than fifty essays by leading media scholars, including concise overviews of modern genre theory, as well as sharply drawn analyses of the major issues in the history and cultural context of virtually every modern American and British TV genre.

In his book *Genre and Television: From Cop Shows to Cartoons in American Culture,*[84] Jason Mittell moved away from a text-based study of genre and instead proposed a more poststructuralist, cultural studies model, which emphasized the interrelationships among media industries, audiences, various media texts, and specific historical contexts. Mittell viewed genres as complex discursive practices and stressed the diverse ways that genres change their cultural meanings and values over time. His book offered detailed explorations of five different aspects of genre study, including history (the quiz show scandal), industrial practices (animated programming), audience practices (how viewers make use of labels in terms of talk shows), textual analysis (the police show), and genre mixing (parody shows like *The Simpsons* and *Soap*) as a way to demonstrate the scope and versatility of his broad-based cultural approach to genre.

At the dawn of the twenty-first century, television programming throughout the world is becoming ever more diverse in its formats, styles, and audience appeals. The critical study of TV genres, as these recent books confirm, promises to be one of the most exciting areas of modern media analysis.

Notes

1. David Boroff, "Television and the Problem Play," in *TV as Art,* ed. Patrick D. Hazard (Champaign, Ill.: National Council of Teachers of English, 1966), 97–116.

2. Sheldon Leonard and Carl Reiner, "Comedy on Television: A Dialogue," in *Television: The Creative Experience,* ed. A. William Bleum and Roger Manvell (New York: Hastings House, 1967), 93–103.

3. Horace Newcomb, *TV: The Most Popular Art* (New York: Anchor Press, 1974).

4. John G. Cawelti, *The Six-Gun Mystique* (Bowling Green, Ohio: Bowling Green University Popular Press, 1970).

5. Ibid., 29.

6. Newcomb, *TV: The Most Popular Art,* 242.

7. Horace Newcomb, ed., *Television: The Critical View* (New York: Oxford University Press, 1976).

8. Renata Adler, "Afternoon Television: Unhappiness Enough and Time," in Newcomb, *Television,* 54–65.

9. Michael Arlen, "The Media Dramas of Norman Lear," in Newcomb, *Television,* 26–34.

10. Daniel Menaker, "Art and Artifice in Network News," in Newcomb, *Television,* 113–19.

11. Carol Traynor Williams, "It's Not So Much, 'You've Come a Long Way, Baby,'—as "You're Gonna Make It After All," in Newcomb, *Television,* 43–53.

12. James W. Chesebro and Caroline D. Hamsher, "Communication, Values, and Popular Television Series," in Newcomb, *Television,* 6–25.

13. Richard P. Adler, ed., *Understanding Television* (New York: Praeger, 1981).

14. Tania Modleski, "Search for Tomorrow in Today's Soap Operas," in Adler, *Understanding Television,* 183–200.

15. Tania Modleski, *Loving with a Vengeance: Mass-Produced Fantasies for Women* (New York: Archon, 1982).

16. David Thorburn, "Television Melodrama," in Adler, *Understanding Television,* 73–90.

17. Arthur Hough, "Trials and Tribulations: Thirty Years of Sitcom," in Adler, *Understanding Television,* 201–24.

18. E. Ann Kaplan, ed., *Regarding Television* (Frederick, Md.: University Publications of America, 1983).

19. Raymond Williams, *Television: Technology and Cultural Form* (New York: Schocken Books, 1974).

20. Robert Stam, "Television News and Its Spectator," in Kaplan, *Regarding Television,* 23–43.

21. Ibid., 23.

22. Margaret Morse, "Sport on Television: Replay and Display," in Kaplan, *Regarding Television,* 44–66.

23. Tania Modleski, "The Rhythms of Reception: Daytime Television and Women's Work," in Kaplan, *Regarding Television,* 67–75.

24. Charlotte Brunsdon, "*Crossroads:* Notes on Soap Opera," in Kaplan, *Regarding Television,* 76–83.

25. Sandy Flitterman, "The *Real* Soap Operas: TV Commercials," in Kaplan, *Regarding Television,* 84–96.

26. Robert C. Allen, "On Reading Soaps: A Semiotic Primer," in Kaplan, *Regarding Television,* 97–108.

27. Hal Himmelstein, *Television Myth and the American Mind* (New York: Praeger, 1984).

28. Ibid, 71.

29. Stuart M. Kaminsky with Jeffrey H. Mahan, *American Television Genres* (Chicago: Nelson-Hall, 1985).

30. Brian G. Rose, ed., *TV Genres* (Westport, Conn.: Greenwood Press, 1985).

31. Stuart Kaminsky, *American Film Genres: Approaches to a Critical Theory of Popular Film* (Dayton, Ohio: Pflaum, 1974).

32. Northrop Frye, *Anatomy of Criticism* (New York: Atheneum, 1966).

33. Kaminsky with Mahan, *American Television Genres,* 8.

34. Ibid., 33.

35. Ibid., 21.

36. Rose, *TV Genres,* 5.

37. Ibid., 9.

38. Ibid.

39. Jane Feuer, "Genre Study," in *Channels of Discourse,* ed. Robert C. Allen (Chapel Hill: University of North Carolina Press, 1987), 113–33.

40. Ibid, 119.

41. Ibid.

42. Ibid.

43. Ibid., 131.

44. John Fiske, *Television Culture* (London: Methuen, 1987).

45. Ibid., 111.

46. Ibid.

47. Ibid., 114.

48. Dorothy Hobson, *"Crossroads": The Drama of a Soap Opera* (London: Methuen, 1982).

49. Modleski, *Loving with a Vengeance*.

50. Muriel G. Cantor and Suzanne Pingree, *The Soap Opera* (Beverly Hills, Calif.: Sage, 1983).

51. Ien Ang, *Watching "Dallas": Soap Opera and the Melodramatic Imagination* (London: Methuen, 1985).

52. Robert C. Allen, *Speaking of Soap Operas* (Chapel Hill: University of North Carolina Press, 1985).

53. Martha Nochimson, *No End to Her: Soap Opera and the Female Subject* (Berkeley: University of California Press, 1992).

54. Laura Stempel Mumford, *Love and Ideology in the Afternoon: Soap Opera, Women, and Television Genre* (Bloomington: Indiana University Press, 1995).

55. Dannielle Blumenthal, *Women and Soap Opera: A Cultural Feminist Perspective* (Westport, Conn.: Praeger, 1997).

56. Charlotte Brunsdon, *The Feminist, the Housewife, and the Soap Opera* (Oxford: Oxford University Press, 2000).

57. Nancy K. Baym, *Tune In, Log On: Soaps, Fandom, and Online Community* (Beverly Hills, Calif.: Sage, 2000).

58. David Grote, *The End of Comedy: The Sit-Com and the Comedic Tradition* (Hamden, Conn.: Shoestring Press, 1983).

59. David Marc, *Demographic Vistas: Television in American Culture* (Philadelphia: University of Pennsylvania Press, 1984).

60. David Marc, *Comic Visions: Television Comedy and American Culture* (New York: Blackwell, 1989).

61. David Marc, *Demographic Vistas: Television and American Culture,* rev. ed. (Philadelphia: University of Pennsylvania Press, 1996); David Marc, *Comic Visions: Television Comedy and American Culture,* 2nd ed. (Malden, Mass.: Blackwell, 1997).

62. Jane Feuer, Paul Kerr, and Tise Vahimagi, eds., *MTM "Quality Television"* (London: BFI Publishing, 1984).

63. Ella Taylor, *Prime-Time Families: Television Culture in Post-war America* (Berkeley: University of California Press, 1989).

64. Kathleen Rowe, *The Unruly Woman: Gender and the Genres of Laughter* (Austin: University of Texas Press, 1995).

65. J. Fred MacDonald, *Who Shot the Sheriff? The Rise and Fall of the Television Western* (New York: Praeger, 1987).

66. Julie D'Acci, *Defining Women: Television and the Case of* Cagney & Lacey (Chapel Hill: University of North Carolina Pres, 1994).

67. Heather Hendershot, *Saturday Morning Censors: Television Regulation before the V-Chip* (Durham, N.C.: Duke University Press, 1998).

68. Thomas DeLong, *Quiz Craze: America's Infatuation with the Radio and Television Game Show* (Westport, Conn.: Praeger, 1991).

69. Vicki Abt and Leonard Mustazza, *Coming after Oprah: Cultural Fallout in the Age of the TV Talk Show* (Bowling Green: Bowling Green State University Popular Press, 1997).

70. Joshua Gamson, *Freaks Talk Back: Tabloid Talk Shows and Sexual Non-Conformity* (Chicago: University of Chicago Press, 1998).

71. Kathleen S. Lowney, *Baring Our Souls: TV Talk Shows and the Religion of Recovery* (New York: de Gruyter, 1999).

72. Laura Grindstaff, *The Money Shot: Taste, Class and the Making of TV Talk Shows* (Chicago: University of Chicago Press, 2002).

73. Julie Engel Manga, *Talking Trash: The Cultural Politics of Daytime TV Talk Shows* (New York: New York University Press, 2003).

74. Bernard Timberg, *Television Talk: A History of the TV Talk Show* (Austin: University of Texas Press, 2002).

75. John Tulloch, *Television Drama: Agency, Audience, and Myth* (London: Routledge, 1990).

76. James Chapman, *Saints and Avengers: British Adventures Series of the 1960s* (London: Taurus, 2002).

77. Jeffrey S. Miller, *Something Completely Different: British Television and American Culture* (Minneapolis: University of Minnesota Press, 2000).

78. Robert C. Allen, *To Be Continued . . . Soap Operas around the World* (London: Routledge, 1995).

79. Lisa Parks and Shanti Kumar, eds., *Planet TV: A Global Television Reader* (New York: New York University Press, 2003).

80. Gregory A. Waller, "Flow, Genre, and the Television Text," in *In the Eye of the Beholder: Critical Perspectives in Popular Film and Television,* ed. Gary R. Edgerton, Michael T. Marsden, and Jack Nachbar (Bowling Green, Ohio: Bowling Green State University Popular Press, 1997), 62.

81. Ibid., 63.

82. John Corner, *Studying Media* (Oxford: Oxford University Press, 1998), 121, 123.

83. Glen Creeber, ed., *The Television Genre Book* (London: British Film Institute, 2001).

84. Jason Mittell, *Genre and Television: From Cop Shows to Cartoons in American Culture* (New York: Routledge, 2004).

contributors

Christopher Anderson teaches in the Department of Communication and Culture at Indiana University and is the author of *Hollywood TV: The Studio System in the Fifties* (1994).

Al Auster is associate professor in the Department of Communication and Media Studies at Fordham University at Lincoln Center. He is the author of four previous books and of articles that have appeared in *Television Quarterly,* the *Journal of Popular Film and Television,* and the *Chronicle of Higher Education.* He is currently working on a book on the television series *thirtysomething* (Wayne State University Press).

Richard Butsch is professor of sociology and American studies at Rider University. He is the author of *The Making of American Audiences from Stage to Television, 1750–1990,* which won the International Communication Association Best Book Award and the American Culture Association Cawelti Prize. He is currently writing a book on audiences characterized as crowds, publics, and isolated individuals.

Michael Curtin is professor of media and cultural studies in the Department of Communication Arts at the University of Wisconsin–Madison and director of Global Studies at the UW International Institute. His books include *Redeeming the Wasteland: Television Documentary and Cold War Politics* (Rutgers, 1995), *Making and Selling Culture* (coeditor; Wesleyan, 1996) and *The Revolution Wasn't Televised: Sixties Television and Social*

Conflict (coeditor; Routledge, 1997). He is currently working on two books: *Playing to the World's Biggest Audience: The Globalization of Chinese Film and TV* and *Media Capital: The Cultural Geography of Global TV*.

Gary R. Edgerton is professor and chair of the Department of Communication and Theatre Arts at Old Dominion University. He has published five books (including *Television Histories* for the University Press of Kentucky) and more than fifty book chapters and journal articles on a wide assortment of media and culture topics and is coeditor of the *Journal of Popular Film and Television*. He received the 2004 American Culture Association Governing Board Award for Outstanding Contributions to American Cultural Studies.

Timothy Havens teaches television studies and media globalization in the Department of Communication Studies at the University of Iowa. His research examines how worldwide cultural differences (race, gender, nation, age) shape the business practices of international television trade. He is a former Senior Fulbright Scholar to Hungary, and his book *Global Television Marketplace* is forthcoming from the British Film Institute Press.

Jeffrey P. Jones teaches television studies and political communication in the Department of Communication and Theatre Arts at Old Dominion University. He is the author of *Entertaining Politics: New Political Television and Civic Culture* (Rowman and Littlefield, 2004), as well as numerous articles and chapters on the intersection of popular culture and politics.

Shanti Kumar is assistant professor of media and cultural studies in the Department of Communication Arts at the University of Wisconsin–Madison. He is the author of *Gandhi Meets Primetime: Television and the Politics of Nationalism in Postcolonial India* (forthcoming) and the coeditor of *Planet TV: A Global Television Reader* (2003). He has also published book chapters in edited anthologies and articles in journals such as *Television and New Media*, *Jump Cut*, *South Asian Popular Culture*, and the *Quarterly Review of Film and Video*.

Jason Mittell is assistant professor of American civilization and film and media culture at Middlebury College. His book *Genre and Television:*

From Cop Shows to Cartoons in American Culture (Routledge, 2004) explores the concepts developed in the chapter included in the current volume.

Horace Newcomb holds the Lambdin Kay Chair for the Peabody Awards and is professor of telecommunications at the University of Georgia, where he is also the director of the George Foster Peabody Awards Programs. He is the author of numerous works about television and editor of *The Museum of Broadcast Communications Encyclopedia of Television*.

Kyle Nicholas is assistant professor in the Department of Communication and Theatre Arts at Old Dominion University. His scholarly interests include media production and the media industries, telecommunications policy, and the use of new media and the World Wide Web in cultural production. His publications include "Stronger Than Barbed Wire: How Geo-policy Barriers Construct Rural Internet Access," in *Communication Policy and Information Technology: Problems, Promises, Prospects,* and "Geo-Policy Barriers and the Digital Divide," in *The Information Society.* His most recent research focuses on converging media, with special attention to Web-based televisual and streaming media.

Norma Pecora is associate professor in the School of Telecommunications at Ohio University. She is currently the coeditor (with Sharon R. Mazzarella at Clemson University) of the journal *Popular Communication.* Her recent work includes a forthcoming edited book, *50 Years of Research on Children and Television,* with John P. Murray and Ellen Wartella (Erlbaum); "Nickelodeon Grows Up," in *Nickelodeon Nation;* and *Growing Up Girls* (coeditor; Peter Lang, 2003).

Brian G. Rose is the editor of *TV Genres* (1985) and the author of *Television and the Performing Arts* (1992), *Televising the Performing Arts* (1996), and *Directing for Television* (1999). He teaches at Fordham University.

Ellen Seiter is a professor in the School of Cinema-Television, University of Southern California, where she holds the Stephen K. Nenno Chair in Critical Studies. She is the author of *The Internet Playground* (Peter Lang, 2005), *Television and New Media Audiences* (Oxford, 1999), and *Sold Separately: Children and Parents in Consumer Culture* (Rutgers, 1993).

Ron Simon has been curator of television at The Museum of Television & Radio since the early eighties. Among the numerous exhibitions he has curated are The Television of Dennis Potter, Witness to History, Jack Benny: The Television and Radio Work, and Worlds without End: The Art and History of the Soap Opera, all of which featured screenings and a catalog. Simon is an associate adjunct professor at Columbia University and New York University, where he teaches courses in the history of the media. He has written for many publications, including *The Encyclopedia of Television* and *The Encyclopedia of New York State,* as well as serving as host and creative consultant of the CD-ROM *Total Television.* He is a member of the editorial board of *Television Quarterly* and has lectured at museums and educational institutions throughout the country.

Rhonda Wilcox is professor of English at Gordon College in Barnesville, Georgia. She has published numerous works on popular culture, including the chapter on television in *The Greenwood Guide to American Popular Culture.* The author of one of the first scholarly essays on *Buffy the Vampire Slayer* and of *Why Buffy Matters: The Art of* Buffy the Vampire Slayer, she is coeditor, with David Lavery, of the first American collection of scholarly essays on the series (*Fighting the Forces: What's at Stake in* Buffy the Vampire Slayer) and of *Slayage: The Online International Journal of Buffy Studies* (http://www.slayage.tv), a peer-reviewed quarterly currently producing its seventeenth issue.

Mary Jeanne Wilson is a doctoral candidate at the University of Southern California School of Cinema-Television in the Department of Critical Studies. Her dissertation explores issues surrounding the collecting and archiving of soap operas and fan pleasure in rerunning the serial narrative.

television index

general index

Films originally shot for television are listed in the Television Index